WORKING THIN WATERS

Other Books by the Author

Turpin
Drifting
From Cape May to Montauk (with photographs by David Plowden)
The Flann O'Brien Reader (editor)
Backwaters
Short Voyages
Harbor of Refuge
Noank: The Ethereal Years

Stephen Jones

WORKING THIN WATERS

Conversations with Captain Lawrence H. Malloy, Jr.

University Press of New England

Hanover and London

University Press of New England, Hanover, NH 03755
Printed in the United States of America

5 4 3 2 1

Library of Congress Cataloging-in-Publication Data

Jones, Stephen, 1935 –
  Working thin waters: conversations with Captain Lawrence H. Malloy, Jr. /
by Stephen Jones.
    p. cm.
Includes bibliographical references.
  ISBN 1– 58465 –103 –2 (alk. paper)
1. Malloy, Lawrence H., 1918 –   . 2. Fishers—New England—Biography.
3. Oyster fisheries—New England—History. I. Malloy, Lawrence H., 1918 –   .
II. Title.
  SH20.M35 J66 2001
  639.2'092—dc21   00–012289

To the gang under the maple tree at West Mystic Wooden Boat Company.

Although we ourselves were formed by imperceptible growth we do not know how to create anything in that way . . . and are unable to visualize a movement so slow that a perceptible result springs from an imperceptible change. We can imagine the living process only by lending it a rhythm which is specifically ours and has no connection with what happens in the creature we are observing.

—Paul Valery, "Man and the Sea Shell"

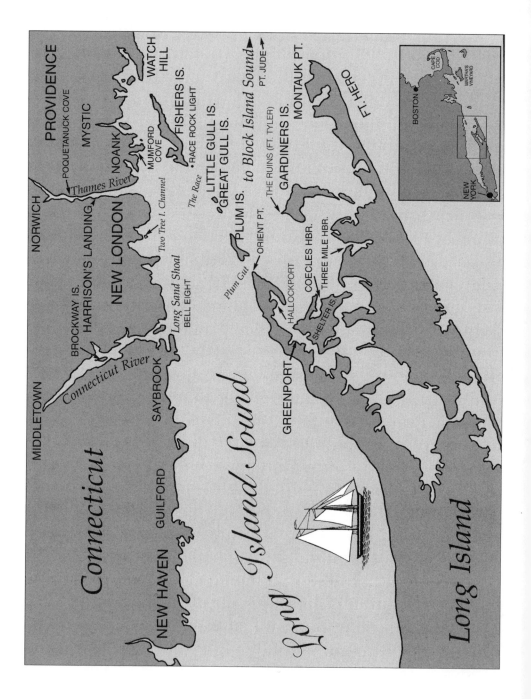

CONTENTS

PART THREE: SWALLOWING THE ANCHOR

ACKNOWLEDGMENTS

In addition to the many who helped with this book and who are mentioned in the appropriate place in the text, I'd like to thank Sina Wright who read the entire manuscript and to excuse her from any errors that, despite her efforts, may persist.

Part One

KEDGING

. . . bear in mind that [this book] . . . may be received for that which it is intended to be, a Kedge-Anchor . . .

— *William N. Brady,*

The Kedge-Anchor or Young Sailor's Assistant, 1864

To kedge. When a ship cannot move ahead, either due to grounding or calm, the crew may place a small anchor in a boat and set it out ahead in the direction desired. The crew aboard the ship will then pull their vessel up to the kedge anchor either by means of machinery or dint of hand.

— *Falorp's Vade Mecum for Crew in these Distracted Times*

1

OYSTER GROUNDS

You will never enjoy the world aright till the sea itself floweth

in your veins . . .

—Thos. Traherne

THERE IS A BOATYARD at the bend in the river just below the railroad bridge that carries the New York to Boston Line. The yard is not much more than a mudhole in the bend of the watercourse that runs another few miles into Fishers Island Sound and thence to Long Island Sound and the Atlantic Ocean. An assortment of venerable shallow-draft boats cling to a pair of wobbly float piers tentatively suspended over water that is barely two feet deep at low tide. There are at the moment a pair of Earl Brockway's plywood oyster scows, a pair of Brockway lobster boats, various wooden yacht tenders, and a pair of Nathaniel Herreshoff fantasies that depend upon Low Country drop leeboards to prevent their leewarding. Seen from the boat yard's ventilation tower, where I write this, these small wooden ketches crouch at the floats, their leeboards hunched, like winged insects contemplating a takeoff that is infinitely postponed.

When we bought this place a dozen years ago it was to run a deep-water venture. From the water at the edge of the federal channel a quarter-mile off we once ran an old eighty-foot schooner drawing eight feet of water in what is known as the "windjammer trade." Built in 1911, *Sylvina W. Beal* had plied from eastern Maine to St. John's, Newfoundland, and the outports to the east. My son Geoffrey had sailed her from Beal Island, Maine, to Cumina, Venezuela. Today in an early summer mist I can barely see the orange balls that marked her mooring and at which now rides a different boat. The old schooner is, in any case, an even remoter vision.

What we have now for glamour out on the mooring is the oysterboat *Anne*, a vessel a quarter-century older than the schooner, and herself once a sailboat. She had been docked a dozen miles to the west at Harrison's Landing on the Thames River at New London, where a family named Malloy had worked her for nearly three-quarters of a century. In his late seventies, Lawrence Malloy, Jr., had recently sold her to a relatively young ship carpenter named Thom Janke. Thom had wisely maintained Larry as part of the crew in a kind of emeritus status.

Anne had an arrangement to provide the Grossmans' seafood shack on the Noank-Mystic Road with oysters for summer weekends, and so every Thursday Larry would come down to the boat yard, ease into one of the beat-up conglomerations of plywood, tar, and roofing nails built by Earl Brockway, and sputter out the shallow bye-channel to the moorings. Once Larry was aboard, *Anne* would cast off and chug downriver, around the bend to the Noank grounds. At the end of the day the Brockway would return from the mooring. Larry and I would sit in the shade on a bench at the top of the ramp with our backs to the Bath House and observe the younger members of *Anne*'s crew heft the twenty-three onion bags filled with oysters up the ramp to the pickup truck.

"I don't think there's a better thing to do," said Larry one day, "than sit in the shade and watch other people do the work you done all your life."

We took this opportunity to discuss everything that mattered at the moment and a good many things that probably didn't. In addition to being in the presence of his old boat and the activity associated with her, Larry felt especially comfortable at the boat yard because he and Captain Thomas Watt had built the carpentry shop there half a century before.

Larry and Tommy had been informal partners in a variety of maritime enterprises ranging from running the Block Island ferry to towing targets in World War Two. I had known Larry and his family for some forty years. His daughter Carol had been a student of mine my first year of teaching in one of the local high schools.

When I first knew Carol she was a quiet young freckle-faced woman who sat near the coat hooks. Somehow I was aware that she was connected to the famous Malloy oystering family. Occasionally I learned about the family businesses of some of her classmates. There were hilarious, dyslexic compositions about a family septic tank company. There were colorful compositions featuring a father's pool hall business. One of Carol Malloy's classmates favored me in home room with monologues about his family's house-wrecking outfit. Another, the son of a marvelous saloon musician, informed me daily on the relative merits of Protestant church business structures. Alas, I recall no accounts from Carol about oystering or any of the other waterfront endeavors for which her father had been famous.

· · ·

A few years after I met Carol there was in my hometown an effort to revive the local Oyster Ground Committee. The oyster grounds in Groton, like most of those in Eastern Connecticut, had lain fallow for a number of years. The last person to serve on the committee that I had even heard of was the late Otto Grossman himself, the man who had run the shellfish shack up the Noank-Mystic road.

The person responsible for the revival was a man named Mortimer Wright. He had made his first great public service commitment by driving an ambulance for the American Field Service in North Africa during World War Two. Ostensibly an insurance and real estate man, Mort was the first person I knew who believed you could do something about the environment besides sitting around the local pub complaining. A Democrat, he had somehow gotten himself elected in a town that had gone Republican since the nineteenth century. I'd met him when I was attempting a percolation test for my septic tank and, standing knee-deep in mud in my yard, I looked up and there was a man in a suit, white shirt, and tie. "You look like you might be a good person to be on the Oyster Ground Committee," he said.

"What's an Oyster Ground Committee?" I said. I barely knew what an oyster was, so long had taking them been prohibited in our waters. As for the "committee" part, what I knew of that particular structure of human enterprise did not strike me as particularly digestible, either. Mort suggested that I might profit from attending a meeting of the Noank Historical Society, another of his projects. As an inducement he announced that Captain Lawrence Malloy, Sr., would address the membership.

"Captain Malloy?"

"The famous oysterman. You see his old green boat *Anne* working out on the grounds here." He pointed to the harbor, which even then was filling up with white fiberglass sloops. "Well, it's not there now."

"I've seen her," I admitted. "Watched her working off the Noank grounds from my lobster boat. As you say, old and green. Low-slung with the wheelhouse aft. Usually seems to be going around in circles." In truth I'd been in love with her.

"At the firehouse. Seven o'clock."

· · ·

In those days the Noank firehouse did not have a separate meeting room and anyone making a speech had to share the space with what was proudly known as the "apparatus." Usually the speaker was badly upstaged by the prewar Seagrave.

By the time I got there that night Mort must have just made his introduction. Other later arrivals were just settling in around me. Judging by the pace of the guest speaker's discourse, however, it seemed as if the famous captain had already been well on his way down the narrative road. A silver-haired man dressed in crisp gray work clothes, he was more than holding his own against the gaudy competition of the fire gear.

Seated behind the flimsy folding table, which cut him off at the chest, Captain Lawrence Malloy, Sr., nevertheless gave the impression of a tall man. Furthermore he was clearly equipped with what seemed to me even then as dangerously long arms. Years later his son, Larry, Jr., confirmed the range of these limbs. They could, he claimed, cover the most remote sector of any wheelhouse. But on this particular night, it was the Captain's verbal range that impressed me. He roamed all over the waterfront, claiming era after era, port after port, job after job. *Anne* was an oysterboat built in 1884. Originally she had been a sloop designed for freighting.

It became clear that the Malloys were not merely oystermen, but had in the interest of survival taken on all manner of work legally available to someone with a boat. They had junked, freighted, and towed. They had dredged, transported scientists, and done a little science themselves. As for illegal waterfront activity such as bootlegging, well, wasn't that why God had created the wink?

This saga of the Malloys continued at breakneck speed for close to two hours, running totally without notes or, alas, structure. Those whom this performance did not merely alarm were enchanted. The Captain especially pleased those who themselves had earned at least part of their living off the water. As I walked out of the firehouse, it occurred to me that in spite of the oral deluge, there must have been a good deal more to this story.

"You ought to go visit the Captain in his lair," said Mort.

2

ABOARD *ANNE*

The only way to know all about an oyster is to be an oyster.

—L. H. Malloy, Sr.

WHILE MORT HAD presumably made the social arrangements, logistics had been left up to me. He had merely told me *Anne* was moored ten miles west at a place called Harrison's Landing in the Quaker Hill section of Waterford. The Landing was on the Thames River directly opposite the United States Navy Submarine Base. The day I went it was hot, and as I drove down the steep riverbank onto the flat that supported the village the mist hung tight on the river. A half-mile off in the glare were the sinister gray shapes of the submarines. This was at the height of the Cold War. Just downstream loomed the mammoth floating dry dock of the Thames Shipyard. Beyond it poked the three spars of the United States Coast Guard Academy barque *Eagle*. In the far mist arched the Gold Star Memorial Bridge, across whose dinosaur hump hummed a steady twinkle of semis, and whose transit I had somehow just accomplished in my pickup. It was, in short, an intimidating neighborhood for someone like me, coming from the sleepy fishing village of Noank.

But what hit me immediately was that Harrison's Landing was very much its own world. Protected—hidden down a steep bank and across the Vermont Central tracks—perhaps a dozen houses were scattered on the flat peninsula. Unlike Noank, or nearby Stonington village, or even the New London waterfront downriver, not one of these buildings had been distinguished by a single architectural feature. It was as if that section of the river valley had already consumed the entire ration of the spectacular allotted to the area. There would have been, in any case, no point in competing with the surroundings. The Malloy house was no exception.

There were in fact two Malloy houses, not in those days much more than stark boxes dressed in white clapboards. One was perched up on the road level, the other was hunkered maybe fifty yards downhill toward the water. Figuring that *Anne* must be in that direction, I bounced down the dirt road past an assortment of what looked like parts of heavy marine construction equipment to the dock. In the tangle there was the top of a tripod mast and the top of a wheelhouse that I hoped would be *Anne*. Was I at last about to go aboard? There were, after all, various dismembered parts of boats about on the land, so I could not assume that the particular sequence of rigging and structure I had spotted was indeed assembled at some point, as yet out of sight, as *Anne*.

To get the last ten yards to her was not easy. There was a shack that seemed to be a product of a trailer truck collision with a load of cinder block and asbestos. The plywood door to this edifice stood ajar, guarding a rank residency. It was probably the only shack I never felt the slightest desire to peep into. Outside were rusty iron devices that looked like bear traps, but that I figured were probably oyster dredges. There were twenty-five-gallon drums of grease and lube oil standing about like amputees. At last I saw a certain coherence that I confidently recognized as *Anne*. She was, however, completely ringed by heaps of junk. If I could ever actually arrive at her, the question would then be how she would ever extract herself from all this. Perhaps we would spend the day here in the heat, broiling, beset by decaying gear.

And then there was the thought of a day spent trapped by my host, Captain Malloy, Sr. It was one thing to be part of an enthralled audience at a public meeting from which one could, like the Seagrave pumper, at any time escape. It was quite another to cast off and go to sea, trapped with this same man of long wind and longer arms in a wheelhouse no bigger than a large telephone booth. (Indeed, years later I found out that the Malloys had provided the Mystic Seaport Museum with just such a telephone booth made from just such a wheelhouse.)

The engine, however, was already running. It was a heavy diesel and made the already thick morning air weigh even more.

"Well, you're late." There he was, already aboard, a tall man stooping slightly, the better to close the distance to his pocket watch. "Good thing we had something to do." I did not, of course, dare look at my own watch right away, but when I sneaked a peek I could see he had a point. There must have been five minutes in which he had found the *something to do*.

To get right up to the boat I picked my way through an obstacle course of rusty iron gear whose function I did not know and made my way across broken planks whose job I hoped was to support people exactly like me over water.

As I began my trip across the plank I noticed that *Anne* was by now tethered to the land merely by her port bow spring. Up close, I could see there actually was open water aft. And there must have been three feet between her rail and the pier, such as it was. Teetering on the plank, I had the feeling that I was not quite going to make it aboard. She had a series of tires strung down her topside to act as fenders. I calculated that if I didn't quite make it across, I could land on one of these, or at least pull myself up out of the water onto the nearest one, as they dangled right to the waterline. The only question was whether I would go ungentle into that good water between the boat and the pier or remain standing foolishly upon the land.

While I was thus meditating, a hand reached out and swung me aboard. This was not the Captain, but a lean man with a face more battered than weatherbeaten. I don't recall a formal introduction, but looking back through the years, I realize that this was the man known as *Walt*. He seemed to have his own space aboard *Anne*. When we were underway he vanished entirely for long periods to emerge mysteriously in the midst of some complicated piece of deck business as if he'd been there all along. It became clear the wheelhouse was not his territory.

As Captain Malloy backed *Anne* down, I peeped out the little square window in the back of the house. The water boiled aft and looked refreshingly cool. Above us on all sides, the junk subsided deferentially. Very little of it actually followed us out into the channel.

. . .

Up in the wheelhouse one had a lordly feeling. Captain Malloy had lowered some of the windows. The air that had been so oppressive ashore and even in the slipway now poured exhilaratingly in over the wooden sash.

Captain Malloy was talking continuously, in a tone somewhere between his firehouse manner and the gruff greeting at the dock. *Anne*, he explained, was what is known as a *ten-knot boat*. That meant that she would go a little over eleven miles per hour under most any conditions, although she would probably most economically cruise at eight knots, or nine miles per hour. As this was double the rate of even the strongest adverse currents, such a turn of speed was considered perfectly adequate for the sort of work *Anne* would be called upon to perform. He also wanted me to know that should she be asked to tow another boat or a barge full of oysters, she would probably still be capable of the same speed. "Working or just cruising, that's what she is."

I was listening, but I was also looking around the wheelhouse. The helm was a huge mahogany affair with spokes. To the right was something like a shift lever, a piece of mahogany hinged to the deck. The lever had a handle on top and a hole through it just below the handle. Captain Malloy explained that this was "a locking pawl" and when you placed the hole in the lever over a particular spoke in the helm the device held the wheel right there, freeing you for other duties. "There's a lot more to running an oyster-boat than just steering," he said. He then showed me the "hyster" controls, which were actually clotheslines running just under the overhead and passing through blocks down through the deck. In various places along the line were clothespins that apparently served as toggles, to act as stops in crucial moments of the "hysting" evolution. From what I could see of the line, it seemed to me that the condition of the rope would have made a housewife hesitate to commit a pair of soggy long johns to a gentle breeze in the back yard. As for what the line looked like as it passed down through the bowels of the boat, one could only imagine. For emergencies, there was a small ship-to-shore radio up in the overhead, but there were no other electron-ics—no radar, depth finder, or radio direction finder, the global positioning device of its day. There was a flat compass in a box ahead of the helm.

. . .

The beautiful mahogany spoke helm was worth another look. "It seems as if it's off a yacht," I said.

"The Roosevelt family on Long Island."

I asked him if he meant Teddy.

"Teddy, oh yes, I met Teddy all right. I was a young feller down in Oyster Bay workin' for Flowers."

I'd heard of people working in the hard days for food, but never merely to supply their minimum daily requirement for bouquets. But then I fig-ured when you were with Captain Malloy, especially on his own turf, you might believe anything. Besides, the wheelhouse was a bit noisy, and I didn't always catch his accent, which was a hodgepodge of Down East and New York. In any case, I hadn't yet developed the courage to pick him up on anything. Years later I was walking up from the harbor at Oyster Bay and saw a sign announcing I was trespassing upon the property of Frank M. Flower & Son Oyster Company. It was right in that stretch that Malloy's encounter had apparently taken place.

"They sent me up off the boat to fetch some milk and eggs. That's what they did with the kids. Sent 'em on shoreside errands. I was a kid all right, but I was a big kid. Long arms." He stretched one out, and I stepped aside. "So I see this little guy bouncing down the street. Steel-rim glasses, mous-tache, hair parted in the middle, a high squeaky voice. *'Well, well,'* he says to me." Here the old fisherman got into a comic voice. *"'It's about time you showed up. Here put these on.'* And what's he got in his arms but a pair of boxing gloves! *'Come on, hurry up!'* he says. *'Put 'em on. I haven't got all day. You know I'm a very busy man.'* Well, I just thought he was a *crazy* man. I just thought what has happened to me but a *crazy* man. Shoves these boxing gloves on me and is about to put on a pair himself."

"And that was—Teddy Roosevelt?"

"He'd sent down to the docks for a sparring partner. He was very athletic, you know. Or thought he was. *Vigorous. Very vigorous.* The other kid, the real sparring partner that was supposed to be, he was late, I guess. Roosevelt sees me coming along, about the right age. I can't say he must have been too pleased with the long arms."

When I was in Oyster Bay, I tried to pace off the logistics of this yarn. The way old Malloy had told it to me, Roosevelt had been standing up on Sagamore Hill, or at least that's how I remembered him remembering it. But Sagamore Hill, of course, is way out of town. If you pace Malloy's narrative off from the Flowers' Oyster Company, just as the path rises up into the village of Oyster Bay, you come to what is now known as "Teddy's," a bar on the ground floor of an old hotel on the corner of downtown. There's a sign inside that tells you the site used to be the location of the Summer White House during T. R.'s incumbency. There are photos of the President conducting the nation's business there in shirtsleeves. With that minor logistical alteration, the story makes perfect sense. Young Lawrence Malloy, the oysterman, must have been a break in the nation's business.

· · ·

The story of *Anne*'s birth came to me on that day from Captain Malloy himself. Thirty years later his son, then himself probably older than his father had been when he told the story, found news in this account, as indeed he had in the Teddy Roosevelt story. "But then the old man didn't always tell me everything."

Are these the sort of stories a father withholds from his son? Or are these the kind of yarns a man might well "embroider" for a young stranger?

According to old Malloy, *Anne* had been constructed in 1884 at Smithtown, a Long Island community about halfway out from New York City. She had been built as a square-stern sloop with a centerboard and was some six feet shorter than her present length.

The man who commissioned her, if that is the word, owned a general store in Smithtown and during the depression of the early 1880s found that he had two problems. The first was that many of his customers had run up a considerable tab. The other was that there was, in those pre-Expressway days, no reliable road over which to ship goods to Smithtown. It occurred to him that a small vessel that could transport freight might be the answer. Several of his debtors were handy with tools, a few were actually shipwrights. "But we have no money for materials," they told him. He pointed out that there was a wealthy man from the City who owned a swamp with white oak nearby. The man would not be back out until spring. If the boat was built by then, they would at least have their timber. Actually it took them two seasons, and they merely covered the project up with leaves during the season when the man was out on the island. The leaves not only served as camouflage but kept the hull from drying out too much. As for nails, the men found some locust and fashioned treenails (or "trunnels," as boat builders call them). At the time I was aboard in the 1960s, Captain Malloy assured me there were yet a number of the planks held to the frames by these wooden pegs.

. . .

That day there wasn't a rock or a rowboat we passed for which Captain Malloy lacked information. It is true that the navigators of the Pulewat Islands in the South Seas teach their profession in the narrative rather than numerical manner—that, as Thomas Gladwin points out, "east is a big bird" and not 090 degrees. To a Pulewat sailor, a story about what happened to an uncle with a blue-footed booby thirty years ago was relevant information in identifying a sea mark. Captain Malloy's filibuster, however, seemed to have more of hedge marking in it than of pedagogy. As with many self-educated men of his generation, he seemed to strike an uncomfortable rhetorical stance in the company of someone he perceived to be "educated" and fell into a bookish stiffness, relieved by what he must have seen as "racy material."

Some of his stories I, as a local, had grown up with. Some, I thought, had actually been better told by my own elders. Many seemed worn flat by what might have been years of repetition. It wasn't until years later when I'd come to know his son Larry that I found a comfortable voice for this material. In any case, old Captain Malloy could not match his narration to his navigation. No amount of accelerating his speech could keep pace with the relentless diesel, and the objects of his anecdotes had long receded in *Anne*'s wash as new inspirations crowded in on her bows.

There was, of course, business of a nonnarrative nature to accomplish. Precisely what this was going to be he preferred to keep secret. His manner was that of a slightly wicked uncle pulling dubious treats out of odd pockets. In any case, once we were free of the lighthouses at the mouth of the Thames estuary there was open sea, before whose expanse the raconteur fell suitably silent. It wasn't until we began to close with the line of New York islands that seemed to nail down the southern horizon that he started up again. The islands were part of the terminal moraine that was the North Fork of Long Island, and Captain Malloy, in a kind of circus barker style, took a shot at the geology. In his view great and mysterious things had happened here. He even allowed as to how some of these grand moments had occurred prior to his arrival on earth. Where we were headed, however, was one of his sly secrets. He pointed *Anne*'s blunt, round bow at the middle island, which was, I knew, Great Gull.

What I knew at the time was rather vague. It wasn't until years later I learned that like its neighboring islands, Great Gull had once been the location of a fort built to ward off the Spaniards in 1898. In those days military intelligence was sufficiently vague. Following the sinking of the battleship *Maine* in Havana there were sightings of the Spanish fleet from Nova Scotia to Cuba. Eventually, of course, the United States fleet did sink the Spanish ships, which had been flushed out of a southern Cuban harbor by Teddy Roosevelt, among others. The Gull Island fort had been upgraded in World War One and again for the next war, after which the island was taken over by the Museum of Natural History (founded in part by Teddy Roosevelt's father).

The Museum wanted to set up a sanctuary for terns. In order to encourage the quick, shy little sea birds, the ornithologists felt they needed to demolish any structures that might look threatening. The Malloys got the contract and two of Captain Malloy's sons, Bill and Larry, had spent a year on the island taking apart the fort doorknob by doorknob. There were "scientists" on the island in summer as part of an ongoing tagging program. There's a wonderful account of this in Michael Harwood's book *The View from Great Gull*, which even has a short account of our man.

As *Anne* approached the island, however, Captain Malloy kept all this under wraps. All my life the island had been a mystery to me: a hump of green or purple or in winter sometimes a smudge of white. There were many days when, in fog or rain, it simply ceased to exist. I naturally looked forward to going ashore.

As we closed with the land, the eye-smarting smell of the island flowed in over the wheelhouse sill. From under the wheelhouse window there was a groan that must have come from Walt. Ahead a pier materialized. Its very existence suggested a complex life on the island of which I'd never dreamed. From what seemed to be a low building under the hill a single figure emerged and began the long walk down to the water. She was there waiting for us as we steamed into dock, a slender woman in brown work clothes. There were dozens of terns twitching about in the air, but as for humans, she was it. There did not seem to be another human in sight.

Captain Malloy nestled *Anne*'s bow against a spiling, and when Walt made to loop a line around, he waved him off. With hardly a squeak from the tires hung on the rail, the Captain held her bow against the pier with the engine. (In all my years later on *Anne* it never ceased to amaze me how often the Malloys would leave *Anne* to her own benign devices.) Then he jumped down from the wheelhouse and brandished a small white card aloft. Apparently it was a postcard. The ornithologist laughed and snatched the card from him. The Captain trotted back to the wheelhouse, mounted the steps and backed the boat down. The woman was halfway up the hill to her home by the time we lost sight of her. All that expanse of water, then the little piece of paper handed over to her.

"Mail run," explained the Captain. "Get paid the same for a postcard as for a ton of fruitcake."

. . .

We skipped the next island, Little Gull with its tall white lighthouse, and angled down the edge of the rip of the Race where Captain Malloy informed me all of Long Island Sound west of Stamford was running out over a two-hundred-foot drop. The far end of the Race was marked by Fishers Island, at the western end of which was another fort. We steamed past the jetties that led up into Silver Eel Pond and rounded North Hill. Leaving the Dumplings and Flat Hammock to port, we swung up through the yacht fleet into West Harbor. At a mooring was Pierre S. duPont's powerful seventy-one-foot 1959 Abeking & Rasmussen steel deep-sea ketch *Barlovento II*. We threaded our way through a mooring field packed with other lesser yachts. Walt trundled out onto the foredeck a twenty-five gallon barrel of Vedol lube. The joke of the moral superiority of *Anne*'s mission among the gleaming toys was not lost on her owner. When he nosed his boat into the Powerhouse Dock with but a mild sigh from the tires on the rail, he greeted the small knot of gathered populace like a returning hero.

Indeed, the arrival of *Anne* was an event. Great significance, of course, tends to load up around the simplest transfer of the most banal goods on almost any island. Every exchange is like Christmas. Yet I sensed there was something special about *Anne*: Gull Island Tern Colony; Fishers Island Gas Dock—we were on a world tour! At the next pier lay Mrs. Pierre S. duPont's fifty-five-foot 1927 Endeavor blue, wooden *Maid of Honor*. With her jaunty Edwardian vertical cutwater, the great brass funnel amidships that the hands kept perpetually radiant, and the pair of brass dolphin sideboys that guarded each side of the cockpit, she had served as Admiralty Pinnace #1694, ferrying the British admiral at Gibraltar.

. . .

Shed of our freight, we were now free at last to visit the oyster grounds. These were back across Fishers Island Sound three miles due north under the hill at the fishing village of Noank at the mouth of the Mystic River.

These grounds stretched across the southern end of the harbor between the moored yacht fleet and the east channel that ran out past Ram Island.

Identified as such, they went back to the turn of the twentieth century and were the chief reason I was aboard. By reading the State Statutes and an agricultural bulletin I had already learned that grounds had been granted by commissions such as the one I was on for "the purposes of the propagation of shellfish." There was clearly going to be an opportunity for me to learn the finer points of my new job. As we chugged up to the Noank spindle and slowed into a turn out over the flats below the mooring field, I was preparing to discuss aquatic husbandry with the Captain when he announced:

"I was told you know how to shovel."

There was no one else in the wheelhouse.

. . .

It was funny how in all my checking out of *Anne* I had not noticed that pile of shell upon her deck or for that matter the two big shovels leaning up against the bulwarks. I did, of course, know how to shovel. Not only had I been doing just that when I'd been recruited by Mortimer Wright, but I had worked my way through the first two years of college by digging ditches in the summer. Shoveling had been a talent I had put to use while serving in the Coast Guard at a lifeboat station (conveniently situated on sandy ground). I also knew, even without checking on the wicked gleam in the old man's eye, that whatever I had known about handling a shovel was now of absolutely no use. I wondered how Teddy Roosevelt must have felt putting on those boxing gloves.

The old man had slowed the boat so that she was just barely creeping ahead against the last of the ebb. The sun was right over the mast now, and the shells, which I had assumed to be part of the smell of Gull Island, now had their own piquancy. I had worked near a shell pile at the lifeboat station and there had been days there when the sun was high when I'd felt as if someone were kicking me in the stomach. It was not quite that bad now, but the notion that with each shovelful thrown overboard I'd be reducing the source of the stench was a bright inspiration.

There was also Walt, the other shovel. When I'd begun as a day laborer, the boss advised me, "Watch the old colored folks. They're not as fast as the white boys from the football team, but by ten o'clock all the football players will be under the tree, and the colored men will be going to four-thirty."

Imitating Walt's methodical, accurate strokes as best I could, I fell to work pitching the shells over the rail. The temptation was to lean on the shovel, WPA style, and observe the oyster shells twittering their way down into cool obscurity, but I felt the Captain's hard eye on my neck. It was true I had let a few dribble down onto the tires that hung from the side, but I figured they would sooner or later dribble off in the natural motion of the ship. The fact was there was damn little motion; beamy *Anne* sat there like a church. I reached over the rail to flick a few recalcitrant shells off the tires. The old man snatched the tool from my hand and demonstrated the proper technique, which included a flourish at the far end of the fling that indeed did give a festive air to the task. (More to the point, this flourish guaranteed there would not be any residue sticking to the shovel that might end up back aboard.) This was not quite Walt's style, but no doubt he had earned the right to merely pitch without the woo.

Later, ashore, I learned that the purpose of putting the shell overboard is to provide a hard substrate for the "set" to—well—set upon. Without some such obdurate floor upon the bottom, the young oyster is apt to sift down through the top fine layer of mud and suffocate. Eleanor Clark, in her lyrical evocation of the oyster industry, *The Oysters of Locmariaquer,* has a wonderful description of how the Brittany oyster workers lay down tiles that in many cases go back generations. Clark would have us believe that these tiles are of household quality. Using oyster shells themselves, however, has the advantage that not only are they cheaper, but the irregularities in the craggy surfaces make for more hiding places against predators. At the moment, however, I had no overview of the tradition. I had the shovel.

The shovel was much like a coal shovel, wide and deep, but the sides did not go all the way to the lip, which gave you a chance to sneak in under the pile. I worried at first about scraping the deck, but I could see it was paved with a thick, dark surface that I later learned was "bridge tile." Eventually the deck was free of shell and I leaned my shovel against the rail next to Walt's. There was a rumble from under my feet and a wheeze from above. The dredge was swinging out over the rail. Down it went into the water. Oh, my God, I thought. Are we now going to scoop all these shells up again?

What we were going to do was eat lunch. The dredge had apparently been lowered to serve as an anchor. Walt had already broken out a newspaper in which something was wrapped into which he plunged his face. There was a thermos standing next to him on the corner of the cabin, which, with the wheelhouse rising behind him, made a seat. As the current and wind swung the boat on the dredge, his spot was in the shade.

"You bring anything to eat?" said a voice from the wheelhouse.

"I didn't," I said.

A hand shot out from the window above and handed me half of a sandwich. It was Spam on Wonder Bread.

"Thank you," I said.

"You always eat on this boat," said the Captain. "But I ain't got extra coffee. You eat on this boat, but you don't always drink."

"Fine," I said, and ate the Spam and Wonder Bread slowly. There was butter in there, too.

A twin-screw, flybridge sportfisherman roared past. "Another man who's late," said the voice from the wheelhouse. "You see 'em all the time. I figure they're going so fast they must all be late."

When the sportfisherman's wake got to us it slapped against the hull, but it did not raise it.

After lunch, Walt disappeared. In a moment I heard what I had at first thought was the raw water discharge at the stern. In a moment he was back. The engine started again, and the dredge added its noises as it rose creaking and squeaking from the harbor and, dripping mud, weed and water, swung aboard.

As we headed home the narration was pretty much abandoned, but we did spot several more boats that were judged by the Captain to "be late."

. . .

After that day, from shore or afloat on other craft, I watched *Anne* work the Noank grounds with a different eye. Mostly she made odd little circles round and round on the dredge wire like a dog tethered in the back yard. Occasionally you could actually see the dredge itself rising triumphant from the sea. (Or what you hoped was triumphant.) When sport yachts flashed past her at her stolid work, I could imagine the old man making his jokes. If I had binoculars handy I thought I could see the old man up in the wheelhouse, peering out above Walt, who was leaning back against the cabin. As time passed, of course, I no longer thought of her in any detail, and she eventually receded into the background. At some imperceptible point I must have stopped seeing her entirely. Then I heard a distressing story.

NOTE

MALLOY SENIOR'S YOUTH (p. 10): Lawrence Malloy Senior's father was an engineer on the New York–Jacksonville steamer, where he met his future wife whose Vermont family owned orange groves. Lawrence was born in 1890, and his mother died when he was only three. As the son of a sailor he was brought up by an aunt who lived at Peck's Slip near the Fulton Market in lower Manhattan. He went to sea at age nine as mess boy aboard the smack (fishing schooner) *Columbia*, which worked the Georges Bank. The experience was enough to give him his fill of deep water.

At 6' 4", Malloy Senior was a giant among the rougher element on the New York waterfront at the turn of the twentieth century. A contemporary neighbor, the young Al Capone, was an effective bouncer at 5'11" when, according to Robert J. Schoenberg in *Mr. Capone*, the average New York "arrestee" was 5'3".

3

ENTER LAWRENCE MALLOY, JR.

SOMEONE TOLD ME that Captain Malloy had retired. *Anne* herself was in her slip at Harrison's Landing, her engine removed. Slowly the story began to take form. Apparently what had happened was that, unable to get anyone to go with him, the old man had taken to working *Anne* alone. Walt was out of the picture. It was January. Oystering does not stop for winter and there he was, now a man in his seventies, out on the Noank grounds in a boat older than he was. He evidently had had the dredge overboard and had locked the helm in the Roosevelt's pawl so *Anne* was dutifully making her circles. For whatever reason he came down from the wheelhouse. How many times had he done this? This time, however, for some reason, his rhythm was off. His first step was on the narrow deck, his second on the rail cap, and the third was in Noank harbor.

And there he was, treading water in January in a deserted harbor as his boat went away from him. "But I knew *Anne,* she'd come back for me," he later said.

With the helm locked over in the pawl, of course, she did circle back, and because he had not panicked, the old man was able to grab her as she chugged on by. There were those old tires arranged all along the rail. On this occasion they made a handy boarding ladder. (He was to claim that they never really were intended as fenders. A good boat handler didn't need fenders. They were aboard for just such overboard emergencies. Somebody pointed out that for that matter, a good seaman didn't fall overboard. In any case, his son Larry continued the practice of carrying the tires.) Once he'd gotten his hands into a tire, it was a small matter to scramble up *Anne's* low freeboard and dash aft into the engine room, where he stripped off his clothes, including his long underwear, and did a keep-warm dance before the big, greasy diesel Hercules. I've often wondered if any of us in Noank had been idly looking out on the harbor that winter day, and if so if any of us who might have caught sight of *Anne* had had any sense of the drama we were witnessing.

That it was indeed drama to the old man led to his undoing. He made mention of his little adventure that night at home. His sons Bill and Larry conspired to prevent further adventures. You might say it was a kind of *Driving Miss Daisy* moment. I recall a similar crisis in my family when my uncle, to make sure he always accompanied his aging father's automotive excursions, would remove the rotor from the distributor in his father's car. In their father the Malloy brothers faced a far more formidable mechanic. To forestall him from any more driving of *Anne* they set up an A-frame with a come-along and removed the Hercules. As Larry later put it, "We decided that he didn't need a boat at that time, and anything short of taking out the entire engine would not have stopped him from going to sea."

. . .

That was the last I heard of either *Anne* or Malloy Senior until I read his obit when he died just shy of ninety. My next contact with the family was through his son, Lawrence Malloy Jr. In all the things I do remember about the Malloy family, I'm amazed that I don't recall the first time I met Larry.

I suspect it was when he began attending the monthly meetings of the Groton Shellfish Commission. He was in the basement of the Town Hall sitting toward the back of the room on one of those uncomfortable folding chairs, his cap bill low over his eyes. He was by then maybe only a few years younger than his father had been when I'd first seen him at the Noank firehouse. A solid, stocky figure, Larry was built on a much different frame than his lanky father. His face, however, was that of a man who'd spent his life outdoors. Indeed, in that period frequently there was a bandage or small, curing sores on his cheeks, around his eyes, and on his earlobes. In the general bull session before the meeting got under way I remember him growling something about replacing the garboard plank on *Anne*. He was annoyed, not by having to do the work on the aging boat, for which he clearly had affection, but because work had also been necessary on his own aging body. That very afternoon the surgeon had removed a piece of his ear. Unlike most people complaining of their operations, Larry Malloy then proceeded to launch into a bit of history that made me realize that here was a life that deserved close study.

"It must be because it's the ear I stick out the wheelhouse window." He went on to tell us that his father also had a piece of his ear missing. "The old man claimed it was from a fight he had in New York back at the turn of the century. A man driving a beer wagon hit him with his horse whip when he wouldn't get out of the way, but Pappy, he grabbed the whip and pulled the driver off the cart seat. They had it out there on South Street. Me, I had always thought the missing ear part was from a rat that had nibbled him. You know: one night when he was asleep aboard *Anne*."

There was a gentler side of Larry that appealed to me as well. Lorraine Chappell tells the story of the time her husband Ron, the Shellfish Commission chairman, was recovering from a major lung problem, and Larry came calling with a bucket of oysters. "I'd never met the man," says Lorraine, " and here he was in his boots and all at the front door. He's got a bucket of oysters, or at least I think that's what it's going to be when he reaches in and pulls out this dog collar which had oyster set growing on it like rhinestones applied by a drunken hand. I gather that his idea was to show Ron that there was still hope in the river. 'You can see that the oysters are doing real good,' he says. 'I'm sorry I can't say the same for the dog.' I've been a visiting nurse all my adult life. You know some people bring flowers. Some people bring candy. Some people even bring whiskey to cheer up the patient, but Larry Malloy and that dog collar with the oyster set was the best. "

. . .

Through the years I began spending more and more time with Larry. We not only traveled about on *Anne,* but he shipped often with my son and me on our schooner *Sylvina W. Beal.* He presided aboard the schooner when we took out Girl Scout troops. We went to sail training rendezvous at the yachting center at Newport. We attended civic celebrations in his hometown of Greenport. On two occasions Larry joined us in the Leeward Islands. We celebrated his seventy-eighth birthday aboard *Beal* in Marigot Bay, St. Lucia. What emerged from all these exchanges was the life story of a complete waterfront person.

. . .

It turned out that not only was Larry Malloy an oysterman, but an all-round marine contractor whose activities included cable layer, channel and basin dredger, lighthouse repairer, target boat operator, crash boat coxswain, tour boat spieler, dock builder, painter, rigger, ferryboat quartermaster, submarine salvager, carpenter, mechanic, oyster runner . . .

As we traveled about together on the water or along its edge, it was hard to get past a job without coming to realize that a Malloy had had something to do with it. One day we started upriver at Mystic Seaport where I had made a phone call in the shoreside booth made from the pilothouse of a vessel named *Miranda* , a small building that Malloy had transported athwartships the foredeck of another of his oysterboats, the former 1910 bumboat *Alice*. Downriver we passed over his oyster grounds, then out to Groton Long Point, where he had laid the cable to Fishers Island; thence to Dumpling Island, where he had removed the skeletal tower when the old lighthouse lantern had been restored. We proceeded out to Silver Eel Pond, Fishers Island, where he had freighted coal; thence to Race Rock Light, the foundation of which he had rebuilt; and back into Pirate's Cove, West Harbor, where there was a barge rotting that he had left there after the Race Rock Light project. Nor did this cover everything. Eighty feet down in what is known as "the well" off Dumpling, we had passed over another Malloy project that is perhaps best left in the murk.

. . .

While Larry Malloy was definitely a man's man in a predominantly man's world, I discovered that women also enjoyed his company. They cared about him not for his ingenuity in recycling old maritime gear or his skills in handling a boat. It has something to do with the twinkle in his eye and an accompanying courteousness that, if his English were more formal, one might be tempted to call Old World. He did not, of course, kiss hands or dangle handkerchiefs. I don't recall him actually bowing and I don't remember him holding doors or proffering cloaks. He was simply courtly without being a flatterer. Beyond that, I am guessing. I just know that a variety of women whom I observed in our travels together had a warm feeling for him and would in his absence ask after him. In fact you could see that they found him even downright lovable.

What women find lovable in an old man is probably not quite what they find lovable in a young one, if that indeed is love. The affection of women for such men may not quite be the love they have for children, but there is some of the maternal in it. The emotion may be more what some women have for a favorite animal, something larger, say, than a cat, but not threatening. Perhaps it is more what those who know nothing of the actual beady-eyed viciousness of the ursine think of when they imagine a bear.

Old photos, however, show that Larry had what might be characterized as a "dashing phase," complete with mustache and a more svelte figure. If this were not quite Errol Flynn it certainly was not Kris Kringle. In another phase in his youth Larry wore glasses and looked so much like his son Wayne that to peer at a photo of the 1940s is to fall through a time warp. On the other hand, the man in the photo on his Merchant Marine "Z" card from some forty years back is a complete stranger to me, though there may be a relative of his whom I have not met who now carries that face. When Larry and I went to the Caribbean together a few years ago the man in his passport photo looked like a Noriega hit man. While I recognized that most passport images have a way of criminalizing the visage of their holders, so sinister was this portrait that I insisted he get a new picture and even drove him to the photographer. What emerged from the darkroom was still a thug, but instead of a hood in the hire of a banana republic dictator, he was someone who might have been hired as a bodyguard by Winnie-the-Pooh.

4

THE WATERFRONT LIFE

BEYOND THE TWINKLE in the eye, the manners, and the huggability, Larry's appeal, of course, is his romantic life, or the life that is perceived as romantic. Such a life is a candidate for romance not only because of the sea, but because of the charming disjunction between work and the monetary system that seems to go with the Malloys' line of business. The majority of readers at the close of the twentieth century who are engaged in legitimate enterprise are either on salary or work by the hour on more or less regular schedules. In either case there is an agreed-upon payday, and, the odd accounting office snafu aside, the pay is a predictable amount. The tax system and the bookkeeping practices based upon the tax system are not congenial to other methods. In fact, going outside this system gives the appearance of a willful evasion of the law. Alternative ways to finance labor and commodities seem either shady or romantic or possibly romantic because shady. The fact is that the tax-driven bookkeeping system is largely a late twentieth century phenomenon of the urban and its satellite suburban culture.

The waterfront culture, in its complex use of what might loosely be called barter, however, is not a recent criminal attempt to evade the norm. It is actually the tradition; the modern tax system is the deviate. Zoning regulations in many waterfront communities recognize traditional uses of property that are not in phase with recent suburbanization and that permit existing nonconforming uses. There is, however, no such thing as a "grandfathered" system of bookkeeping. The issue is one that far transcends accounting—if one can, in these days of the Reign of the Bean Counters, accept that there is anything that transcends accounting. In many ways this is not even about taxation or the government's right to spend those taxes on certain items. Rather, it is about the way people relate to their work and to all the other people who are involved in that work.

The way in which labor and commodities are exchanged is at the heart of the traditional waterfront style of life. Larry's daughter Donna dropped by the boatyard one day.

"I never knew then and I don't know now how the money worked in our family. I was always brought up to believe we were poor. Very poor. But then . . ." Her voice trailed off in a shrug.

Ironically, her remark echoed a statement I'd heard her father make about his father several times. It was also something I'd heard in other fishing families and families involved in other kinds of waterfront work during the middle of the century. On one level we may be looking at what is called by nervous taxmen "the underground economy." Even economists call it "the black economy" and attempt to salvage it for the taxman through the notion of imputed income. Under that term, sweat equity and barter are given precise quantitative values, a notion in whose reality only an accountant could have faith. Much of waterfront work is driven by logistics and weather. Most deals are made on a "while-you're-at-it" basis, the "it" that you are "at" being an entirely different job, very likely for a different customer. Such economy of movement makes it difficult to arrive at a realistic hourly rate, to say nothing of mileage, fuel, and other contingencies. What makes one waterman more skillful than another, and presumably therefore entitled to more reward, is this very ability to improvise his way in and out of these "while-you're-at-its."

On another level such mysterious ways with a buck may well be just a cultural difference in handling what the more abstract types would call commerce. As John Kenneth Galbraith shows in *Money*, the abstract manipulation of the economy that we take as the norm these days is a relatively new concept, confined to certain strata and regions of society. Work on the water exists in a kind of self-contained, improvised, salvage culture of complex barter and mutual assistance, or, as we have recently called it, "networking" and "sweat equity." It is the work of the hand and the tool in a context of tide and weather. Money is a remoter way to understand what you are doing moment by moment and what you are all about in the longer run. To contract manipulators such as the insurance lawyer Wallace Stevens, "money is a kind of poetry." To people in Malloy's line of work, the poetry is more what Gerard Manley Hopkins had in mind when he wrote: "Glory be to God for . . . all trades, their gear and tackle and trim." Of course, no Malloy would admit to so pious a conception.

. . .

This is not a matter confined to taxes. There is the whole area of licensing and permits. When George McGugan used to dredge in the Mystic River he did it in the *Captain Frank,* a barge he'd cobbled together out of odd parts and named for Larry Malloy's father-in-law. George went to work with a plan sketched on the back of an envelope, his contract a handshake. Nowadays his son has had to create an entire company with a two-story office building to handle what used to be filed in his father's hip pocket.

When Larry Malloy was in business the hand that took the cash was the hand that did the work. In the event there was no exchange of cash, there was a swapping of labor for gear. In the case of the potato business, the seasonal services of the boat as a produce freighter were exchanged in part for year-round space at the Halyoake Farm pier, a tenure that included the Malloys' oystering business, which ostensibly had nothing to do with the Hallocks' farm. In another case Malloy worked out a deal with a small marine engine company for a landing spot by simply building the modest facility, bulkheading by jetting the spiles with his washdown pump and backfilling with his daily load of oyster shells. If economy of means is one field mark of the poetic, compression or concentration is another, and concreteness is a third, then doing business without pausing to divert the process into the verbose abstraction of the monetary system would seem to make a superior poetry.

While John Ruskin struggled mightily in the nineteenth century to compose an ethical aesthetics of work, and Marx was at his best in exposing the ugly effects of the worker being alienated from his task, the sentimentalization of physical labor on land or sea is neither ethical nor aesthetic. Larry Malloy's kitchen overlooks the docks where his family has kept their boats. On the walls are photographs and paintings of some of the vessels he has worked on: the oysterboat *Anne,* the bumboat *Alice,* the ferryboat *Catskill.* When all is said and done very few fishermen have pictures of stockbrokers at work on the walls of their homes. Nor, for that matter, do stockbrokers themselves.

· · ·

Working the waters, especially in the days of the Malloys, seems to be something like being a jazz musician. Just as with jazz, where you may not always have a gig but are always a musician, whether you have a job or not you are always a boatman. You may play in different combinations of other instruments. While you may specialize on a particular instrument yourself you may double on other instruments and maybe even from time to time be required to sing for your supper or at least develop a patter between maneuvers. Fads for music and seafood come and go. The pay is uncertain. Sometimes it seems ridiculously easy. You are being paid for something that other people may do as a hobby or recreation. You develop unfrugal habits that come back to haunt you in hard times. Go with the large organizations and there is some sense of security, but there is always the nagging feeling you are somehow selling out. Even if the benefits are not as good, you'd be truer to yourself with your own small group. You try to adapt and wonder how much adapting will turn you into somebody you no longer recognize as yourself. Part of the adapting is to move about. After awhile it's hard to know if you're doing this because you have to for economic reasons or because it's your psychic nature. Some places are better than others. There are the equivalents of concert halls and low dives. There is always the threat of the criminal element taking over. After a while it doesn't matter why you are traveling or what the venue is. This is what you do. You develop a great deal of affection for the one part of your life that you always have with you and over which you have control; you come to love your tools.

As for plans and procedures, the whole way you go about your business, here is where you find your challenge. There are elaborately scored arrangements where everybody knows what to do ahead of time. There are improvisations that range from those based on charts to traditional head arrangements and on out to the ragged edges of convention where you jury-rig solutions that strike observers as so without precedence as to be what they perceive as "free."

You have your rivals, but unlike other business there is the feeling that if you're not all in the same boat you're at least in the same water. Because of this sense of community there may be a certain amount of swapping of gear and even borrowing of personnel. Beyond this community, however, you are outlaws. Even your own domestic relationships develop and decay when you are far away on the job. You are often mistrusted or idealized. There are few ordinary relationships for ordinary matters. You develop your own lingo that outsiders find either offputting or colorful, in which case they adopt it in ways that further alienate you. There is probably more drinking than is wise.

What with booms, winches, dredges, and other unforgiving gear, the working water environment is not as benign as a bandstand. Although there are occasional moments of violence in the jazz culture, maiming is not inherent in the playing of the music. There are no recorded cases of saxophonists accidentally getting their necks caught in neighboring trombone slides, broken drumsticks piercing trombonists, or overly pizzicatoed G-strings garroting their bassists. Few pianos let go their soundboards upon the shins of their performers. While both jazz and water work are apt to be seasonal, the chief difference is that jazz is less weather dependent.

Formal studies of the waterman's life, especially when he or now she comes ashore, are growing into an industry. One of the best early ones is *Seamen Ashore: A Study of the United Seamen's Service and of Merchant Seamen in Port* by Elmo P. Hohman. While directed toward the deep-water male at mid-twentieth century, there are a number of points that apply equally well to the shallow-water worker who may make home port most nights. Even a mere twelve-hour day out on the water, especially if there are several in succession, can make one susceptible to what Hohman refers to as "the problems of adjustment faced by the seaman in his contacts with the half-forgotten and often uncongenial requirements of life ashore."

. . .

As David Tedone points out, "the oyster . . . leads a discreet life in shallow water. It inhabits estuarine regions (where fresh water mingles with salt water) and spends the majority of its life affixed underwater to a rock or other hard object." The Malloys' work therefore was predominantly done in what Larry called "thin water." To contemplate the Malloys' life is a thalassophobic's dream. Their boats moved over depths rarely more than thirty feet and most often did the work in half that. If the bottom were your living room rug, Larry Malloy would just be somebody upstairs walking around on your bed, occasionally going up to the attic. Furthermore, once the commute from Harrison's Landing to the job at hand was accomplished, he'd attach the boat to something solid. If it were oystering he'd reach down to the bottom with his dredge and maintain intermittent contact with ground, like a tentative swimmer touching the bottom of the pool with a toe. If it were construction or salvage there would be the grappling of the gear to the task. In any case the nature of the metier was to avoid being tossed about in a boundless blue-water wilderness like some stunt sailor writing the sort of book that tends to dominate the literature of the sea.

Mariners debate the relative skill required in working the thin waters versus the great adventures of blue-water sailing. The *American Practical Navigator,* originally by New Englander Nathaniel Bowditch, has been looked upon as the mariner's bible in this country almost since its inception in 1802. In the edition published in 1918, the year of Larry Malloy Jr.'s birth, the "epitome of navigation and nautical astronomy" has this to say on the relative skills involved:

> Piloting . . . is the art of conducting a vessel in channels and harbors and
> along coasts, where landmarks and aids to navigation are available for
> fixing the position, and where the depth of water and dangers to navigation
> are such as to require a constant watch to be kept upon the vessel's course
> and frequent changes to be made therein.
>
> Piloting is the most important part of navigation and the part requiring
> the most experience and nicest judgement. An error in position on the high
> seas may be rectified by later observation, but an error in position while

piloting usually results in disaster. Therefore the navigator should make every effort to be proficient in this important branch, bearing in mind that a modern vessel is usually safe on the high seas and in danger when approaching the land and making the harbor.

To facilitate the work on board, the boats of the Malloys were wide, their beam-to-length ratio giving them the stability of a platform, though I have never heard Larry Malloy employ that inelegant term so favored by naval theorists and recently by commercial fishermen and even those who fish for what they call "sport." While weather was certainly a factor, as it is in any outdoor job, I don't recall Larry ever discussing seasickness as a phenomenon, nor did it even seem to play a part in any of his stories.

NOTE

WORKING, DRINKING, AND ALL THAT JAZZ (p. 26): "A ship at sea may be, as is sometimes pointed out, a world in microcosm; but if so, it is a world apart—a seagoing world and not a terra firma world. The differences between these two worlds can be fully appreciated, perhaps, only by a true seaman, for he is the only one who understands the peculiar psychology and philosophy of the one and at the same time knows enough of the other to offer a basis of comparison. For the seamen, after all, spends not inconsiderable periods of time on shore as a participant, however spasmodic and temporary, in the affairs of the land; whereas the landsmen spends far less time at sea, and then usually as a passive and only mildly interested observer" (Hohman, p. 202).

5

YARN SPINNING

LIKE MANY WATERFRONT veterans who eventually get "discovered," Larry Malloy, like his father, did develop a kind of patter to put between himself and the world. In fact the shtick was perfected into a day job in the Cold War era, when the waterfront entrepreneur Clarence Sharp ran the "See Submarines by Boat" tour boat. Operating out of the Whaling City Dock and Dredge Company, Larry ran a launch up and down the Thames River, grazing the restricted zones of the sub pens and the factory downriver that had spawned the sinister gray fleet.

Unlike the narratives of his father, however, Larry's stories were not merely turf markings. There was a generosity of spirit heard in turns of phrase revealing a mind that saw beyond the limits of the ego's need to triumph. The Italian movie director Federico Fellini says that "improvisation is merely a form of sensitivity to the demands of the moment." In Larry Malloy I saw a man who clearly delighted in the joys of that sort of sensitivity. Moreover, his own role in the event was almost always subordinate to someone else's—his father, a brother, or his favorite shipmate, Captain Tommy Watt. He could, in Robert Louis Stevenson's phrase, "play the fool for the yarn's sake." His take on events was often a wry one. As in the case of his employment of used trailer truck tires as bungee cords to hold *Alice* to the work in the surge at Race Rock Light, there was usually some sort of marvelous bit of adaptive reuse technology—an enthusiasm that appealed to me as the son of a World War Two Seabee.

Like the Connecticut River resident actor William Gillette, who played Sherlock Holmes hundreds of times on stage, and unlike Malloy Senior, Larry always gave his audience what Gillette called the "illusion of the first time." You had the feeling that this marvelous tumble of lore, technology, fiasco, and perseverance had just occurred to him fresh. "Stories, like oysters, got to be fresh," he says, "or at least seem so."

Not that Larry was always able to escape his father's style. On some of those occasions the Malloy narration mode was appropriately parodied by the youngest of Larry's three sons. Larry, Jr., had been born with Down's syndrome and lived with his dad at Harrison's Landing. He worked as a dishwasher at nearby restaurants and sometimes shipped as crew on his father's boats. He was a better deckhand than many I've known because he did not get bored and improvise basic evolutions such as making off a dock line. In fact he'd call his father if the old man deviated from the usual. Especially alarming was the Captain's casual vacating of the wheelhouse to go down on the deck, leaving the stately *Anne* to track for herself. "Dad! Dad!" Larry, Jr., would shout, "Who's in the boat? Who's in the boat?"

One day father, son, and I were all properly up in the wheelhouse of *Anne* steaming south on the Thames River past the United States Submarine Base. The father commenced a monologue in which he described the passing scene. Perhaps he had fallen into the old narrative groove that he had churned when giving the "See Submarines by Boat" tour back in the sixties. I was looking out the windows, trying to follow the spiel, when I became aware of a kind of counterchant emanating from behind me. It had the same rhythms and intonations as the main narration, all the rises and falls and pauses. It's just that the words themselves were slightly off, as in doubletalk. I turned around and there was Larry, Jr., a solidly built fellow of thirty-five, sitting up on the bench at the back of the wheelhouse, thumbing through one of his comic books and talking away as if from a script. Meanwhile, his father, at my side, continued placidly to steer the boat and narrate. Bit by bit, however, Larry, Jr., picked up the volume, and the parody became not only louder, but more accurate. Finally the Captain turned and said, "For God's sakes, Larry, I can't hear myself think!"

This unfortunately was followed by its own parody as Larry, Jr., innocently read the lines from his comic book.

The Captain stared at him for a moment. For an instant I was transported to what it must have been like a generation back. Could such sassing ever have occurred in this same wheelhouse? I thought of Larry's comment that there was not a spot in the place from which his long-armed father could not reach him without so much as shuffling a foot. Larry, Jr., peeped up over the top of his comic book. His logo cap was set at an angle just that magic inch off from his father's. He caught my eye and burst out in laughter. His father just shook his head and went back to steering.

Much of Captain Larry Malloy's material rises on the spur of the moment. I was talking one day about a two-man curragh I'd seen in the West of Ireland coming the twenty miles across from Connemara with a cow as cargo. I explained how the curraghs were made of cattle skins covered with pitch. The men had the cow fettered on her side in the bilge, but it was yet a wonder to me that the animal hadn't holed the skin boat somehow with horn or hoof. "Well," said Larry, "it wasn't like they weren't carrying spare parts."

At some point I thought it might be nice to write some of this down. Larry cooperated by sitting at his kitchen table at Harrison's Landing and writing out in longhand on yellow pads a chronology, with forays into the occasional anecdote as best he could. His principle of selection was the successive (and sometimes simultaneous) biographies of the boats in his life. He would bring these sheaves to me at the boat yard at odd intervals in the spring of 1999. I would then type them up, inserting queries in boldface and comments in italics. Next time he dropped by with new manuscript, and sometimes Wonder Bread sandwiches that he had made just as in the old *Anne* days, and we would go over the emendations. As Boswell paraphrases Johnson on the Doctor's collaboration with Goldsmith on "The Deserted Village," "both . . . the sentiments and expression were derived from conversation with him."

. . .

The act of painstakingly writing out the past had apparently become at times for him more a matter of nailing down a date or name at the expense of his usual colorful oral narration. I had the process of restoring "the expression" to the quality I had remembered aboard *Anne* or *Sylvina Beal* where his style had more of the raconteur than the litigant about it. The necessary process was more time-consuming than I think he appreciated. Looking at these sometimes dry written phrases, I had to ambush the latent color at times. He writes: "It was at this time my wife and I lived in a trailer near Little Creek." I ask, "Was this the period when at the dance you accidentally backed her into the fan and her blood went all over the dance hall?" Another time he writes, "We had a lot to talk about that day." I ask, "Was this the time the Army officer was calling in fire on your boat by using a board with nails stuck in it?" He writes, "We flew these planes until they passed inspection." I ask, "Was this the time you were eating your lunch with the cargo door open and the plane hit an air pocket and you drifted out over Norfolk?"

An odd phrase or name or date here and there would spark a memory. I would try to run down a stray detail from a story that he had told us aboard the schooner under the moon in Cumberland Bay, St. Vincent's, or sitting on an old friend's porch on a back street of Greenport. One day I asked him to tell me again the story of running aground with the potatoes in the Connecticut River. In trying to straighten out the geography in my mind, I challenged him on the distance between two key places. He said it was a mile and a half. There happened to be a Connecticut River chart rolled up in the overhead rack of the boatyard office and he challenged me to pull it down and check him out. We spread the chart on the counter top and broke out the dividers. The distance was one mile as the crow flies; a mile and a half if you were doing it as he had, half a century before, in a boat, following the bend of the river.

To aid his memory, he raided the family pay books, licenses, Navy documents. There were dozens of photographs, some more artistic than others, most of which had careful notations on the back as to names and dates. There was even a brown paper bag full of old 8 mm. film of backyard picnics, wedding parties, and oystering, that we had converted to video. On May 6, 1999, at the boatyard, he turned to a May 6 entry for 1937 in the pay book. "I don't know what you was doing on this day," he said.

"Probably sucking my thumb."

"Well, we was taking the *Emma Frances* up as far as we could into Mumford Cove. Then we anchored her, off-loaded bushels of oysters into the skiff—not all at once, mind you—and poled the skiff up over the flats up to Thomas Story's Oyster House at the head of the cove."

In poking through my stuff I found the photographs I'd taken in 1969 aboard *Anne* with his father. Larry gave a running commentary on what I had been looking at thirty years earlier with his father. "You see that cleat there on the hyster post, right there where he got the dredge tied off? That piece o' hardware came off the Cup Defender *Rainbow*—Vanderbilt's boat. Her skipper was a Monsell, a Greenport man, and when they were breaking her up, Johnny Monsell, he put us wise to some of the scrap coming out of the job. Now that engine in *Anne* when you was on her was the Hercules. You can tell without even looking at the engine itself, but by looking at the flag mast aft of the funnel. You see how it's all spit over with soot. Well, that was the Hercules in her last days: getting tired and spitting soot."

As we reconstructed the chronology, certain themes seemed to develop. When I found something conceptual growing I'd shut down the "and-then-and-then" and try to get us to concentrate on a theme: labor relations, pay, living conditions, the environment, tools, rigs, and one that he found very odd when considered in this fashion: innovations in the business. Some of these themes sneaked up on me.

One day I found myself staring at the stark fact that *Emma Frances* was built in 1869, almost a generation before *Anne,* the boat we had come to think of as defining the backward-looking limit of the Malloys' technology in 1884. *Captain* also had long preceded *Anne,* being built only two years after *Emma Frances.* True, all these craft had been modified, some from sail to power, some from steam to gasoline to diesel, some lengthened. All had been rerigged several times for changes in fishing gear. Nevertheless, it struck me that the Malloys had made their living for a hundred years using basic vessels that had been conceived before the major technical developments that marked the twentieth century.

From time to time, when it came to a technical point, Larry would stump me with a reference to a mysterious reference work. "It's all in Hotchkiss," he'd say. Eventually I discovered that "Hotchkiss" was actually *Oystering from New York to Boston* by John M. Kochiss (Mystic Seaport Press, 1974), a copy of which I fortunately possessed thanks to Mary Maynard, the maritime writer. Larry and I would park "Hotchkiss" on the counter at the boatyard and he'd poke his finger here and there, emending the text. "Now, you see right there. You see where that guy's standing? Well, that's right where I was standing when Elijah Ball said to me, 'You want to come work in the oyster shack?' "

We had similar sessions with *The Oyster* by William Brooks, a book recommended to me by my colleague Dr. Evan Ward at the University of Connecticut, and *The Pearl Makers* by Old Lyme Shellfish Commissioner Mervin F. Roberts. There were numerous minor excursions with other printed materials. Larry was an inveterate newspaper clipper. He read not only the New London *Day,* but *The National Fisherman* and the weekly *Suffolk County Times,* which contained waterfront gossip from his old home town of Greenport.

His filing system was an old, woven oak oyster basket made by George Stevens in Guilford in 1950. "I stood right there and watched George Stevens weave this one. There were times we had the deck stacked over your head with them. Nowadays you got to have everything plastic." These baskets went for three dollars and fifty cents the year they were made. Recently I had seen one, very much stove in and bespattered by grime, in a Guilford shop for $350.

It is a fond illusion of the casual observer of colorful narrators, however, that all that is needed is to "stick a tape recorder in front of them and just sit back." As Albert Murray says in a review of several books on, with, and "by" Louis Armstrong:

> Of course the accurate representation of one's voice on the page should not be confused with verbatim transcript of one's voice in person or on stage.
>
> As any competent student of literary composition knows, the more natural and casual a voice sounds in print, the more likely it has been edited time and again. It is not a matter of making a record of things, memories, opinions and notions as they come to mind. It is a matter of composition.

Well into the process of this book Larry announced, "I had a sixteen-foot power sharpie when I was a kid. I don't know if I ever told you about that one. She was mine. She had a one-cylinder make'n'break engine."

In thirty years he had not mentioned this boat, at least not as such, that is, as *his* boat. It might have been something like: "and then we came alongside *Anne* in the sharpie." It became clear to me that at that stage of his youth, Larry's personal craft was his foot outside the family circle. It represented a significant move toward independence and potential growth, to talk like a social psychologist. When he was telling me about the boat, however, he seemed chiefly interested in the way the engine worked. (There was also a dog that somehow crept into the story, his dog.) The one-lunger make'n'break is indeed an interesting bit of primitive, transitional technology (as if all technology weren't transitional). But it is characteristic of Larry's style that the human side, like the Pomeranian that shows up in his sharpie story, often stows away until, once safely at sea, it wriggles forth from under the gear with its tail wagging.

After some two hundred pages of fleshed-out manuscript, I reversed the process and winnowed a two-page chronology of what seemed to have been the key moments as actually established in the texture of the emended narration. He had just told me, for instance, that one of his first memories of his father was when the old man had set him up on a chopping block so he could see to steer the *Anne.* With a list of these highlights before me one afternoon, I had him filling in the dates, numbers that he most often instantly locked on. It was certainly more than I could have done for my own life. Pencil poised, I got to the line in the list where it said: Father died. Here is what he said:

"July 11, 1979. I had just joined brother Bill planting shells on the Milford grounds in his barge *Carnesee.* We felt good because we had them out there at the right time to be catching the set. Pappy, though, he was back home in bed and not doing too well. We was steaming into the Mill River in New Haven and was just coming in through the Chappell Street Bridge. Bloom's dock was there around to the other side across from United Illuminating. I was winding her around to get up alongside the pier. *Carnesee,* she was 128 feet long and 14 and a half wide. The marine operator come on just above my ear in the wheelhouse with the call that Pappy had died in bed. 'Jesus Christ,' I said, 'are we gonna make this? Are we longer than the slip?' It didn't look like we was going to make that turn! I look over the stern and see the prop wash slamming up against the bulwark at United Illuminating."

. . .

In the days when I came to know him, the house of Larry Malloy was always crowded. Through the years the Malloys had cobbled it up out of various buildings and parts of buildings from across the river and, as in the case of the kitchen, from Fort Wright across Long Island Sound on Fishers

Island. In later years the front yard was dominated by the twenty-eight-foot lobster boat *Dream*. Around to the side by the Vermont Central Railroad were parts and hints of other beached watercraft. If you were resisting the boats you went up the three concrete steps through the front doorway where to the right you encountered a parlor with a TV set constantly athrob with soap operas. The performance was surrounded by various chairs, couches, and other seats upon which there seemed to be a permanent audience of various ages in more or less repose. One day the room was clear of people, and while the TV was still on, I saw neatly arranged on the floor against the far wall a collection of knee-high ceramic owls and angels. At the end of a couch was an "old salt" lamp stand. Presumably these had been there all along.

Opposite the parlor, to your left, was a table upon which toys and animal cages competed for the horizontal space. The cages seemed to be empty, the toys missing parts. There was an upright piano against the street side wall. As a collector of old musical instruments, I once took the liberty of moving the three items of bric-a-brac, including a "perpetual motion" clock (whose perpetuity my curiosity threatened), from the key cover and discovered the instrument to have been built by the Leslie Bros. Of New York. It was years before I learned that his wife had played this instrument, and I did not learn this from him. On the wall across from the piano lurked an aquarium in which aquatic species may well have been existing. I know there were miniature shipwrecks.

Straight ahead was a shallow hall that led to the bathroom and Larry, Jr.'s room off to the right. This was a compartment best not looked into, but one day the door was ajar as if pushed open by a cascade of comic books and devices ancillary to a weightlifting program.

Through the hall to the left was an orderly kitchen with the usual appliances, the refrigerator bright with magnets celebrating lightships. Onions and bananas hung in baskets. The counters and sinks were of the sort that if there were any food about you were tempted to steal it.

The showplace of the house, however, was the dining room. It was this section that had been the Fort Wright army nurse's barracks and that the Malloys had floated the dozen miles from Fishers Island in New York waters across the Sound and up the Thames. You did not feel that you were truly in the house until you reached it, with its sliding glass door that opened out onto the deck and the spectacular view. It was as if the river, the Thames Shipyard, Coast Guard Academy, and highway bridges were visually a part of the house, though all were sufficiently far downstream to be rendered more or less silent by distance. It was years before I noticed the rest of the room. To take the curse off the gas station origins, the room had been paneled in vertical planks that displayed the following: a *National*

Geographic map of the Caribbean; a photo of the steam ferry *Catskill*; a poster of the oysterboat *Anne* in company at Claudio's pier with the schooner *Sylvina W. Beal* at a Greenport festival; a head of Jesus on a slice of wood with the bark still on; a computer; a tiny cuckoo clock; and photographic portraits of the next generation by the dozen. On the wall between the head of Jesus and the cuckoo clock was a tide clock, registering the daily occasions of low and high water. It was from this end of the dining room table in the midst of this spectacle that Larry would on festive occasions materialize amid the familial din, carrying not a tray of martinis, but folders flopping with boat pictures and waterfront news clippings. Many of these items he plucked from the oyster basket woven by George Stevens of Guilford in 1954. Behind him was the door to his bedroom, evidently the ultimate archive, and into which he would occasionally retreat to emerge with historical reinforcements consisting of more waterfront clippings or photos of boats.

A door led upstairs to bedrooms. It was up there that presumably the mysteries of the actual residency of the house were resolved. It was in those regions, for instance, that the shadowy presence known as Neil, the Iguana, moved and had its being.

The family had evolved in a manner similar to the design of the house. By the time I knew Larry, the five children—two daughters and three boys—had all grown up, and with the exception of Larry, Jr., moved out. Larry himself was divorced from his wife, who had gone west to Kansas to join their daughter Donna where she had subsequently died. Larry's companion of over twenty-five years, Shirley Monez, had moved in, and Larry had provided a roof for some of her children from a previous marriage. Some of these children in turn had had children, who frequently seemed to be staying at the house. In addition, Shirley's mother and her twin sister, Shirley's aunt, were frequent visitors. The fact that these women were twins added to my confusion, if not Larry's. Just down the street at the Landing lived one of Shirley's daughters, Sandy, who had children of her own.

A taxi driver in New London, Sandy was a cheerful woman who would only put up with so much. When she was taking Larry and me to the airport once she related a recent encounter with a cab-jacker. She had picked him up as a fare at the New London Railroad Station. Almost immediately he'd threatened her with a broken bottle and ordered her to drive about town in what degenerated into a random selection of streets. Eventually, in an especially desolate neighborhood, he ordered her out of the cab and demanded the keys, which she obligingly surrendered. Then he told her to climb into the trunk. "That was it," she told us. "*I ain't getting in no trunk. And that's what I told him. And by the way, gimme my keys back.*" She proceeded to disarm and subdue the man by a sequence of moves that do not bear thinking about. Having rendered him helpless, she called in to the police, who took him away. "I ain't getting into no trunk," she informed us again.

"OK," said Larry, "We won't ask you."

Not everyone who came into and out of the Malloy house was related to Larry or even necessarily to Shirley. It was years before I began to sort all this out. There was, for instance, a man the age of Larry's son Wayne whom I had assumed to be a cousin but who was actually a mere protégé of Larry's. The interesting thing is that their relationship did not seem to revolve around boats, although the young man did own a wooden motorboat about which Larry gave advice. Occasionally he even piloted it. The chief axis of their partnership seemed to be an electronic device, the precise working of which I never quite understood. It was about as big as a full loaf of bread and it was going to make their fortune. Larry had a kind of franchise arrangement, and while I sympathized with his entrepreneurial enthusiasm, the price for my participation would have been close to a thousand dollars. Larry once paid a visit to the boat yard and held the device up in front of various buildings as if to model the effect it might have on our life. He seemed to fall into playing the role of a jaunty, old time drummer bouncing about on his toes and waving his arms. He reminded me of a lightning rod salesman who had once zapped me years ago when I owned a barn far inland. It was the one time he ever bored me. By the time he was done I must confess I began to feel a little like Sandy when she was asked to get into the trunk. Oh well, I thought, this is what happens when a waterman tries to make his living ashore in a "normal" job.

. . .

In a kind of summing-up moment one day I asked Larry what he would call his profession. I offered "waterman." I myself was somewhat dissatisfied with this term, as I'd always felt that admirable epithet belonged to the Chesapeake. "'Waterman' is strictly reserved for different kinds of fishing, isn't it?"

"How about 'Bay Man'?" I said.

"Good Jesus Christ, I never was a 'Bay Man.' What a 'Bay Man' is—well, he's what other people might call a 'natural growther'—someone who works the public beds where the oysters grow naturally, that is, without cleaning the bottom, laying down shell, transplanting stock, liming the starfish—without really farming the ground. A 'Bay Man' doesn't farm. He registers, pays a fee, and is given a license to be a 'Bay Man.' It's a legal form, not some sort of cute way to refer to a man working on a bay. You look out on the Bay all those years, you see me, a man, right?"

"Yes."

"You see me, a man, working on the Bay, or in the Bay—depending upon how much we was leaking that day—but what you see is no 'Bay Man.' In other words, I was a man working in the Bay. I was not, however, a 'Bay Man.'"

"Well, then," I said, "what would you call a person who used his boat in all the ways you did?"

"I'd guess I'd call him a damn fool." Then he said, "Hey, what are we writing here, a novel or a joke book?"

. . .

There are moments in this book when memories collide, when it is clear, say, that a particular vessel cannot have ended her days in two different coves. While considerable effort has been made to document such facts as the final resting places of the formerly floating, for me the ultimate truth has always been in the voice of the elders' debate. This threnody for vessels long in the primal mud, after all, is not the mere trivia of the treasure dabbler. It is the sense of finality these facts bring to what has been the family business. These are, after all, concerns beyond making a living. They are the very stuff of living itself.

What emerges here then is not a biography of the sort that attempts to probe into and account for everything in a person's life. It is a conversation, that is, a verbal exchange between the writer and his subject about matters of mutual interest. What ends up at the center of this interest, and what gets nudged to the periphery and beyond, is, as it is in any conversation, a matter of mutual taste. There were occasions when Larry said to me, "You know my life ain't been no bed of roses." His daughter Donna's comments on the bewildering family finances are another indication of the lurking complexities. A life seen then from the inside: roses, beds, poverty, and the mysteries of family finance . . . who does not at some point report to us that they have led such an existence?

In one of those oracular utterances of his, Wallace Stevens once announced: "only the rich remember the past." If one thinks in terms other than merely financial, the remembrances of Captain Lawrence Malloy, Jr., are indeed those of a rich man.

NOTES

LARRY'S STORIES (p. 29): With narrators of Malloy's immediacy, the problem in dating an event that is the ostensible subject of the yarn is complex. When is it really happening? In 1938 to a twenty year old? Or 2001 to an eighty-three year old? A local bookstore owner just the other day had received advanced word about this book.

"Oh, yes," she said, "that's the book about the old fellow."

I relayed this to "the old fellow" himself a week later. It was after supper of a winter Sunday. He was looking forward with dread to a doctor's appointment the next morning. The purpose of the visit was to prepare a narrative of his condition in order to determine if he could withstand what might be a life-ending operation.

"Oh, well," he said, "'Old Fellow,' eh. I suppose it depends upon how you look at it. Most of the stuff in here was done by a young fellow."

BED OF ROSES . . . (p. 38): "But life at sea for the worker, as distinct from the passenger, has never been a bed of roses" (Hohman, p. 209). If I understand Larry Malloy, I suspect there were more roses at sea than ashore.

All photos aboard Anne *or at Harrison's landing were taken by the author during the 1969 trip related in this part.*

Anne port side to wharf at Harrison's Landing. This was before the overshot wheelhouse with vertical staving was removed. Another obsolete item, oysters in wooden bushel baskets. Captain Lawrence Malloy, Sr., in suspenders. Walt at the culling table. Fuel tank on pier.

One of the Malloy residences, Harrison's Landing. The capstan in the foreground was used to raise the anchor on a sizable vessel and was part of the salvaging operation.

Anne, port side amidships alongside wharf. Captain Elmer "Eddie" Edwards (with goatee), chairman of Groton Oyster Ground Committee, asking question of Captain Malloy, Sr. The Oyster Ground Committee was the predecessor of the Shell Fish Committee. Note roller on hyster post, used for bringing oyster dredge aboard, in right foreground.

On the Noank grounds. Captain Malloy, Sr., in the wheelhouse. Walt at his station on deck.

Captain Malloy, Sr., and Captain Edwards at work on *Anne*'s culling table.

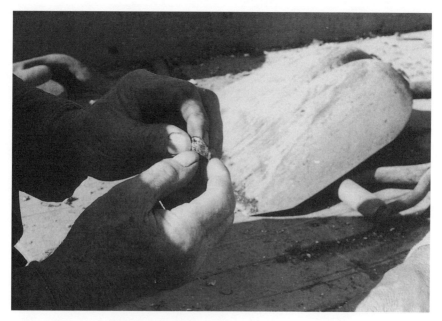

Captain Malloy, Sr., displays a seed oyster.

A pair of #9 shovels lean against the culling table among wooden and wire oyster baskets. The yellow pine deck has not yet been covered with "bridge tile."

Anne's hyster post with the cleat from Vanderbilt's 1934 Cup Defender *Rainbow*. The same piece of hardware may be observed in a different posture in a Rosenfeld photo, where it functions as if to trim sail among the cuffs of the yachting togs of Mike Vanderbilt and the man who specified it, naval architect Starling Burgess. Found on page 110 of Olin Stephen's autobiography *All This and Sailing, Too*.

Up in *Anne*'s wheelhouse. Sunlight streams in from the windows overlooking the bow and lights the mahogany helm, obtained from a yacht in Theodore Roosevelt's family. The spoke to the right is in the locking pawl that saved Captain Malloy, Sr.'s, life off Noank. To release the pawl, the helmsman merely grabs the handle and moves it to the right. The correspondence in the rack lies at the ready to substantiate the Captain's points about marine science and government regulation. The gauge leads to the dim lower regions, reporting on the engine's electrical condition.

Just above and ahead of the helm is *Anne*'s sole navigation instrument, the compass on a shelf inside the windows. At night, the carefully shielded light illuminates the compass card with its red bulb, friendly to the helmsman's night vision. The rumpled cloth is handy to wipe off the glass.

In the galley, below and aft the wheelhouse and sharing space with the engine. The enamel sink that serves as dishwasher, laundry, and hand basin is hanging up on a nail. Plates are held in the shelf above by high "fiddles" to prevent them from flinging about in a sea, in those rare moments when the wide-beamed vessel altered her otherwise stately progress. The empty hanger hints at shore-going attire, but more likely lies in wait to be twisted into something more useful.

Captain Malloy, Sr., was not a man to don dark glasses. The long-peaked "swordfishing" cap was as far as he'd give in. The tube running over the window on the face of the sheathing was another concession to natural light, or in this case to the lack of it.

Part Two

UNDER WAY

... and how everything was made by themselves, right there on shipboard.

—Gertrude Stein, "Melanctha"

6.

DEAD RECKONING

Tracking the life of a waterman such as Larry Malloy is a little like the navigational mode known as *dead reckoning*. The *American Practical Navigator* edition that was printed in the year of his birth defines dead reckoning as "the process by which the position of a ship at any instant is found by applying to the last well-documented position the run that has since been made, using for the purpose the ship's course and the distance indicated by the log." The 1918 *Navigator* also offers this warning:

> The correctness of dead reckoning depends upon the accuracy of the estimate of the run, and this is always liable to a fault to a greater or lesser extent. . . . Notwithstanding its recognized defects as compared with the more exact methods the dead reckoning is an invaluable aid to the mariner.

With this caveat in mind we may begin with what Bowditch would call "a well-determined position." Captain Lawrence Harris Malloy, Jr., was born in Greenport in 1918 at Ludlum Place near Main Street.

Larry Malloy's own personal, first, "well-determined position" was up in the air, being held by his father, Captain Lawrence Malloy, Sr., at the Greenport Shipyard, just around the corner from Sterling Basin. They were looking at an oysterboat undergoing a major overhaul.

"I remember my father saying, '*Don't fall in that hole.*' The 'hole' I was looking at was the back end of *Anne*. I found out much later the reason why that part of the boat was missing was because they were converting her old, square sloop stern into a round or horseshoe stern. What yachtsmen call a 'fantail.' What we call a 'tugboat stern.' They did this to strengthen her for dragging under power. You compare the way a wheel is held together, the rim to the spokes, you see how this is a stronger unit than just a box with the sides going into the corners.

"Of course, I didn't know all that then. To me it was just a hole I wasn't supposed to fall into. A lot of my life has been just trying to figure out all the things my father showed me before I knew what it was I was looking at. One of the things I found out is that he didn't always know what he was looking at himself. That isn't because he was stupid. It's because some things take time figuring out. And then they change 'em, as soon as you got it figured out. Just who this is that keeps changing things, I'm not sure. Sometimes it's the government, but sometimes it's just that what with *conditions,* hey, you got to change stuff yourself.

"That business in Greenport Shipyard must have been sometime in the early 1920s. *Anne* was already around forty years old. I sure didn't know that I'd spend the rest of my life on and off that old girl making my living. I didn't know that when I got to be an old man over in Connecticut I'd someday be looking at that same *Anne* propped up in a boat shed getting her stern rebuilt again."

. . .

Larry Malloy spent his early childhood in Greenport. The 1918 *Coast Pilot* tells us:

> Greenport is an important town and the terminus of a branch of the Long Island Railroad. There are several shipyards, marine railways the and a well-equipped machine shop. The depths at the wharves range from 7 to 10 feet, according to location. The steamship and railroad wharves are on the south front of the town.

Perhaps the town was already beginning to wane. The 1892 *Coast Pilot* had called Greenport "flourishing" with "extensive fishing interests and a large coasting trade; it is also engaged in shipbuilding to some extent. The carrying trade employs a considerable number of vessels, some transient, some owned in the vicinity," and lists the number of marine railways at six. (By 1938, even before the Great Hurricane, they were down to three.) In 1892 steamboats ran in summer not only across Long Island Sound due north to New London, but up the Sound to the west, where the Connecticut River debouched at Saybrook and gave access upriver to Hartford. Ferries continued further west to New York City and out to the eastern end of Long Island to Montauk, a service that just now at the beginning of the twenty-first century is being contemplated again.

. . .

As Larry Malloy grew older he came to appreciate the geographic position of his hometown, which had now become his home port. Greenport sits near the end of Long Island's North Fork just off the northwest corner of its principal oyster resource, Gardiners Bay

Gardiners Bay is what Larry calls "a mighty thin" body of water. The average depth in feet is in the mid-twenties, with long shelves that average only fifteen feet. This is contrasted with Long Island Sound where the depths between Orient Point and New London run in the middle hundreds. Thin water is ideal for oyster dredging, but "mean as hell in a chop." The water behaves much like a lake. Gardiners is nearly ringed by the North and South forks of Long Island and is further enclosed by two big islands within the forks, Shelter Island and the island from which the bay's name derives.

In the early days of chartmaking, depth soundings were only taken where ships customarily traveled and only where the surveying vessel was actually able to maneuver using the wind. The chart published in 1777 shows considerably more soundings in Gardiners Bay than on the New London side of Long Island Sound. At the beginning of the nineteenth century, there was an oyster industry in these waters not unlike what the Malloys knew. James Fenimore Cooper, famed for his loosely stitched but historically important Indian novels, spun several maritime yarns, including one, *The Sea Lions,* which commences, as he would say, on the North Fork. Set in the first quarter of the nineteenth century, *The Sea Lions* anticipates many of the themes of the Eastern Fork for the next century. A hundred and fifty years later, despite Cooper's lament for a lost rural culture, Larry Malloy was still bumping about in the same waters, worrying about war and moving manure, among the same sort of folk and employing gear that would not have shocked Cooper's Oyster Pond folk:

> In that day [1819] Oyster Pond was, in one of the best acceptances of the word, a rural district. It is true that the inhabitants were accustomed to the water, and to the sight of vessels, from the two-decker to the shabby-looking craft that brought ashes from town to meliorate the sandy fields of Suffolk [County]....
>
> The name of Oyster Pond Point was formerly applied to a long, low, fertile, and pleasant reach of lands that extended several miles from the point itself, westward, toward the spot where the two points of the prongs of the [Long Island] fork are united. It was not easy, during the first part of the present [nineteenth] century to find a more secluded spot on the whole island than Oyster Pond. Recent enterprises have since converted it into the terminus of a railroad; and Green Port, once called Sterling, is a name well known to travelers between New York and Boston.

Cooper goes on to marvel at the "eye of the railroad projector to bring this spot in connection with anything"; nor could it be done, he notes, without having recourse to the water by which it is almost surrounded.

> Gone is the region's seclusion, [he continues] its simplicity, its peculiarities and we almost said its happiness. It is to us ever a painful sight to see the rustic virtues rudely thrown aside by the intrusion of what are termed improvements. . . . How many delightful hamlets, pleasant villages, and even tranquil country towns, are losing their primitive characters for simplicity and contentment by the passage of these fiery trains, that drag after them a sort of bastard elegance, a pretension that is destructive of peace of mind, and an uneasy sense in all who dwell by the wayside to pry into the mysteries of the whole length and breadth of the region it traverses!

Cooper addresses what, eighty years later, will become the Malloys' chief occupation at midcentury when they were involved in servicing the Race forts between Greenport and New London. Cooper refers to the "checkered sides of two-decked ships, and the venerable and beautiful ensign of Old England" as the squadron lay in Gardiners Bay "watching the Race, or eastern outlet of the Sound, with a view to cut off the trade and annoy their enemy."

This was the British squadron that sailed in 1812 under the command of Thomas Masterman Hardy (1769–1839). Hardy was with Nelson against Napoleon's admirals at the Nile, at Copenhagen, and most famously at Trafalgar in 1805, where he commanded the flagship H.M.S. *Victory*. It was Hardy whom Nelson leaned on for tactical advice: sounding at Copenhagen; the precise point of attack in the French line of battle at Trafalgar.

It was Hardy whom Nelson was standing next to when he was fatally sniped from the French rigging; it was Hardy in whose arms Nelson died 'tween decks; it was Hardy to whom he turned over command at the end of the greatest ship-to-ship battle in naval history. The "checkered sides of two-decked ships" Cooper refers to includes Hardy's flagship in the American campaign, H.M.S. *Ramillies*. She was the third English ship of that name, a seventy-four-gun square rigger that saw service with Nelson at the battle of Copenhagen in 1801 and ended her glory as a lazaretto, or hospital ship, in 1832. Hardy had her and his squadron patrolling from Gardiners Bay to Block Island. In the key engagement of her duty, she cut off and annoyed Stephen Decatur (1779–1820), son of the American hero of the Revolution. Decatur was himself the daring star of Tripoli and aboard the U.S.S. *United States*, one of the six original frigates in the American Navy, had captured the British frigate *Macedonia* only that fall. In May of 1813 Decatur attempted to bolt from New London to Block Island. Hardy pounced upon him in Block Island Sound and sent him scooting back up the Thames River, where Decatur wisely remained for the duration, cowering back of

Allyn's Point—the next turn of the river above Harrison's Landing. One of Larry Malloy's finds while oyster dredging in the region of that blockade was part of a great sailing ship mast of such diameter as to suggest the Napoleonic wars.

Cooper, however, goes into a brave patriotic dance to convince us that "that game is up forever. No hostile squadron, the English, French, Dutch, or all united, will ever again blockade an American port for any serious length of time."

Cooper is right as far as he goes, but dying well before the Civil War, he cannot see into the era when the international maritime power shall shift to three nations whose potential aggression in these waters gives a variety of employment to the Malloys: the Spanish, the Germans, and the Russians. His sense of the more local aspects, however, is on course for the twentieth century:

> Nor was it only by these distant views, and by means of hostilities, that the good folk of Oyster Pond were acquainted with vessels. New York is necessary to all on the coast, both as market and as a place to procure supplies and every creek, or inlet, or basin, of any sort within a hundred leagues of it, is sure to possess one or more craft that ply between the favorite haven and the particular spot in question. Thus was it with Oyster Pond. There is scarce a better harbor on the whole American coast than that which divides the point from Shelter Island; and even in the simple times of which we are writing Sterling had its two or three coasters, such as they were. . . . Wharves were constructed, at favorable points . . . and occasionally a sloop was seen at them loading its truck, or discharging its ashes or street manure; the latter being a very common return cargo for a Long Island coaster.

Cooper's interest in *The Sea Lions* turns out to be not with this "inside" traffic but with " a vessel of a different mold . . . one which was manifestly intended to go *outside*." This is to say, in Cooper's novel, seal hunting is the story, and there, heading for the blue waters of the North Atlantic, we leave him. To follow the Malloys we need a man interested in what goes on *inside* the Forks.

A better man to report the longshore culture is Walt Whitman. We pick up America's first world-class poet some thirty years after Cooper's "Oyster Pond Point" tale. For better or worse, Whitman got around all the edges of Long Island, and before he got thrown out of the North Fork for questionable pedagoguery, he wandered "On the north, Long Island Sound, a beautiful, varied and picturesque series of inlets, 'necks,' and sea-like expansions, for a hundred miles to Orient Point." Whitman frequently visited his sister who lived in Greenport (now one word). One day he goes walking along the narrow road that connected Greenport to Orient Point. He comes across an old man in "faded" blue patched trousers who is lugging a clam hoe and a bucket, which to the reader proclaims the old man to be "an original." In the tradition of poets such as Basho and Wordsworth, Whitman is eager to see in interviews with such men not merely local color or comic relief, but potential revelations of the cosmos's larger secrets. It is no surprise that to the good gray poet, a solitary Eastern Fork man exhuming shellfish from the mud beneath the brine by means of a simple hand-wrought tool, was eligible to be just such a totem.

. . .

In many ways, however, the true venue for the Malloys was neither Greenport nor New London, but the waters between. The maritime corridor between Greenport and New London, now largely ignored except for ferrying passengers to the Connecticut casinos, goes back even earlier than Admiral Hardy and the British Squadron in 1813.

In the uneasiness just preceding the outbreak of the American Revolution there was, according to Walter Powell, a steady trafficking between Greenport and New London in "illicit commerce and spies." The illicit goods were chiefly items that were not necessarily illegal in themselves, but were under embargo restrictions. While the spies apparently sailed both ways, it was, according to Powell, chiefly the British spies from Long Island who were scoping out the strength of New London. At the time, Powell tells us, "New London was the chief seaport of Connecticut and the most important naval station between New York and Newport, Rhode Island. [It was] a storehouse for naval stores, ammunition, foodstuffs and a repository for British naval prisoners." The corridor came alive when the Revolutionary forces made a raid on Sag Harbor, a half dozen miles south across the bays from Greenport. Powell quotes Yankee hero and non-speller William Ledyard, commander of the colonist's fort on Groton Heights, as understanding the ramifications of the raid. In a February 4, 1774, letter Ledyard wrote:

> the enemy now at the East end of Long Island intended to visit the place [New London] in order to destroy the shipping as well as the Town. It thought that the two prizes [British] Brigs taken [by the colonists] near Sag Harbour & brot here was Intended for Transports with Others to have brot off some of their light Horse & other troops.

When the British struck back north across the Greenport-New London corridor in 1781 under the leadership of the treacherous Norwich resident

Benedict Arnold, they came ashore at the two points of land on either side of the Thames, then marched inland to burn much of New London and the shipping in the harbor. Storming Fort Griswold on the Groton heights, a British officer ran Colonel Ledyard through with what is generally believed to have been the Colonel's own sword, an implement that he had ceremoniously offered up in surrender.

. . .

When the Malloys closed their Greenport home and crossed the Sound to live in New London when Larry was ten years old, the family was far from done with Greenport. The Malloys' business constantly had them back and forth between the two towns all of Larry's life. The 1918 *Coast Pilot* illustrates the kind of maritime relationship that existed between the two ports, and the versatile role that Greenport oyster boats played in the larger scheme: "Towboats are rarely used [in Greenport], but they can be obtained from New London. The oyster steamers are available in case of necessity."

Well after the Malloys shifted their residence to New London, the family continued to own oyster ground in Gardiners Bay, work with people from that area, and provision and repair their vessels chiefly in Greenport shops and yards that were set up to support the oyster fleet. As late as the mid-1990s Larry received a longevity award from a Greenport fraternal organization and continued to read the weekly *Suffolk Times,* which his mother received in New London.

NOTE

GREENPORT–NEW LONDON CORRIDOR (p. 54): Walter Powell's lecture, "The New London Raid, 1781," University of Connecticut at Avery Point, April 9, 2000. Mr. Powell's remarks were part of his forthcoming book on this topic.

7

RUM, ICE CREAM, AND BLACK POWDER

To Larry Malloy, looking back, it wasn't long after viewing *Anne*'s rebuilding that he was aboard her and working.

"My father put me up on a chopping block in the wheelhouse and pointed out the window to where I was supposed to steer. I guess he needed me to steer while he tried to keep his pipe lit. Later I found out people called him 'Snake.' That is not an especially pleasant name, and I guess my father wasn't always an especially pleasant man. There are some unpleasant stories that go with that name, but the story to explain his name that *I* like best is the one that has to do with this business of steering the boat.

"Pappy, he was always trying to keep his pipe lit. I don't know if it was the tobacco. In fact we used to say he didn't have any tobacco, just matches. Matches was for sure all he seemed to smoke. Maybe it was the way he packed it—something wrong with the pipe—maybe just too much draft in the wheelhouse, even with the windows all up—Each time he'd go to light the damn thing he'd take his hands off the wheel, and off she'd go, off course. Now right there, that's odd to me because years later when I steered her without him aboard she'd stay right down the track. Anyway, then he'd see what was happening and he'd grab the wheel and steer back on course. Except there already behind him was the evidence. You know, the wake coming out behind the stern looked like a snake, and there it would lay a while crooked and wriggling. That wake lay there in full view for anyone to see coming along from any direction, and you couldn't erase it 'till it just died out of natural causes. A minute later, the pipe would be out again. *'Break a snake's back.'* That was the expression people used for a wake like that."

There were other vices besides pipe smoking and erratic steering in Greenport in Larry's youth. Shelter Island's Robert Carse in his *Rum Row* sets the scene:

Famous once during Colonial rule when smugglers had used Sterling Cove as a haven, prominent in the eighteenth and early nineteenth centuries in the whaling trade along with adjacent Sag Harbor, Greenport had lived through the good days created by the oyster business, slid into a decline that was halted by the increase of interest in yachting, built up fine local yards and then was given wealth by the rum-running traffic. The town was ideally suited as a depot where rum-runners and bootleggers could meet, with Shelter Island, indented with numerous coves and inlets, to the south; the narrow extension of Orient Point to the east; Long Island Sound directly north of that; and out beyond to the southeastward, past Gardiner's Bay, the open Atlantic and Rum Row.

Greenport in the 1920s was a town of indiscriminate architecture where upon two streets, the stores, a movie theater, a restaurant or so, a few garages, a pair of bowling alleys, a sailmaker and a chandlery served the residents and the neighboring fishermen, farmers and summer folks. The bootleggers, in collusion with the rum-runners, took it over after dark. The town police did very little to hinder the illegal operations, and there was very little that they could do.

Most of the town's population of less than ten thousand derived some form of profit from their disregard of the Prohibition law. Unemployment was practically non-existent. Men strong enough to carry a case of liquor were hired and paid an average of twenty dollars a night to transfer the loads from the contact boats to the waiting trucks. The boatyards were busy at work on craft for which no contracts had been drawn, but none were needed; everything the rum-runners ordered done was on a cash-in-advance basis. Gasoline was sold in five-hundred-gallon quantities. The town banks kept on hand large-denomination bills—one hundreds, five hundreds, thousands—for the deals out on Rum Row, and opened accounts for citizens who had never in their lives owned more than a pair of seaboots and a clamming rake.

The trucks came in from New York with the approach of darkness. They were accompanied by the cars that would form the escort on the return, usually gray Buick touring cars. The Buicks, when the contact boats were in, took their own freight underneath the seats or concealed in false bottoms. While the bootleggers waited for the boats to appear from seaward, a group of four or five men attended to each car. They hefted it up and introduced between the chassis and the leaf springs a set of powerful coil springs about the size of a pound coffee can. These supported the extra weight of the loads; down the road to New York, if suspicious police or Revenue agents ranged close, there would be no telltale sag to inform them.

A good hour prior to the arrival of the contact boats, the bootleggers occupied the shore end of Main Street and the docks beside it. Nobody but their own people and others in their hire could enter the area. Hoodlums with pistols in their hands stood guard. A fisherman waiting to return aboard his own boat, customers seeking to cross on the Shelter Island ferry, were told to stay away until after dawn. If anyone insisted, he was clubbed over the head, kicked, hustled out of sight and kept very much incommunicado until after dawn.

An eight- or nine-year-old boy had his own kind of knowledge of this scene, and in his eighties, Larry Malloy recalled:

"Father would tote me around to the oyster shops, take me clamming, fishing (dragging), oystering on *Anne,* eeling, visiting many places by boat on the eastern end of Long Island.

"We'd moved from Main Street to Ludlum Place, which meant we lived right on Sterling Cove, which I guess is now famous for the rumrunning days. To us it was just a creek on the north side of Greenport that was a damn good place to keep boats. Sterling Cove was close to open water, yet sheltered; it was right there in Greenport without being out in that nasty roll you can get from fish boat wakes or a nor'easterly in the commercial harbor; and while it was close to shipyards and suppliers, it was a couple of blocks away from the busier section of town. I guess that makes it a nice location because it's now all marinas, bed and breakfast, and a tennis court."

The United States Coast Pilot, Atlantic Coast, Section B, Cape Cod to Sandy Hook, published the year Larry was born, informs us that Sterling Basin is "on the northeast side of Greenport, has a depth of about six feet in the entrance and 2 to 3 feet inside. There is a railway for small motor boats at the head of the basin. A staked channel good for 2½ feet leads to oyster wharves in the northern part."

"We kept *Anne* and *Emma Frances* right there to the dock. It was the house behind us where they stored all the booze. Just who this 'they' was I could never be sure of. I really don't think my Pappy had anything directly to do with that bunch. You just kept out of their way. Before us that building used to be a boatbuilder's place. I remember as a kid all night long our house shakin'—the sound of engines at night. Them trucks in those days didn't have no air in the rubber on the tires. Tires was solid rubber, like wagon wheels. The roads, they were all oyster shells, all the way up to the corner where you turn out of Ludlum Place. In fact I remember watching by the side of the road the day they paved Route 25, the road that leads out of town to New York City. It would keep you awake with them steamin' in and out all night.

"Come to think of it, there was a mysterious room in our house—the pantry. A lot of people don't remember pantries. Well, that's where I wasn't supposed to look. That's where all the 'prunes' were stored. I asked the old man why the door to the pantry was locked and I couldn't go in there. '*Prunes*,' he said.

"'Prunes?' I said, "'My God, Pappy, but that's an awful lot of prunes.'"

"The thing is I think I was with him when he collected them (prunes), somewheres around the Gut.

"We saw these cases bobbin' in the water. He was fishing, dragging with the otter trawl. That's a net you use with underwater 'doors' on it that you rig to sheer out to keep the mouth of the net spread sideways. To keep it spread up and down you got cork floats on the top line and chain on the bottom. Where the *otters* come in I never could figure out because we never caught no otters, nor would've known what to do with them if we had. That was when we were doing a lot of dragging. I can remember standing in fish up to my knees. Fluke and skates. I know it was skates because that was my job, to throw them back overboard. Them days you didn't save them for lobster bait. And swell bellies. Plenty of swell bellies, blowfish. You tickle their bellies; they swell up like a football. It was several years later they found you could eat them. Then they became 'chicken of the sea'; right after that they became *extinct*. When we was oystering we'd get a whole dredge full. We'd play with them. Bouncing them on the decks. Oh, as for the 'prunes,' in Plum Gut. That sounds like we're eating a lot of fruit. Plum Gut, the tidal race runs between Plum Island and Orient Point. Like the Race between Little Gull and Fishers Island, but worse because you've got less room to maneuver. It was *Anne* caught the prunes. I'll tell you when we ran into these floating cases, we gave up fishing right away.

"To tell the truth, that's the way most regular fisherman crept into that line of work—just stuff you'd find because the real rummies had ditched it under hot pursuit. It wasn't something you did full time. It was sort of like a government subsidy. It was the government, after all, that made the basic setup. Prohibition.

"There was, of course, locals known to be or suspected to be in the business. Locals and strangers. The fast boats would come in all the way from Rum Row off Montauk where the big schooners lay just outside the twelve-mile federal limit. Greenport had most of the business that went to New York City.

"What happened to the 'prunes'? I don't know. All of a sudden the room was—well, *the cupboards was bare*. I guess the old man got a quick buyer.

"The enforcement was more like a joke. Later I was aboard a couple of those 'six-bitters,' that is, the seventy-five-footers the Coast Guard had to chase down the rummies. By the time you walked from one end to the other of them six-bitters you'd be drunk just from the smell. I guess the idea was a lot of the bottles got broken in transit. Or something like that. Hey, glass is glass. And, of course, sailors is sailors.

"You have to understand that in those days there weren't that many boats around. You'd see one maybe every two or three weeks, especially in the colder months which was when you was out and about, poking into places, catching oysters. And there weren't that many docks. So when you saw another boat, you'd be more likely to say a hello or two. Back in those days you knew everybody. You didn't always *like* everybody, but you *knew* them. When we were in the oyster shop on the pier in New London, there was all kinds of people coming in, coming by. That's the kind of place we were in. The Coast Guard didn't have its own dock, so if you was any size and not a yacht, if you was *commercial,* you'd be right in there at the same dock with the Coast Guard. At the end of the day's work you'd walk over and, hey, make a visit. You might be there an hour or two. Have a cup of coffee. They was mostly always local boys anyway. You knew their uncle or their cousin or someone. Hell, we was all in the same business; we was all workin' the same waters.

"Nowadays the Coast Guard, I don't know, they always try to keep you at some kind of distance. That is, unless they're coming to pounce on you and rip up your life preservers. And now they're mostly boys from Ohio or some place where I guess they ain't been brought up with life preservers, so they just tears into them like they was going to make a meal out of it. Maybe that's what they do in Ohio. I don't really know. Hell, *I* never been to Ohio. Sometimes the Coast Guard I think they don't want you makin' any visits. They got fences and all these what they call '*secrets.*' Maybe they don't want you to catch them doing anything illegal. Like taking parts of the galley home at night."

· · ·

Greenport retained much of its prewar ambience well into the 1980s. In the 1950s I spent time there with my father, who'd known it on his schooner in the rumrunning days. In the sixties, seventies, and eighties I visited it by boat on my own. It seemed to me a magical place out of the past, in a way that, say, New London never did. During the time my son ran the schooner out of Claudio's dock at the end of Monkey Wrench Corner in the nineties, Larry Malloy and I spent many days and nights revisiting the old haunts.

There had been an attempt on the part of some locals to bring the town into the last half of the century. Tolerating our 1911 schooner and the oysterboat *Anne* was even seen by some as visionary. There was a project to restore the old mansard-roof aid to navigation known as "Bug Light," for years familiar to yachtsman by its *nom de cart,* Aban Light. You could not, however, in that fishing town, buy block ice or coal, and the second-best restaurant in town was named "Rhum Runner," a cute confection of navigational wordplay and retrofitting. More amusing to Larry was a narrow way between buildings on Front Street with the cheerful sign "Rum Runner's Alley."

"The boats didn't go to a *dock* in the middle of town to unload! They would run the boats to a beach, most any place. Jam in on the beach. As they unloaded, they'd keep pulling the boat further up the beach. Forty or fifty cases at most, then get the hell out of there. They wouldn't hang around. I wasn't quite old enough to get into that. I did have one chance to unload a boat, but I guess my mother wouldn't let me out that night. I didn't make that."

Larry had been showing me a bulkhead he had built long ago down the so-called Rum Runner's Alley. It had actually been back of what had been an engine shop run by two German brothers. "In those days your marine engines were often built locally. At least in towns like Greenport or like Lathrop's in Mystic. It wasn't as if they started from scratch. They got the blocks from automobile engines or concrete mixers or tractors and modified them for marine use. At that time we needed a place to lay at night, so the German said, 'Go ahead, build a bulkhead.' The ground kind of sloped down to the water there so we jetted in some wooden piles and some bulkheading at the edge. Every night for a while we'd come in from oystering and lay alongside and dump the day's shells over the wall. Hey, you're standin' on that ground right now."

There were indeed a few oyster shells showing through the dirt, but no real sense that 90 percent of the material we were standing on had been secreted layer by layer by the silent creatures of the bay bottom and then day by day transported in *Anne* to their present location.

"These days that little job would violate how many laws?"

The modest engine works that had been run by the two Germans was now a bait shop. The large building next to it, Claudio's Restaurant, however, was still owned by the man who had founded it back in the days of Prohibition. In the schooner business we used one of the booths as a kind of office, and Larry and I would often eat lunch at one of the tables overlooking the harbor. Bill Claudio, Sr., and Larry would reminisce about the days when the bowsprits of other schooners menaced the window of the very booth at which we sat. "Those schooners were used mainly for transporting the oysters," Larry explained. "They didn't do the actual catching. Sometimes they'd be used for shelling, carrying shells to the grounds to put down for cultch, to make a hard bottom for the spat to set."

. . .

Bill Claudio, Jr., built a bar and bandstand at the end of the next pier down that summer. One hot night we were trying to get to sleep on the schooner—she was moored aft of *Anne* on the first pier. I was awakened by a trumpet playing on the inboard end of the pier. This was clearly not one of the musicians from the bandstand on the next pier, but a trumpet player whose style was from the era of the great swing bands. He was playing "Stardust" with a sure, wide tone:

> And now the purple dusk of twilight
> Runs along across the meadows of my soul

His embouchure was a bit out of shape, and he was missing notes, but you could tell he knew exactly where each of those notes belonged. Their ghosts hung on the night air. Drawn out of my bunk and up the ladder, I found myself walking along the pier.

The asphalt on the pier still held the heat of the day although it was getting on close to midnight, and the soft updraft floated me toward the trumpet music. Behind me from the next pier came the house band, a slick amalgam of flawless, synthesized virtual instruments.

The sulfur dock light illuminated the balding dome of the man playing the trumpet. A barrel of a fellow in a striped jersey, with a great mustache, he looked like a weight lifter out of the gaslight era. He was standing with his legs braced wide apart, elbows out, in that artillery stance favored by trumpeters in the pre–Miles Davis era. He was pointing his silver bell at the back balcony—in this case, at the stars themselves. His audience, however, was right next to him. Seated at a table made from a large rope spool into which was stuck a beach umbrella was an ancient African American man, apparently the parking lot attendant. Standing a little to one side was Larry Malloy.

"Just like the old days," said Larry. "Except the bands was bigger."

"Yeah, well," said the trumpet player pointing with his bell to the end of the next pier where the house band was clicking and blipping through its gluey electronic arrangements. "I got kicked out."

"You were in that band?" I said.

"*Them?*" He looked over at the pier to make sure he was still onto what was out there. "Me, I played with Krupa and Dorsey, Harry James and Tony Bennett, Cab Calloway . . ."

We all looked out toward the end of the pier from whence came the music, none of which approached the work of anyone he'd just mentioned.

"Naw, I'm on that other schooner over there. Helping out Teddy Charles, the vibraharpist. He's got that schooner over there."

The small black schooner *Mary E,* her stern hogged down into the shadows, might well have been a refugee from Rum Row.

"I used to play section with all the big boys. These guys today. They don't understand. You bring a real horn over there . . . and *sitting-in!* The whole concept, the *tradition* of *sitting in.* . . . It's beyond these guys. These guys. . . . They got these charts and off the charts, they're lost. Charts and electronics. They thought I was a drunk."

We all agreed that once *these guys these days* got off the charts they were lost.

"It's the same way in the oyster business," said Larry.

"That's right," laughed the parking lot attendant and slapped the rope spool that was his table. "Off the charts is *lost* !"

The attendant turned out to have worked on the menhaden boats, long gone south. Before that he'd crewed on the oyster schooners. He and Larry exchanged some names. There were not the names of people, but the names of boats, some, of course, named for people, but you could tell the names uttered were of the boats.

The trumpeter and I exchanged some musician's names. He played a couple of other old tunes, then, since I had been talking a good game, he offered me the horn. I wiped off his mouthpiece, let out the spit from the water key, wiggled the valves and groped my way carefully into a kind of blues. Though much less adventurous than the section man, I achieved about the same number of fluffs. For a few moments I had the illusion I was back in the days when my father and uncle and their gang had played in the old harbors. The ancient fisherman under the umbrella was kind.

We got to talking about boats. The trumpet player had worked in a Brooklyn boatyard in the forties with his cousin and between them had managed to spirit away enough materials to build their own craft, which I gathered was modeled after the feluccas of their native Italy. "We were confined to short planks," he said, "which, as you know, do not make for a very strong hull. We were basically crazy. We fished the western end of Long Island Sound for a few weeks. Then we went to Nantucket in it."

"Nantucket!"

"Had a hell of a time getting back."

It was perhaps inevitable that even a brief account of such a voyage to windward in the open Atlantic aboard a Mediterranean design constructed out of materials carried out beneath the coats of short men would lead to a discussion of the infirmities of old age. Larry introduced his constant companion, "Arthur Ritus." The trumpet player had just the thing for "Arthur." He excused himself and limped over to the next pier where he disappeared aboard his rheumatoid schooner.

"What's he going to bring back?" said Larry. "Some old prohibition hooch?"

"I sure hope not," said the parking lot man. "Man, some of that stuff give you the *dark* nights."

The bottle that accompanied the trumpeter's return contained selenium, an over-the-counter supplement.

There was a certain amount of pharmaceutical talk that drove all before it. Gone now forever were the days of the oyster schooners and big bands. When the medical talk was done, there was nothing for us to do but limp home to our damp holes.

Back at Harrison's Landing Larry took this nostrum with enough success to encourage him to continue for the next several years. I could never figure out the purely somatic value of this remedy, and the VA doctors who treated him were even more skeptical. It was, however, hard to argue with the persuasiveness of a prescription given under such circumstances, and Larry often remarked on the superiority of Greenport pier trumpeters to other types of "so-called physicians."

· · ·

One summer afternoon that year Larry and I paid a visit to one of his ancient Greenport cronies. While in many ways a New England town, Greenport has often felt to me more mid-Atlantic, like something in southern Jersey on Delaware Bay or southern Delaware, one of those sleepy, shallow-water oyster ports down behind the barrier beaches of the Delmarva Peninsula. Never did the sense of geographic dislocation seem more apparent than on this day. We walked back from the harbor a few blocks through leafy streets, still as the old days in the sun, and sure enough, up on a veranda of a modest frame house, found an old fisherman in his nineties. We sat on his veranda, our backs to the asbestos siding, and looked out over a short chain-link fence where ice cream wrappers fluttered softly, like blow-bellies caught in a gill net. We fell into discussing oysters and chanting the litany of vessels and crews long departed. The old fisherman, by now a high-waisted creature of bags and tubes below the belt, nevertheless brightened when a pretty girl strolled past on the opposite side of the street, muttering his gummy desire. Larry made the minimum supporting grunt that our role as guests required. Later Larry remarked on the old guy's persistence in pursuing memories of things long past. "With the way he's rigged now, I'm not sure what he thinks would happen if he ever caught up to her."

I met many of Larry's old Greenport cronies in a more formal setting.

He had apparently belonged to a fraternal order in Greenport for so long that they'd voted him what seemed to be a longevity award. The whole thing bewildered him a bit. He explained that while not all of the members had been watermen, there were few whose business had not been touched by the way in which maritime Greenport had done its business over the last century. These were not necessarily the Rotarians, but they were the men of competence who had seen that the things that needed to get done with hands and backs had indeed gotten done. I looked forward then to the opportunity of seeing into Greenport's past and the sort of social milieu in which Larry Malloy had operated.

The quarters of Larry's fraternal order were upstairs over an antique shop, opposite another ancient Greenport social institution, The Chinese Yacht Club just off Monkey Wrench Corner. The center of Greenport has been known through the years as "Monkey Wrench Corner" because of the way Main Street coming in from the outskirts meets Front Street, which runs along the harbor. The end of Main Street continues past this intersection onto a pier in such a manner as to suggest, to those whose daily bread often hinges on matters mechanical, the shape of a monkey wrench.

As we walked down the street, Larry's step accelerated in anticipation and he pointed to the second story of a shop. It occurred to me that the second stories above shop fronts in small American towns often go unnoticed. There was probably, in many a sleepy town like this, a whole other culture going on above street level, one that from my experience often seemed to be decades in the past. Entrance is usually through the sort of narrow door to the side of the plate glass that you pass a hundred times and never think about. If anything, these narrow doors seem to be the way to a long-closed barbershop, or a dentist who has been defrocked by the health board. There is often no sign on the door, or one that is so faded or obscure in word or symbol as to offer no hint as to what is within. Such was the place we had come to on this hot evening.

The door was ajar, and we swam our way up what seemed an endless column of dust motes kept alive by the setting sun. Aloft, the place had the odor of old attics where one might find the wool and paper of long departed relatives. Here indeed were people who, by physique and clothing, seemed to be the owners of the stuff you find in such attics. In a room in which kitchen furniture was scattered, several men were standing about. Surely some were younger than Larry. They moved through the motes with care and kindness and greeted Larry with formal affection. He had clearly been one of them.

Because I was Larry Malloy's guest, they invited me into their meeting room. It was an oblong chamber with a bare wooden floor suitable for dancing but which was furnished solely with high-backed ceremonial chairs elevated on a terrace that ran all around the side walls. It was as if just the back row of seats in the English Parliament were present. I was invited to sit next to Larry in one of the high-backed chairs along the wall. I sat down and hoped that nothing would be required of me that might embarrass Larry.

The work of the meeting was handled from both ends of the chamber. There was a secretary and lectern at one end and a president behind a lectern at the other. The rest of us faced in, as if observing a tennis match between the two officers. The sun from the street outside was streaming in low behind the president, which gave him a bit of an aura, but aside from the American flag in a floor standard to one side, there was no other attempt to juice the place up.

We commenced by bowing our heads. *Ah,* I thought, *here is where the religious orientation of the old waterfront community will out.* We recited the Lord's Prayer with all the Protestant bells and whistles followed by a pledge to the flag, which hung profoundly becalmed upon its stand at the president's right. I could not count the number of the stars, and while I had no real reason to doubt it did not possess the number that currently corresponded to the extent of our nation's amplitude, I had the feeling that that very flag had stood there since World War Two.

There was a public part of the meeting during which Larry received his award, and I proudly joined the dozen or so members in applause. It was again clear that these men had not forgotten him, and that they looked upon him with respect and affection, two emotions that are not automatically found together in waterfront communities.

The secretary read some correspondence from within the fraternal order and then came to an item " from," as he put it, "the *outside.*" This epistle from "outside" was a bit bewildering as to its claim on the members. Some of us looked toward the window, which was nearly opaque in golden dust. The sounds from the street were remote. There was a good deal of patriotic rhetoric in the communication. Some of this language flowed in phrases that seemed to make it easier for the secretary to read out loud. Other parts that seemed to be asking for action were evidently very difficult to pronounce. Eventually the letter became clear enough in its intent. It was nothing less than a request for an endorsement in behalf of President George Walker Bush in his coming election against Bill Clinton. When the secretary had valiantly concluded the reading there was a discussion. *Ah,* I thought, *here is where the political ideology of the waterfront community shall out.*

Some of the members seemed to think that Bush was indeed the obvious choice. No one spoke up for Clinton. Everyone agreed that the patriotic phrases that had flowed so smoothly were just the sort of thing the organization could without problems endorse. Then someone suggested that the organization was not really a political one. While they could gladly applaud the patriotic sentiments, they should not endorse any particular candidates. Everyone, even the Bush supporters, agreed to this distinction. The chief Bush supporter apologized for even having brought up the matter. "I don't know what I was thinking of," he said.

"Well," said the secretary, "it was just something we got in the mail." Everyone agreed that that was exactly what the item had been.

There was a brief discussion about precisely what obligations the mere receiving of mail actually did incur. Some members felt that the organization did not receive all that much mail of *any* kind. Did this paucity of material therefore somehow increase the obligations on the organization to respond to each and every item that they did receive? Did this particular request, for instance, require an acknowledgment even if not an acquiescence? Did any one actually *know* the man who signed it ?

There was a brief flurry in which members recalled men they knew with similar names. One man actually thought he knew a man with that very name. Someone suggested the letter writer's address become public knowledge. It turned out the writer was from a Western state, and the local member withdrew his claim of familiarity. Through all this the secretary continued to hold the letter firmly out before him, indicating the exact position of the item in relation to the agenda at that moment. Finally, someone suggested that the reading of correspondence go on to the next item. Gratefully the secretary retired the request to the lectern and proceeded to open up another piece of mail.

This letter was a request for a donation to a charity. Everyone agreed that they recognized the charity. One man reminded them it was even one of the causes to which they had traditionally donated. Another member reminded them that donating to charitable causes was indeed an integral part of their mission. With a sense of great relief, the membership enthusiastically voted the donation. With that vote, the regular part of the meeting apparently had concluded.

At this point Larry's sponsor bent over to him and whispered something in his ear. It was time for me to go into the back room while the secret part of the meeting, the ritual, was performed. The president in his halo of sunlight was already nervously fumbling at a thick book that evidently was going to have to be read out loud.

The back room was a kind of old-time kitchen, and one of the men gave me a plate of vanilla ice cream out of an icebox that my mother might have had in our kitchen in the 1940s. He excused himself to return to the ritual, and left me alone to listen to the hum of an ancient electric fan and the sounds that managed to make their way up from the street below. I sat in a green wooden chair at a round table covered with oilcloth and pitched into the ice cream. It was delicious, creamy vanilla, and upstairs in the back room by myself, I felt a contrary mixture of being dislocated and yet somehow at home.

With no one about now, free at last from the anxieties of procedures, I wondered: had I arrived at last, after all these years, at the true heart of Greenport in the days of Larry Malloy's youth?

The evening breeze had just begun to pick up a little, wafting in over the worn, peeling windowsills, when there was an alarming explosion. The window panes rattled, and I thought of the patriotic sentiments expressed so recently in the next room. Not knowing if the world, or at least Monkey Wrench Corner, Greenport, had come to an end, I set about finishing my ice cream. It now tasted of what could only be black powder. Ah, the detonation had been nothing more than my son firing the Lyle gun on the schooner to celebrate the ritual of Evening Colors. We were that close to the harbor.

In a moment the door to the meeting room opened and the men poured in, relaxed and ready for their treat. The ritual in the other room was behind them. Reading out loud was over. Larry himself emerged, apparently none the worse for it all, and we all had what my grandmother would have called "a plate of cream." I asked my hosts if *their* ice cream tasted of black powder. No one admitted to such. The acrid smoke yet hung in my nostrils, and I apologized, explaining my culpability in the matter.

A sunset gun, one man said, was perfectly appropriate to our nation's well-being. The only pity was that one was not fired off routinely.

. . .

"But you know," Larry said later, "I'm not sure I ever really understood that club. We had a pin we could wear if you was all dressed up, and I was at one of them big oyster meetings, you know where you all get together to decide everything about oysters and end up deciding nothing, but sometimes at least you have a good time. This fellow spots my pin, I guess, and comes up to me and says, 'I see you're traveling east.' I sez, 'Hey, sometimes I travel west, too, just so's I can get back to where I started from. I even travels north and south and sometimes nor'by'nor-east.' Well, he starts playing with my hand. You know, tickling my palm with his fingers. *Jesus, I didn't think it was supposed to be that kind of a party,* I thought, but I got to thinking later it was all because of the pin. But, you know, I don't think that Greenport gang was one of them Traveling East outfits because I know we never played with each other's hands."

NOTES

LAW ENFORCEMENT A JOKE (p. 59): In fairness to the New London law enforcement units, in 1931 alone, according to the New London *Day* for December 29, 1999, "local police and the Coast Guard seized 53 vessels and captured 27 boats with liquor on board."

ABAN LIGHT (p. 61): For a generation in mid century this major aid to navigation outside Greenport had no other name on the chart but the abbreviation for abandoned. Its name before and after was and is Long Beach Bar Lighthouse. The 1918 *Coast Pilot* tells us, "Long Beach Point is a low spit from which a bar of little depth extends to Long Beach Bar lighthouse, a white tower and dwelling on piles." During its discontinuation the paint peeled, weather and vandals broke the windows, and eventually some locals set it afire. In the 1990s money was raised, in part by bids on a painting showing the perfectly maintained structure erupting in flames. Rebuilt ashore at the edge of the Greenport Shipyard, the building was transported to its old foundation on the spit by Larry Malloy's brother and nephews.

RUNS ALONG ACROSS THE MEADOWS OF MY SOUL (p. 62): Michael Parish's gorgeous lyric misquoted to indicate the misquoting by the horn player in his playing of Hoagy Carmichael's air.

8

NEW LONDON

In passing the west end of Fisher's Island, you must give it a berth of 3½ miles, as there are several rocks to the westward of it; then your course to the light-house is N.N.W. distant 2 leagues; but in going in here you must not make long hitches; you will leave a sunken ledge on your larboard, and one on your starboard hand. When within one mile of the light-house, you may stand on to the eastward till the light bears N.N.W. and then run up about N.N.E.

— "Directions from Gardiner's Island to New-London,"
The American Coast Pilot, Fourth Edition, 1804

All the bright June afternoon Thad Putnam, a tall, wiry boy in his late teens, stood on a spider-legged wharf at New London watching the life of the harbor.

— Alfred F. Loomis, *Tracks Across the Sea,* 1932

Dusk is gathering in the living room, an early dusk due to the fog, which has rolled in from the Sound and is like a white curtain drawn outside the windows. From a lighthouse beyond the harbor's mouth, a foghorn is heard at regular intervals, moaning like a mournful whale in labor, and from the harbor itself, intermittently, comes the warning bells of yachts at anchor.

— Eugene O'Neill, *A Long Day's Journey into Night,*
Act Three, Scene One

We went to New London. . . . I got in touch with my schooner
[*Arethusa*] that had been jogging patiently off No Man's Land,
and we sold some more of her cargo to Connecticut purchasers.
I enjoyed myself in New London. . . . I was happy, but I played
my hunches. Something woke me early one morning, saying in
my ear: "Time to get out of here." Fifteen minutes later we were
on a launch, heading out across the Sound and, as I learned
later, Jim Lynch, a Treasury agent's man, was asking at the hotel
for me.

—*The Real McCoy*, Bill McCoy quoted by

Frederic F. Van de Water

We at last arrived at New London.

—Captain Joseph J. Fuller, *Master of Desolation*

TRYING TO FOLLOW the life of an oysterman is a bit like tracing the
growth of an oyster. I used to think that an oyster lays down a new ring of
shell for each year of growth, but one day on the Hatchery float at Noank
Captain Jim Markow straightened me out on that. "It's a ring of shell for
each *stop*. It just so happens that winter is your usual stop. But you may
have other stops than that caused by a dip below fifty degrees." There are
certain moments, certain stoppings and goings, then, that do serve to mark
a life, even one that seems to ebb and flow like the Malloys'.

New London, like Greenport, is one of those towns that always seems to
have seen better days. John Ruddy in his published collection of old New
London photographs says, "When the camera's infant eyes first beheld New
London, the city was in the midst of its greatest days."

Like any deep-water seaport, however, its fame was based on things that
happened elsewhere, usually far away. Names like Lahaina and Desolation
Island conjure wonders, but the actual places could hardly be more distant.
As for what did happen right in New London, a lot of that was merely dismal. Benedict Arnold burnt much of it in the Revolution. But there was always this idea that somewhere, in some part of New London, there was elegance. At the conclusion of the 1812 War, which featured Decatur skulking

up above Harrison's Landing, there was a fancy ball in New London in which the officers of Thomas Masterman's British navy danced with the belles of New London's society. There certainly was some money. Joseph Gribbins of Mystic Seaport tells us that "at the height of U.S. whaling in the middle of the nineteenth century New London was, along with Nantucket, second only to New Bedford in the size of its whaling fleet." In the later years of the twentieth century New London clung to its whaling past, touting itself as "The Whaling City." The local high school sports teams are named "The Whalers," and in the gym is a life-sized wooden harpooner leering out over the bow of his boat, weapon at the ready. "Whale Oil Row," a short sequence of matching Federal-era houses, is a prestigious office address for lawyers, nautical magazines, and psychiatrists. There had also been a sealing trade, that is, a business built on the clubbing to death of seals as they lay out on polar ice. Sometimes the particular species were elephant seals, so this activity was known as "elephanting," not to be confused with the "ivory trade" that was feeding the elegance of the nearby Connecticut River ports. One of the principals in this sealing trade was Captain Joseph J. Fuller. A retired blue-water ship master of unquestionable skill, resourcefulness, and bravery, with successful voyages to Desolation Island in the high latitudes of the Southern Ocean, Captain Fuller was later a keeper of Race Rock Light. In his last years he was ashore in New London itself, slumped on a small round fold-out seat, operating the clutch and door in the elevator in the Harris Building (now Lena Building). The same moral reading might be made for an earlier glory, which was euphemistically called the "three-cornered trade," or "the West Indian trade."

There was a time when New London was noted for shipbuilding, with forty different shipyards when Boston had a mere twenty. Presumably the majority of these craft went on to engage in the more benign trades. In the middle of the twentieth century, New London's glory was its submarines. (Actually both the Atlantic base for the United States submarine fleet and the factory that produced most of these vessels, the Electric Boat Division of General Dynamics was on the Groton side of the river. As Larry Malloy points out, "in those days the idea was that New London went right to the high tide mark on the Groton shore.")

Perhaps the harbor's most innocent glory was based on two premier sporting events associated with it: the Bermuda Race and America's oldest intercollegiate athletic event, the Yale-Harvard rowing regatta. No doubt Marxists would have a field day juxtaposing the consumption so conspicuous on these Race Days with the hard life of the harbor's commercial mariners.

As commercial blue-water sailing began to wane there were a number of people who grew up as worthy, if nonprofessional, sailors. As their chief chronicler, Alfred F. Loomis, put it in one of his books about the New London-Bermuda Race (now simply called "the Bermuda Race" and starting biannually out of Newport, Rhode Island): "In the decade since the World War a distinct ocean racing personnel had been created. The members of this amateur navy were devotees of the hardest kind of sailing."

New London then was seldom without some sort of major activity, even if at times on a small scale. Perhaps the most startling part of the time line is that the last whaling vessel was in New London in 1910; the first submarine arrived but six years later.

At the time the Malloys sailed into the harbor, however, naval activities were at their lowest point since before World War One. In fact the biggest naval activity was when two years prior to the Malloy's arrival the 320-foot German underwater experimental freighter *Deutschland* made two voyages to the port bringing chemical dyes and departing with zinc, nickel, and rubber. Four years earlier, John Holland's Electric Boat Company had just taken over the New London Ship and Engine Company, which had made heavy diesel engines for submarines. The United States Coast Guard Academy, which was to be built just below Harrison's Landing, was three years away. The present road between New London and Norwich, the next city upriver, petered out into a dirt trail just above Harrison's Landing. If you were interested in moving goods between the two principal cities of Eastern Connecticut, either the river or the railroads that ran along both banks were your best bet.

It was during these years that Captain Frank Thompson was running the *Governor Winthrop,* which in the absence of a highway bridge between New London and Groton moved passengers from one side of the Thames to the other. Thompson was father of the famous draggerman-author-painter Ellery Thompson. The younger Thompson was a writer far more celebrated locally than the long-winded Eugene O'Neill, a man promoted largely by such out-of-towners as the Swedish Academy. This was the period when O'Neill, a summer New London native, was doing the work that made him the most renowned American playwright of the first half of the century. O'Neill set many of these award-winning dramas in New London, but those locals who bothered with these productions at all saw them as betrayals of their town's seedier side to the outside world for the author's fame and profit.

Most of O'Neill's plays were influenced by what critics like to call "the sea." Actually, O'Neill was chiefly attracted to the New London estuarine waterfront, many of whose citizens he depicted as washed-up blue-water men. In his work there is always the notion that blue water is a redeeming spiritual force in the life of otherwise doomed lubbers. Wharfside activity is demeaning, fit only to illustrate, like Captain Joseph J. Fuller's elevator job in the Lena Building, the poignancy of departed oceanic glory. The closest O'Neill comes to celebrating the sort of maritime environment that shallow-water sailors such as the Malloys made their living in is with *Anna Christie*.

The mercifully short (for O'Neill) play is the story of a New London immigrant barge captain's daughter who has had to work Bank Street in order to maintain her father's indolent, beery lifestyle. Stage productions feature much back-and-forth with buckets of beer fetched to the barge from Bank Street establishments of the sort to which the young Larry Malloy lugged his oyster pails. When I asked Larry what he thought of Eugene O'Neill he said, "Until they renamed Main Street after him, I'd never heard of the guy." Other old-time New Londoners are nowhere near so kind.

Thompson, on the other hand, although known for some of the same vices as O'Neill, was the darling of the town. He was, after all, a real boatman. The wonderful waterfront writer Joseph Mitchell wrote him up in a two-part profile in the *New Yorker* (January 4 and 11, 1947), later reprinted in Mitchell's 1951 collection *The Bottom of the Harbor*. *Life* magazine also discovered him, and in 1950 Viking Press got a writer to ghost a pleasant book more or less in Ellery's voice, *Draggerman's Haul*. Ellery told me one day, up in his Mystic apartment over the paint store, that "Hollywood had even come a-calling." He had held out for Gary Cooper to play him, "but Gary was on another picture and the whole thing fizzled." There was also supposed to be a literary sequel, "but Mr. Pope, the ghostwriter, dropped dead of a heart attack and so that fizzled." Ellery did write a pair of sequels on his own, *Come Aboard the Draggers* and *Sea Sketches* In these locally published volumes you can read him without the late Mr. Pope's doing the prose for him. As for the activities of the Thompson family as recounted in Ellery's literary productions, Larry did get a little closer than he did to Eugene O'Neill. "I never read any of them books, but I did know the family. As a matter of fact, I have Captain Frank's safe in my basement. That's Ellery's father, the ferryboat captain. It's still got his name on it."

O'Neill was thinking of New London before the First World War. As the century progressed, the oceanfront aristocracy he loathed was pushed by the advent of the income tax, the Depression, and eventually the 1938 Hurricane, into decline. Up in the harbor itself the outbound blue-water life oozed into a kind of unliterary funk.

In World War Two I remember Bank Street as thronged with pungent sailors, often in foreign uniforms, startling in their burst of gaudy ribbons. On each side of the street, even in full daylight, in summer, white-belted in dress blues, men in SP armbands paraded in pairs back and forth, pounding their palms with fat clubs. "Nightsticks," my mother explained. "Shore Patrol." Every time we passed a bar, we had to keep an eye out for the door, as it was apt to fling forth a sodden mariner whose over-the-shoulder anger was ripe with the courage of the sidewalk. There was a tattoo parlor and a pawnshop crammed with fishing gear, foul weather coats, guitars and euphoniums. I sensed that behind the buildings on the east side of Bank Street great gray armed ships pressed in upon the town. My mother, however, warned me not to collect the bottles that lured me into the entrances of those sea-seeking alleys. "Men," she assured me, *do terrible things in bottles.*"

In the early 1960s I signed up for the Coast Guard in the New London Custom House and was comforted in New Jersey, Delaware, and even New Orleans with Off Limits notices that posted Bank Street bars and that tattoo parlor. New London strutted a couple of Irish bars that were, in truth, more Irish than many I later saw in the Auld Country. The ferryboat to Long Island was a partially converted World War Two LST. She had seen action on D-Day and the wind still howled through the holes in the superstructure where the antiaircraft guns had been bolted. My father had a story about how coming across the Sound from Greenport on a cold day one of the truckers dropped a sack of Long Island potatoes, broke it open, and baked potatoes for the passengers on his muffler. This seemed to me a wonderfully romantic image of potato transportation until I got to know Larry Malloy, who had moved barrels of them as deck cargo on his oyster boats. Yet, for all its history, there has always seemed to me to be a damp melancholy hanging over New London.

Unlike Greenport, however, the melancholy of New London, despite its gory glory, has often been seen not so much in its departed past as in its failure to achieve a potential. (Perhaps, after all, it is the sad suspirations of all those expiring cetaceans that hangs over the "Whaling City.") Situated on the mainland nearly halfway between Boston and New York, easily accessible to deep water and inland routes, New London suggests itself as what is now known as an "intermodal transportation center." Visitors to San Francisco compare it to New London's "situation" as do those who have seen the gas-lit restoration of nearby Newport. (In fact, city planners have actually taken a bus tour to look at Newport so that they might think more about all this.)

One afternoon in the mid-1970s when I lived in New London I was standing on the corner of Bank Street and State, a confluence that is called "the Parade" after an old military tradition. Up State Street was the former site of the City Hotel, where Andrew Jackson, Martin Van Buren, and Abraham Lincoln had each spent a night. Down Bank was the former site of Bacon's Hotel, where Daniel Webster, George Washington, and the Marquis de Lafayette had bedded down. When that building burned in 1897, the Royal Hotel rose in its place, but now the only marquee was the leaky canopy lurching off the façade that announced the hotel's name. Its foyer was the sort of lurk hole in which, if men were not doing terrible things with bottles, bottles had done terrible things with them. I was but a minute's stroll from where the Malloys once had their oyster shop. Two blue-haired women with a pretty teenage granddaughter in tow approached me.

"Is this it?" they wanted to know. The "it" they were seeking, of course, was the authentic New London waterfront. I suggested they stroll down Bank Street to the 1833 Custom House, which was just around the gentle curve of the road. I sketched some of the history of that noble edifice. The door had been made of wood from the *Constitution;* the landing out back had been the place where the people on the liberated slave ship *Amistad* first officially landed. Back there on the pier there was presently a fine assortment of aids to navigation. The aids were interesting, I naively informed the ladies, because the parts usually hidden beneath the water's surface were now exposed for all to see. (As for the sleeping presidents, I let them lie.) The two elder women strained in their tennis shoes, but did not move them. I followed their eyes past the bars and former tattoo parlor, the military uniform store, the emporium for adult books, the drooping marquee of the abandoned Capitol Theater, the smaller, bulb-spattered marquee of the Royal Hotel. "Perhaps," I suggested, "you would prefer Mystic Seaport Museum."

The older generation thought that a capital idea; the granddaughter caught my eye.

. . .

Larry Malloy's New London began just prior to the stock market crash. "We moved to Connecticut (Thames River) January 1928 aboard the oysterboat *Lieutenant,* lock, stock, and furniture, including father, mother, sisters, two brothers, and me. I was about eleven years old.

"We had chairs and beds and tables and bureaus and a piano. What I guess you call a baby grand, because it wasn't an upright like later Tommy Watt had at his West Mystic Boatyard, and it probably wasn't a full size like you'd have in a concert hall. Not that I've ever been in a concert hall that you'd probably call a *concert* hall.

"I don't know what caused it, what caused the sudden move out of Greenport, but one day I come home and my father said, 'Get aboard the boat.' There were days when he could talk up a storm. This wasn't one of them. He was like that. Either he'd talk your head off, especially if you was part of an audience, or he'd clam up. I still don't know all these years later what caused it, our sudden departure, that is. I think he may have had a disagreement with a neighbor. I'm not sure you'd call it a *brawl.* My father was a big man and sometimes didn't think it necessary to reason things out.

"I got to thinking about this the other night, and it hit me that maybe Connecticut was someplace the old man knew from eeling. He used to do a lot of eeling, setting out pots in Gardiners Bay with Josh Moore, but Pappy, he got the bait from seining for what they called 'silver eels' over on the Connecticut side. You know the little basin on Fishers Island, the western-most harbor on the place, is the one with Fort Wright and the ferry landing. Technically that's still New York waters, but Connecticut's right there. That's still called Silver Eel Pond. I'm not sure what the right names for the different kinds of eels are, but to us there was two kinds: *silver eels* that we netted for bait; *regular, eating eels* that we caught in the baited pots and sold. So maybe I'm in Connecticut because of eels. Hey, this stuff all fits together if you get to thinking about it. You just have to live long enough, because, at the time, a lot of it don't make sense. But then that kind of sense ain't usually what you're looking for then.

"Another thing about that sudden move out of Greenport: when we moved over to Connecticut—it wasn't exactly the season to be traveling. We managed to get across the Sound into the Thames River about midnight and encountered twenty-four inches of ice at the swing bridge, which then was the only highway bridge across the Thames at New London. That's the bridge that put Ellery Thompson's father's ferryboat out of business. Unable to proceed any further upriver in the heavy ice, my father decided to moor at the Valvolene Oil Company pier just south of the bridge. Here we lived for a while until the ice disappeared. That must have been several days. It's hard to tell things like *days* when you're eleven years old. *Hours* can seem like days.

"When the ice cleared we proceeded upriver looking for a new home. The *Lieutenant* was forty-four feet long and almost fifteen feet wide. She'd been built in 1906 in Tottenville, Staten Island—drew almost five feet. For an oysterboat, she was comfortable, but, hey, she was still just that: an oysterboat. My father had in mind a house at the Narrows in Montville between Robert Gear and the railroad coal station, which is now Dow Chemical. Only problem was it was right under the high-tension lines. When my mother saw the towers and high-tension lines Pappy's plans were shattered.

"So we continued to live aboard *Lieutenant*, now moored at the pier at Robert Gear paper plant. These arrangements went on for close to a month before father located a two-family house at Harrison's Landing, a little distance down on the New London side. The house was empty; we chose the west end. This house had been a blacksmith shop at the United States Submarine Base across the river, but had been moved, in a year unknown to me, across the river by barge. The river was good to us in other ways. We got our electric power from telephone poles that just seemed to wash up on the beach. Hey, they must have just got away. Things like that happen, you know, when you pile them too close to the river. Look what happened to us in the 1938 Hurricane."

"The River giveth," I intoned, "and the River taketh away."

"Only problem is," he said, "it always seemed a lot harder work to get the river to *giveth* you something."

"Ah ..."

"Anyway, this was home until 1940. The Savings Bank of New London owned the property (which was in an estate) with the idea they were to sell it off later. Before that it had all been farmland. Eventually, many years later, Father and I did purchase the lots where we are today."

"Getting settled in a house and in Quaker Hill School, I became more active. As it was quite a severe winter I learned how to shovel snow. New London's only a dozen miles north of Greenport, but it's that dozen miles across the Sound that make it just a bit colder. I tried ice skating, skiing, bobsledding, all the things you would do if you lived in Canada. I helped in maintaining heat in the *Lieutenant,* cutting wood and stoking the coal fire.

"When spring arrived, it was oystering in a big way. I did get considerable play time in, however: swimming, power boating, fishing, eeling, and sailing, all that good boat stuff.

"I tried eeling in the Thames with the hundred and fifty or so pots left over from the Greenport days. I would set twenty-five or thirty pots in late afternoon and haul them early in the morning before school. Some mornings I would arrive at school a little slimy. Other kids would arrive a little skunky. Hey, it was a rural population. And both eels and skunks were items that were fun to catch and you could sell. I also did that with crabs. I had a holding car—you know, like a lobster pot—I would keep the eels in until I sold them. There was a door-to-door fish peddler named Daniels that came around in those days who would buy them from me. I would sell them in the skin or dressed. Whatever he wanted. I shipped several tubs of eels to New York Fulton Market by Frank Maria's fish transportation located at Bentley's Creek, which is south and west of Fort Trumbull down below the main part of the city of New London. I found that if I shipped the eels from Greenport I could get more money per tub. When the time was right my father would take the tubs of eels to Greenport and ship them to Fulton Market by Sweezy's Trucking, which was at the foot of Main Street.

"We shipped the eels in three-pound butter tubs, which I purchased from the Mohegan Market which was next to the Mohegan Hotel in New London. I think the price was a nickel or maybe a dime a tub. Eels were shipped alive in the tub. We'd throw a handful of pipe tobacco in on top of them to quiet them down so we could put the cover on and fasten it down.

There must have been something about the nicotine. I don't know who discovered that trick. Must have been some old cud chewer who was frustrated one day when the bastards wouldn't lay still for him. Well, none of us chewed, but Pappy, he had that pipe. We also used butter tubs to ship scallops to Fulton Market. You didn't need tobacco to quiet them, which pleased Pappy who was always running short for his pipe. We did this kind of commercial fishing up until September 21, 1938 (hurricane)."

. . .

In many ways Larry Malloy's life is not so much a trail of places or even a succession of jobs as it is a sequence of boats. The boats helped him do different jobs and, being portable, took him different places. Some of these boats are pre–New London. Some he first encounters in Greenport. They drop out of the Malloys' life, then return again, like *Anne*, now the only one yet running. In some cases the boat passes in and out of the Malloys' life without benefit of clear ownership on their part, but as in the case of the *G. H. Church*, not without tangible results.

"Pappy never did actually ever own the *G. H. Church*, but he was always looking for an opportunity to horse-trade boats. Find a way to make some money off the water. If not by something the boat could do better than another boat, then by just plain trading the boat—I suppose like you would on the stock market. Pappy made himself the chance to go master aboard of *G. H. Church*. The idea here was Pappy was to go down to New Haven to work on the Great Oyster Set of 1930. Down off New Haven, the oysters set three-foot thick on the bottom and pretty much all over. It was like a bonanza. Suddenly everybody needed a big boat to work the New Haven grounds. The *G. H. Church* was perfect for this job. She was fifty-four-and-a-half-feet long. Hotchkiss [Kochiss] says she was built in Noank in 1911 as a freighter and a fishing boat.

"Of course we didn't know things like that until [Kochiss] came out in 1974. Pappy, he just knew she was an old boat, but a serviceable one. She had lain in the Sterling Basin at Greenport back of *Anne* for years. If you look at the photo in the Wash White calendar you find just her bow to the left of *Anne*—right down at the wharf below where them running-board cars are parked. Nobody paid her any attention. People thought she was all done because her stem was rotten. Pappy he looks over at this old girl been just layin' there to the bulkhead near *Anne*. He pokes around the *G. H. Church*'s stem a bit and finds it's only rotten in the top foot or so and so he saws that off, splices in a piece, daubs a bit of paint. Off he goes in her to the Big Set. A few weeks later after working the set, he arranges a sale of the *G. H. Church* to somebody down to the westward and he makes himself a nice piece of change."

. . .

At first I thought to straighten out this boat chronology a bit, but I'm now beginning to be convinced Larry's narrative instincts in this matter are right. Or at least basically right. The bedbug incident below, however, still strikes me as out of sequence, or at least confusing.

The buildings in which the Malloys lived were also the products of the maritime industry. While their original house—the blacksmith shop at the Submarine Base—had been ferried the half-mile across the Thames by somebody else, it was the Malloys themselves who floated the kitchen that had been the gasoline station at Fort Michie on Great Gull Island a dozen miles across Long Island Sound and up the Thames. "We slid her off the boat on some planks—high tide, of course. The lucky thing was that the doorway was such as to fit right over the hyster post on the boat.

"We had a vegetable patch, like you had and Tommy Watt had at Willow Point. And we had chickens and even had a cow. Geese. We ate pretty good even though there wasn't much money around. It was my job to cut the heads off the chickens. You know how you do that? You got to go at 'em with a broom handle in one hand and the hatchet in the other. They'll watch you out of the corner of their eye and move that head just enough at the last minute. You got to stun them with the broom handle across the neck and they'll stretch that right out then so you can get a good whack in. Of course, sometimes they run around pretty good afterwards. They're liable to jump right in the pot. Hey, this is kind of gruesome, ain't it? But you know in them days you didn't think so much about what was gruesome. You was hungry!"

. . .

"Maybe New London between the world wars wasn't exactly the *glory days*, but to me it was a thriving place. People used to come over from Long Island just to walk around and shop. They must have stayed the night, too, because the *Catskill* only run one boat a day. At Harrison's Landing we may have been literally at the end of the trolley line and the concrete road as far as New London was concerned, but the place seemed lively. That wasn't so much because of automobile traffic north and south, because like I said, there wasn't much. The traffic was east-west, across the river by boat. A lot of the sailors who were stationed across the river at the Base lived on the Landing. In fact the Navy used to send a liberty launch to pick them up in the morning and bring them home at night. Pappy had the only dock, so all that activity went on right at our house. My sister, the one that later married Captain George Sanford, she went out with one of those sailors for quite a while. On Race Day, when the Yale-Harvards got going, the Navy sent a shore patrol over to the Landing to keep law and order.

"I used to go over to the Submarine Base all the time. We'd row over in the sharpie and had permission to pick up the brass and other scrap they dumped off the piers. They dumped all kinds of things, including the batteries that had worn out from driving the subs under water. I swam over there to Bailey Point once with Bob Hart. We got to the bank and he said, 'It don't count as having made it over unless you touch bottom on this side.' I didn't want to try that because I knew that all them oysters were on the bottom there. Well, I guess he got to be official because he come up with two feet that looked like he'd been in an alley fight. So you see what the oysters in the Thames River was like in them days, right at the Sub Base!

"That big test tank over there. The Momson device. I was there twice when they was building it and I was there the day they opened it up. I was in the Boy Scouts and was standing at the edge of the apron around the tank where they send the divers down. They had a line with buoys at regular intervals. The idea was the divers would go to those intervals and wait until they were told to go to the next level. This guy turns to me and says, 'Here, you hold the line.' So there I was holding the buoy line in the test tank the first day it opened. Later on they'd shoot you for any of that.

"I never personally saw the *Deutschland,* but Pappy had quite a bit to say about it. She was supposed to be OK because she was bringing in a lot of dye. But he said she did 'a lot more spying than dyeing.'

"As for bars I never went into any except to deliver oysters. We did go into the Empire Theater, which was down on the far end of Bank Street beyond the Custom House and which has long since been torn down. We saw all the big movies that came around in those days, or at least thought we did: Mickey Mouse and cowboys. Sometimes the action in the theater was even more exciting. You had to keep your legs up or the rats running over your feet might break off your toes. One day George Sanford stood up and shouted. Something had gotten a hold of him, and you know George Sanford's gone and I don't have the answer to that one to this day.

"I used to do some roller skating in a rink a man named Rudd had up over the Hygienic Restaurant. Outdoors, my brother Frank and some other fellows and I would go over to what is now the Coast Guard Academy. We'd crawl up that cliff where they have the officers quarters now. When they built that, they must have glued that building to the rock. Then there was a short golf course over there. The tee was on the hill where the Lyman Allyn Art Museum is now. They drove the ball over the trolley tracks to where the Coast Guard Academy now is. There was a lot of woods around, and we'd find the golf balls in there and take them back to the Landing. We had a baseball bat and would throw the golf balls up in the air and hit them back down almost to the golf course again."

I remarked that this was one of the few instances of pure play that I'd ever heard him mention.

"I keep thinking work was all I done. I didn't know that girls were to play with. I guess the old man took care of that."

. . .

To get to his grammar school, Larry Malloy climbed up out of the Landing to Quaker Hill, which was so far up that even the trolley didn't attempt the ascent. For high school, which followed directly from grammar school, he went to Buckley in downtown New London. There were three secondary schools then for New London County, all in the city. Buckley High School was for what we would now call the college-bound males. Williams Memorial Institute was for women, and there was also Chapman Technical High School. Larry was chosen for Buckley, which does not surprise me but did him. He attended through his junior year, where there was the sort of misunderstanding that seems inconceivable today, but that was all too common in those times. Students were required to keep a notebook in English and pass it in on the final day to be checked off. As Larry stood in line the student behind him tapped him on the shoulder. He had not done his work and wanted to copy Larry's. Obligingly, Larry loaned him the book, which the student simply then submitted as his own. When Larry had nothing to hand in, the teacher said, "I'll see you next year."

"I don't think so," he said, and that was that. Larry Malloy's formal education was over.

NOTE

ELECTRICITY FROM FLOTSAM (p. 77): A characteristic Malloy trope here blended with a bit of Malloy mysticism. Having received a number of queries about this in the editorial process, I asked Larry for exegesis. "You get the poles from the river, stick them in the ground, then string wires between the house and the power lines."

9

OYSTERING

I will not be sworn but love may transform me to an oyster.

—*Much Ado About Nothing*, II, iii, 23

"THE REASON OYSTERMEN need boats is because they ain't figured out a way to make the boots tall enough. I don't know how deep in the water an oyster can grow, but I do know how deep it can get before you start wishing you'd found somewhere shallower because you got too much chain running out. Not only out, but out and back. Then how you gonna manage all that, especially after it's been out and back a few times? You take a look at the chart of Gardiners Bay and except for the northern edges of it at Plum Gut and at the Race you haven't got but forty feet or less up and down in all that. You got plenty of sideways water, but it's the up and down that's thin. With so much land that's shallow under you there's no point in looking for the few holes that's in it just so you can lose your chain down in there. Besides, at the Gut and the Race the water's running too hard most of the time to let you hold your boat where you want it.

"As far as all them stories about Indians in canoes, I don't see how leaning over the side of one of those light boats would be better than just getting out of them entirely and scratching around on your own two feet. Walk along, and if you got to have a canoe, maybe tow the canoe like a big rubber tire around a basket—like you see the recreational people do it. Another thing, out on the Bay you need a sufficient boat under you because wind against the tide, shallow water gets to be pretty choppy water. When it gets choppy you're going to be bounced around like a cork in anything that draws under six feet. Up in the rivers you can maybe get away with four foot of draft.

"To many people today oysters are a mystery. They don't really know much about a clam either, but what they do know pretty much takes care of it for them. Especially since it's likely to be in a chowder: Down there in the murk with potatoes and something from the garden so in any one spoonful what you got may not even be a clam at all. But oysters, hey, they're one of those things that kind of bewilders you, looking at it. Even when you're not looking at it. And that's where you got to do most of your thinking about oysters. When you're not looking right at them, when you can't see them at all, and maybe, hey, they ain't even there anywheres about. That's when they're the most problem.

"Then there's the times you're looking at what you think is an oyster, but when you open it up, you ain't so sure. Some strange things can happen to an oyster. Maybe it's even an oyster that you know from before. You might have known this oyster for two, three years, what with moving it around from here to there, catching and setting it and catching and setting it again out on different grounds. I don't mean to say you give them names or anything. But you *do* know what *lot* it come from and what you expect from that lot depending upon all the things you know that have gone on out there on that particular piece of ground. You either rent [lease] or own [been granted] that land, so it gets to be like the potato patch back of your house. Oystering's more like farming that way than fishing. But more unpredictable even than farming. Rainfall, water temperature, salinity, storms, the usual spills and thrills you got to put up with on the water—all the different things that can change an oyster for better or worse, usually worse. Things you got no goddamn control over, but for which you're responsible.

"I been in the business all my life, and oysters still confuse me. I suppose it's silly to admit that a blob of a thing in a shell that would fit in your hand, a thing that can't walk or talk or even sing much can outsmart you. My father used to say that 'the only way to know all about an oyster was to *be* an oyster.'"

. . .

"My father, he never bothered with *clams*. 'You want the clams on my grounds?' he'd say. 'Have at 'em, but just don't touch the oysters.' Of course just how you'd dig the clams out from under the oysters without touching one or two was always a mystery to me. I just know that Pappy never had much use for clams or clammers. He didn't make a long speech about clams. But you bring up the idea of clams, he just looked at you in a certain way that, well, made you feel like maybe you was some kind of clam yourself.

"Scallops are exciting, but they move around so much that it's hard to get a bead on them. It's not so much one year you got them, the next you don't. It's one *day* they ain't anywhere around; the next morning they're all over the place. Most of the ones I eat I find in the oyster dredge, a handful maybe here and there. Some people seem to learn a lot about scallops from reading cookbooks. Hey, they don't last long when you're standing on deck and already got an oyster knife in your hand. From my experience on deck it's pretty hard to get any cooking in between a fresh scallop and my mouth. Mussels, now they grow on the spilings and they'll grow on the bottom of your boat if you don't move around much. Some people eat them, but I think you have to be French or at least have a cookbook written in French."

. . .

The other side of the public's perception of the oyster is exotic. Oystering is, after all, as Larry Malloy's father indicated, the queen of shellfishing. Having recognized that, people go overboard the other way and get too ambitious about oysters. People think oysters produce pearls. "I never found a pearl in all my shucking days," said Malloy, "and never heard of anybody doing that. The best place to get pearls is in a jewelry store. Maybe in the South Seas."

In stories that usually go along with people going over Niagara Falls in a barrel or Teddy Roosevelt shooting something, there are the yarns about gourmandizers of a hundred years ago. Large-bellied men with top hats aslant ate dozens of raw oysters at a sitting and washed them down with vast quantities of beer. Oysters also were, or maybe still are, a kind of pre-Pfizer Viagra. I asked Larry Malloy what he thought about the aphrodisiac properties of *Crassotrea virginica,* which he has, after all, spent a lifetime pursuing. "I always found the biggest aphro-whatever about oysters was in that oysters sometimes allowed you to make enough money to impress the girls. What happened after, well, I'm not sure if that was due to the oyster, I mean the partakin' of a few."

Then there is the whole business of *catching* oysters. That clams are caught both along shore and from boats does not seem to most people a problem. That scallops move about on their own and are caught with spotters and small scoop nets on long handles is something so far beyond most people's experience that there is no need to consider the matter here. Oysters, however, may be picked up along shore and then there are those oyster boats, some in the range of the larger yachts. Evolved out of nineteenth-century sailing craft, the wooden oysterboat you may now see a half-mile off some suburban shore seems like some conscious effort to recreate a piece of nostalgia. In an age of steel trawlers that look like float-ing ray guns, surely what you see is not a serious commercial enterprise. If these boats *are* the best way to harvest this product, is there something about the oyster then that insists on maintaining its connection with an-cient ways?

Your classic oysterboat, encrusted, disheveled, even dilapidated though she may be, yet has her lines or the evidence of what used to be her lines, that graceful sloop sheer connecting the fantail stern to the plumb bow. The oysterboat superstructures, unlike the encumbered clammer who lugs about a raging beast upon its back in the form of a conveyor, is relatively clean, with its wheelhouse, engine box, and mast. The mast, while stubby, is redeemed by a boom and its attendant tackle. The engine box, which in some cases is big enough to be considered a cabin, is modest enough, a low structure aft of the wheelhouse and considerably lower, so that the captain can see out over it when backing down. But it is the wheelhouse itself that is the glory of the craft.

In fact, so attractive are these structures that they often survive the vessel herself, living on as everything from ticket and telephone booths to roadside tomato stands. Their design is well proportioned, and the texture of their execution is a delight. Rounded on the forward end with a permanent awning visor, the wheelhouse was often built with a slight overbite to allow its sash-hung windows to drain, yet another nice adjustment of form and function on the old work boats. Oysterboat wheelhouses are sheathed vertically with tongue-and-groove barrel staving dressed with bullnose moldings. Inside is the large mahogany helm with big-fisted spokes that would do justice to a Cup defender of the old school. Sometimes, as in *Anne,* there is a locking pawl, that is, a wooden hinged lever that rises from the wheelhouse deck to capture in a small aperture at its end one of the spokes and so hold the wheel hard over when the boat is turning on its dredge. The furnishings may vary but the interior doorknobs are usually brass or porcelain. There is a settee across the back of the house which, when cleared of oil cans, Primus stoves, log books, pliers, screw drivers, hammers, tide books, boots, logo caps, foul weather jackets, and lunch may, in theory, be used as a bunk. From the overhead dangles a squawking radio. Some boats recently have added the ambiguous red glow of a depth finder, but your old timers carry that kind of information all in their head. What is unique to an oysterboat is the cat's cradle of lines and blocks that control the hoisting rig (pronounced "hyster"). The line is often merely of the sort used to hang out the laundry, and the hardware through which it runs suggests backyard pulleys more than seagoing blocks. Wooden toggles interspersed here and there give hope of some sort of mastery on the part of the operator. In any case, the lines vanish through the floor of the wheelhouse, and a yank on one of the toggles may well produce a rumbling in the bowels of the vessel with the eventual squeak and wheeze of machinery located out the window down below you on the foredeck.

The wheelhouse is high so that it offers a good view of this machinery, and it is from there that the captain controls everything. The winch under the mast takes its power off the main engine. In the old days the main engine was steam, but is now some great, midcentury, diesel-drinking behemoth whose moods are known only to operators of at least the same vintage. The purpose of the winch is to lift the dredge from the deck where it has been reposing. Because of the thumping returns of the dredge, the deck is the only truly ugly thing on an oysterboat. *Anne*'s long-leaf yellow pine had to be covered with what Larry euphemistically calls "bridge tile": squares of asphalt. On the winch drum is laid cable, which passes up through the sheaves of a series of big diamond-shaped steel construction blocks to the upper end of the mast. The cable bends back down to the apparatus winch below deck, which commences operations up in the wheelhouse with the tug on the clothesline. As the boom swings the dredge over the bulwarks, the winch lowers it in a controlled manner into the sea.

Through the years there has been some mild experimentation with the dredge, but it has remained basically the same through the lifetimes of the Malloys. Kochiss traces the basic design of the dredge back to the Middle Ages in England and speculates that the fishermen of Colchester and Whitstable may have stolen the idea from the Romans. An armspan wide and maybe half as deep, the dredge is a steel frame at the front of whose maw is blade a handspan wide. At the back of the frame's mouth is not a stomach but a chain bag. The flat bar angle of the blade is crucial, as it is this surface that first contacts the bottom and, as Larry Malloy says, "encourages the oyster to come aboard." Oysters tend to live either on the surface of the bottom or slightly below, so it is important to set the dredge at just the right angle so as to pick up the product without burying the rig needlessly in the mud, possibly even inadvertently anchoring you.

Greenporters' dredges were made by a blacksmith along the harborfront for $125 a pair. "Or at least that's what I think they cost," said Malloy, "because that's just about all the money we had. That blacksmith kept the oyster fleet going for years, made all kinds of gear and repaired gear, often in an emergency. Not only dredges but also basic workboat hardware like blocks, right down to the sheaves in the blocks. Whatever you wanted. Sketch it out on the back of an envelope or, hell, in the dirt outside using a stick. Whatever you wanted. His name was Paul Nossolik, up that alley back of Holse Brothers Engines. People now are trying to reconstruct his shop over there on the edge of the harbor, but in 1987, when he was ready to retire, somebody stole his anvil. Some fellows came by to purchase his tools. They said they wanted to be, you know, 'authentic.' They walked off with them, including the anvil, and never paid him. Hell, they even stole all the timbers that had made up his shop."

The course steered by an oysterboat, unlike trawlers after flounder, say, is not in straight furrows but in a series of circles in which the boat's stern and screw propeller is turned away from the dredge. (This is why, when Larry Malloy's father fell overboard on the Noank grounds, he knew *Anne,* her helm locked down on her pawl, would come back to him.) That is, if *Anne* has the dredge over the starboard side, Malloy will put her helm to starboard, which throws the screw away from the cable. "I *can* turn back toward the dredge because I'm *acquainted* with exactly how far I can go that way without catching the dredge in the screw. It's something you got to be real careful about, especially in shallow water where the angle gives you a much longer target of cable to hit. If you do get the cable in the screw . . . well, I don't recall ever doing that."

If he's got two dredges over, one on each side, the crew keeps them alternating. That is, one dredge is overboard while the other is on the table being culled. This alternating process produces an S-shaped course to the edge of the grounds, where the boat turns around and comes back, making a the S into a figure 8. Just how long the time of the drag is to be and how much cable should be out and what speed the boat should be going are all matters of judgment based on long years of experience.

"It depends upon the shape of the ground under you and what you know about what you put down there and how long since you been there and what you think might have happened down there while you was gone. As for speed, if you go too fast, you skip over the bed; if you go too slow you end up anchoring or at least taking too long to get aboard the day's *order*. Usually you go out with some sense of the amount to bring back. You've got orders from the middlemen or some sort of transplanting project you yourself has in mind. You don't just go out there and wander around in circles until you get tired and you sure don't go out and strip the grounds."

When *Anne* was working out of West Mystic Wooden Boat Company in the mid-nineties, she would chug the two miles downriver to the Noank grounds every Thursday and bring back exactly twenty-three onion bags of oysters for the local markets. When Larry Malloy and Johnny Bartlett were moving oysters off the Milford ground in the middle of the century, they loaded the boat up to the bottom of the windowsill in the wheelhouse and wallowed back to New London with decks awash. Of course the twenty-three bags was a tactical routine order for local markets; the Milford binge was part of a strategic shift in "soaking" the product. *Soaking* is one of the procedures by which oystermen enhance a crop, in this case by moving it to waters of increased salinity.

When the drag has been completed, the winch hoists the dredge back aboard, and the boom swings it over the culling table under the mast. At the right moment the deckhand yanks the purse string on the bottom of the dredge bag and the goodies tumble down onto the culling table, raining and clattering onto the stainless steel surface. As with lobstering, each load is slightly different from the last. Some catches are more vegetative; others may wriggle with diverse members of the benthic community. If crabs are preying on the oysters there will be no mystery about their work. There they are rioting among their prey, *Carcinides maernas,* the green crab, a relatively recent invader of New England waters, its commercial use confined to blackfish (tautog) bait. Market-sized oysters are too big for the green crab, but in the juvenile stage no oyster can withstand them. Even in the intermediate stage an oyster will have its growth mantle trimmed by the green crab. "Years ago it was starfish," says Larry Malloy. "We used to dump lime in them. Some people just boiled them. Sometimes it's *drills,* which is really just another kind of shellfish, more of a snail, and it bores through oyster shell. It's always some kind of thing wants your product."

Besides the odd lunch scallop or two, occasionally the bycatch will include an artifact: a clay pipe where old whalers once moored or a spoon from a World War One warship's mess deck.

The culling table is just aft of the mast and is about chest high and a bit wider than the dredge basket. *Anne*'s has a back lip to it to keep the catch from oozing on over onto the foredeck and into the winch drum.

In the meantime, the deckhand's oilskinned belly and hands keep most of the catch from falling off the aft end of the table, from where, if a few creatures do tumble, it is no great task to retrieve them. Errant oysters usually manage to get themselves retrieved quickly. For crabs, there's less enthusiasm, so that by the end of a grab the deck can be a lively dance of twittering and scuttling.

The characteristic sound of this part of the process is the clink of the culling iron against the oysters. A culling iron is an elegant solution to what at times are baroque problems. Nothing more than a straight piece of flat stock about two inches wide and maybe a foot long that looks like a burglar's pry, the culling iron is the key tool in separating clumps of oysters that have grown either into other oysters or onto some other material such as a rock. It is handy for moving the catch around on the table and saves the hands from the rougher encounters with shells and crabs. It is also helpful in sounding the shell to see if it might be empty. Most dead oysters will open, and with the hinge decayed, fall into two half-shells. There are conditions, however, when the shell might be closed and yet there's "nobody home." The ping of the culling iron makes a kind of "Anvil Chorus" to the circling gulls who hope for scraps. A veteran such as Larry Malloy would need to tap far less often, but he was up in the wheelhouse, and today's man, much to Larry's amusement, was performing a veritable xylophone concerto.

"Everything had a place where it was made. The cullin' iron was made by a guy you knew and was used in a particular place in a particular way and had a place where you put it when you was done. Paul Nossolik, who made our dredges, also made our cullin' irons. You could tell his cullin' irons because they had a hole on one end so you could hang them up.

"Sometimes these days you see people using welder's knives, instead of cullin' irons. These are pointed on one end. Sure you can pry apart a clump faster than with a cullin' iron, but you also spoil a lot of the product by poking holes and breaking the shell. This all comes from growing the oysters too tight so you get these monster clumps. Some of it may have to do with *where* you're growing them. You know: *conditions.* Now don't ask me what is *in* those *conditions.* I ain't no scientist and I don't see nothing yet where even the scientists know all about these *conditions.* What I do know is Thames River, for instance, it's good for single oysters. It's extraordinary if you get a clump of even five."

Defective and undersized shells get dropped to the bridge tile deck. Marketable oysters are flipped into bushel baskets. In the old days these were the beautiful woven oak baskets made by people like Stephens of Guilford, Connecticut. Now they are plastic containers such as you see in laundromats, an aesthetic disaster that pleases the State Sanitarians who see the relatively impervious surface of plastics as a detriment to disease.

From time to time, when the debris gets too deep or there is a moment between drags or when the boss decides the grounds below either require or can at least tolerate a dumping, the stuff on the deck gets shoveled overboard. The shell makes an ideal substrate for future seeds. The rest of the garbage is quickly degradable. Bottles and other artifacts remain on board, both for what may be their intrinsic value and in order to preempt the necessity of having to catch them over and over. There is also the possibility a bottle or piece of junk will get caught on a dredge tong or jammed in the latching mechanism or in some as yet unknown way sabotage the rig. "You want to clean the place up," says Larry, "just as you don't want a lot of junk in your garden."

The deckhand clears the deck, in the old days wielding a number 9 shovel, which is somewhat like a coal shovel with raised lips on its sides. Recent ones are rubber, which are more forgiving for the deck and even for the crew, who sooner or later will just miss clearing the rail or a stanchion if they are shoving the stuff out a freeing port below the rail. Larry Malloy has a story about the importance of these shovels.

"Each man had his own shovel he was used to. They might have all started out as standard number nines, but with work they grew to fit your hand and your style. You carried a file in your back pocket and in spare moments out on the grounds you filed the edges when they got ragged. You don't want to catch on anything. If by mistake you picked up your mate's shovel and began to work with it, you knew right away it wasn't your shovel. You couldn't get them in just any port, and so we would get extras from Wash White in Greenport and bring them to New London and hide them up in the rafters of the oyster shop down on the pier. You needed extra ones because from time to time one might go missing. People would lean them up against the bulwarks and sometimes the shovel would see that as an opportunity to get overboard. We was working down for Elijah Ball in Stony Creek one day and this fellow, well he'd been drinking that night before and wasn't feeling all that good next day. Something upset him, so he throws the shovel down on the deck. It hits just so and bounces up over his shoulder right on overboard. Five minutes later, Elijah Ball, he's alongside in a small boat. 'That's coming out of your pay, that shovel,' he says. The old guy had been up in the office watching us through a telescope.

"Nowadays everything gets hosed back overboard with the washdown pump. The problem is you don't get a good scattering pattern that way. You can end up dumping everything straight down. That was one of the things you had with a good deckhand; you had a good pattern of shell on the bottom. You had a *floor,* not a lot of clumps and then bare spaces. Depends a bit on the current. And, of course, the depth—how far the shell's got to flutter down there to the bottom. And there's no question shovels is hard on the deck. That's why we lay down this asphalt bridge tile. Before that we used maple, which was hard, but stayed put. Sometimes we used oak, which, of course, is hard, but it don't stay put. It can curl up on you when it gets wet. Then you're stumbling all over the place. In any case, you don't nail or fasten that top decking down. You got to be able to pick up the decking from time to time to make sure nothing's going on underneath. No rot or maybe something flopped in under there and died. The DEP wants you to make all that stainless steel now, like you was in an operating room. Aside from the expense, which is considerable, you do most of your work when it's cold out there, maybe on the edge of freezing. You want some fun? Just try working on stainless steel that's got just a film of ice on it. As I keep telling them: you won't have to worry about regulating the business after a season of that. All the crews will have skated on overboard."

· · ·

Whenever you get into the elaborate procedures of oyster fishers, especially contrasted to the relatively simple methods of clammers, one of the first questions that comes up is: Come on now, this is all nonsense. What did the Indians do? They certainly didn't go through all this planting and moving. The simplest answer to that is that the ratio of native Americans to oysters and the technology by which that vast resource was harvested had not yet put the resources into crisis. The same is true of the Colonial period and right on up to the middle of the nineteenth century, when population and technology developed at an unprecedented rate. Not only did the seaboard population grow but through the railroad the expanding inland market could now be tapped. Technology in the form of engines dramatically increased the rate of harvest. Bigger boats could get on and off the grounds faster and, while there, employ larger rigs in the harvesting. Meanwhile, ashore, the rise of today's urban structures with attendant manufacturing and sewage discharges created pollution on a scale previously unknown. With the "natural beds" that the native and colonial populations took for granted nearly exhausted, people began to think of various ways to assist the oysters' natural development.

Regulation and oyster culture pretty much grow up hand in hand, both initially being responses to an exhausted resource. Kochiss gives 1845 as the first date when oysters were regulated in Long Island Sound. There were other laws to follow in the next ten years, but it wasn't until 1881 that the regulations came into effect that pretty much stood as the basis for management for the next 120 years. Born only nine years later, in 1890, Larry Malloy's father was at work in the oystering business by the time he was in his early teens.

. . .

The need to move and "re-catch" oysters to which Larry Malloy refers is one of the most distinctive, if confusing, of the aspects that distinguish oystering from other types of shellfishing, and for that matter most other types of fishing. The idea of taking the trouble to catch something and haul it aboard, only to move it somewhere else and throw it back in the water with the pious hope of finding it again, seems like pure madness. Indeed, these days, with smaller numbers of oysters, many oystermen are no longer merely casting their product overboard, but containing it in buoyed "cages" similar to lobster pots. The cost of the cages aside, this is a vastly more labor-intensive procedure that only justifies itself under particular local and market conditions.

In Connecticut, all underwater land is under the control of either the state or the local town. The boundary between state and town ground is usually laid out point to point. The original concept was based roughly on a boats/boots distinction. Such an arrangement gives the deeper water, which is perforce accessible only to heavy mechanical gear, to the commercial interests (boats), while maintaining local control of the inshore waters for the towns, who regulate and supervise the recreational shellfisher with hand tools (boots). While this division of jurisdiction and client remains largely appropriate today, there are notable exceptions.

Because of the varied nature of the Connecticut coastline, the relative proportion of town to state water may vary markedly from town to town.

Added to this anomaly, the amount of certified water within those jurisdictions might vary greatly. It is up to the State Sanitarian, now fortunately at last associated with the Department of Agriculture/Aquaculture, to classify both state and town waters. (A decade ago this same Sanitarian was in the office that inspected chickens and restaurants.)

The state accomplishes this carving up and labeling on maps of the waters through the help of the Town Sanitarians and the local shellfish commissions. The locals usually provide the small boats necessary to get to the stations selected by the state, not all of them reachable by people in boots. Through the years, the Malloys helped out on some of these tests. One day Larry called me up. He was going to be transporting a young woman from the State Sanitarian Office up the Thames on *Anne*. He was looking for a deckhand.

"What's wrong with Walt?" I said.

"This ain't gonna be a Walt type of trip."

10

AN EXCURSION INTO THE BACKWATERS

ALTHOUGH IT WASN'T going to be a Walt type of trip, Larry still needed somebody to lend a hand. Something about helping him keep a skiff's bow line out of the *Anne*'s screw. I wasn't sure what this business of the small boat was all about, but I agreed to come.

"There's going to be a Sanitarian," he warned.

"OK," I said. My experience through the years was that some Sanitarians were not dour. I had, in fact, known some to be quite Rabelaisian.

The woman waiting on *Anne*'s deck did not, however, look as if she had escaped from the fantasies of a medieval French monk turned doctor, nor did she seem, despite the clipboard, poised for petulance. She appeared, in fact, to embrace neither extreme of the Sanitarian personality spectrum. If her appearance suggested anything it was that of a pleasant young woman about to get in a tennis match before going to work in one of the vaguer professions.

We began by slowing so she could take her samples out in the main channel up past the Submarine Base. It always amused me to be on *Anne* as we chugged by this haze of high-tech might, but on this day when we were, as Larry put it, "operating scientifically," the contrast between our weary wood and the nation's finest steel seemed even more ludicrous. Larry slowed *Anne*, and the Sanitarian set aside her clipboard to scoop water into a jar that was rigged to a long pole. So far, so good.

Larry, however, soon began working on her about a side trip. She really should also do the Poquetonuck, he suggested, a tributary that ran in from the east above the Submarine Base and just below the state mental hospital. He had once maintained oyster ground in the Poquetonuck. The young woman searched her clipboard for some sort of confirmation that such a digression was a valid mission. Larry, however, soon charmed her by means of a paean to the past that somehow made an argument that science owed the future a look. I had seen him have that effect before on women of a certain age.

It was here that I also began to understand the need for the small boat. To reach up into this watercourse, it was necessary to get under the Providence-Worcester railroad. Just off the channel, we dropped the dredge and anchor *Anne* and climbed in to take the little varnished skiff Larry called his "*Yot.*" It was for this we had apparently been towing the boat with just this sentimental side excursion in mind.

Slipping off the mother ship onto the *Yot* had been easy, but it wasn't until we'd moved away from *Anne* that I realized why: her freeboard was shockingly low. It seemed as if her fantail was virtually awash! Had we been that close to the water that day off Bell Eight? Had we been that near things going through the Race? I guessed we had. In any case, I said nothing, but ducked just in time as we went under the bridge that brought the railroad down the east bank of the Thames.

"We had ground all up in here," Larry was rhapsodizing, "but when they upgraded the bridge, they made it so you could hardly get in here. To add to the problem, they threw a lot of boulders overboard just outside. Now you tell me, why would they do a thing like that?"

In spite of being Someone From the State, the Sanitarian had no suggestion as to why the railroad had been allowed to impede the channel.

"You may have noticed I was swerving quite a bit," he said to me. "That was to avoid hitting those boulders."

I hadn't noticed, having been occupied with the thinness of *Anne*'s freeboard. Now, inside the cove, I was smitten by the idyllic qualities of this meandering water. There were trees and marsh grass on either side. A great blue heron watched us from the grass. At the head of the cove, hard by where the brook ran in, was a tavern that in an earlier life had been a mill. Right up to the back door, Larry told us, ships had come. The Sanitarian was, of course, by now interested in her numbers. I myself became convinced that if the data came out okay, this whole lovely backwater would soon once again be producing oysters.

"This used to be Playland," Larry said. "That is, up at the head of the cove, a little beyond. An amusement park. Wheels and lights and a bandstand."

He sat grinning in the stern with the outboard clucking under his arm. Outboards are the great levelers. Because the propeller doubles as the rudder, the response time of the steering is almost instantaneous. All those tasteful anticipations, those nuances of action and suspended reaction between helm and rudder and prop blades that the helmsman cultivates over a lifetime—in short, the art of handling the single screw inboard—

the outboard renders obsolete. An eight-year-old can "run" an outboard. So watching Larry Malloy, nearer eighty, master of the oyster boat *Anne,* run his outboard was like seeing Charlie Parker tooting a kazoo or Segovia strumming a ukulele. Nevertheless, he seemed to enjoy running his outboard. It was as if maybe the silly simplicity did make him feel like an eight-year-old again. And here he was up a gunkhole with a couple of skeptical buddies to show off to.

The Sanitarian crouched on the middle thwart, her blue jeans among her bottles and her clipboard across her lap. I looked over the bow into the tea-colored water. After all, wasn't that what the expedition was about? I could not see the bottom. But then, if deep draft ships had nosed their way in here, and if the railroad had not caused the cove to shoal as it seemed to have done in nearby coastline embayments, then maybe the fact that I could not see the bottom was okay.

The newspapers had been running the complaints of Poquetonuck citizens who decried the fetid odors of their waters. On this day, however, the air seemed more bracing than pungent. It was tangy with the leaf mold of fresh water intrusion from tumbling Crowley Brook at the head of the cove. It was precisely this sort of lowering of salinity that could actually be helpful in oyster spawning. In fact out in the open sea, the high salinity all but prevents oysters from propagating. A cove like this was important. Perhaps something major was about to happen. In any case, the Sanitarian had her bottle rigged.

"So you do approve of my little *Yot,*" said Larry.

"Very much," said the Sanitarian.

. . .

Samples are sent by automobile either to Hartford or the State Shellfish Laboratory in Milford, each at least two hours round trip from southeastern Connecticut in summer traffic. Unless instructed to look for additional problems, the laboratories test for coliform count. The coliform bacterium is found in the intestines of humans and other animals such as dogs and cattle and is therefore useful as an indicator of fecal matter, which, of course, can carry a wide spectrum of disease. Based on these results, repeated in some cases over a period of years, all waters are classified, subject to change, by the State Sanitarian as "certified," "conditional," "closed," or "prohibited."

"Prohibited" waters are closed without option of reprieve through depuration. Usually the "prohibited" ground is the site of toxic metal dumping. From such substances, the animal cannot ever free itself. These blighted underwater lands are therefore written off as potential grounds for shellfish production.

Local shellfish commissions may close an area as part of a reseeding or some experimental program, but in Connecticut they must reopen them in a year. Shellfish from "certified" waters can be marketed directly.

Products taken from "conditional" waters can only be removed under certain conditions—usually some function of rainfall as recorded by the official gauge in that particular town. The idea is that run-off from the land will carry animal droppings, the effluvia of marginal septic systems and other undesirables into the backwaters and thus produce a temporary rise in coliform. These conditionally closed waters are retested after a certain number of rainless days, usually ten days to two weeks.

Waters classified as "closed" may be fished if the product is depurated. That is, the oysters are bagged and tagged, then set out in open or certified waters of 50 degrees or above for a certain length of time. The notion is that at fifty degrees the animals are filtering and therefore, in theory, eventually clearing themselves of what they had taken in. The soak time is usually two weeks, after which the filter feeding oysters are presumed to have cleansed themselves and are now eligible to have their actual meats tested. In the last fifteen years or so, the use of this system of classification and depuration has provided much of the commercial shellfish consumed.

The process of depuration is closely regulated and monitored. The grounds selected upon which the cleansing is to take place must not only be in classified water but offer some sort of hope for the fisher that the product will be protected from poachers or heavy weather that might shift the bags and lose them. These depuration grounds are leased by individual shellfishers for this purpose, and buffer zones must be maintained between lots. Strictly speaking, nothing forbids a recreational fisherman from going through this tedious and risky process. What sort of powers would be refreshed by the combination of red tape and weather-dependency involved, however, is hard to imagine. Depuration is hardly the same sort of stuff as an afternoon's pleasure, boot deep with a rake and a bucket. In any case, anyone going through the depuration process would be, by the conclusion of the process, either *de facto* a commercial operator or a patient in a mental ward.

While all of the above classification process is as true for clammers as oystermen, there is a point at which the procedures of the two chief shellfishing pursuits divide. In oystering, the analogy to farming is key. As in agriculture, the ground and the product thereon are "owned" at all stages of development.

The parallel with other food raising businesses is, however, more with farming than any of the other fisheries. The land that oystermen use, unlike the ground that a lobsterpot or trawl net happens to fall upon, is legally considered as real estate. All underwater ground is initially owned by either the state or the adjacent town. To obtain the exclusive right to work a piece of ground for oystering, the applicant must either obtain a *grant,* in which case the applicant owns the ground, or a *lease,* in which case some condition of time is imposed by the granting body. Grants may be sold by the party holding the grant or even passed down through probate, which may result in monopolies on the one hand or abandoned "ghost grants" on the other. Leases, however, are subject to the particular conditions of the contract, which gives the governmental body involved considerably more control over the conduct of the lessee, and over the termination and transfer of the property. As a result, in Connecticut for the past few decades the policy has been that no new grants be issued. In the case of either grant or lease, the holder of the property is granted exclusive use of that bottom for the purposes of oystering. Trespassers are treated as poachers. (As Larry Malloy says, "Catching poachers is not necessarily easier or harder than catching oysters.")

To obtain this ground, the oysterman must go through an elaborate process. The oysterman pays fees, both an initial amount and yearly taxes. Competition for ground may look at times like a land rush. At such moments, there will be what seems like a roomful of people at the Shellfish Commission meeting.

Many of those potential applicants these days tend to be *wanna-bes,* who envision picking up a buck an oyster off the ground as if they were the same things, just there for the stooping. These folks soon dry up when they find out what's involved. The good ground has usually been taken two generations back. As one cynic put it, "By now it's like last call at the single's bar. If anything is left, there must be something wrong with it. "

Unlike the lobsterman or the bass fisherman or even the clammer, the oysterman is allowed his exclusivity because he has at some point "planted" his product. Furthermore, he has in many ways nurtured it and grown it through a series of tendings, the most spectacular of which is transplanting. Planting is not a simple matter of broadcasting small or "seed" oyster overboard but involves geographical precision as to the optimum site and timing to assure that conditions are most favorable. (The matter of where this "seed" comes from is a whole story in itself. "Seed" are oysters below market size, that are transplanted to grow.) The bottom must be prepared so that the oysters will not sink into smothering mud. To do this, the oysterman must "work" the ground by dragging his dredge with the chain bag open over the ground to "clean" all rubble, silt, and other impediments to the oyster's delicate life, impediments that, in the colonial and native days, were largely not present.

Timmy Visel, when he worked for Connecticut Sea Grant, was fond of telling how he had discovered that, in the transition between the natural abundance and the present state, men were known to clean the backwaters by hauling bedsprings with oxen on an ebbing tide. It was not clear whether the bedsprings were then returned to their position of repose.

If the particular area is to be used to set spat, that is, to provide a benign substrate for free-swimming oysters in their larval stage, then some sort of cultch has to be provided. In Eleanor Clark's *Locmariaquer,* this cultch is made up of the lovely tiles that constitute the central image of her book. In Japan, branches stuck in the mud have sufficed. Larry Malloy once arrived at a Town of Groton Shellfish Commission meeting with his now famous dog collar upon which small oysters had set. The usual cultch on Long Island Sound and the mid-Atlantic states has been the oyster shells themselves. These shells have to be brought from the big piles outside shucking houses and wheelbarrowed or front-loaded back onto oysterboats which take them back to the grounds where they are thrown overboard shovel by shovel, a process known as "shelling" and usually performed in late spring before the July set. Shell itself has become a valuable product and laws forbid the old practice of paving roads and walks with it.

The oyster spat, or free-swimming young, attaches itself to this cultch, but not until it has tested the suitability of its new home, "wiping," as Ed Ricketts puts it, "its large and turgid foot over the area and extruding enough cement to affix the left valve."

Secreted by a gland, the cement hardens in ten minutes.

The transplanting has not necessarily been for the purpose of cleansing the coliform, but was practiced long before formal depuration as a way to fatten the product, or to enhance the taste by increasing the salinity. As some regions have become famous, such as Chincoteague, Virginia, and Blue Point on Long Island, there has even been transplantings solely for marketing purposes. An oyster that has soaked a couple of weeks in the waters of Chincoteaugue becomes, ipso facto, a Chincoteague oyster.

But human factors such as regulation and marketing are far from the only factors involved in oystering. As Larry Malloy says: "Sometimes you get so concerned with what people got to say about everything you forget that the oyster is something that is out there in the water and the water's out there in the weather." There are certainly specific days when nature says definite things must happen. The summer set, sometime in mid-July in Long Island Sound, depending on the water temperature, takes place for only a matter of a few days, if that. Cultch scattered too soon slimes over; scattered too late, it is, well, too late.

Other times, however, an oysterman may be involved in almost any one of the activities in the cycle, in some cases anticipating a future need, at other times responding to a present crisis. There is even time to do something else entirely, though since you have the boat with its deck space and hoisting gear you might as well use it. You might, say, take somebody's Stutz to Block Island or a load of potatoes up the Connecticut River, fix a lighthouse, raise a submarine or maybe just deliver a postcard to an island bird sanctuary. There is, or at least there was before licensing got so compartmentalized, a lot of *"while you're at it"* that gets done if you have a broad-beamed, shallow-draft, low-fuel-consumption old girl that doesn't mind a bit of banging around, as long as you leave her in the water. "Besides," says Larry Malloy, "thinking up other stuff to do with the boat was a way to get back at the oyster for being so goddamn tricky."

NOTE

THE HISTORY OF OYSTER CULTURE is a fascinating study in itself, brilliantly put forth in Eleanor Clark's 1964 book *The Oysters of Locmariaquer,* which, among other things, traces the history of oyster culture to Roman days. See also Kochiss and Bridges.

11

RIGOR

Not only should you replace the rocks you overturn, you should leave the animals where they are unless you have a good reason for taking a very few of them.

—Edward F. Ricketts

THAT OYSTERS ARE, as Larry Malloy says, "so goddamn tricky" no doubt gives them some of their appeal, and DeQuincy's axiom that "knowledge is power" has some strange ways of manifesting itself on the waterfront. Exactly what consitutes knowledge, however, is a question that finds divergent answers—and never so dramatically divergent as when scientists meet the working fishers. Each knows the oyster in a professional way, which is to say each has its own discipline, its own language, its own, to use the scientists' word, *rigor*. Surprisingly enough, I have not found the mutual distrust to focus so much on methodology as on motive.

The mission of the one who catches and merchandizes the product is clear, with the rewards and punishments all lined up in classic market fashion. The scientist comes draped in the mantle of a more sacred mission having to do with the pursuit of Objective Truth. It is, in these secular days, the closest we have to a mission from God. But the fisher knows that, no matter how holy the scientist, this person, like everyone else, must feed. And indeed, the fact is that each needs to fashion some kind of economic return in order to justify proceeding further. While the way of the market in the oyster industry can be complex, even nuanced to the point of deviousness, it is ultimately a matter familiar to everyone in a capitalistic economy. Just how the scientist gets paid is a matter so displaced, deferred, and circumambulatory, as to leave even those in the profession often bewildered.

The other day I was going through some things that had been thrown out of a marine biology laboratory, and came across a notebook that had been meticulously maintained by one of the employees at the lab. It consisted of page after page of data, graphs, diagrams, and notes. I handed it to an oysterman of the new generation, an educated man. He fanned the pages.

"Just look at this! All this and for what? In the trash." And he tossed it back into the can from which I'd plucked it. "Well, I hope he or she got a good job for life out of it."

The satire that follows—Larry Malloy (from the old generation), on Professor Victor L. Loosanoff—may seem a bit harsh. Mervin F. Roberts in his *Pearl Makers* finds that Loosanoff "provides good solid original source material." Here, however, is Eleanor Clark, incidentally an admirer of Loosanoff, whom she elsewhere in her oysterbook calls "our leading scientist in this [shellfish] domain":

> In 1890 a marine biologist named Bashford Dean, working for the United States Fish and Wildlife Service, was sent on a journey of investigation to all the main oyster centers of Europe, and wrote two extraordinary reports, one on ostreiculture in France, the other on the rest of Europe. Extraordinary, in that they were as good as they were useless; everything has gone on as if they were never written. They are in the archives, among the publications of the Department of the Interior. Not that our scientists, to be repetitious, aren't as informed and dedicated as any. The question is only whether their hard work and knowledge has any serious relation to the survival of mollusks and fish, and the answer to date [1964] is no, it has not. Every year, speaking collectively, we know more and have fewer oysters, and most that we do have less taste.

When I ran this by Larry Malloy in 1999, he said Ms. Clark's comments struck him as being as sound now as when she wrote them.

"We done a lot of different kind of work on the water through the years, whatever it took to keep going, but what most people think when they think about us at all, is that we were in the oyster business.

"Now the oyster business comes and goes depending upon the seasons and sometimes the seasons themselves come and go depending upon God knows what. We've asked the scientists about this and they agree that this coming and going is an interesting question all right and sometimes they do a little science about it in our direction, but mostly they just collect their *grants*. Now we have *grants* in the oyster business, but there a *grant* means you got to produce something because you've been granted the ground and you got to pay taxes on it so you might as well make something happen that gets your money back. It don't seem to work that way with what a scientist calls a *grant*. Pappy had scientists aboard and I had scientists aboard. They're always nice enough people. It's just you don't know what happens to them after they go ashore.

"Pappy had a very famous scientist who seemed like a real scientist, all right, because he had a German name and even a German accent. Pappy'd say: 'Don't miss today. We've got Professor Hopping Stance coming aboard.'

"You'd crack open an oyster and show the Professor the insides and point at something in there that didn't look right to you and say 'What about that?' The Professor, he'd look at it a minute and say, 'Umm, dat's a case of *Hopping Stance*.' You'd show him your figures in the book and then point out something on the grounds and ask him for some sort of reason why this condition was going on and he'd think a minute and say, 'Ummm, dat's a case of *Hopping Stance*.' *Hopping Stance,* that was a pretty bad disease we figured, because it sure seemed to raise hell with our business, and there was no cure for it. Now, maybe he knew more than he was letting on. I know that when you got a real bad disease on you, it usually comes out in Latin, so that by calling it *Hopping Stance,* he was either making it simple for us poor oystermen or maybe he was protecting us from getting any of the real stuff on us. The Professor came out a number of times with us, and we always had a good time. People tell me he was very famous for years. That must have been because he had discovered this disease that no one else I knew had ever heard of: *Hopping Stance.*

One of these interchanges with science had major implications. During the height of the Cold War, in July 1966, there is a letter between the acting city manager of New London and Dr. John S. Rankin, Jr., Director of the Marine Research Laboratory of the University of Connecticut. The letter grants "Mr. Malloy permission to continue using the region just north of the Gold Star Memorial Bridge, west side, to put down clean shell to catch young oysters for the purpose of studying radioactivity . . ." The location is just upriver from the Electric Boat Company, builder of nuclear submarines, and the State Pier, where a small squadron of submarines was moored, and downriver from the United States Naval Submarine Base. Close readers will appreciate the "to continue."

Three years later, a Mr. Robert H. Lessard of Salt Lake City, Utah, wrote Malloy, requesting fifteen hundred starfish in order to start a "scientific supply house in North Dakota (North Dakota Scientific, Inc.). Mr. Lessard had been informed by the biologist of the Bureau of Commercial Fisheries located in Milford, Connecticut, that "large numbers of starfish, *Asterias forbesi,* occur along the shores of Connecticut, invading the oyster beds." He asks, "Perhaps you might be able to supply our company with much-needed starfish." Captain Malloy, Sr., replies:

We are willing to supply the Starfish at a very low cost, however we cannot assume the packing for transportation or the transportation of the Starfish from our Dock to your Supply House.

If you or your representative wish to examine our facilities with the thought of your assuming the transporting of the Starfish, please contact us by calling. . . . Our dock is located at Harrison Landing, Quaker Hill, Connecticut.

Looking through the scattering of Malloy papers that touch on science, one is tempted to ask, like Leonardo, "What ever happened to—?" As for the Dakota starfish project, Larry seems to think that the logistics broke down pretty much with his father's letter. "Pappy had a way of presenting matters that, while he didn't exactly say you couldn't do it, he made it clear that you would have to be pretty stupid to try. I mean he *laid it out* for you so you knew exactly what to expect from his side of it."

As for the study of radioactive oysters in the Thames, Dr. Rankin apparently discovered that there was contamination all right. "The funny thing was, though," says Larry, "it wasn't in the oysters. It was in the kelp and the sand. It didn't come from the submarine factory; it didn't come from the squadron; it didn't even come from the Base. It come from the sand that the city of New London trucked in from somewhere else inland to make a beach in what they called Riverside Park!"

Some of the "science" was clearly more pleasurable, more in line with our Poquontunck excursion with the sanitarian. There is a photo of *Anne* that documents Captain Malloy, Sr.'s, "ecology trips." The photo was evidently taken from another boat running alongside the steaming oysterboat at a distance of about one length on the starboard. *Anne*'s functional tarp is stretched on a boom between mast and wheelhouse and here looks uncommonly festive. Four female students dressed in shorts have arranged themselves with their backs to the wheelhouse in a group pose reminiscent of the old Rheingold Girls calendars of that era. One woman, in white shorts and white shirt rolled up at the sleeves, straddles the bulwark and has extended her leg down to the guard halfway to the water, as Captain Malloy, Sr., leans coyly out of the wheelhouse door in suspenders. Three young men are segregated up forward under the tarp. A crewman stands outside the wheelhouse. (Walt?)

When I had Larry examine this photo, he peered at it a moment. There was the festive tarp; there was the old man in the wheelhouse; there were the girls in shorts; there was the girl straddling the rail, her toes teasing the very waters by which the Malloys made their living. I wondered if he'd rise to the bait.

Larry placed his finger just forward of her thigh. It was exactly there, he said, that they used to have the hyster post. That had been an up-and-down roller on a post that ran from the sheer plank along the port quarter and was bolted on its lower end to the round of the hull planking. It had seemed much simpler than the mast set in the middle of the foredeck, except for the fact that the hyster post frequently had to be replaced, especially after the dredge hit a rock. Then it had been quite a job to remove the broken one.

"We called that *digging out the post*," he said, and handed me back the photo without batting an eye.

THE GLORY OF THE SHALLOWS

But I should think of shallows and of flats.

— The Merchant of Venice

T HE SUITABILITY OF the tool to the task is one of the great themes of civilization. Nowhere is this theme better illustrated than in the relationship between an oysterboat and the particular grounds she works, in this case *Emma Frances* and Mumford Cove.

"We had oyster grounds in the Thames and Greenport. In fact, right where the Coast Guard Academy now has that causeway out to Jacob's Rock where their boathouse is for *yachts*. That's right where we used to drag for oysters in the *Emma Frances*.

"*Emma Frances* became part of what you might call our *fleet* in 1929, when she was already sixty years old. She was a very capable vessel, though, for the oyster business until she was destroyed in the 1938 Hurricane at Harrison's Landing along with the *Captain, Sir Thomas, Mary A. Brewer*, and *Virginia*. Like *Anne* she was built as a sloop and like *Anne* she was lengthened. She'd been down to Great South Bay, Long Island. It kept getting shallower and shallower down there so they lengthened her *at least* three times. Every time they'd lengthened her, she'd draw less, so that she got so as she could carry three hundred tons in three feet of water. She started out just thirty-four feet, and by the time we had her, she'd got herself up to sixty-one feet! Problem was, you do that to a boat, and she can get kind of *weak*. You'd be up in the wheelhouse and could look forward and see her flexing. Of course, better bending than breaking. The boom was very long. It started at the mast up by the hyster post in the bow and ran all the way aft to where it rested on chalks on top of the pilot house. *Emma Frances*, she wiggled so much she wore the boom where it went through that chalk. We couldn't keep paint on that foot or so of the boom—all on account of the wiggle. We eventually double planked her. George Stanford, my brother-in-law, was on that project.

"I remember *Emma Frances*'s stiffening being done at Sweet's Shipyard in Greenport, and the men grabbing the planks right out of the steambox with their gloves and shouting, '*Hot Plank!*' When you heard that, you either got the hell out of the way or, if you had gloves, you grabbed a piece of the plank and helped run it to the boat before the wood cooled out. When the wood was hot like that, you had a chance to bend it to the shape of your frames.

"Back in those days we always carried a jib, even if you was powered. You had twenty-nine-horsepower engines, granted equal to ninety horsepower today. *Emma Frances* was twin screw. One was six horse, the other twelve. So with any little breeze, you was looking for a push. Oyster boats were so beamy you didn't need a sail to steady you, as you did aboard the draggers. But they was handy for that extra knot or two getting home. Sometimes that was the difference between making it back in the light or the dark. Of course, we run a lot in the dark as it was. Still, if you had the choice, you'd take the light.

"We sold *Anne* to Washington 'Wash' White, who had an oyster business in the Sterling Basin around back of Greenport Harbor in 1926."

The photo that Larry had used to show his house and the rumrunners' stash house was preserved on a calendar that had been issued by Wash White. The picture included *Anne* moored port side to a pier in front of a two-story building with a Texaco Star logo. Written across the front, just beneath a loft dormer with yard arm and bull wheel, was:

WASHINGTON WHITE OYSTER DEALER

The photo also showed *Emma Frances,* bow on, with her hysting post sticking up above two low cabins. There was as yet no wheelhouse. "You steered from right out there on deck like a sailboat," explained Larry. "Take the weather as it come."

When Larry and I were in Greenport, we matched the old calendar photo with the actual view as it was then in the mid-nineties. The Basin is now a slicked-up marina with a big tennis court right where Wash White's oyster shack had stood. In the photo there is an alley with a trio of running board sedans parked under a pair of trees. When we tried to walk into this space we were prevented by an anchor chain fence. "I guess you need a tennis racquet to get through here now," said Larry.

"By the way, old sport," I said. "Did you ever *play* tennis?"

"I never even *watched* tennis."

Because of her capacity to carry a big deck cargo in shallow water, the ancient, elongated *Emma Frances* was the boat they used to do a job in Mumford Cove on the Connecticut side of the Sound.

A mile east of New London, Mumford Cove is a shallow, mile-long sheet of water. It lies between Groton Long Point—at the beginning of the twentieth century a barren sand spit with stagnant lagoons and marshes—and Mumford's Point. Now the Bluff Point Coastal Reserve, Mumford's Point was then a great hump of farmland gone to second growth since the days when the Winthrops of *Mayflower* fame had built a farm house, a white, frame building that still stood atop the ridge until the 1960s. Ephraim Chesebrough's chart, made from actual surveys by Stephan Decatur's American Squadron in 1811 and Admiral Hardy's British squadron in 1813 and 1814, shows "Mumfords Cove" with a "Marsh Island" in its mouth. The island has shown considerable mobility in the last two centuries, morphing into a peninsula hooked to Mumford Point, stretching out straight and sandy for more than halfway across the cove, and last year fragmenting back into an island again. The west side of the cove is now sufficiently pristine so that, when Steven Spielberg was looking for a place to simulate his *Amistad*'s escaped slaves landing in nineteenth-century New England, he chose the land that overlooks Malloy's oyster grounds.

When the Malloys began working Mumford Cove, the grounds were not yet actually theirs. According to the Town of Groton's *Oyster Book*, Thomas H. Story of the City of Norwich received four acres in a "section of this Tide Water of *Mumford's Cove*" on "15 May 1889" from Van R. Ball, who in turn obtained it from James W. Rathbun of Groton in 1885, a year after *Anne* was completed and only seven years after the first entry in the Groton *Oyster Book*. When I pointed this out to Larry, he said, "That's the year, 1884, when all the oyster boats seem to begin. I don't know what they had before that. I don't think they just went from Indians to oyster dredges. And where did all the money come to build those boats if there wasn't some kind of an industry? The government wasn't about to put up the money for a fishing fleet in those days. You take *Alice* in 1907; $550 was a lot of money."

Gaps in chronology can make you nervous. It's not that, like a human resource director processing curriculum vitae, you require that all time be accounted for. It's just that in the odd mood now and then when you actually stand before certain places, your mind might demand a coherent image of what you're looking at. Histories that begin with, *"Ever since the beginning of time, Man has..."* will not do. Attempts to imagine Early Man poking at things in the water with pointed sticks tend to be somewhere between Gary Larson and *The National Geographic*. What, after all, did the year 1884 mean on the waterfront?

In 1884, the senior uniformed man in the Navy, Admiral David D. Porter, was to urge that new warships continue to be rigged for sail in the interests of avoiding dependence on coaling ports. Up at the head of steamboat navigation on the Connecticut River at Hartford, Mark Twain was working on that paean to shallow craft, *The Adventures of Huckleberry Finn*. It was the year France presented the Statue of Liberty to the United States a couple of dozen miles from Smithtown. (It was not actually put together and erected on an island in the big harbor until two years later.) Eighteen-eighty-four was the year the Brooklyn Bridge was completed, and you see all those pictures of that celebration showing the watercraft of the time.

One of the best evocations of the 1884 waterfront is Gordon Grant's evocative oil titled *"The Great Admiral" Brooklyn Bridge–East River 1884,* in which schooners, square riggers, and Whitehall pulling boats share the busy scene with a steam tug. We have a print torn from an old calendar that we display in honor of *Anne*'s birth. It's tacked over the toilet in the boat yard bath house, and, following good museum practice, we have arranged this acquisition so that with the right eye one can admire the 1884 scene, while at the same time, check out the window where *Anne* herself actually lies to her mooring with the left eye.

The picture by Grant is a juxtaposition much admired by Captain Malloy on numerous occasions. For him, this depiction, however, is not an occasion for nostalgia but for contemporary problem-solving. In spite of what Hart Crane called the "choiring strings" of the Brooklyn Bridge poised above, and the magnificence of the featured, full-rigged square rigger, *The Great Admiral* herself, for Larry the picture is stolen by the two men in the foreground. One is rowing a twelve-foot-long Whitehall while the other reaches over the wine glass stern, endeavoring to adjust a line to a long flotsam plank so that they might tow it out of the way and, as Larry points out, "probably take it home to add to their own building." Furthermore, he notes, "the nice thing about using a rowboat for that job is you can get in the nooks and crannies of the harbor and don't have to worry about getting the hawser caught in the screw."

· · ·

The gap between the Indians and the settlers' regulated oyster industry, of course, is noted in Larry's favorite book, *Oystering from New York to Boston,* by Kochiss. Why Larry had forgotten this information, I don't know. Perhaps because it was just that, *information*. The chronology was not something material (as is so much of what is in this wonderful book) that confirmed his own life. Indeed, there is a picture of Larry Malloy working in Elijah Ball's oyster house.

In his second chapter, Kochiss traces the history of oyster cultivation in Long Island Sound, which he finds begins with the an 1845 ordinance permitting "any state citizen to plant in Connecticut waters oysters brought in from another state." Such an act recognized an activity that had grown up in the face of the depletion of natural, local stocks and marked the official recognition that man was making conscious and extensive attempts to manipulate the oyster environment. Ten years later, the Connecticut General Assembly passed the "two-acre law," which gave coastal towns the right to make grants of underwater land in that amount to "individuals for planting oysters."

Malloy was right, however, in that it wasn't until 1881 that the oyster industry came of age, when it was regularized in Connecticut with the formation of the State Shell-Fish Commission. Kochiss claims that the enabling legislation "became a model for oyster legislation in other states." The 1881 Act continues to this day to be the bible for oyster law, and we have appended large gobs of it as ballast to the *Town of Groton Shellfish Management Plan.* On land granted just three years after the State Shell-Fish Commission came into existence, Thomas Story's Mumford Cove enterprise was one of the pioneers in the new dispensation. His shop was at the head of the cove between the water and the New York to Boston railroad line. It was there that he also had his home, a two-story structure painted yellow and surmounted by an odd-looking roof.

I had no idea of what I was looking at in the 1940s when I was a boy at Groton Long Point, then already crowded with summer cottages. To us, the head of Mumford Cove was a mysterious foreign land. Whenever we'd come in or leave the narrow entrance into the Groton Long Point Lagoon, we'd glance up into Mumford Cove. There were no buildings except way at the very northern end, where there seemed to float this yellow house.

In those days, before the dredging for Mumford Cove Estates, the water was too shallow to sail or even to traverse by outboard, and to reach the far end was too far for a casual row. Furthermore, there were rumors that this was a strange community of squatters presided over by a man with a shotgun. These were people "left over" from a pocket in history before the war. Some of the older people called it *"Hooverville. "* To some, such a designation produced a snicker, at which time other people, usually even older, would admonish the mirthful.

In the 1940s, the past was something we were all trying not so much to improve upon as to flee, especially the immediate past of the 1930s. There was very little attempt to recapture it. There was no nostalgia. There were no Civil War Roundtables, nor retro-shows, no *American Heritage* magazine, no Williamsburg paint colors on the market. Historical societies, where they existed at all, did so largely in the interests of confirming the genealogy of the elite. The Mystic Seaport was a small local repository of moldy artifacts in glass cases and one rotting ship that stank like a bad cellar. The head of Mumford Cove and the yellow house took on the aura of a blighted community trapped somehow in hard times. You were thankful that all that water continued to separate you from the past.

Nevertheless, one day, under the lure of the forbidden, and seemingly encouraged by a following wind, we opened an umbrella and, under the protection of that goofy rig, sailed into the past. Because of the legendary man with the shotgun, we did not go ashore but folded our umbrella and lay off a bit on our oars, gazing at the strange settlement. It was the only settlement on either side of the cove. The house was surrounded by half a dozen Airfoil trailers left over from the Depression. There seemed to be no one around, though the bit of lawn by the house looked recently mowed.

The house we'd been looking at all these years from afar was two stories and, like the lighthouse, way out the other way in the Sound, also what my father called a "Mansard roof." The funny thing was that up close it didn't seem anywhere near as big as we'd imagined it would be when we were far away. We tried to imagine the man who would emerge from the screen door. Would he be a regular-sized man, made huge by the small house, or a tiny man, eerily to scale? What *did* people trapped back there in *hard times* look like? Had they started out that way, or had they somehow, by their fate, been altered? We did not wait to find out. From somewhere a screen door banged. We began the long row home, wondering if the umbrella would ward off the shot.

Other times we dug for quahogs down near the mouth of the cove, just back of the jetties into Groton Long Point Lagoon. We dressed in old sneakers and equipped ourselves with a garden fork and an inner tube in which we set an apple basket. We never gave a thought to pollution, limits, or permits, and my mother made chowder that was not much more spooky than the stuff you got out of cans. One night, my father, too impatient to be a rod and reel fisherman, rowed us around the jetties and into Mumford Cove in a flat iron skiff. We hovered over the mud in six inches of water with a lantern and eel fork to spear a half dozen flounder. Back in the bright kitchen later, he himself, though not a cook, prepared the meal for us. The flounder had the deliciousness of forbidden fruit. The whole expedition had an air of illegal hilarity and was something my father talked about for years but had the sense never to repeat.

Later the *verboten* reputation of Mumford Cove was made more palpable by the presence of the Groton sewer outfall, and the state officially pronounced condemnation upon the waters for shellfishing.

The Malloys and *Emma Frances* worked Mumford Cove in those hard times. In the thirties, for all the blight elsewhere, there was actually considerable oyster ground up there, owned and active.

"With Mumford Cove in mind, Pappy bought *Emma Frances* from Wash White for ten thousand bushels of oysters. It took us a week to bring that many over to Greenport from New London. She was perfect for Mumford Cove."

The lengthened-out *Emma Frances,* though capacious, was sufficiently shallow to be ideal for going up into Mumford's Cove, to Thomas Story's ground. For Larry, however, the place was spooky for far different reasons than mine. "That *was* a strange place, all right. There'd be water up there one day, none the next *on the very same tide.* You often had to push and pole *Emma Frances* up to the head of the cove there, where Tom Story had a little house and his business.

"I don't remember any trailers, though. I think they come after the government shut Tom Story down. There *was* an oyster shack where he opened oysters and packed them. You didn't need much of a building, and them days it could be right on the water where you wanted it. That was before the big hurricane of 1938 and, of course, before the DEP and all that. Waterfront structures were just that, right on the water or, in many cases, *over* it on pilings. The New York–Boston rails was right behind his place. Tom Story, he'd get word out somehow, and, even though there was no station there, the train would stop, and he'd carry a basket or two up to the chef on the dining car. That wasn't the regular way he'd ship to New York, but it was the way the dining car got fresh oysters to serve to passengers right there on the train. Nowadays they'd figure out a way to run them oysters back and forth between New York and Boston two or three days before they'd let you serve them. And they'd call that *fresh* oysters!"

. . .

One day in May of 1999, May 4, to be precise, Larry stopped by West Mystic Wooden Boat Company with a battered little tan book in his hand. It was a round-cornered, mitt-sized volume with a water-stained, tan cardboard cover on which was printed:

WEEKLY TIME BOOK

I examined it as I thought such an artifact deserved. There was a drawing of an eagle below the title. At first I thought it was the same bird that's on our money, with the olive branch in one claw and the arrows in the other. When I looked more closely, there was a hammer in the left claw and a spanner in the other. A banner across the eagle's chest, extending out on both sides the width of the wing span, said:

NATIONAL

Here seemed to be a vision of labor's dignity that you will not find on time books printed in our age. Maybe such things don't matter, but the logo, as we'd call it today, did make me think of Larry's fraternal order in Greenport.

Written in big script across the top in pencil was:

Emma Frances
1933 –1934 –1935 –1936

Since it was May 4, we turned to that date in 1933 and found a penciled entry. Under "Names" was a very faded *"J. Moore,"* and there were marks on his line under M T W T F S. There was nothing under "Total Time," and nothing under "Rate p. day." Under "amount" was $5.

"That's Josh Moore," said Larry. "It means he got fifteen dollars that week for six days' work. An early version of Walt, but different from Walt."

On the bottom half of the page, ignoring all printed columns, the pencil had written:

Loaded 359 bu[shels] oysters from T[homas]s Storey.

"Story would plant them out front of his shop until they got market size. It would take but only a couple of months to get to market size. He didn't want anything that wasn't three years old already. He was a tall man, and since I don't think he was around after the war and, from what you say about when he got his grounds, he must have been pretty old by then. He didn't wear no stovepipe hat or anything like that as I remember. But you know most of them oystermen, they were *stately* men, like Chamberlain. You know, Chamberlain?"

"You mean Neville Chamberlain, the prime minister of England? 'Peace in our Time' Chamberlain?"

"Yeah, that fellow," said Larry.

It startled me to be derricked out of the mud of upper Mumford Cove in the thirties to the Munich Crisis, but, of course, there it was: a time line in spite of myself. But Larry quickly had me back in the oyster business.

"Elijah S. Ball, he was always dressed up like he was going to a wedding every day."

We got into a little discussion about work clothes before the Second World War. In the building trades, say, men did not wear work clothes as such, but only their second-best suit. My father had once traced the advent of work clothes in American construction to the masons, especially the bricklayers, who like to go hunting and, after the war began, to wear their red-and-black plaid shirts and mackinaws to work.

"Yes," said Larry, "When you stop to look back and really pay attention you notice a lot that's different from now. You don't stop to think of it when it's going on, but you pick up a picture or a tool from the past and you think, *My God, is* that *the way we did it?*"

In the *Weekly Time Book* the penciled figure of $45 was at the bottom of the page. I asked: "If that's what Tom Story paid for the 359 bushels of oysters; and if this Josh Moore got six days at five dollars a day makes thirty dollars; and you only got paid forty-five dollars for the whole trip, your father, the boat, and you—how did you make any money?"

"What you see there in that book only represents the oyster transaction that week. And that trip maybe took only one day. Pappy'd get the oysters off the Thames River ground and bring them around to Mumford Cove."

"And how much did you get?" I asked. "I don't see anything in there listing you."

"My mother got a check for the house same as we got. Pappy, he kept his own money in a roll with a rubber band. Sometimes that pocket really bulged out. We did have a checkbook that we used to pay for the grounds such as Mumford Cove."

"That's very interesting," I said. "But here in this particular book, as you say, you worked, but I don't see you actually *listed*."

"When you're working for the old man you don't always get listed."

. . .

Since oyster grounds were leased or owned outright through grants and were considered private, if damp, property, it was necessary at times to protect them from the depredations of poachers. The practice of hiring people to watch this property has interesting variations. The shacks, perched on stilts, where watchers sat equipped with binoculars and shotguns, have their own history.

In Noank, the late postmaster Bill Banks used to tell the story of the old man hired to watch the beds in Palmer's Cove on the west side of the village, one cove to the east of Mumford. The trolley line used to run right across the grounds, and in summer the local lads such as himself liked to use the trestle as a diving platform. While they were down there in the water it was a temptation to duck under and pluck a few oysters . . . sometimes not such a few. The oyster watcher soon became their adversary. The old man lived alone in his shack. He was pathetically susceptible to the occasional communication from the outside world, so the boys tapped into the system by which he was notified of special deliveries at the post office a mile away. Bill Banks told me this story some thirty years ago and, alas, he is now gone. All I can recall is that this notification of mail and retrieval system was complex. Part of my problem is that I'm not quite sure which part of the process was the notification aspect and which the retrieval. In any case, the whole evolution involved a flag, a bicycle, a light generated by pedaling the bicycle, and a series of steep hills. I suppose those boys were the early twentieth-century equivalent of computer hackers. In any case they would lure the watcher away from his watch. By the time he returned empty-handed on his bike, the boys had made their snatch. This method, of course, could only be worked so many times until the old man wised up. It was then that the lads noticed that the trolley also had another effect on the oyster beds. On Tuesdays and Thursdays the old man took it to New London. The story was that he visited "the ladies" in the colorful port city on these days, apparently to take advantage of midweek rates. That he visited at all was connected with the theory that oysters were the Viagra of the day. Taking advantage of the old man's romances, the cynical lads would dive with impunity on the beds.

Larry Malloy spoke of an oyster watcher whose domain was in between the Long Island Fork and so used a boat:

"'Red' Fernier, I think that's how you spelled his name. We paid him twenty dollars a month to watch our ground. He watched other ground, of course, for other people, and he was a 'Bay Man,' that is, what some people call a 'natural growther.' In other words he didn't have any beds of his own, but worked the State Grounds. Bay men would apply to the state and pay a fee.

"I remember we'd be laying over in Kerk-ells Harbor [Coecles on the chart—a long skinny inlet around the back side of Shelter Island from Greenport]. Red, he'd come in about supper time and tie alongside us. He had a thirty-four-foot centerboard sloop—gaff, of course, with a six horsepower make'n'break. *Pretty soon you'd notice him go; pretty soon you'd notice he'd be back.* I mean he'd be like that. He wouldn't just sit out there over a ground like those men you read about down in the Chesapeake hunched up in their huts on stilts, or your man in Palmer's Cove. In New Haven they had watchers that would just sit there.

"'Red' he didn't really make what you'd call *raids.* He'd go out on the grounds, and you know, depending upon the wind and the tide, he'd cut his engine and just drift around or sail around a bit. The sail was important because that way he could hear people. They would always have heavier equipment, so he could just hear them working. He did that a lot at night. Days he might be doing his own natural growthing and while he was at that, he'd, of course, be out there where he could keep an eye cocked.

"Them days everybody knew everybody else. Just to know there was a watchman out there helped. I guess there used to be a lot of problems earlier. Another method was Red would walk along the docks at Greenport, and he knew everybody and everybody's boats. He'd see who was tied up at night. If one was missing, he'd try to find out where it was. You know, like your neighborhood cop in the old days knew every car and who was in it and probably just where they was going. If they was going the *other* way, he might wonder. There were some guys who would poach. Everybody pretty much knew who they was. It was like lobstering where people develop reputations. We didn't have any real gangsters, just a few of the captains for one company. They was told by the big bosses to go out and come back with so many oysters. They'd go get what they could find.

"'Red' did have a shotgun, but I don't recall him ever firing it at anyone except maybe a duck. There were some pretty good ducks out there. Of course just knowing he had that duck gun was something people probably kept in their minds."

It wasn't until after the war that oyster pirating on a grand scale hit the Malloys, and I only found out about that myself much later and by accident.

NOTES

WHEN ALL THE OYSTER BOATS BEGIN (p. 108): Thomas C. Gillmer also shows this period as the height of the working oyster sloop in *Chesapeake Bay Sloops*, p. 13. See also: *Under Sail: The Dredgeboats of Delaware Bay, A Pictorial and Maritime History* by Donald H. Rolfs, Wheaton Historical association, 1971. Kochiss has a good chapter on the history of sailing oyster dredges in New England. He points out that unlike the Chesapeake skipjack or bugeye "no northern dredger type appears at the forefront." Mystic Seaport has an example of one of the smaller sailing dredges in *Nellie*, built, like *Anne*, in Smithtown, Long Island, eight years later in 1891.

ADMIRAL URGES SAIL (p. 109): *Yangtze Patrol: The U.S. Navy in China*, Kemp Tolley, Naval Institute Press, 1971, p. 48.

GROTON SHELLFISH MANAGEMENT PLAN (p. 110): This is itself a model for other coastal towns, according to John Volk, Commissioner of Aquaculture for the State of Connecticut.

WHAT MOTHER GOT (p. 114): According to a slip from Preston Nurseries and Florist up the Norwich New London Road from Harrison's Landing, Mrs. Malloy also received "Gardenia" on March 25, 1964, from her husband, L. H. Malloy, Sr., for which he paid $6.50 and a card from Lawrence, Helen & Children. I'm not sure why Larry kept this particular item for forty-seven years, but as he might say, "it sure lasted longer than the gardenia."

13

MASTER

. . . the proudest moment they had known in that calling which is never embraced on rational or practical grounds, because of the glamour of its associations. It was the moment when they had passed their first [Marine Board] examination and left the seamanship Examiner with the little precious slip of blue paper in their hands.

"That day I wouldn't have called the Queen my cousin."

—Joseph Conrad, *Chance*

Tyrone: Where's Edmund?

Mary: *[With a vague far-away air.]* He went out. Perhaps he's going uptown again to find Jamie. He has some money left, I suppose it's burning a hole in his pocket.

—Eugene O'Neill, *A Long Day's Journey into Night*

SOME FAMILIES NOT only have a sense of their history, but operate consistently with conscious reference to that past. No doubt this is stronger in families that have been in business together ("together" being in this context a loose concept). This familial historical sense is not just the chronology, or even a story that defines a key family member. The stories are those that are perceived by the family as marking the high point in a trajectory of family progress. In the Malloy family the Oyster Shack on the City

Pier in New London seems such a moment. As Larry wrote on his yellow pad: "At that time we were well established."

There was, first of all, the central location in the city. No longer were the Malloys relegated to the literal fringes of society stuck out on the tidal flats. The fruits of their labor were now acknowledged in the vibrant center of the city, at the foot of the Parade, as it was called, where the railroad station and the Civil War monument and a ferry service all stood at the confluence of Main, State, and Bank streets. This was the "uptown" for which the O'Neill family felt such a mothlike fatal attraction. Second, the Malloys had cobbled together a small fleet of working watercraft.

Typical of the way human structures rise and fall, however, it was at this high point in the family fortunes that the wheel turned, and young Larry Malloy sought a measure of independence in two very different ways. The first was in the flow of the maritime life; the other was in what seemed to me to be a totally irrelevant field. The more I studied Larry's life, however, the more the Parking Garage Phase and other such lubberly ventures made their own comment on the seagoing life upon which these occupations seemed to turn their back.

The Central Vermont Railway, which figures in other Malloy stories, was an interesting phenomenon on its own. A freight line running almost due south from northern New England, its tracks terminated on the Sound in New London. Unable to negotiate roadbed rights along the Connecticut coast, the Vermont Central was forced to transport its cars from New London to Manhattan by barge. I'll never forget the sight of seeing what looked like a freight train going down Long Island Sound one day off Bell Eight on Long Sand Shoal at the mouth of the Connecticut River. We were far enough away so that the barges themselves were just over the horizon and the many-colored freight cars seemed to be chugging their way merrily along at sea with a tugboat out front instead of a locomotive. The Vermont line eventually stopped going to sea when the owner apparently fell overboard one night, and his body was never found. In such cases, to discourage scams, the victim cannot be declared legally dead for seven years. As the owner had sole signatory authority, this was a tragedy with disastrous financial repercussions for the company. The railroad station Larry refers to is not, however, part of the Vermont line, but the main line between Boston and New York, about halfway between the two cities.

· · ·

"We were now well established. Father had the oyster shop on Central Wharf, across from the railroad station in New London. This business thrived from 1934 until it was swept away in the 1938 Hurricane, which also sunk the *Emma Frances,* and several of our other boats. We leased Central

Vermont Railroad property where there was already a building that had been used as the place for the mail to come in. There was a platform for the trucks to come in. Those buildings hadn't been used in quite a while. When Pappy's crew was revamping the place they found a mail bag there that had fallen down under the platform. They turned that in. I've often wondered what them people must have thought when they got those letters. Of course a lot of them maybe was beyond caring. The oyster shack was both a wholesale and a retail operation for us. They were all our own oysters— oysters we caught—except when we had to get some because we had an unusual order.

"After school every day, I'd rush down there, put on my apron, and go to work, opening oysters, handling lines on the dock, sweeping up—doing whatever had to be done. We had the *Emma Frances* and the *Captain* operating, but we also owned the *Sarah Thomas* and the *Mary Brewer*. As far as pay went, well, I was still eating the old man's food.

"We even had an oyster route: Montauk Avenue all the way to Ocean Beach. We had a Dodge truck. It looked like a prisoner's van, wire on it and all. It was actually an ex–produce truck. I got my motor vehicle license in 1936. Any driving I did before that was just around Harrison's Landing in a 1922 Buick coupe, a jewel which I purchased for seven dollars in running condition from Al Fox, a mechanic who'd done work for my father on the boat machinery. I drove this vehicle all around the Landing through the woods. This is where I learned to drive. People didn't think that much about licenses in those days. I was a good boy; I never done anything illegal. [LHM was telling me this over the speaker phone and said he was getting loud laughter from his "audience," i.e., Shirley Monez and son Larry, Jr.]

"You had Otto Grossman over on the Noank-Mystic Road. You had Manny Costa on Groton Bank who started out of the back of his car with a box of ice and fish he'd just bought off the draggers. You had fish peddlers going from door to door who would buy from us. I myself delivered lots of gallons to the Hygienic Restaurant on Bank Street which is now an art gallery, I guess, with big naked women painted on the side of the building that people write letters to the editor about. I'd go up Bank Street on foot with a gallon can under each arm. Those cans didn't have handles on them so that was the way you had to lug them and hope you wouldn't drop them on the sidewalk.

"There was one bar on Main Street which was owned by a guy who had a Stutz. Later he and I were the only two in town at the time with a Stutz. His was a bit newer. Mine had a real low windshield, a squatty windshield, but was a big car in all other ways. Anyway, before I had my Stutz, I used to get calls at what seemed all hours to run up to that bar with a gallon of oysters. A man named Payne worked for us in the oyster shop opening oysters by day. At night he'd go up to this bar and drink and the bartender would say to him across the bar, 'Hey, Payne, get us a pail of oysters.' Then Payne would call the house at Harrison's Landing and I'd have to go down to the oyster house and get together what he wanted. Sometimes Payne, he would walk down to the shop and help me sort out the oysters. Most of the time, he didn't help but put in the call. All I ever got off him was a Waltham pocket watch for two dollars when he needed two dollars one time. I had that watch until I took a trip to Canada after the war and I left it on my bureau, not wanting to risk it in a foreign country. Turns out that when I come back it's missing. One of my relatives says that it's just hanging there on the wall behind the new paneling in my bedroom. Someday I'm going to smack the wall and see if I can start it ticking.

"Oysters in those days were shipped by truck to Fulton Market, New York, in three-peck butter tubs, which demanded the high price of a dollar and a quarter per tub. There were times at that shop we was selling them thirty cents a pint. Hey, oysters was cheaper than hamburger.

"But even in the Depression, we always had enough to eat. Not necessarily oysters—-hey, we could buy a bag of corn once in a while! We could always make a day's pay just scratching stuff up. I never had to eat too many oysters."

. . .

Larry came by the other day with three photos of the oyster shop operation at the Central Wharf on the east side of the railroad station. Unfortunately, the pictures consist chiefly of the shell pile next to the shop, but maybe this makes the point. The wooden structure that housed the operation was not what was important. As Larry put it: "What mattered was how much stuff you got *out* of the building." Of the three snaps, only one shows even a corner of the building, a clapboard affair with overhanging roof suggesting Victorian railroad Gothic. The shell pile comes nearly up to that overhang. In the background is the old overpass that allowed pedestrians to mount a number of steps and cross the tracks between Union Station and the City Pier. Featured in one photo is Ira "Ike" Edwards trundling a wheelbarrow full of shell up the single twelve-inch scaffold plank to the top of the heap. I have personally never known a shell pile that lacked a certain pungent kick, especially in summer. Of course the more careful the shuckers are in removing all of the animal, the less strong will be the olfactory assault. One can only assume that old Captain Malloy's austere hand inspired the leaving of a minimal residue to haunt the already sometimes too vibrant heart of New London in that era.

. . .

It was about this time in New London that Larry also began to assert himself in the family business. He wrote on his yellow pad: "I was made master of the *Emma Frances* in 1937 at nineteen." I didn't think anything of this until I came across another note where Larry had said, "My father said to me just before the storm [1938 Hurricane] struck, 'OK, she's [*Emma Frances*] yours.'"

On the phone now Larry has just admitted he was made master about a whole year ahead of the storm, but this quip about the father handing him the boat just before the storm struck is the way he seems to prefer to remember it. What to make of this? In any case, what comes out now is a sidebar about the people at the Post Office whose job it was then to handle the paperwork on the master's certificates, and it is the Marine Inspection Office, after all, that is the final authority on being a master, whether you have a boat to go with your paperwork or no.

The master/captain distinction is a technical one, not, however, without its considerable emotional weight. Anyone can "captain" a boat merely by purchasing the vessel or having been given the authority by someone who has made that purchase. To be a *master,* however, requires a license issued by the federal government. The certificate is awarded only after a rigorous oral and written test. In the days Larry discusses below, the issuing agency was the Merchant Marine. Now the job is done by the Marine Inspection Division of the United States Coast Guard. To be even eligible to sit for this test, the applicant must present documentation of having performed upon vessels with an appropriate combination of time and tonnage. It is also interesting to note that while Larry Malloy's father *owned* all the boats and was without question their *captain,* he was never officially a *master.*

. . .

"Let me tell you something about licenses. There were two men, Mr. Brooks and Mr. Macdonald, in New London in the Post Office when it was the Merchant Marine Inspection Office for the Merchant Marine. That was before that office got moved down to the Coast Guard in the Custom House on Bank Street with all them buoys up on the pier.

Mr. Brooks and Mr. Macdonald had New London and they had Greenport. They had to run back and forth to Greenport on business but the ferry only operated summers then and even then not always when you needed it. So they'd hitch rides with Pappy on whatever he was running that day. These individuals were very cheap. Gee, they always wanted something for nothing. They wanted clams. They wanted oysters. During Prohibition, hell—they wanted booze! And, of course, they wanted the rides.

After a while they felt kind of guilty about this so they offered to pay him for the trip. Give him two dollars as a tip. Now he knew that he couldn't do that on account of he didn't have no license *to transport passengers for hire,* and here these were the guys who controlled those licenses! He looked down and saw the briefcases them two always carried full of official documents. '*You* ride free. Two dollars for the freight,' he says, 'Per case.'

"They agreed. It was sure a lot better than driving down Route One to the Whitestone Bridge then all the way back out east to Greenport.

"One day as we were setting out down the river, Mr. Brooks, he looks at me and he says, 'You should pick up a proper license, even if your old man won't. There's nothin' to it.' So I says, 'What'll it cost me?' He says, 'It won't cost you anything. There's nothing to it.'

"So I go over to the New London Post Office, and Mr. Brooks, he's glad to see me and all. Shakes my hand and all. Then he sends me in the back room, sits me down at this big, long table so I thought maybe we was going to have to be the Knights of the Long Table. Christ, he sits me down four hours. Then he begins walking back and forth, back and forth. He asks me what happens from the time you put gas in the tank to when it comes out the tailpipe. All the steps. For two-cycle and four-cycle. Then when I sit there scratching my head, he leaves the room. I had believed him when he said there was nothing to it. I hadn't studied or nothing, I was just in there with what I had. I don't know what he was doing in the other room, maybe washing the windows or something. I'm sure they was pretty busy with other things. In a minute he comes back. 'OK,' he says, 'Now what's the answer?' I had to write down the answer while he kept walking back and forth, back and forth. You had to write down what you thought was the proper answer. I give it to him all right, two-cycle and four-cycle. In those days you had updraft carburetors. A two-cycle got 'ports,' not cylinders. He put me through the mill. Then Mr. Macdonald, he was an old deck man, had been a sea captain. He asked me the rules of the road which was a book I had home and which, of course, I'd been operating under all my life. That is all my life which was only up to eighteen years old at the time. At least it was all my life since I had been standing on the chopping block steering *Anne.* I don't think Mr. Macdonald cared much for Mr. Brooks being the boss, seeing as how he was a deck man himself and with a whole lot more sea time to boot.

"Mr. Macdonald was real nice, kept me relaxed, none of that nervous business. It wasn't any stuff using the chart. That was much later with my hundred-ton license which I still got. Still it seemed to go on for hours, well, all morning anyway and was not my idea of 'real easy' at all. Hey, I was a little snotty eighteen-year-old kid.

"Eventually he walks over to Mr. Graham who was sitting at a desk by the door. He was the secretary or receptionist or stenographer, or maybe all three. Mr. Macdonald tells him to write up the license. Mr. Graham pulls out a book and tears out the license, like you would postage stamp, but of course it's a lot bigger. It's already got printing on it and the picture of a ship. Mr. Graham adds in your name and the date. His handwriting was out of this world, a masterpiece, old English—something you'd be proud to paste up on the bulkhead of your steamboat. It took him ten minutes just to write my name and the date. Meanwhile I sat in the chair. They had steamer chairs in there, probably some chairs they stole out of steamboats they was inspecting. You know: *condemned.*

"During the war they called all the licenses in. They made you come down and reapply. If you was working on the water you had a better chance of getting your license back than if you was, say, a farmer living inland who just happened to have a license, a sailor come ashore."

NOTE

PICTURES OF SHIPS ON LICENSE (p. 124): See "The Marine Licensing Tradition: What Are Those Ships?" by Captain Robert S. Bates, in *Nautical World: The Arts, Allure and Traditions of the Sea,* June 1998.

14

JIBBOOMER AND THE GREAT STORM

TWO RITES OF passage besides the master's certification occured about this time. The first was social, the second meteorological.

Larry was invited to join New London's venerable Jibboom Club. Named after the furthest point forward on the rig of a traditional sailing ship, the jib boom, the Jibboom Club was actually an organization that honored more where the maritime culture had been than where it was going. Founded circa 1870 by officers of whaling ships, the club was formally chartered in 1891 and incorporated in 1894. At its peak there were 280 members. When Sebastian Lawrence of the great New London whaling, shipping, and banking family died in 1909, he left money to a wide range of charities, including "dinners on Thanksgiving and July 4 for those at the Alms House," a church spire for St. Mary's Star of the Sea, the land on which the present New London Hospital is located, and $1,000 to the Jibboom Club. As Larry says: "So where your kids were born and you're likely to die, you might say, all come out of an old Jibboomer." Less mystically, the Jibboom Club was what we would now call a "networking operation." (Critics would see it as the ultimate old boys' club.) Most of Larry's friends were in the marine business and many of them, sooner or later, were Jibboomers.

In the beginning the membership was exclusively blue-watermen, but as New London's maritime culture drifted inshore, so did the prerequisites for belonging to the Jibboom Club. Eventually after World War Two the membership could not keep up with the rent and the organization was disbanded and the artifacts dispersed, some going to various historical societies and the Mystic Seaport.

. . .

"By the time they got to me in 1936, they was taking people in pretty shallow water. I was the youngest member. It wasn't long they'd come right ashore taking railroad engineers. I guess the idea was because of the Vermont Central, which had ships. In fact most of the New London pilots and the men getting passenger licenses then had come up through the Vermont Central barges that took the cars from New London to New York. Tommy Watt, he come up that way. It was getting to be the only way you could get the time and tonnage. I was one of the few who didn't go that route.

"The Jibboomer commodore sat up on a stage behind a big ship's wheel with the binnacle and everything. On either side were quartermasters. I was port quartermaster. I was in charge of paraphernalia, which included the initiation rollers. Those were round timbers I had to lay down on the floor so when people come up to get initiated they had to navigate on rollers. By the time you got up to the ship's wheel you didn't know where you were or how you got there. I had to memorize my duties: 'My duties are to take position on the port side of the wheel, to assist in taking up the password, and perform any other duties that the officers require.' One of the passwords I recall was 'piss pot.' Apparently that was for historical reasons. There is another Jibboom Club in England. That's number two. This was Jibboom Club number one. They had a lot of models of whaling ships in glass cases and *implements* and other gear. All of these things had traditions behind them and around them and hell, sometimes it seemed on top of them. The 'piss pot' tradition had to do with conserving water aboard a whaleship. We had quite a discussion on that. Seems on whaling ships they never threw any liquids overboard no matter what spigot it come out of. They washed their clothes in the piss pot. At least that's what the old timers said around the pool table. That's where most of this 'sea lore' got passed along, the whaling vessel *Colgate* for instance. Now she had been owned by Sebastian Lawrence, a Jibboomer, and had been picked apart at the Lawrence wharf, but then they run her up into Winthrop Cove where I used to see her whole shape and her ribs sticking out of the mud for years until with Redevelopment they filled a lot of that in. You knew exactly whose ribs those were through the Jibboom Club. Those old guys played a lot of pool and when they was at it with the sticks and balls and the corner pocket they was always talking about the old days.

"We moved the club a lot in the time I was in. Always up on the second story of some place down around Bank Street. The pool table always came along. Had to get it down from upstairs, along the street, then back up again. You'd think at some point they'd leave it behind, but hey, them old guys had to play their piano. Did I say 'piano'? I meant pool.

"They moved that pool table. That and the big ship's wheel and all the delicate relics. I gave them relics myself, *implements* and novelties like clay pipes with oysters growing in the bowls. The old sailors used those clay pipes, kept breaking off the stems if somebody else had been using them. When the stems got too short, they just tossed them away. Sometimes they find them in the old bilges. I found them in the oyster dredge.

"The dues was something like a dollar and a quarter a month. The best part was we all had keys, so if you're in New London you always knew where you could find a bathroom. You didn't always necessarily need to use it, but, hey, it was there for you. That is, if you could find where they moved the club that week. I always figured it was a good idea to help out in the moving for that reason.

"Jibboom Club was famous for a traditional 'plum duff' dinner in December. It was supposed to be a *secret* recipe. *Secret people* doing *secret things*. There was a certain amount of that. Hey, you really can't have it be a club otherwise, can you? I don't remember much about the plums. I do know they put a lot of liquor in it. There was also a parade through town on Washington's Birthday and a dinner dance afterwards. Again, I don't recall the parade. As a matter of fact I don't recall the dinner dance either except that it was held up in the Sky Room of the tallest building in the city, the Mohegan Hotel. I guess I was missing from work about three days after one of those Sky Room adventures, and the old man, he got tramped and raved. He put the crew in charge of *Anne*, and damn but they backed down over a floating two-by-four that got in the screw, and she had to be hauled. When I come back to work, there she was up high and dry in the Greenport Shipyard with no explanation from Pappy. I had to find out from old Otto Hulse who run an engine company over there on the harbor front."

. . .

Besides the Jibboom Club New London had another venerable social organization, the Thames Club. The membership consists of prominent professional people. I knew a New London man, graduate of an Ivy League college, who said, "I'd give my right arm and my wife just to be allowed to crawl in the front door of the Thames Club." When I asked Larry Malloy if he knew anything about this organization, he said, "I never heard of the Thames Club."

. . .

In checking some of the above out on the phone, we make a date to meet tomorrow (March 6, 1999) if the weather isn't bad. "Well, you know what to do if the weather's bad. You go down on the dock and put out more lines."

As both of us can see out our windows to a river, he the Thames and I the Mystic, we also discuss the tide streaks in the late winter afternoon light.

Next day there's a driving raw rain. When I call Larry, he's looking out onto the Thames from his kitchen table; I'm up in the boat yard's ventilation tower. We speculate on what happens when the Antarctic western shelf melts and the water comes up the predicted twenty feet. He figures at Harrison's Landing he'll be just above it, "but I'd like a little more land under me in case of storms." Somehow this leads us into a discussion of his cremation. "Shirley asked me what I want done with the ashes. I think she figures there's gonna be a whole lot of them. Spread 'em on the walk for the ice, I guess." I suggest the sea. "Well, old Captain George Sanford, he told me he been on some of them trips with ashes and everybody ends up eatin' them. They don't seem to understand that just because it's a funeral the wind won't blow the way it always does when you put the bow into it."

To get him on a more cheerful topic, I read him back some of the notes he'd made on the yellow pad. According to the yellow pad, he'd gotten to what biographers would usually call a *breakthrough* moment in his career by earning his master's certificate; I had been expecting the narration to be a kind of onward and upward in the maritime profession, or at least that it be so at this moment.

. . .

"When I got my license I guess I went around and told everybody I knew. Some of them said, 'Hey, that's good.' Some of them—well, I don't remember what they said.

"My father, he did have a license; it was to operate a gasoline engine on a boat. He was one of the first to have that, and the subject of that license came up quite a bit, but, of course, it wasn't really a *deck* license, that is, one that permitted you to decide where the boat was going to go. The gasoline license permitted you to be below running a gasoline engine that somebody else was up on deck deciding where it would go. I do know I posted that license of mine up in a frame on the bulkhead wall of *Anne*. And I took it with me to whatever boat I was running. It was on the bulkhead of *Emma Frances* when the hurricane hit, so I had to send away for a new one.

"But, hey, you know my life didn't really change that much. I just went sailing every day like on *Anne*. In fact, four years later I'd progressed to working for George Young in the New London Parking Garage on Water Street opposite the railroad station."

. . .

Watershed moments are usually wars, but in the eastern end of Long Island Sound, a single storm altered the lives of waterfront workers almost more than what happened in World War Two. On September 21, 1938, a storm of force unprecedented in the memory of the settlers of New England swept over eastern Long Island, crossed the Sound, and pushed up the estuaries. The effects of the storm were made all the worse for coming totally without warning. At the end of the century, the New London *Day* voted hands down that it was "The natural disaster of the century."

"Pappy and I looked out and saw the neighbor's boat start to drag, so we got aboard the *Captain* and started her up. Without too many problems we towed the neighbor's boat off the beach and over to the Submarine Base. Just who gave us permission to do this, I can't imagine, but, hey, in a storm, you did stuff like that and before the War people understood. Coming back across the river, we began having a bit of a problem in the wind. I was up on the bow and had the line ready to put over the spile on our dock. This was the same dock we'd just left a little while earlier. The line started running, and I stepped in the coil as the boat pitched. The line pulled my foot so all I could do was go overboard with it. There was a lot of debris already in the water. At one point I thought, '*Well, I ain't lived too long, but it's been fun.*' I kept ahold of the line. I looked up and saw the spiling that had been sticking up hip high above the deck of the pier when I'd begun to put the line over it was now almost under water. It didn't seem to me to be blowing all that hard, so I guess that was what they later called 'the *surge.*' The surge had happened just as I was trying to get that line over the spile. I remember getting ashore and then going out on the boat again to try to take care of her. A lot of stuff happened so fast you don't know now how you got it all in."

When the storm was over the Malloys had lost all of their boats and the oyster shop downriver. A New London *Day* article quotes Malloy, Sr., as listing the loss at $120,000, which may be broken down into 75,000 bushels of oysters and four boats. The national average income was $1,731. Minimum wage was set at forty cents an hour. In 1938 a new car averaged $860, a house less than $4,000, a loaf of bread nine cents, a gallon of gas ten cents, and a quart of milk fifty cents.

"It was very difficult to find anything in all that wreckage that anyone could say that for sure this was theirs. Court Culver, later the outboard king of Eastern Connecticut, borrowed a pair of oyster tongs from Pappy to try to find his tools. Down off the City Pier, we did find one oyster container in which we chucked the spare change each night. It was a soggy mess, but my mother found the thirteen cents or whatever inside. That's when we found Captain Frank Thompson's big iron safe and it was full of nothing but water. That's Ellery Thompson, the draggerman, painter, and author's old man. I don't know if Ellery ever knew we had that."

One of their neighbor's boats was saved merely because by the time it came ashore there was so much debris floating about that it was protected from the rocks. As for the neighbor's boat, which they had towed across for refuge to the Submarine Base, she did not have a scratch on her. "People ask me, when the 1938 Hurricane swept our shop away did we ever have a thought of going back to open up another oyster shop? Well, we never did go back."

The Depression was still very much in effect. World War Two was less than three years away. In between it and the Great Hurricane, there was in the lives of the Malloys a curiously idyllic interlude.

15

SALVAGE

Salvage is man's most noble art.

—Falorp

ONE DAY RECENTLY down at Orion Ford's gas dock in Noank, I was with the eel-grass specialist Fred Short pursuing the hypothesis, common enough in sea-grass circles, that the disease that had ravaged *Zostera marina* in the early 1930s had ultimately contributed in a major way to the economic woes of local fishermen toward the decade's end. The thesis had been that the eel-grass blight had ruined the hiding places for all the nursery stock, which ultimately led to a crash in fin fish landings. Among the old-timers sitting around on the ruptured auto seats set outside Orion's shack was Depression veteran lobsterman Alfie Foster. "Eel-grass blight?" he said, "Hell, there wasn't enough money in town to go buy gas to take the boats out to see if there even was an *eel-grass blight!*"

In any case, while this had been the most disastrous period in the history of the country, the 1930s locally had included not only the Great Depression but the 1938 Hurricane. Add the repeal of Prohibition in 1932, which had deprived many fishermen of what had amounted to an unintended government subsidy in the form of a smuggling trade. In my own childhood I'd wandered among the wrecks of the era: cellars into which houses had collapsed, boats in pastures, houses in lagoons. Even many of the houses still standing on their foundations were unpainted. More to the point was the attitude of the people, often hard-bitten, stripped, like their houses, of any adornment. If ever New England swamp Yankee Puritanism needed a revival, this period was ripe. Even now when you meet someone at the Noank or West Mystic post office on the first spring day you're set straight: "We'll pay for it."

The glib view is that the Grim Thirties were rescued by the boom economy brought on by the military-industrial complex in the mid-1940s. In southern New England, however, there is a subset of the Great Depression, the period between the Great Hurricane in the fall of 1938 and the days in mid-1942 when the effects of World War Two began to kick in. These three-and-a-half years are often seen in retrospect, even by people who lived through them, as comprising a kind of waking dream, as if it were then everyday knowledge that somehow the war would change all. Greenport writer Milt Heitzman calls it a "shadow time" that hung over the waterfront.

It is true that the boom was especially dramatic along the waterfront where commercial fishermen such as Alfie Foster and boat builders like Bob Whittaker went to work in the submarine factory or, like Howard Davis, into the service. This boom continued on through most of the Cold War. There was hardly a lobsterman as late as into the 1970s who did not work a shift at Electric Boat.

It is in the years between the Great Hurricane and the time that the Second World War actually had an economic effect on southeastern Connecticut that we see the Malloys scrambling to survive without any foreknowledge of rescue. It is salutary and instructive to note how a family living so close to the edge, both literally and metaphorically, managed to do this. It is hard to imagine an American family of the mid-twentieth century that was more Depression-proof than the Malloys. Their success was based on understanding salvage. It is almost as if they were a family designed to survive a national collapse.

What the Malloys have always understood about salvage is not only the particular techniques in the nuts-and-bolts phase, but the vision behind the concept. Whether it is a life, a career, or an engine, salvaging in great and small matters has been so much a part of the Malloys' life as to transcend merely being a habit of doing business. It almost seems that the Malloys salvaged not only out of necessity, but for some sort of gleeful retribution. To paraphrase the old Spanish proverb: *Salvaging well is the best revenge.* And it is not only the initial triumph of the act itself, but the twice-chewed delight in the telling of it. Salvage is, after all, a classic reversal of fortune, a kind of jujitsu joke on fate. Salvage contains all the elements of art, improvisation, creative recasting, social purpose, design, and economy of means.

There is another point that may be found lurking in the following account of *Virginia*'s new engine, and that is the sturdy simplicity of a bygone age, when an engine could be sunk in salt water and retrieved and still function. On one level this has to do with technical matters such as the thickness of castings and the absence of dependence on electrical parts. On another, however, this is political. As with the now forbidden multitasking illustrated by the regulations prohibiting the mixing of freighting and fishing, salvaging is yet another case of how in midcentury an oyster-man could improvise his way out of difficulties and even into a kind of glory.

In Larry Malloy's narrative, Point Jude (Point Judith on the chart) comes in for some attention from time to time, as in "Pappy was rounding Point Jude when . . ." While not in the same league as Cape Hatteras, the Rhode Island peninsula has its share of shipwrecks and horror stories. At the often obstreperous confluence of Narragansett Bay and the Atlantic Ocean (on the chart euphemistically called Block Island Sound), Point Judith can be as harrowing a challenge as a mariner can experience between Cape Cod and Hatteras. Most of the Malloys' craft were built for thinner waters, but the necessity of moving a boat from one venue to another occasionally forced them into a blue-water nightmare.

. . .

"In 1939, we were lucky to purchase the *Virginia* from H. J. Lewis Oyster Company of Bridgeport, Connecticut, where she had somehow survived the [1938] Hurricane. *Virginia* had been built in New Haven and, like *Anne*, had first touched the water in 1884. She was much bigger, however, being sixty-four and a half feet long and displacing fifty-four gross tons to *Anne*'s mere thirteen.

"All that tonnage gave *Virginia* a thousand-bushel capacity. She had, at the time we bought her, one drawback. She had no power. H. J. Lewis had been experimenting with her, installing various rigs. We salvaged the engine out of *Captain,* which had sunk out front of the Landing in the 1938 Hurricane. You could do that in them days with engines that had gone down even in salt water because you didn't have so much goddamn electronics on them. *Captain*'s engine was a standard six-cylinder model 48-56. We trucked it down to Bridgeport to Hitchcock Engine Works where they installed it in *Virginia*.

"*Virginia* was a closed-in oyster steamer, like the oysterboats were in the late 1880s and early 1900s. The deck was completely closed in. The wheelhouse was up over the deckhouse near the bow. She was an eighty-foot long steamboat and proved to be more boat than Pappy and I could handle.

"Her length was made even more unwieldy because she was not wheelhouse-controlled. That is, there were no gadgets connecting the man steering the boat down to the engine. What we had was a trap door in the bottom of the wheelhouse floor. I was the one to be down in the engine room to answer the bells. Not that we actually had real bells, mind you, you know like, *one bell ahead, two reverse with a jingle for more power*. Also, we didn't have a clothesline long enough, probably would have had too much play in that long a run in any case, so we had to control the dredge hyster the same way: Pappy hollering through the trap door at me. I run and throw a lever and stuff starts spinning. Oh, we used to have some real rattles about the engine room stuff. We come into the Valvolene Dock in New London and there's the old man with the hatch open, his head hanging like a bat capsized throwing down bells to me. But I didn't miss a stroke. I don't know how he could steer the boat, see where he's going, and hang upside down hollering at me all day."

. . .

The Crosby family has been continuously building boats on the same site longer than any family in the United States. While they have built a variety of craft since the eighteenth century, they are best known for a mid-nineteenth-century innovation, the Crosby catboat. The cat rig is one of the best examples of indigenous boat design in history. It is a wide, shallow-draft, single-sailed vessel adapted for the local waters working fishing fleet. Many of these hulls were later down-rigged and converted to motorcraft, and their wide beam provided excellent stability for an oyster-man to stand out on the gunnels at the very edge of the boat and work his tongs. A converted cat made a good platform that also had grace and maneuvering ability, unlike the current bandage boxes one sees at such venerable oyster haunts as Blue Point on the south shore of Long Island. Evidently, however, Crosby's *Hooker*, despite her noble lineage, did not prove suitable to Gardiners Bay.

"Being boatless after the 1938 Hurricane, we went to Osterville, Cape Cod, Mass., at Crosby's where the Hurricane had not hit so hard. We picked up the oysterboat *Hooker*, which we brought to Harrison's Landing. Sometime later, Father, Captain Frank Staplin, and myself left with *Hooker* bound for Greenport to deliver her over to Sid Smith. Wind blowing a gale southwest right on the nose in Gardiners Bay and it seemed like it took forever to get to Greenport. We must have arrived back home somehow, but I can't remember how. Frank said it was the slowest trip he'd ever been aboard of anything! For sure she was never a boat to work Gardiners Bay. In those short, choppy seas she bounced like a cork. You can't be an oysterboat out there without some *weight*."

I used to be puzzled as to why this particular story sticks out in Larry's mind among all the other voyages of his life. He's mentioned it a number of times. Was it one of those defining moments? Precisely what would it have defined? An attitude toward a particular boat design? Maybe it's about something between his father and himself or Captain Frank, his "future father-in-law." Voyages, both good and bad, certainly bond men, to each other and to the sea. It is often the bad voyages that provide the best cement. The voyage of the *Hooker* seems to have been such a one. It occurs to me now that at the time the Malloys must have thought that this was going to be it for them after the Hurricane: the comically cumbersome *Hooker*. But fate stepped forward in the form of an old friend.

"About that time, we received word from Mr. Robert M. Utz Oyster Company, owner of *Anne,* to stop in and talk to him. My father did this and much to our surprise he became owner of *Anne* once more. She was over in Sterling Basin in Greenport moored port side to, bow out, next to the spot where you see her on that Wash White calendar. There she had been during the Hurricane and as a result had survived just fine as the breeze had kept her off from the dock—unlike what happened at Harrison's Landing when everything come ashore.

"*Virginia* was now used as our oyster shop, basically a shore structure tied up where she couldn't get us into too much trouble. As for having bells shouted at me, them days were over. There was no more need to be hollering from one end to the other to keep her from running into something. She just stayed put. She was already *there.* Her size and the fact that she was closed in now were help instead of a hindrance. And she wasn't yet a breakwater like she ended up. She was still afloat. You hate to see a boat go that way. Even if she was a problem. I mean you don't go to all the trouble to build a boat just to make it into a breakwater. But, hey, when it's her time, you do the best you can with what you have. We use what we got for the reason of the time when it happens we need something particular. We didn't think of *Virginia* as any the lesser just because she was now a shop. And hey, we hadn't done nothing to her to keep her from ever being used as a boat again. And later we did use her as a boat again.

"*Anne* was now our oysterboat to catch oysters and unload them onto *Virginia* for processing and loading into trucks. We had a crew on *Anne.* Captain Frank Staplin was our cook on *Virginia.* We needed a cook because we was working long hours out in Gardiners Bay aboard *Anne* and sleeping back aboard the *Virginia,* which had six berths in the fo'c's'l."

NOTE

SPELLING STIRLING (p. 135): When Malloy was born, *The U.S. Coast Pilot* spells it "Sterling Basin." By 1933, it is "Stirling Basin." More to the point, the inner basin itself was a mere two to three feet deep. "On top of that was all eel grass," according to Malloy. "You could barely get around in there, real slow. Wheel got wound up in the grass. We didn't call it a 'basin.' To us it was just a *creek*." Not until a year after the hurricane was a hundred-foot-wide swath dredged to eight feet right up the creek.

16

POTATO PORT

I met a traveler from an antique land

—"Ozymandias"

To any one who has not seen this place for the past twenty

years, it would seem almost like coming into another world.

—Charles L. Young, writing in *The Rural New Yorker,*

July 30, 1893, about the Halyoake Farm

IT WAS DURING this interlude between storm and war that the Malloys added another product to their business, the lowly potato.

"We had mooring space in Pete's Neck Bay Orient at Halyoake Potato House. We ran potatoes in summer, up to October, then we went to oystering around to next summer. They let us stay there during the oyster season, which was good because we had grounds in Gardiners Bay and we had no waterfront left after the Hurricane back at Harrison's Landing. It was quite the place, all irrigated with big piston pumps, wheels going around, valve wheels . . ."

. . .

Sometimes, when trying to fall asleep, I'll imagine visiting harbors . . . odd nooks that are not quite harbors, or perhaps once were, but have now become for some reason abandoned. "Pete's Neck" is such a place, a dreamy mix of land and sea.

Looking at a chart for Long Island–Eastern Part (C.&G.S. #1212) you can muse your way only so far. There are soundings of 4, 5, then ½ with a sprinkling of cartographer's ink that is likely to be unforgiving if met in real space. Of Larry Malloy's "Pete's Neck Bay," here is what a water-stained, cloth-covered 1918 *Coast Pilot* says:

A dredged channel, with a least width of 35 feet and protected by dikes in places, leads through [Long Beach Bay] to a wharf on the west side near its north end. In 1917 there was at least a depth of 5 feet in the channel and 6 feet at the wharf. This channel is marked by the dikes and private aids and easily followed. The black buoy at the entrance lies midway between the shores 600 yards westward of Peter's Neck Point. Leave the entrance buoys, the first dike, and the buoys near Peter's Neck Point on the port hand, then follow the next dike, leaving it on the starboard hand, until in the channel between the dikes, and when past them follow the bush stakes, leaving them on the port hand. The aids and dikes should be passed at a distance of about 20 feet.

I read this to Larry over the phone. "That's it," he said. "The dikes was so to speed up the water and deepen the channel. That's the same channel we used to take up to Halyoake Potato House. Except we didn't call it 'Peter's Neck'; we called it 'Pete's.' That channel was so long I guess that saved some time."

I asked him how long he thought that channel had been there, and if it had been built and maintained only for the potatoes. "It was there before my time. As for other reasons for the channel besides just the potatoes, well, there was cabbage."

"Somebody built an elaborate channel like that with dikes and spiles just for potatoes and cabbage?"

"Produce."

"Oh."

"You don't understand. How the hell else was they gonna get things to people to eat. You didn't have all these goddamn trucks and highways."

"Ah."

. . .

We were talking on the phone the next day. It was a little difficult as his son Larry, Jr., was enthusiastically "mowing the carpet," by which I took it that he was vacuuming. "I was talking to my brother Frank," said Larry, "and he remembers Halyoake Potato House."

"Does he remember that channel with the spiles and dikes?"

"He remembers the *Walter Raleigh*. She was built in 1901 'right there on the farm,' as Frank says. A steamboat with side paddle wheels, they used her to tow the potato schooners up in that crooked, shallow channel. They called them *schooners,* but that don't mean they was always still rigged out with two masts. A lot of the time the main mast had been cut down and the foremast shortened. Hey, sometimes maybe they never had even been what you'd call a proper schooner rig. It's just that they did work a schooner used to do. It's like we say *trucking* when we usually mean the stuff was brought in on a boat. What the hell, don't we say *shipped* all the time when we mean *trucked?*

"Brother Frank remembers that Long Beach Bay as being choked up pretty good with eel grass. The schooners, they had an air-cooled donkey engine on the bow to run the cargo boom, but they didn't have no main engine to drive the boat through the water. They had an engine in a little yawl boat they kept on davits over the stern. If they found a place they couldn't manipulate by sail, they'd throw those yawl boats over, snug 'em up tight to the transom and try to push their way in with that out back shoving them along at a couple knots—if they was lucky on the current.

"They also used the sidewheeler to drive in those spiles you keep talking about. The pile-driving barge itself wasn't big enough to carry her own steam engine, so *Walter Raleigh*'d come alongside and run a hose over from her boiler to run the hammer that knocked every one of them spiles in. *Walter Raleigh* was sponsored out, like steamboat *Sabino* you see go by every afternoon now on the Mystic River as a special treat. Well, *Walter Raleigh*, she wasn't treating anybody; she just did her work. Or I should say had done her work, because by the time we got over there to Pete's Neck, they had her up on the beach north of the point. We used to go over there and get aboard her but she was all done. Frank says they broke her up right there.

"But that channel, it really was something. I remember one day on the *Captain* we're following the *Charles W. Lynn,* one of those schooners, but she had her own engine aboard of her. Old Johnny Monsell—I never thought he could see too well. He was tearing along. Well, those engines, you got to run them a while and get them hot. Fairbanks Morse diesels. They've got no clutch, so you start 'em up in gear. At the dock. You have to have good dock lines. Hey, the *Elizabeth Ann* was the Block Island ferry out of Point Jude and she had a Fairbanks Morse. Undermined the whole bulkhead in there just warming up so the pier fell down. It was *ca-tass-triss!* So there's Johnny Monsell screaming down the old potato channel right in front of us. The current out at Pete's Neck can get going pretty good and took him on the side. You had to be in the deep water, especially when you were laden, and the deep water, of course, has all the tide in it, deep water's where the current runs fastest. That channel, the minute you left the Potato House you was never steering straight. There was quite a turn this way, then that. It's the kind of place that if things don't go *all* right somehow they go *all* wrong. Those spiles you keep talking about, the ones the *Coast Pilot* says you're supposed to keep at least twenty feet off of, well, Johnny Monsell in that old potato schooner, he hit every one of them. I wouldn't say he *bounced* from one to the other. They was close together, and he just went really tight, and there we were right behind listening to the *Charles W. Lynn* screaming and whistling against those spiles. Well, you know they was nice spiles at that, no knots in them or anything so that when you rubbed up against them you wouldn't be in trouble, and they had some *give* to them. You'd have to say they were there to be of help."

. . .

Larry once took me to this place. I tried to match the dream with the actual scene, "Pete's Neck," as he kept calling it, despite the chart's insistence. "Peter's Neck Point," is indeed on the Gardiners Bay side of Orient Point, that tenuous last thought of the North Fork of Long Island. The Neck is protected from the Bay by Long Beach, which is exactly that, and itself protects Long Beach Bay from the southwest. On the chart Orient Point looks like a crab with Long Beach an extended left arm reaching round almost to shake claws with the shorter right arm which is Peter's Neck Point. When we visited the site it was deserted, the point tentatively pushing its spartina well out into Long Beach Bay. "Look on my works, ye Mighty, and despair!" It seemed a watery Ozymandian vista:

> Nothing besides remains. Round the decay
> Of that colossal wreck, boundless and bare
> The lone and level sands stretch far away.

Except there wasn't even a wreck.

"The *Halyoake* was built right there on the farm, a regular flat-bottomed sharpie, but bigger, that is, longer. Just a great big rowboat hull, really, with decking and wheelhouse and all over that. They built her that way because they didn't know how to build anything other than rowboats, but it worked out for them because there wasn't much water in the Bay. Of course, being built like a rowboat didn't make her a good sea boat for when you had to run off across the Sound and up around Point Jude and up to Providence or even across the Sound to Long Sand Shoal and up the Connecticut to Middletown and Hartford. But having some weight in her helped keep her from spanking. Otherwise she'd knock your teeth out. Pappy and Ed Adams, the captain, were going around Point Jude on her one day with Pappy sitting on the rail. His backside was almost in the water, so he suggested to Ed he add another deck a bit higher to keep everyone's ass out of the sea. Of course he couldn't do that right then, but eventually Ed Adams, he did this, adding another deck on top of the old one, but up about two feet, which not only worked fine on the outside for keeping Point Judith out of your hip pockets. The new deck also allowed the crew to have some shelving below to store their tools and gear. She ended up over in Mumford Cove as an oyster freighter. When I was over there a few years ago though I didn't see so much as a rib of her."

As Larry and I stood at the water's edge at Pete's Neck the bay looked beautifully protected, but so empty you wondered if it really were suitable as a harbor. I didn't see any of the famous spiles, though I did think for a moment I caught the sound of the *Charles W. Lynn* slithering its way out.

"That's just the wind in the sea grass," said Larry.

The longer we sat there, the more the water seemed stagnant rather than secure. We stayed in the truck while I guess Larry gathered his memories. He began sketching on the back of an envelope. "Here's where the dock was, *Virginia* port side to, bow heading in. Then *Anne* alongside of her at night, port side to, same thing, bow heading in. The suction dredge *Michael J. Fitzsimmons* was laying over on the far side as part of the breakwater. She's discarded. Away from the water, where there's no room on this envelope, you had all the other farm buildings. You had the well where they got the irrigation, places for onions, carrots, and Brussels sprouts—they had two sizes of Brussels sprouts, your little ones and your great big ones—and cauliflower. Way in the back out by Route 25 from Orient to Greenport they had the shacks, really more barracks than shacks, where the workers lived. In closer to the water was the coal shed.

"They kept a lot of stuff growing in the cold inside buildings by having potbelly stoves, and they also had a coal business, some of which we shipped out. On ships. *Our* ships. The potato house was here, right on the dock so it was connected by a chute to the boats. Everything gets weighed twice, before and after you unload. Just like when you go to a sand and gravel pit or the dump. The wagons, two horses, they come in the gate and over the scales, then on through the potato house where they are unloaded and out and back around outside on the far side the building, away from the boats. Now you know that everything in this world weighs *something*, even things that aren't necessarily potatoes. As a result you used to find all kind of stuff on that back side of the potato house. Stuff that got thrown off before the wagon got weighed the second time. Most of it was gravel, but there was other stuff, too. Hey, every job's got its little tricks."

With so much gone Larry appeared to be wondering if it were going to be worthwhile getting himself out of the cab. Certainly by now there was more to see on the back of the envelope right there in the truck.

"What the hell," he said, "we've come this far."

Loosed from the confinement of the truck, we soon broke out of our melancholy to play archeologist. Larry hiked off ahead as if he were exploring a site where a man he had once known had spent an important part of his life. Just who this man might have been was not entirely clear.

I was left to sift. Where *were* the remnants of the great Hallock Potato Company and its wharf? More than a company, it had evidently been virtually a whole village. In the mud, overgrown with spartina, we found a few rotting timbers, the sort of thing one often comes across in poking about backwaters. The timbers, even in their half-eaten condition, however, seemed to suggest something a good deal more substantial than some mere marsh dweller's spindly improvisation in the days before the DEP. I was still thoroughly confused between Larry's adventures in the potato trade and those yarns involving oysters. I had no understanding of where one began and the other let go. Standing on the deserted point, to me it all seemed a fantasy. I didn't expect to see the *Virginia*. I knew where *Anne* was. Yet there should have been some sign of the structures. There simply could not have been all this bustle he was going on about. We were not, after all, talking about ancient Egypt. The place had been thriving after the Great Hurricane in years since I myself had been born. There had been no more recent great storm, fire, or invasion. All that he had spoken about had been laid waste by the slow sulk and squirt of the marsh.

A year or two later Larry digs out a tiny snapshot that shows a farm cart laden with what looks like five layers of dead pigs, which, upon application of the magnifying glass, turn out to be sacks of potatoes. A man sits atop the forward end of the load. Although you cannot see the animals that are pulling, the man clearly is driving them. The cart is just about to turn a corner around a ramshackle wooden shack. The land ahead is flat except for a distant line of trees. You could be in Iowa but for the foreground, where three spilings insist upon the proximity of the sea.

"There," he says, "just like I said it was." The back of the photo bears a wobbly scrawl: *Hallocks farm 1936 or 1937.* He also comes up with a bill of sale:

POTATOES	**The Halyoake Farm**	PRODUCE DEALERS
PRODUCE	Farm Garden Products	FEDERAL LICENSE
COAL		NO. 3420.
	Geo. W. Hallock & Son	

ESTATE OF *LUCIUS H. HALLOCK*, PROPRIETOR

John H. Jagger

Orient, Suffolk County N.Y. April 14, 1937:

Received from Capt. L. H. Malloy payment in full for gas screw boat "Captain"

[Signed]

John H. Jagger.

Larry also brings forth an article from the Friday, July 16, 1937, edition of the Providence *Evening Bulletin*. Surrounding a four-column photo of *Captain* is this text:

Big event of the year, rushing new cobblers from Long Island to Rhode Island's dining tables is an 82-mile trip concluding with speed contests for unloading, because the more trips the more profits to the potato boat skippers. Growers and dealers can worry about market prices; the boatmen don't. Shown in action here is Capt. Lawrence H. Malloy of Waterford, Conn. [Harrison's Landing is technically in the town of Waterford], guiding laden barrels from the oysterboat *Captain* onto the dock at State Pier, while son Bill, 15, stands nearby, and another son, Lawrence Jr., 19, engineer, manipulates the gasoline powered hoist from the pilot house and tallies the unloading.

Captain is moored port side to with a ramshackle urban wharf in the background. Visible on deck are over fifty sack-capped casks on end with their tops wrapped in burlap marked **H H**. Bill stands on the foredeck with his jacket still on, suggesting that even on this mid-July day, the air was cool at sea. His father is in shirtsleeves and suspenders with a swordfisherman's long-billed cap, and gloves with which he is hauling upon a line leading up out of frame at a 45-degree angle. Larry in shirtsleeves is in the vertically staved wheelhouse looking in the same direction as his father. A single spoke of the great wooden wheel pokes up above the wheelhouse sash. A one-column ad beneath the article advertises a clambake "at Grimshaw's, Fort Phoenix, Fairhaven, Mass every Sunday & Wednesday Open at 1 p.m. Tickets $1."

The article itself hangs on the idea that what is going on with the oyster-boats is the "Annual Potato Race." The reporter has evidently tried to interview the first Long Island boat into the Providence dock, the 42-ton *Hal-yoake*. Her master, however, one Robert Adams, sixty-one, caught up in the rush, has just cast off his lines, and advises the writer to talk to the next boat. Anxious for "a more enthusiastic picture of the potato racers and their thrills and perils, if any," the reporter moves on to a Captain Lawrence H. Malloy, forty-nine, who "owns his own boat." Fortunately, Malloy is yet unloading the oysterboat *Captain* and is willing, as the reporter puts it, to take "the race question calmly."

Captain Malloy explains that the running time from Orient to Providence is nine and a half to ten hours for the eighty-two-mile trip. There follows a characteristic bit of Malloy mischief. He informs the reporter:

With a breeze and the boat jumping up and down you have to go twice as far. It isn't like an auto, where if the wheels are spinning around, you're going somewhere.

Going home unloaded, Malloy says, is usually quicker. The point is to make as many trips as possible.

A Malloy lecture on the nuances of hauling "Long Island Irish cobblers" at sea follows. Salt water rots potatoes. Sun can weaken the skin so that water will blister them. Barrels, holding 165 pounds and costing thirty cents apiece, are therefore used for the first two weeks of the season because the potatoes are too fragile. Later, when the skins are tougher, hundred-pound burlap bags at five or six cents apiece will do. As for the teenage crew aboard the *Captain,* their father/skipper says hauling potatoes "keeps 'em out of mischief and gives them something to do."

IN SEARCH OF A VANISHED SIEVE

> The owl and the pussycat went to sea in a sieve.
>
> —Mother Goose, more or less

I CONTINUED TO be haunted by the world that was once at the edge of Orient Bay in the days when the Malloys lived and worked there between the Great Hurricane and World War Two. For one thing, what on earth was the relevance of that Elizabethan explorer and con man, Sir Walter Raleigh, to the Hallock project that they should name their steamboat after him? While prowling through Thomas Jefferson's garden and farm books in search of something resonant on the lowly potato, I found the answer in a letter he had written from Monticello to Horatio G. Spofford on May 14, 1809:

> a vessel of Sir Walter Raleigh's, returning from Guiana, put into the west of Ireland in distress, having on board some potatoes which they called earth apples. That the season of the year, and circumstances of their being already sprouted, induced them to give them all out there, and they were no more heard of or thought of, till they had been spread considerably into that island.

Someone told me that on the North Fork was something called the Hallocksville Museum Farm that apparently memorializes some of those days. On the phone no one at the Museum, however, can tell me anything about the maritime aspects of the farm. They've never heard of anything to do with Halyoake at Peter's Neck. Their brochure promises a harvest day miles away.

"Damn it," says Larry, "You got the completely wrong place. Call Ed Adams of Route 25, Orient Point. That's his father in the 1937 Providence article."

It was Columbus Day, a clear blue sky with a northerly that had just enough muscle in it to keep you honest. Mrs. Estelle Adams answered the phone.

"I'm sorry, Ned's not here right now."

Oh-oh, I thought. Well into his eighties, he's probably in a rest home.

"He's out on the Bay scalloping. He needs to use a walker to get to the boat, but once he's aboard, he's fine. They need someone to tell them what to do anyway, and when they come back, they all just sit down in chairs and shuck. Then they'll see how fast he is."

When I told Mrs. Adams about Walter Raleigh and the potato she said, "Well, that's very interesting indeed, but the name of the boat was not *Walter Raleigh,* it was *Walter Royal.* It was so named because the Hallocks had a little boy who was rather sickly named Walter Royal Hallock and while they were building the boat, they took him down there in his wheelchair or whatever to watch the construction. He enjoyed that. Watching the building of that boat was the big thing in his life. In fact it was pretty much the only thing in his life. He died soon after and so they named the boat for him." She not only knew about the boat, she had a painting of the *Walter Royal* on her living room wall. The same for the *Halyoake.* "She was big all right. Seventy feet overall, though we called her sixty-five because that was her waterline measurement. But, Lord, no, she didn't end up in— where was it you said—Mumford Cove. Larry ought to know exactly where she is because every time he looks out his back window there at Harrison's Landing, at least at low tide, there she is downriver at the Thames Shipyard. She wasn't a schooner, but a single-master. People kept calling her a schooner. I suppose you could call her a sloop, though the mast was mainly for the potato boom and the only sail was just a little one, a kind of help-alonger like those boats always had to help the engine if the wind was right. From Larry's back porch, you should be able to see that stub of a mast at low tide. Ned bought that *Halyoake*—there was at least one earlier that was a steamboat—. Ned didn't remember her, that is, the first *Halyoake*—except one time from a distance when he was four and they were taking her away to destroy her. That stayed in his mind, you know as it would with a child, a thing like that. When he heard they were just going to junk the second *Halyoake,* he bought her from the Hallock family in 1939 for four thousand dollars. She was nineteen years old then and had a three-cylinder Wolverine.

"That was the last they were shipping potatoes out of the farm. By shipping I mean in actual ships. Later it was all trucks. In 1939 they didn't seem to know what to do with boats anymore, so Ned bought her. He had her for seventeen years. Although she was seventy feet, she was pretty much just a three-handed boat. Ned's father ran the boat while Ned and Curt Tabor did the heavy work. She moved as many as eight thousand bushels of oysters. She was good at transferring oysters from bed to bed, from New Haven to Greenport, even out to Cape Cod. He worked her with the people who had leased Gardiners Island. She was their freighter, you know, loads of pheasants and the tractor. Ned sold her to Larry's brother Bill in 1960. She wasn't under her own power by then, and I think Bill used her as a barge.

"Earlier at Halyoake they would barge in horse manure from the streets of New York. Barge after barge of manure right up that channel. The sandy soil wasn't much good for anything until they built it up with the manure from the city, barges of it.

"They had a big coal business at Halyoake, too, and used barges for that. The coal shed was right there on the farm opposite where they did the potatoes. There were lots of buildings on the farm and right up the road. The workers lived there in shanties. Migrant workers, but that was before the black workers came. These people spoke Russian. [One thinks of the baseball player Carl Yastremski's father.] Ned didn't own the farm. His father managed it.

"Ned worked on boats most of his life. When we tried to explain that, how he wasn't necessarily a fisherman all the time, but still was on boats, well, we usually said he was, well—*a workboat man.* That meant he wasn't on yachts.

"Those valves and wheels Larry speaks of, well, they were there because of the irrigation system. We don't have rivers out this way, so the water had to be pumped in and distributed. One pipe could service quite an area when it was rigged up right.

"As for that channel coming into Hallock Bay. We call it Hallock Bay inside Pete's Neck, though I guess it does say Long Beach Bay on the chart. That tide does run in there very strong, especially toward the last part of the cycle. I know when I go swimming at a certain point out there at that stage I can hardly hold my place. I don't swim much anymore, at least in the last four years.

"But you know those pilings. Well, they're still there, only they don't stick up above the water anymore, but you can still hit them. You're still supposed to stay twenty feet away from the edge of the channel, but just the other day a boat came in banging up against them just like Larry said about Johnny Monsell all those years ago. I knew Johnny's father. It's the same tide, only you can't see the pilings above the water."

Mrs. Adams asked me when Larry and I were out at Pete's Neck Point if we ever got out of the car. I admitted that in the face of all that desolation, we nearly had chickened out. "But we did finally climb out of the truck."

"Well," she said, "did you ever walk to the water and look over the edge?"

I admitted we had not been so intrepid.

"Well, as I said, I haven't been swimming there myself the past four years."

I laughed and asked her what her husband had done since the *Halyoake* days.

"Ned worked with Larry's brother, Bill Malloy, on and off through the years. They did that wharf at Mystic Seaport where the whaleship *Charles Morgan* is. When Ned was working over on that side, I'd often come with him and visit the elder Malloys, that is, Bill and Larry's mother and father. They were nice people to talk to. One time the Historical Society here in Oyster Pond [Orient Point] asked me to see if I could get anything down from the people who had been here long ago. I took a tape recorder over to 'Snakes,' that's Larry's father, and he was very cooperative, very affable and all, but he was awful hard to keep on the subject. I remember one story about sinking off Plum Island in a potato boat.

"Mrs. Malloy was very nice. She was a 'Bonaker,' as they called people from over on the South Fork then. I tried to catch some of that accent. Usually she talked just like you and me, but sometimes if she got excited, especially talking of the old days, she'd go into that Bonaker and that's what I tried to catch.

"I got time to talk because I don't know when Ned's getting back for supper. It all depends on how many scallops they catch up in Hallock's [Long Beach] Bay. The more they catch, the more they've got to shuck and it's been a pretty day."

. . .

Larry was pleased to hear that Ed Adams was still out on the water and gracious about Mrs. Adam's additions and corrections to the record. "Hey," he said, "there was a lot of boats in a lot of years and sometimes one will get away from me in the mud somewheres. Stell's right. She was a school-teacher, you know. *Halyoake* is right down the river here. She caught afire when Bill had her, and they nosed her into the mud. You say Stell said when Ned was running *Halyoake* for the Gardiners they shipped pheasants and tractors to the island on her. How about deer? I know that Pappy shipped deer over there. Not that they couldn't swim across by themselves. Come to think of it, that was Tommy Watt's *Carrie H.*, the one that ended her days up in Mumford Cove. As for *Walter Raleigh* or *Walter Royal*, hey, now you got me. Me and Frank are going to have to do some *research* on our own."

Mrs. Adams calls the boat yard. She has located an article written July 30, 1892, by a Mr. Charles L. Young for the *Rural New Yorker*. A couple of days later I'm reading a typewritten copy. We are a step closer to recreating the vanished world of the great saltwater potato farm.

"A 'Sieve Farm' Clogged with Manure:
Something New in Agriculture"

Charles Young, writing a hundred years ago, has the sort of straight-ahead, no-nonsense, go-getter prose of the American journalist who worked for one of the practical magazines that survived on exhorting the populace to brace up to the American Dream. Mr. Young wants to hear nothing from those farmers who whine about failure. He wants to hear from the "successful farms all over the country showing the methods of work and explaining the principles upon which success is based." There is "Mr. Terry farming with clover in Ohio, Mr. Lewis with chemicals in New Jersey, Mr. Johnson's poultry and the cranberry bogs that stretch along the shores of Cape Cod." The farm of "Geo. W. Hallock & Son" is another story of success. "Mr. Hallock is what may be termed a market gardener. Living 100 miles from New York, and still further from Boston, all the produce must be barreled and shipped by steamer or sail or both, to commission dealers to be sold at wholesale. . . . The bunch-stuff such as rhubarb, beets and radishes, is out of his line, for he does only a barrel business."

Young tells us how this "abandoned farm [was] rescued from salt water":

Mr. Hallock bought the original farm in 1870, and since then has bought several strips of land adjoining, and the past Fall [1891] has added ten acres more, making the total for the season of 1892 about sixty-eight acres. When purchased, the place was practically an abandoned farm. It had frequently changed owners, was almost always mortgaged, and it was said that if a man lived on it long enough he would starve to death. The land was said to be gravelly, and was intersected by salt meadows that permitted high tides to wash over the lower lots. People thought manuring that land was like pouring water into a sieve, and for an owner to spend money for manure was as foolish as to throw it into the bay, but manuring for twenty years has clogged the sieve. Then it was the poorest farm in Orient; now it is the richest in Suffolk County. No farmer can blame anyone but himself if he does not have a crop as big as Mr. Hallock; for no one in Orient has as poor a farm as his was twenty years ago. When he first commenced to buy manure in company with some of his neighbors, he bought a schooner-load of [New York] city stable manure; the next year he bought a whole load himself, and now buys a dozen or so. For 1892 he will use nearly 1,000 tons of city stable manure, 65 tons of fish-scrap and 12½ tons of chemicals. He is a strong believer in the good effects of fertilizers.

Young goes on to chronicle the arrival of George Hallock's son Lucius H. into the business. It was Lucius who "proceeded to do it in a business like manner." Avoiding what Young sees as a common problem in partnerships, the overlapping of responsibilities and authority, Lucius and his father divided the labor between production and marketing. This conceptual breakthrough, along with "willing hands and stout hearts, and what is more, the best of common-sense," got the job done. One of the more interesting techniques employed by the "junior Hallock" is "the book of maps. Each year the junior member draws in his book maps of the different lots showing where each crop is to be placed the following season. The maps are drawn to scale and the foreman [Mr. W. S. Jaggar], by applying a rule, can tell just where the potatoes are to be planted and where to start the plowing for early cabbage. Imaginary lines form the boundaries of the fields; for like parallels of latitude, they exist only on paper. There are no fences on the farm". These maps are all keyed to records of production so that crops that don't make money are abandoned. "No guesswork is done here."

So well thought out was this enterprise that nearly half a century later when the Hallock operation bailed the Malloys out after the Hurricane much of the layout remained what Young described in his *Rural New Yorker* piece:

Coming from the west [New York City], we arrive at the residence of the proprietors, a large, two-story double house, or rather two houses under one roof, as one side is the duplicate of the other, and they are separated only by a large hall. It was built some three or four years ago, and the elder Mr. Hallock occupies the east side and his son the west. A steam heater in the cellar warms the whole house in the most economical manner. Just to the east stands the old house which sheltered our friends during their struggles with fate and fortune years ago, and which is now occupied by one of their foremen. On the other side of the new road stands the barn, sheds, stables, cribs, ice-house, etc. In 1890 three cold-storage rooms, with a capacity of about 2,000 bushels, were placed in the east end of the old barn, and the ice-house was built adjoining. The barn is surmounted by a large Challenge windmill, with two eight-foot wheels furnishing the motive power to run a feed-mill, rip-saw, pump, a drill and a small circular saw for sawing crate laths. . . . The shed on the west side of the barn contains the tools, and all of them that are used during the day are cleaned, greased and hung up at night. To the south across the farm-yard stands the two-story shop, with the smithy in the rear. The little room in the corner of the shop is the office, the headquarters of the whole business, which has grown so that it is already being enlarged.

To knit this operation together internally and with the outside world, the Hallocks had a telegraph service. Not only was there an instrument in the office, but there was one in the residence and another down on the dock. By using the telegraph the Hallocks could fine-tune their operation to market shifts in Boston, Norwich, Worcester, and Hartford.

Reporter Young gets enough of a peek at the Hallocks' books to determine that the payroll during harvest season was fifty people. The key to signing on and keeping this crew, Young feels, is that there is a full-time cook. There is a cook house, which includes a kitchen, pantry, and dining room with a dormitory above.

Most interesting in terms of the scene that the Malloys found in the 1930s is Young's account of the waterfront:

As their farm adjoined the bay, they conceived the idea of having a dock of their own and a vessel also, as this plan would enable them to ship this bulky produce just where and when they had a mind to. The difficulties in the way were that the channel leading out into the bay was crooked and narrow, and the water was so shallow that the mud had to be dug out before a vessel could reach their dock. The son built a mud-digger to open a channel out into the bay. People laughed at him, said he was a fool, and that he was throwing his money away; that he would never dig a channel, and that it would not pay him if he did, and if he had never done any more business than his critics, they would have been right. They did not realize that the man who had the enterprise to build a dock would have enterprise enough to use it after it had been built, and the dock of Messers. Hallock & Son is worth $1,000 a year to them now. At last steam had to supplant the uncertainty of sails, and three years ago [1889] they bought the steamer *Jed Field*, converted her into a freighter, and she has steamed in and out of her owner's dock, bearing his produce and also that of the very men who called him a fool for digging mud.

...A bulkhead dock is used long enough for the *Jed Field* and a schooner to lie together, and now there are seven feet of water at high tide. The south end of the dock is covered by a large two-story freight house having rolling doors on each end and on the side next the water, so that teams can drive in at one end, unload, and drive out at the other. Three teams can stand in line and unload under cover regardless of rain, and as they drive on out, all clogging, which is so common on the village wharf, is prevented. Upstairs is used for storage purpose. North of the freight house are the coal-bins, and an elevated track carries a coal car to the edge of the dock so as to leave the north end of the dock free for unloading manure. It is a pleasing sight to see the raw material pitched off at one end of the dock and the manufactured product trucked aboard at the other. Up the creek a little way is the "Navy Yard," where the *Jed Field* has her Winter quarters and it is the home of Mr. Lucius' donkey. This is simply a little side-wheel steamboat used for towing schooners in and out of the bay and for operating the mud-digger. They estimate that the dock saves them $600 or $800 per year besides being a necessity. In fact, what these men make is what they save, and they save what most men would throw away.

As a further example of the Hallock's economy is how the potato farm got in the coal business:

> The purchase of the steamer, which was a necessity for marketing the early crops, led [Hallock] incidentally to another business apart from the farm. The expense of running the *Jed Field* back from New York would be no greater if she were also loaded than if she were light, so the proprietors wished to freight the coal for the other dealers here, but were refused. The consequence was that they put up coal-bins of their own and went into the business of selling coal on their own hook, and in a few years Messrs. Hallock & Son will be the only coal dealers here, because they buy and sell for cash only.

Larry calls. "Hey, you and Stell ain't the only ones can do research. Here's what Frank found out about the Hallocks' steamboat. He looked up *Walter Raleigh* in a beat-up copy he got of *List of Merchant Vessels of the United States.* Now that's published by the Treasury Department for 1901. In there we found out her real name, which like Stell said was *Walter Royal.* She was thirty-four feet, two inches long and fourteen feet, eight inches wide with a depth of hold of three feet, seven inches."

As for the coaling operation at Hallocks', with the demise of the Hallock's own freighter *Jed Field,* thanks to the flexibility of *Anne,* even this Depression-era problem would turn out to be good luck for the Malloys.

FREIGHTING

> Quinquireme of Nineveh from distant Ophir
>
> Rowing home to haven in sunny Palestine,
>
> With a cargo of ivory,
>
> And apes and peacocks,
>
> Sandalwood, cedarwood, and sweet white wine.
>
> —John Masefield, "Cargoes"

PRESENT REGULATIONS FORBID boatmen from going into any line but the one in which they and their vessel are licensed. The Coast Guard will not permit boats to be in both the fisheries and the freight business. It accomplishes this both through the vessel license and the master's license. The Federal Food and Drug and the State Sanitarians may also have something to say about shipping shellfish in boats used for other cargo, such as the various loads of potatoes, oysters, coal, and manure Larry Malloy describes.

A person with a boat used to be able to make a living any way he could. He might go oystering one day, freighting the next, or if he were especially lucky, combine the two. These freighting stories illustrate the multiple activities a waterman needed to practice in order to make a go. Oystering not only has ups and downs, what with weather, disease, and market problems, but even at the best of times has long stretches of natural down time. Aside from all these necessary reasons for diversifying, it seems to me the Malloys enjoyed the challenges and the changes involved in using the boats and their own talents and even their social connections in a variety of modes. Of course there is the sour side of freighting—the dangers, and just plain hard work.

The scuffle between the elder Malloy and Mr. Ellsworth related below would seem to illustrate not only something of the intergenerational problems in communication in a family-held business, but something of the back-and-forth relationship between individual oystermen and the larger oyster companies. This type of relationship in turn illustrates the relationship between the individual, independent shipper-entrepreneur and the less personal corporate paradigm.

. . .

"Around 1930, when I was about twelve, I went to Greenport with Father when he took over the *Ann Elizabeth*. We had her to go shelling, also to freight potatoes. At this point of my life I had little knowledge of boating, or at least boating at night, what you might call 'the boating life.' You know: *the life aboard.* I sure found out about that the same time I found out about bedbugs when I turned in that night. Well, I guess I didn't have much knowledge of bedbugs, either. Like I knew roaches. I knew about roaches from the Ludlow Street house in Greenport. We was renting only the bottom half of that house, but had to acquire the whole house to get rid of the bugs. The people upstairs never did get the idea. Greenport was damp all the time. The place was practically under water. That's how I got to know about roaches. But bedbugs, I could thank old *Elizabeth-Ann* for that.

"On the *Ann Elizabeth* this night I wound up sleeping on a pile of life-jackets on the floor. That's the nice thing about bedbugs as opposed to cockroaches. Bedbugs, they pretty much stay like their name says: *in the bed.* So that makes it simple. All you got to do is just *get out of the bed* and you can sleep alone. That is if you don't mind the floor. And believe me, after a day oystering and an hour in the bed amongst company, I found the floor, she seems pretty good. Now, Pappy, he was up in the wheelhouse on the thwartship bunk. When I told him about the bedbugs down below, hell, he'd been on boats since he was nine years old: '*Oh, they're only bedbugs!*' Goddamn, but the *Ann Elizabeth* she was loaded with 'em. I was worried if all them bedbugs run to one side of the boat she'd roll right over.

"The *Captain* was purchased from J. & J. W. Ellsworth Oyster Company August 14, 1937. Just how she got herself purchased is a bit sticky. She got laundered through our friend John H. Jagger, manager of the Halyoake Farm, because Pappy and Ellsworth, they didn't get along. It was one of those things you couldn't always figure out about why Pappy done something a certain way. I know Ellsworth, he thought he knew more than Pappy, but Pappy knew more than him. Excellent oysterboat and freighter, the *Captain*.

"*Oysterboat and freighter,* that's because those were the days when we wasn't oystering we was carrying potatoes for the Halyoake Farm to

Stamford, Bridgeport, New Haven, Hartford, New London, Norwich, Westerly, and Providence. That was typical, oysterboats carrying Long Island potatoes. You didn't have the semis in those days. You didn't have the roads.

"One night we didn't even have much of a waterway. Coming up the Connecticut River after dark. You did a lot of running after dark in them days, what with having to load the boat to start off with and then makin' maybe only six knots and maybe the current or the wind or both against you, that made for a long day. And, of course, you didn't have any radar or RDF or GPS or even a depth machine. The depth machine was your old heave and ho lead line. 'Stay in the light spots,' my Pappy just got through saying when *bump*! We run aground.

"The theory was that dark spots in the river was caused by a shadow and that was caused, of course, by something substantial. You never quite knew where the bank was. You know how up in under the banks in the shadows you can't tell where you are. We didn't have all these powerful lamps in those days. Just kerosene running lights and a lantern to walk around the deck with to keep from falling down a hole or tripping over something. Nothing you could really use to poke out into the dark looking for a bank. Of course nowadays you got all these fancy lights, but by now it don't make any difference to me 'cause I'm runnin' blind anyhow.

"So this night up on the Connecticut everybody's in the wheelhouse. Eight eyeballs are better than two. Besides, where else you gonna be on those boats when they're running? Boil yourself to death in the engine room and all that noise. On deck's all cargo heaped up. And it's cold out there, even in summer, running at night on the river after dark. Rivers always seem colder than the open ocean. I think there must be something wrong with fresh water.

"Off Brockway Landing with Hamburg Cove on the other side. '*Look for the light spots.*' And there we are: we're running in the sedge grass up to the wheelhouse windows: *slurp*! You talk about *thin water*! She sat upright on her keel, contented—she'd been a centerboard sloop, so was pretty much flat on the bottom.

"We got Bill Reynolds to come on his dragger *Fortuna Margie*. I don't know where the hell you get a name like that: *Fortuna Margie*. Later—much later—Bill Reynolds, he went overboard one winter off his pier with his boots on, and that was it for him. But this night he took off a quarter of our load of potatoes in the middle of the night for us. He had to make several trips to Brockway Landing, which was a mile and a quarter up the bend where the paddle wheelers used to land. Then he put a line aboard of us from *Fortuna Margie*, and seeing we was considerable lightened up by now, Bill Reynolds, he backed us right off that sedge bank. No harm done, but the time.

"Also hauled coal to Gardiners Island. That island, of course, was still in the same family as got it from the King of England, one of the real old ones. In fact some of them Gardiners don't ever want to let go of the place. One of Pappy's first freighting jobs was a Gardiner that had got away and died off island. Job was to lug him back in a box."

. . .

More than most islands, Gardiners (there is no apostrophe on the chart) was in need of freelance freighting such as the Malloys provided. Its port is less than five miles of protected water off Three Mile Harbor on the South Fork of Long Island, but its isolation is less geographical than political.

Gardiners is one of the few manors in North America with an unbroken lineage back to its original patentee, in this case Charles I. Lion and Mary Gardiner came in 1635 and for their work in "pacifying" the natives at Saybrook at the mouth of the Connecticut River were awarded what was known as a "patent" on the large island between Long Island's forks. It was there they made the first permanent English settlement in what is now New York state. The Gardiners were "independent of every other settlement, and subordinate only to the general government of the Colony." The island was then named after the English island of Wight and the patentee for five pounds a month was permitted

> to make Execute & put in practice such any Laws for Church & Civil Government as are according to God the King and the practice of the country without giving any account thereof to any whomsoever.

The deal with the English sovereign was arranged through the Earl of Stirling, who lent his name (if not his spelling) to the cove across the bay on the banks of which Malloy grew up nearly three hundred years later. To further placate the locals, Gardiner paid in May of 1639 "ten coates of trading cloath" to one Yovawan of Pommanocc (the native name for Long Island, a sobriquet beloved of Walt Whitman) and his wife Aswaw Sachem. To this day Gardiners is the largest privately owned island in the United States and is often referred to in the press as a "virtual fiefdom," a designation that certainly beats "enclave" or even "compound." Robert Payne in his 1958 book-length study of Gardiners titled *The Island* says, "In a sense, of course, an island has no history: only a succession of anecdotes." He goes on to say, "The story of Gardiner's Island [Payne puts in the apostrophe that the cartographers eschew] touches American history, but always obliquely."

Most famously Gardiners is the alleged site of the last adventure of Captain William Kidd (1645–1701). After a late, three-year career of more or less legal plundering of non-British vessels in the Indian Ocean, Kidd was summoned to Boston in 1699 by one of his previous patrons, Lord Bellomont, Captain General and Governor-in-Chief of His Majesty's Provinces of New York, Massachusetts, and New Hampshire. Fearing that he might be betrayed, Kidd, on July 17, 1699, moored his sloop *Antonio* in Cherry Harbor on the southwest side of Gardiners opposite the tiny village of Springs. There court dispositions made in his Boston trial state that he sent one Whisking Clarke to represent him to John Gardiner, saying, "I want you to take ashore and keep for me to my order a chest and a box of gold, a bundle of quilts, four bailes of gold clothe. This box of gold is intended for Lord Bellomont."

In addition Gardiner took two thirty-pound bags of silver, which he was handed by two of Kidd's men, Cooke and Parrott. For these items Gardiner gave Kidd a receipt. There were other gifts exchanged, including a barrel of sugar from Kidd to Gardiner. When the court asked Gardiner if he knew who Kidd was, he replied, "I did not know that Kidd was proclaimed pirate."

While it would seem that almost every one else has always known Kidd to be so proclaimed, there was a time when his status was yet to be decided. In any case Kidd sailed off for Block Island and Boston in *Antonio* and never returned. After the trial, at which he was denied counsel, he was sentenced, and was hanged at Execution Dock, London, in 1701. Myths of Captain Kidd's buried treasure sprang up almost immediately. Washington Irving and others made their literary contributions. Digging for Kidd became big business. According to Willard Hallam Bonner in his careful 1947 study *Pirate Laureate: The Life and Legends of Captain Kidd* there were at least nine companies formed in the nineteenth century alone in which shareholders invested in digs for Kidd's stash. In northeastern America, there were reports pinpointing Kidd's locations from the Isle of Shoals off New Hampshire to the Hudson River. Of all of these locations, however, Bonner maintains, after exhaustive research, that "the Gardiner's Island legend . . . is probably the most reasonable," based as it is on the logic of Kidd's movements and the court dispositions. In the nineteenth century members of the Gardiner family reputedly found some 14,000 pounds of treasure.

One of the reasons Gardiners has not been overrun with treasure diggers is that since 1635 there has never been a tradition of what we now call "public access." The island has been basically one large estate with a manor and ancillary buildings, including a windmill and pier on Cherry Harbor, and there is usually a caretaker family in residence all year.

The land is covered in virgin timber. Loads of wood removed from the island by the Malloys were blowdowns from the 1938 Hurricane, the most valuable being white oak and cherry. A 1798 Gardiners account holds true largely today:

> The soil . . . is good & very natural for Wheat and White clover. The timber is various kinds, mostly large White oak. . . . The land is well watered with brooks, springs and ponds. . . . Fish of various kinds may be procured at almost any time.

Through the years various members of the Gardiner family drop in for stays of divers lengths. One penned a memoir, which can be summed up as "idyllic," especially in its ecstatic descriptions of day trips *away* from the island to places such as Montauk. Intrusions are rare and often memorable. In the War of 1812 Admiral Thomas Masterman Hardy of Trafalgar fame sent a party ashore for water and to get information as to the whereabouts of Stephen Decatur. The British assumed that such intelligence would readily be forthcoming from any citizens to be found dwelling on an island that was yet functioning more or less on its original patent from the king. The caretaker, however, for whatever reason, was less than cooperative, cleverly ensconcing himself in bed and surrounding himself with a variety of nostrums, tinctures, and ointments suggestive of a victim of the plague. The representatives of His Majesty's Navy hastily withdrew.

Even the army base established on the island did not contribute in any real way to the population. Fort Tyler was built at the far end of the long northwesterly-tending tombolo whose connection to the island was at best filamental. Duty there was akin to being on Alcatraz. Cart traffic rumbling down the tombolo to supply the men quickly eroded the beach grass, and soon the fort was an island for at least half the tide cycle. After a storm in which the garrison was nearly wiped out, the installation was abandoned. The fort has been known for most of the latter half of the twentieth century by its name on the chart: "The Ruins" and along with "Aban Light" forms the desolate gateway to Greenport from the sea.

Approached as it must be now from long, flat sheets of water, the old fort is more an optical phenomenon than a place. With nothing around it, there is no scale. Its once sharply squared-off walls balloon, shrivel, and pop according to the condition of the atmosphere. Even when you are almost alongside it, the size seems contrary to expectation. With every sighting the illusion is renewed. Each time you approach what had seemed to be a city of most imaginable splendor, suddenly will squat before you a round-shouldered rubble of screaming ammonia. Closer looks reveal a sign announcing

The sign seems to refer to the island's day job as a bomb target. Off-hours it is a bird sanctuary. (Evidently the birds that have survived have learned to check their clocks.)

No one is allowed to visit the island proper without permission of the Gardiners. It is one of the triumphs of Brooklyn's Norman Mailer to have received permission to make a film there. Stewart Udall, then Secretary of the Interior, also visited the island in order to sign a pact that will make the property a limited-access national park following the death of the present Gardiner, who seems destined to pass on with no heir. In the meantime, the place remains mysterious. Treasure myths aside, the idea of romping on primordial turf has its deep appeal. While yachtsmen passing the island may amuse themselves in speculation by peering through their binoculars, the Malloys, in their freighting days, actually worked there in labor that was fitting to the medieval flavor of the island.

. . .

"As for going around with a shovel and a pickaxe digging up Captain Kidd, well, I don't think the Gardiners would have appreciated us doing that. I know other people was always trying to do that, but the caretaker, he drove them off. Besides, we had enough to do with a shovel on Gardiners Island just moving the coal. At least with that we knew what we was doing and what the reward would be. All's I ever heard about the treasure of Captain Kidd was something about *silk*. Now I don't know about you, but digging up half the island for maybe finding some *silk* somebody *maybe* left there three hunded fifty years ago, well, it's not my idea of a way to put in a working day.

"But for the coal the island was self-sufficient. They wanted to keep that virgin forest. They even fed the wildlife: deer, ducks, turkey, pheasant, rabbit. There were maybe a dozen people, though I never saw the windmill at Cherry Harbor actually turn. I suppose it still could. We'd bring the coal from Halyoake Farm into the pier in Cherry Harbor and they'd back the horses down. We'd throw it up shovel by shovel from the deck. We shoveled right along with the locals. You did that—everybody pitch in if you're standing there, hey, grab a shovel. We also delivered coal to the island on *Virginia* by offloading from the deck a bag at a time and only shoveling up what broke out. (All our cargoes on all our boats was deck cargo, the oyster-type boat is too shallow to have any depth of hold.) Then on the *Emma Frances* we had a better way to do that. She was shallower draft so we'd just run her up on the beach next to the pier. They'd back the horses down, and then we was on the same level and could just push it off onto the wagons. You didn't carry any depth of water. If you was too deep alongside, the horses and everybody would drown! The wagons had two-by-fours across the bed so that when they got going where they wanted the coal they could just pull them two-by-fours out and dump the coal right there.

"In 1940, the oyster business shut down as usual the last day of April. The next job was freighting cordwood off of Gardiners Island to Three Mile Harbor, East Hampton, Long Island. That was all virgin timber that went back to the days of the King of England and the Indians before, but the 1938 Hurricane raised hell with the place, went right over the top of the island. The Gardiners contracted a man named Mr. Brown from upstate New York to clean it up. He set up a mill to saw the blowdowns and was in there two years to finish the job. I don't suppose he worked every day at it. In addition to cutting the blowdowns into just logs they turned out a lot of planks, white oak and cherry. Me, I only worked on that three months. *Virginia* carried twenty-five cords each trip. We had plenty of help: father, mother, brothers Frank and William, myself and wife. We were not crowded on *Virginia*. She was a big boat with plenty of room.

"At the time I had a 1935 Buick which I'd got by trading in the 1928 Buick. This was our transportation over to Three Mile Harbor, which was the nearest landing on Long Island proper and what you might call, with a bit of a stretch, our 'liberty port.' At least brothers Frank and Bill used the vehicle there quite often as if they was real sailors. Everything worked out all right until one evening when they borrowed the vehicle for a night on the town. I don't know exactly what they was looking for. I doubt they found any women that was loose out there. The high point of the evening seemed to be when they crossed the railroad tracks at a high rate of speed and the bump blew out every bulb that was lit on my car. I had to replace all the bulbs. Some liberty!"

. . .

"When freighting we also carried drums of gasoline to Fishers Island for Henry Walsh aboard the *Captain*. They don't make men like Henry Walsh anymore. At least we didn't have to shovel that stuff. We rolled the fifty-five-gallon drums up planks to the shore. I suppose there was some danger in that, but in them days, hey, you didn't think about those kind of things. Hell, most everything you did was *some* kind of dangerous. We used to load the gasoline in Shaw's Cove, New London, and the Italian lobstermen in there said to Pappy, "Why you go way out around every time? Do like we do and *cut* across." Only thing, when *we* try this *bango*. We're on the rocks. Broke her keel. We managed to keep her afloat enough so that with the next tide we got off OK. We put a keelson on her, but she always did leak after that so that when she got really wrecked again in the '38 Hurricane, we said, *that's enough,* and as soon as she dried out set her afire.

"One of our best coaling jobs was at the beginning of World War Two. This wasn't anything to do with Halyoake Farm coal. This was strictly government coal. If it had been Halyoake Farm you can bet they would have got it right. There was something wrong with the manifest and the government dumped all the coal for all three islands in the Race at Fort Terry on Plum Island. They had these big barges the government built up the Hudson River. They built them like hot dogs. They'd make them in six-hundred-foot sections, and you could come along and get them to cut 'em off in whatever length you wanted. I never got to see them do that, but Ike Edwards, he told me all about it. I wish I could have seen them do that because, hey, that was in my time. They could carry a lot of coal and they dumped all that lot at once on Plum Island. Now they had to move that coal, redistribute it to the other two island forts. Pappy come along.

"He had a big old 1909 boat with high bulwarks called the *Report.* High-waisted she was, tapering to maybe two foot high at the stern. She was sixty foot long, but narrow, I'd say only fourteen foot beam on her. With them high bulwarks she was perfect for poking along with a big deck cargo sliding along the edge of the Race. Them bulwarks was fine as long as nothing got over the top of them, but once it did, by God, it was damn hard to get rid of what you didn't want. She didn't have much for scuppers. 'Freeing ports'? What's that? We called them all scuppers: holes in the bulwarks that let out deck water. We didn't call some of them 'freeing ports.' That sounds like a draggerman's name. We just called everything that was like something else, that you used for the same purpose, we called that thing by the same name. That way we didn't have a lot of extra names lying around to trip over.

"Seems so to me Pappy spent the first half of the war chugging along out there redistributing that coal that should have been distributed to all three forts by the government in the first place. Hey, it was his part of the war effort at twenty-five tons a trip, and although there was German submarines out there in the Race they didn't bother taking a pop at him.

"*Emma Frances* also carried coal to Gardiners Island, cordwood and cow manure to Fishers Island. Manure running had been a big business over at Halyoake Farms, though we wasn't the one who done that. Like Stell Adams said, Halyoake Farm manure came in big barges from New York City. When we run manure, we dumped the manure right onto the deck. One night at Harrison's Landing as we were getting ready to go to Fishers Island the next morning, the *Emma Frances* got her gunnel hung up on the pier at low tide and as the tide rose she began to tilt over and of course, all the manure slid to one side, which made the situation worse.

"There was a fellow living aboard, and when the water started to run in on him, he woke up and gave a shout. I was up at the house and I came running down to the pier and was going to start shoveling the stuff overboard. I was so excited I jumped down off the pier onto the deck where it was deepest and went into the manure damn near up to my neck. We eventually got straightened away, shoveled enough off into the water so she straightened up and we pumped her out. The next day we went off to Fishers Island with what was left of the load. The cow manure had filled in the deck seams pretty good so she didn't leak. As for the smell, well, cow manure is the sweetest stuff. Sure a lot sweeter than a pile of oyster shells with bits of oyster meat stuck here and there in the shell and then the hot sun.

"I don't know how Pappy got permission to bring anything over to Fishers Island. Ferguson of Fishers Island Farms pretty much had all that sort of thing sewed up. You couldn't land anything on Fishers without his say-so. I don't suppose that gasoline and manure were exactly the cream of the freight.

"Maybe the prettiest thing we ever freighted was the bandstand from Fishers Island, which we pushed across the Sound up to Mystic Seaport on a crane barge with *Alice*. It's now the centerpiece of their Village Green up there and they do have cornet concerts and sea chanteys and picnics and demonstrations in it and all around it."

· · ·

Socony was a small tanker of some seventy-five feet with a capacity of some ten thousand gallons and had more in common with a submarine than it did with, say, *Exxon Valdez*. A one-man submarine at that. It was long and skinny like a submarine and had a tiny wheelhouse like a submarine conning tower except it was way back—an afterthought that was just barely catching up with the rest of the operation. One of the differences between *Socony* and a submarine was that it ran a lot lower in the water than any submarine I'd seen operating inside Fishers Island Sound. The cambered deck was awash to such an alarming degree that whenever I saw it out in the Sound, my stomach sank. I remember passing this wallowing hulk one day when I was young and crying out the alarm to my father. I thought it might be a whale breaching. Closer in I thought it was a Japanese submarine left over from World War Two. (It was the era when the draggermen were picking up unexploded torpedoes.) As we came alongside, the little man in the wheelhouse grimaced out the tiny window. He seemed trapped in there with the whirling helm like Rumplestiltskin caged with his spinning wheel run amok.

The grimace may be a later retrieved memory, because I had the good fortune to know Captain George Sanford when he served aboard the town Shell Fish Commission. By then he was known as "Captain Monday" because he was running the last coal-fired, steam-powered passenger vessel in the United States: *Sabino* out of Mystic Seaport. Sina Wright was working in Personnel the day he came in to get his name tag. She typed onto the formal identification badge the day of the week that he was scheduled to run the boat. "There was just something about George Sanford," she told me at his funeral, "that made you want to go along with a prank like that."

George Sanford was famous for his kindness to animals and was once appointed local chairman of Be Kind To Animals Week. He had rescued a dog from the icy waters of the Thames River, brought him aboard *Socony*, wrapped him in his pea jacket, and given him sandwiches. After a vain attempt to find the dog's owner, Sanford kept the dog aboard his ship for some dozen years as "crew," citing the dog's ability to sniff out land and buoys, "a valuable and comical shipmate." Sanford himself had survived an earlier heart attack in *Socony*'s wheelhouse while running alone from New Haven to New London. "There I was," he told me. "all alone in that little wheelhouse, halfway between New Haven and New London making about six knots in half a gale. I just had to tough it out." And he flashed that grimace, which along with his overall build and cap made him look like Edward G. Robinson in *The Sea Wolf*.

Watch Hill Passage, which figures in Malloy's following *Socony* narration, is the inside way into Long Island Sound and is the site of many a fatal wreck. In Watch Hill, down by the carousel and the ice cream shops, The Book and Tackle Shop does a brisk trade in books and postcards depicting some of these "harrowing tales." The gaudiest is the old paddle wheeler *Larchmont* with a loss of life in the high hundreds on February 11, 1907. The ship sank right at the split in the current, and half the bodies went up on the beach by the great old hotel on the cliff; the others drifted out to Block Island, where they washed up a week later. More recently, and found on nobody's postcard, is the death of a father and son coming in on the same course from Block Island.

Socony's port of call, the Hog Pen, is a deep but narrow slot up at the head of the New Harbor on Block Island around back of the big steamer dock known as "Payne's." It is a wonderful hurricane hole, a hideaway. My father used to put his Friendship sloop up in there with her bowsprit over the road. The place has long held an attraction. Anthropologist Kevin MacBride has discovered early remnants of a shellfishing civilization there that predates the sack of Troy. Nowadays the Hog Pen is considered too ecologically fragile for most mooring purposes.

Putting a tow "on the hip" means to take it alongside and lash it to the towing boat for greater maneuverability in tight waters. In the open sea, the towing boat has to get away from the tow so that they don't smash into each other on the swells and so goes on the "long hawser."

. . .

"I don't know if you'd count this as *freighting*, but we had a job towing a tanker. That would be the *Socony*, captained by my brother-in-law George Sanford. If we only done it once that might be considered *salvage*, but since we kept doing it on her regular schedule, seems so to me it got to be more like *freighting*.

"We done that, whatever it was, with *Alice*, towed the tanker *Socony*, about half a dozen times between New London and Block Island before they figured maybe they needed a new engine. We'd have her on the long tow, then as we come into New Harbor we'd have to heave on the hawser to shorten up and put her on the hip. We didn't have any of those hawser-heaving winch drums you see on the big tugs nowadays. We had hand over hand on the cold, wet line. There was just enough room to get her by Payne's Dock and up into the Hog Pen that way. Going out, we'd reverse that.

"Only problem was on this particular night our own engine broke down on *Alice*. Percy MacDonald, he's the engineer from the tanker, but since the only engine that's working in this operation is aboard *Alice*, he's with me. Now we didn't call him 'Percy,' because who would have even thought of 'Percy'? We called him 'Mac.' Norman Bray was aboard of *Socony*. He's brother to Ray Bray, the shellfish warden. George Sanford, he wasn't on that particular trip. So now we got two boats tied together off Watch Hill Passage with no engine.

"We was coming back from Block, so the tanker she was empty which made her a bit more frisky. It was getting dark. I say it was getting dark, but it was so foggy maybe it wasn't really dark. We was just off the entrance through the Watch Hill Passage into Fishers Island Sound. It's not the best place to be when something like that happens, and we was on the wrong side as far as the open ocean goes. Fortunately it was pancake calm. What had happened is that the engine on *Alice* started racing. It was that 120-horsepower Kermeth. I slowed her down and took the cover off the gear box. Everything in there was flopping around. The bolts had sheered off the reverse gear. I've got a picture of that engine and could show you every-thing that happened. I'd have to do that with just showing you the engine because as far as the view of Watch Hill and all the rest outside was con-cerned, well, there wasn't any—not that I would have had much time to enjoy it, as I had my head in the engine.

"There wasn't much point in trying to figure out what was happening up on deck like navigating anyway because I couldn't have done anything about it. I kept at the part that was where I could do something about it. We looked around and found some bolts. Bolts was very important that night.

Some had round heads. Some had square heads. Some had no heads at all. By four in the morning we had fixed it up. Enough to continue on through the Watch Hill Passage and into Fishers Island Sound and back to New London. In fact it was such a good repair that we forgot all about it for the next few weeks until the oil company, they decided maybe *Socony* should get her own engine.

"As for that night, if indeed it was night, we kept working with the jury rig that was just meant to keep us off the beach. What we were looking around for, like I said, wasn't no reefs. We looked around for some bolts. I guess you could say that was *freighting*."

NOTE

CAPTAIN MONDAY (p. 161): Sina Wright tells the story behind the name. "A child who was a passenger aboard the Mystic Seaport's steamboat *Sabino* asked George Sanford what a 're-lief captain' was, and he replied that he drove the boat on Monday. The child began to call him 'Captain Monday.' The name stuck. When George came to the office to obtain a new badge, I'd heard the story about the child and, out of respect for a very kind and honest man, I typed him up two badges, one saying George Sanford, the other Captain Monday. He took both, but usually wore the Captain Monday while in the wheelhouse of *Sabino*. Years later when he retired he was probably known to more people as Captain Monday than by his real name."

A WORKBOATMAN'S COURTSHIP

Bring with you all the Nymphes that you can heare

Both of the rivers and the forrests greene:

And of the sea that neighbours to her neare,

—Edmund Spenser, "Epithalamion"

A landsman can keep away from the sea indefinitely, whereas a

seafarer cannot long remain from shore.

—Elmo P. Hohman, *Seamen Ashore*

As is common in trades that are in some ways isolated from the larger community, marriages tend to take place within the trade. The name of Captain George Sanford has come up in this narrative a number of times, as has that of Captain Frank Staplin. Both were well known to Larry Malloy before the marriages that made both men his in-laws. George Sanford married Larry's sister and Larry married Frank Staplin's daughter. The story Larry Malloy tells about the *Catskill* in the Great Hurricane is a yarn of the sort heard around the kitchen table at Harrison's Landing. It illustrates not only the fury of the storm but its impact on Larry Malloy's inner circle, as well as the sort of bonding down through the years that making a living on the water can produce. By way of contrast, one thinks of the sort of motivational stunts that desk-bound corporations cook up to put their sedentary staff through: weekend "retreats" where officemates have to belay each other up and down small, carefully chosen cliffs in order to build trust and teamwork.

Frank Staplin, who figures so intimately in the following, was not only Larry Malloy's future father-in-law, he was also the Captain Frank for whom the McGugans named their dredge barge. Originally the MuGugans were going to name it for Gwen McGugan, the matriarch, but she said, "I don't want people to say, 'I was going by Water Street and saw Gwen up on the ways getting her bottom scraped.'" The story is that Captain Frank, the man, in his old age was not permitted by his wife to listen to the baseball games at home. He survived by walking the three blocks downhill to the Mystic River waterfront. There the McGugans would allow him to hang out in their dredging office and listen to the games. "To tell you the truth," said Sandy McGugan one day, "I think the old guy was just looking for an excuse to get out of the house. Hell, we were glad to help him."

In our age of "combining career and family, family values, etc." Larry's relationship with his in-laws might demonstrate a contrasting paradigm. Another anomaly in these days is noting the year and make of the car, a characteristic Larry shares with my father, both of whom were always very proud of their vehicles and often dated their various other activities by the car they had at the time. The car defined their era.

It is also interesting to note how sixty years later Larry recalls in passing the month and year of ship master Clarence Sherman's demise. This truly is what Conrad would call "the fellowship of the craft."

. . .

"Pete's Neck, where we lay at Halyoake Farm, seemed a long way from Greenport, which is now just five or ten minutes by car. Nobody in them days, especially nobody workin' oysters much, had the luxury of a car. And Frank Staplin, he needed a job while he was waiting around for the *Catskill* to get ready for her season. *Catskill,* she was a steam ferry that ran from New London to Orient Point. In those days they didn't run the ferry all year. We shut down oystering May 1, and that was just right for Frank Staplin because he was the mate and pilot under Captain Clarence Sherman, master from Shelter Island. Captain Sherman passed away in November 1939.

"It might seem funny that one minute Frank is working as a cook on an oysterboat, the next as pilot of a ferry without having done nothing in between to upgrade himself. You didn't worry if you was a cook or a captain or what as long as you was workin' somewhere near where you lived. You didn't go too far for a job, and the title of the job wasn't all that important. You couldn't eat titles, and as far as building up a resume by titles, hey people in the business knew what you done whatever you called it. As for the pay, there wasn't all that much difference in what you did on the boats.

For instance, when I was captain of an oysterboat for Elijah Ball, the mate got fourteen dollars a week. I got fifteen dollars a week, a dollar more for the privilege of drivin' the boat. In that kind of job having a license didn't rate you more pay because you didn't even need a license to run an oyster-boat. You didn't need a license unless you was carrying passengers for hire. A lot of the captains picked one up anyway in case something came along: you know, like running somebody else's boat, a freighter or a ferry, like Frank Staplin done.

"With Captain Frank, our cook, leaving, I get assigned his job. Now, I'm not only decking on *Anne,* but I got to do the cooking for three: my dad, George Hildebrand, myself. After breakfast I pack three lunches to take with us out on the bay oystering.

"Our product [oysters] we sold to Mr. Fagan [Fagan Trucking] and we un-loaded from *Virginia* and onto his truck at Halyoake Potato House wharf.

"I finally thought I was doing a little more than my share. Had a short discussion with Dad and packed my few belongings in my 1928 Buick for a lengthy trip home, via the length of Long Island, Bronx Whitestone Bridge, and Route One North, arriving in Mystic (12 Latham Street) early morning (two or three A.M.). There was no place to sleep, so I had to get in bed with Captain Frank, who was later my father-in-law. He just grunted and rolled over. Hey, those days there weren't all these fold-out couches and guest rooms. It was either Captain Frank or the floor.

"In the morning Captain Frank told me to see Captain McClaran if I wanted a job for the summer on the *Catskill.*

"You might wonder why *Catskill* was still afloat after the Hurricane. Well, on September 21, 1938, *Catskill* made an uneventful trip to Orient Point. Edith Staplin, Captain Frank's daughter, was waitress aboard *Catskill* on that trip and all these years later says she will never forget that day. Pre-paring to return to New London, the crew realized something was going to happen with the weather. By the time they had passed through Plum Gut, they decided not to continue on to New London. They chose to come left and run before the wind up Long Island Sound toward New York City, a hundred miles away. They dropped the anchor part way to the bottom, hoping that by towing it, they might to try to steady the boat and keep her from broaching, rolling over sidewise like a barrel. In other words, make a kind of sea anchor. But, of course, with a *sea anchor,* you don't actually *an-chor,* or at least you're not supposed to. You just drag something behind you that will slow you down, like a bucket or some warps or a sail. It ain't supposed to get down on the bottom and fetch up, and, of course, most of the time you're doing this you're way the hell out to sea where the bottom is out of the picture. Or at least so I'm told because I've always managed to stay out of those kind of situations where the bottom ain't part of the picture. Anyway, out there on Long Island Sound that day in 1938 aboard the *Catskill* they paid the anchor out too far, and it hung up on the bottom. The ship jerked and the chain soon parted. With just enough power to keep steerage, she blew all the way past Faulkner's Island. That's twenty-five miles to leeward of their original course as the crow flies, and it wasn't until Faulkner's Island before they dare turn her and head back to New London. When they got there everyone aboard was amazed to see the destruction that this storm had done in New London. Arriving in the early evening, they found the only place suitable to moor at was the Spicer Coal pier just south of the swing bridge on the Groton [east] side of the river.

"So since *Catskill* was still afloat, I was hired on May 25, 1939, as a deck-hand, and on Saturdays as quartermaster. That is, I not only took a turn at the wheel when we was running routine from buoy to buoy out in open water, but I was, as quartermaster, asked to handle the helm when we was coming into the dock at either end.

"The wheelhouse on all them ferries was in the center of the boat, and you couldn't see what you was doing when you come alongside the dock, so she had chain pulls on each wing of her bridge. That is, narrow boxes that were alongside the rail and that come up to your waist with a chain inside and a handle on the end of the chain. When you'd get her lined up about right coming into the slip the captain would step out on the wing and ring down his bells to the engine room on those chain pulls. The bell would ring in the engine room and signal the engineer forward, reverse, neutral, full speed, dead in the water—whatever. I'd be left back in the wheelhouse and he'd signal me with a whistle which way to shift the helm. One whistle: turn to port; two whistles, turn to starboard; three whistles, put her amidships. So you got like they say today: *all the bells and whistles.* Problem is all those chains were exposed at some points in their run down to the engine room and every once in a while somebody'd reach up from below and give them a yank and send the wrong message to the engine room. I always wondered why the steamboat inspectors didn't object to that.

"*Catskill* was a steam-powered, 500 horsepower, 652 gross tons, car and passenger ferry plying from New London to Orient Point, Long Island, from May to September. For the hell of it—being young and full of beans and just quit of the Old Man—I decided one day to show off a bit. I grabbed a shovel when *Catskill* was away from the dock in New London and began heaving coal into the boiler. I figured anybody who could shovel oyster shells all day in the hot sun up on deck ought to be able to heave a lit-tle coal down there in the shade. I lasted from Ocean Beach to about half-way to Plum Gut.

"I signed off *Catskill* on September 11, 1939. Reluctantly I agreed to go back to work for Captain Lawrence H. Malloy, Sr.

"By then the Old Man had another boat, the *Let's Go*. She was a good deal bigger than *Anne*, being sixty-five feet. I was just as glad I had nothing to do with her. She had a flywheel that was a foot wide on the rim and turned 150 r.p.m. To reverse her you had to grab the spokes and wrestle her back the other way. On deck she had a potato boom that was twice as long as the mast was high and ran from the mast, which was up in the eyes of the boat, clear aft to just ahead of the wheelhouse. He run shells with her but didn't catch oysters. She was pretty tired. Going around Point Jude one day he went below to rest and leaned back against one of the ribs and it gave way and water came in.

"After a few weeks of living aboard *Anne* I decided there must be something better. With the help of an aunt I found an apartment on Second Street, in Greenport. Now, however, I needed a cook and housekeeper. I made a journey to Mystic, Connecticut, and on October 29, 1939, married Captain Frank's daughter Helen."

. . .

"Maybe I should go back a little and explain how I think I impressed Helen into marrying me, what you might call our *courting*. Captain Cornelius Rose—we called him Captain Neil, he had the schooner *Aunt Edie* out of Block Island. He would bring cod or whatever the catch was that day, in from Block Island. *Aunt Edie,* she had a live well in her, that is, in the midst of her hull she had, bulkheaded off, a big box with holes through the bottom of the hull so's raw seawater would come through, but not get into the rest of the boat. This was typical of them schooners in those days, and the smaller lobster boats was all rigged that way too in the time before you had circulating pumps and all this refrigeration.

"We had the oyster shop on the City Pier in New London and I got to watching Captain Neil and the *Aunt Edie*. He'd come in off the pier two or three times a day to warm his fingers. He bought some shellfish from us, but it was his business in used automobiles that grabbed my interest. There weren't many cars on Block Island then, and what Captain Neil would do was purchase jalopies in New London and run them down to the City Pier. We'd help him shove out a couple of planks onto the deck of *Aunt Edie*. On the Island he could get twenty-five dollars for most anything that would run off the planks at the other end. Well, one day he shows up with this Stutz Bearcat, 1928. This was in 1936. He'd bought it from a doctor down in Westerly, Rhode Island, which meant that it had run at least that far, which was over twenty miles down Route One. He caught me drooling over it. 'Hey, I'll take that to Block Island,' he says. 'I'll get a *fortune* for her.'

"'OK,' I sez, 'but just in case there's a problem, keep me in mind.' You see the whole while I was drooling over that Stutz I also was measuring her with my eye. What Captain Neil usually done is rig them cars athwartships, and what with that long hood on the Bearcat, I know that in this case the *usual story* just might be a problem. He waited for high water so the Stutz could go right straight across from the pier to the *Aunt Edie.* I was eager to help him rig the planks because I wanted to be right there when he found out that this time the car was going to be too long. We get the Stutz about halfway across them planks to the schooner and even Captain Neil he could see that the car was going to be hanging off both sides of the schooner. You got some pretty bumpy water outside the Watch Hill Passage on your way out to Block Island, and you could see it come to Captain Neil in a flash—all that salt water was pretty much going to put the damper on making this *fortune* he was talking about out of the Stutz. He turns to me and says, "I see you looking at this car. How bad do you need it?"

"About twenty-five dollars worth."

"Sold."

We pushed her back up the planks onto the pier, and I run into the oyster shop and said to Pappy, "Give me twenty-five dollars advance."

This was 1936, the same year I finally actually got my driver's license. So next thing I know I'm off to courting Captain Frank's daughter, Helen Staplin, who's staying out at some farm in the Hope Valley of Rhode Island. Now even these days that ain't exactly the most advanced area in the country. Back there in the thirties it was pretty much what you'd call Appalachia. So here I come flying down the hill into the village that's called Wyoming and there's a bunch of locals hanging around the street corner at night and the Stutz is getting a little overexcited and goes into a slide as I try to brake her. We go into a fishtail U-turn and fetch up right there in a cloud of dust in the midst of all those yokels like I done all that on purpose. There was hardly any cars at all in that town, let alone a Stutz Bearcat being driven by a maniac. Everybody gathered round. Of course 'everybody' in a place like that wasn't very many and what with the size of the back seat in that Bearcat, you could have got them all in there. For sure they never see anything like it.

"She got to be running pretty rough, so I contacted Bob McFee, a mechanic who I knew. Bob took the Stutz to his place, which was up on top of Logger Hill in the Graniteville section of Waterford, the next town over from New London. In a few days, after a valve job and a tune-up, all for seventy-six dollars, she was as good as new. It's a good thing gasoline was only nine cents a gallon.

"Of course once I got lined up to get married I knew I couldn't keep a car like that so I traded it in for a Hudson Essex, what they called a Terraplane. That Terraplane had some severe problems and only lasted me two weeks. I turned it in on a 1928 Buick.

NOTE

TERRAPLANE (p. 170): The Terraplane was a low-priced, conservatively modern sedan offered by the Hudson Motor Company from 1933 to 1938. It was the successor to their Essex and sported a remarkably efficient 6-cylinder 70 horsepower engine. It was designed by Britisher Reid Railton and had a top speed of 88 miles per hour!" (Stephen C. La Vere, *Robert Johnson: The Complete Recordings*). In addition to bluesman Robert Johnson and Larry Malloy, the Terraplane claimed my father's attention. The Terraplane was notorious for its fibroid timing gear and left many a conservatively modern driver in strange surroundings.

20

PARKING AND SHUCKING

Thus a seaman's entire career, whether on land or at sea, is

made up of a never-ending series of adjustments.

—Elmo P. Hohman, *Seamen Ashore*

THE MULTITASKING OF the old waterman is gone forever. The Army Corps has more boats than the Navy. Every college or university now has its own research boat. What is left is prevented by the restrictions of licensing, either of the master or the boat itself. The question always is, in these ancillary duties, just how far ashore can one get and yet be a waterman? This sensitivity to shore duty, however, does not seem to be part of Larry Malloy's makeup. He will wax as eloquently upon his days "In Housing" as upon those in oystering. In fact at first I did not even realize what "housing" was; it was maintenance in a "project." One day in exasperation Larry said of the "housing" job, "That was no job; that was an education."

"An education in what?"

"Oh, Jesus, you don't want to know. The way some people live. I mean we was always poor, but . . ." He thought a moment. "Mainly *language*. Some of them women could tell you places you never seen."

All of this I guess goes under the general discussion of the Romance of the Waterman's Life and the way in which the water part serves as inspiration, or maybe does not. It may be a class thing. It may be a Depression thing. Obviously if a man is going hungry he is not so romantically inclined. A job is a job. The old Irish proverb quoted by Frank McCort says, "After the full belly, all the rest is poetry." If subsistence is not the immediate issue, then identity maybe becomes the point. If I am on my hands and knees scrubbing a toilet, I am at the bottom of the totem pole. If, however, that toilet is on a vessel or even, as with the plumbing at Boat Haven, a waterfront facility, then at least I am above all those lubbers, from custodians all the way up to CEOs (who still dream of running away to sea). In any case, I am a long way off from confronting Larry with this in such stark terms. Even English teachers are on guard to protect their romanticism. As with God and other loves, you have to sneak up on it.

Of course war and the preparations for war are traditionally one way of solving the problem of making work romantic. William James's 1910 essay "The Moral Equivalent of War" was written in the wake of Teddy Roosevelt's "splendid little war" and could just as easily have been called "The Aesthetic Equivalent of War." The 1898 forts of which Larry speaks below include Fort Mansfield down on Napatree Point on the Rhode Island border, and the three forts strung along the New York islands in the Race: Fort H. G. Wright, Fishers Island; Fort Michie, Great Gull Island; Fort Terry, Plum Island.

· · ·

"This is 1940 going into 1941.

"There were already forts on the islands. I used to think they was set up against the Germans or the British, but when we went to work out there the sewer covers said 1898 on them so that must have been for the Spanish American War. There's a bow gun off the flagship of the Spanish American War up on Fort Griswold over here on the mainland in Groton. I don't think that ship actually got this far, but it shows you how we was worried. Seems so we've always been worried somebody was going to be sneaking up on us from off of them islands."

"We were starting to build up greatly. Business in the area picked up rapidly.

"Father with *Virginia* started freighting building material to the forts for the U.S. Army Corps of Engineers. I was only on the boats occasionally as I was working in a parking garage. That may sound funny, but I was making good money at the garage with Mr. George Young.

"How all this happened was the oyster shop and George Young. He was one of the many people who stopped by the oyster shop. Some of the people who stopped by were, well, New London being New London, especially down by the water, they tended to be some odd people. George Young, he was more of what you might call a *normal* man. In fact since I'd been working there in the oyster shop as a kid, George Young was maybe the most normal man I'd met. Because we had a delivery route that went way out to the lighthouse by Ocean Beach and sometimes I went on that, Mr. Young, he knew I could handle vehicles. He'd also seen me drive all those strangers' vehicles off the *Catskill* when I was a deckhand. You couldn't let the passengers park the cars on *Catskill*. We used to park each car because, hey, that ship hadn't been designed for cars. She'd been a sugar carrier up on the Hudson River and had all those stanchions holding up the deckhouse. You had to work the cars in around those stanchions. Mr. Young, he used to come down to the ferry slip when we come in and hawk his wares. *'Hey, come to my parking garage! That other guy, he ain't got a good garage.'* You know, like a circus barker.

"I agreed to pay of sixteen dollars per week. My first pay envelope I opened and found eighteen dollars. I went to Mr. Young and told him that he had made a mistake. He told me that he had made mistakes in the past, but never with money. He said that what I find in my pay envelope is mine. My pay went up several times after that.

"You might figure it's odd for a fellow who just got his boat license to think it was a big deal to work in a parking garage. Back in them days you took any job you could get. Who wanted a boatman? Who was there? My father. A couple of others. Stop and think about it. There was few fishing party boats, and they had their own crew. Cars in those days were pretty interesting, too. Especially to someone my age. I do suppose though that if I'd stuck it out in the garage we wouldn't be having this conversation. But, you know, having that master's license made it easier when I did eventually go to my hundred-ton and my uninspected vessel towing. I didn't have to serve a hundred years on a square rigger.

"You have to understand I ran all over the place looking for a job—Electric Boat, Dart and Bogue, a car dealer—I was living on the hill in Mystic with my in-laws. At least I wasn't sleeping in the same bed as my father-in-law anymore. The most nautical thing I got on was washing dishes on the *Yale,* a ferry to Orient Point. That is, unless you count cording wood with the old man on Gardiners Island, working for my father with my brothers and with my mom as cook.

"I didn't get back into oystering until I met Mr. Elijah Ball, the man who run the whole middle of the state coastline from the Connecticut River to New Haven as far as oyster grounds went. As a matter of fact, his nephew, Ernest E. Ball, still has a lot of them grounds under the name of Certified Shellfish, a company that he runs out of Virginia Beach, Virginia. Elijah Ball was famous as owner of the Thimble Island Oyster Company of Stony Creek, Branford, Connecticut. I'm working in the garage, and Mr. Elijah Ball he opens the trunk of his car. 'You know who I am?' he says.

"Well, I ain't sure quite who the hell *he* is, but, of course, I do know what it is I'm looking at. It's September, ain't it, and I know that's when we start catching oyster set, and that's the part I tell him.

"'That's right,' he says.

"He had a sample of oyster seed that he was taking to Long Island on the ferry to show other oystermen.

"My father's running materials out to the fort. When Elijah Ball comes back from Long Island, he says, 'You want to work for me? I talked to your father. He says take *Anne* up Stony Creek and catch some more of this set.'

"'Well,' says I, 'I'm going to have to talk to Mr. George Young. He's been very good to me.'"

. . .

"I thought this would be a good move. Working in the parking garage had been a good deal; working for Elijah Ball was an even better deal. Mr. Ball, he paid Pappy forty dollars a week for the use of *Anne,* and Pappy said I could keep that plus I got fifty dollars a week direct from Elijah Ball to run her so that ninety dollars was a lot of money when you consider sixteen or eighteen dollars was the average a week on land. And working oysterboats before, the most I ever got was twenty-four dollars for a week of six days.

"So September 1, 1941, I headed for the Thimble Islands with *Anne.*

"Mr. Ball furnished the crew of five men. *Anne* caught two loads a day, 550 bushels in the morning; 450 in the afternoon. The morning load would be put aboard one of two schooners: *Gear,* and *S. Sage,* Captain Clary Morris. Our old friend from Halyoake Potato Farm, the *Charles W. Lynne,* Captain John Monsell, would come out at noon to offload what we had from the morning so we didn't even have to come in off the grounds. So you see, even in them days, you had *efficiency.* The afternoon load we held aboard *Anne* until next morning, when it went aboard one of the schooners.

"As the season progressed, Mr. Ball offered me a job in the oyster shop. It was in the wash and packing room. That was what happened after the seed had been caught up and transported. I delivered *Anne* back to Harrison's Landing and headed down to Stony Brook by vehicle, about an hour down Route One toward New York. I already had a small cottage next to the oyster shop.

"My duties were to keep all equipment clean, wash oysters, pack in cans (pints and half-pints) that we run through a machine that put covers and dates on each can. I was to keep track of the cleanliness of the oyster shuckers—the people who done the shucking—keep track of the ice, and package oysters—in general everything to do with getting the product ready for shipping. All product was shipped to A & P Company, Youngstown, Ohio.

"One day I see this shucker out of the corner of my eye. He's going to get a drink of water every few minutes. Shucking's hard work on the hands. You get paid by the pint. What he's doing to fill out the pint is spitting a mouthful of water into the container. *Topping it off,* you might say. It was my job to see stuff like that didn't happen. I had my eye on him. Over he goes to the spigot, gets a mouthful. You know if he'd just run the water in directly from the spigot it wouldn't have been so bad. Maybe he thought he was *filtering* it by running it through his mouth. We fired him.

"Howard Sheppard was foreman for Mr. Ball. His duties were to pick up oyster shuckers in New Haven, transport them to Stony Creek and back to New Haven at day's end, and also truck oysters to the railroad station in Stony Creek for shipment. Shep also took care of all maintenance and made sure things got done.

"In those days you had regular freight trains stopping at all these little coastal towns to pick up fish. You take Noank with all them barrels of lobsters heading down to the Fulton Market every day. When the Amtrak got up this high-speed rail idea between New York and Boston recently they was pretty annoyed at the rails running around all these bends between New Haven and Rhode Island. They made a lot of cracks about quaint Yankees and their ins and outs with the trains. Them Amtrak electrifiers must have forgot why the train ran that way in the first place. They must have forgot that all that shellfish freight was what paid the way for them those years.

"It so happened that Mr. Ball decided to turn Mrs. Ball's 1936 Club Coupe in on a new Buick for her. Through his generosity, I finally wound up with her car. I still have pictures.

"Just after the war was declared the wife and I, we was living in that little cottage down at Stony Creek belonged to Elijah Ball Oyster Company. We was just preparing to go home for Christmas to Harrison's Landing, forty miles to the eastward on Route One. I noticed the cylinder head of my 1935 Buick was cracked. Water was pouring out of it. In those days we used to drain radiators to keep them from freezing until we could afford to buy the antifreeze. What we had was alcohol. You'd go blind if you drank it. Unless you did something to it, but hey, I never messed with things that required much chemistry. The block was full of sludge that evidently didn't let all the water drain out so she cracked between the valve stems; she was an overhead. It was snowing, and Mr. Ball he looks out the window and sees we're having trouble so he gets in his car and drives my wife and me to Route One where we planned to catch a bus to come home. That wasn't so crazy in them days. You had things like decent public transportation. But this time it was snowing pretty good by then, and the bus was late. We were about to give up when a delivery truck—I think it was a bread truck—in those days bread trucks stopped at the house—the bread truck stopped for us standing by the road. Maybe he thought we was looking for some buns. He picked us up and took us to Madison where we knew Mrs. Parde who owned a restaurant in town. She let us stay inside out of the cold until the bus finally came, and we did get home. It seemed like a dream. This whole trip all in your own car would take less than an hour now.

"You might not think that was much of a thing for your boss to do, giving you a hitch up to the main road, but getting up from the Creek to Route One seemed the hard part of the trip in them days. For him to have taken us all the way the forty miles to the Landing and then for him to come back the same forty miles in a snowstorm was certainly something that I would never expect. Just to be looking out the window after us in the snow and come to help us—well, here I am remembering it as a kindness all these years later. Things were different back then. The spaces between the places seemed different and the spaces between people. Both were further away, yet somehow in ways that meant something, maybe they was closer.

"After Christmas and we'd had a chance to settle down, I checked out the cylinder head crack in my car. It looked hopeless. I went up to Branard's Garage in Stony Creek and explained my dilemma. Mr. Branard took a can of X Welder off a shelf, handed it to me and said, 'Your problem is solved.' He was so right. After I gave her the treatment as per instructions, I could see within minutes the crack sealing up. Never had a bit of trouble after that until months later. Of course, I didn't put in antifreeze. The only problem was that I knew the crack was there. A few months later the crack did let go and fortunately it was then that Mrs. Ball's Buick showed up. I did think though that Mrs. Ball really wanted her car back. She kept telling me how much she missed it.

"My position with Mr. Ball was not only operating boats and taking charge of washing and racking oysters. When not needed in the shop—because of the end of oyster-opening season—I would do maintenance, like tarring shop roofs, gardening, mowing lawns, being watchman, helping with oyster shell planting, staking out grounds, etc. All the things you needed to do from one end to another to keep an oyster operation going. I worked for the Balls for a year and a half. Then things got slow and what with the war now on, I knew my number was coming up."

21

A WORKBOATMAN'S WAR

THE COMPLETE STORY of the inshore coastal defenses of World War Two has yet to be compiled. As a small boy I lived in a house on Fishers Island Sound that my grandfather had bought for $8,000 because the 1938 Hurricane had destroyed half the front porch, the previous owner had hung himself in the linen closet, and the Germans were expected every day on the beach. Each morning I'd climb down off the broken porch onto that collection of kelp, grit, cobbles, roofing slate, and sea glass and look for things that might have happened because of the Germans.

There were indeed strange remnants of packing cases with odd writing. On the horizon our warships stood moored off Avery Point, ten miles away. There were destroyers, cruisers, and small aircraft carriers. There were days when our windows shook with the whack of heavy artillery. I would run inside and hide, but in a way it was worse inside because of the danger from the windows. My grandfather, fearing that our shaking windows would break, urged us back from the glass and snatched the blackout curtains tight. We all thought that this was caused by the gunfire of the great ships. It wasn't until I met Larry Malloy years later that I found out why our window panes rattled.

· · ·

"At the end of 1942 Captain Thomas E. Watt contacted me about a job with the U.S. Army Water Transportation Corps. I had known Tom since 1936 or before. He was an oysterman and an all-round boatman. A Jibboomer who'd gotten his time aboard Vermont Central vessels. He wanted me to help him out aboard the *T-11*. The *T* in that was for targets. Our job was to tow targets for the gunners at Fort Wright on the west end of Fishers Island at the Race. The idea was these gunners weren't too good yet and needed practice so they could hit what they were shooting at. If we didn't get sunk doing that, we were also to deliver mail, supplies, personnel, etc.

"Tom was the skipper. I took the job of deckhand (seaman). When the engineer was transferred to another position on July 28, 1943, I was assigned to be the engineer/deckhand, first watch. This brought my pay up to two thousand per year, for the times, not bad money. Unlike on the *Virginia,* the engine was controlled from the bridge, so as "engineer" all you had to do underway was duck below once an hour and check your gauges. The job was three days on, three days off. Some of the days were very long—like twenty-four hours.

"We took care of the needs of those three forts out on the New York islands: Fort Wright, Fort Michie on Great Gull, and Fort Terry on Plum Island. Fort Michie was the hardest to land at due to its pier being wide open to the north with a fetch of some half-dozen miles all the way from the New London shore. We were often unable to land on our first attempt, so mail and supplies were a few days late. Fortunately everybody involved understood this. Hell, they was all looking at the same water we was.

"The *T-11* was a wooden hull, sixty-five feet in length. She was well equipped, having living space and a galley. When we lay at Silver Eel Pond at Fort Wright, even though we had plenty of food aboard, we had the right to eat at the mess halls on the post. This was very handy, and it saved our food. Several times we shared our food with the target detail if we were out on station in Block Island Sound during mealtime. Eventually the detail would replace the food. It was a good deal for us aboard *T-11* because they always gave us more than we had loaned them.

"We was to tow a target for the gunners on Fort Wright, who had sixteen-inchers—which could throw a projectile maybe, they said, eighteen miles. We usually worked, of course, much closer, maybe four miles off to the south of Fort Wright over off Fort Michie.

"One day they wanted us to just go around Fishers Island to see if they could track us. We headed out through the Race and run down the back of the island as close as we could and come in through Lords Passage and back up through the Sound. Well, damned if they claimed we'd never done any of that. 'You couldn't have done that,' the officer says, 'or we'd have tracked you on the radar.' I told him I thought the point of us doing it was to see *if* they could track us on the radar, and I showed him our log where we'd put down our time for all our way stations. *The log don't lie.* Of course the pencil can, but what would have been the point of that? We *wanted* them to be able to track us. Hell, they was our protection out there, wasn't they? If we could get around the island without being seen, hey, anybody could have done it. And the Germans are a lot smarter than we were. If it weren't for the Germans, we'd be rowing. Diesel, I mean. What ever happened to him, anyway? You say he disappeared overboard one night crossing the English Channel going to England. He must have drunk some of his own fuel oil.

"The target was a canvas diamond shape about eight foot high set up on a ten-by-ten-foot-square float. We had an inch-and-a-quarter manila hawser we let out to eighteen hundred feet. The idea was not for the guns actually to hit the target. They were supposed to bracket one shell over the target, one under, one on each side. Another idea was that they should not actually hit the towboat, either.

"There were six to eight soldiers aboard to handle the hawser. I was mainly in the wheelhouse steering. Tommy, he kind of kept an eye on things and took over the helm when I had to duck below to check the gauges on the eight-cylinder straight Superior. We had one of them big radios you had back then and probably should have had a radioman on board because everything was in code; you know, "Charlie" and "Baker" and "Able"—all them folk. We wasn't up on that. Nevertheless, we usually managed to figure it out anyway. After all, these were waters we was used to working in and once you got the hang of the routine, there wasn't much variation as far as what the people at the fort wanted out of you and only certain places in the water where certain things would make sense for us to be doing anything.

"That is, until one day.

"Fort Wright ordered us to go to 'Course J,' which started from the center of the Race and ran to the east. Captain Thom was on vacation so Captain Al Beckwell took his position as captain. I thought it was strange as they did not send any target detail and told us no target was needed. Captain Al and I were the only personnel aboard. We arrived on 'Course J' and notified the station by radio of our position. We were told to proceed east on this course. About halfway down course a message came over the radio telling us that we'd done a good job and to proceed to some place that was in letter code neither of us knew. This was when we began to think *maybe we really should have carried an operator*. There was a lot of code stuff and, of course, we couldn't just get on the radio and ask them what the code meant. I don't think we was even supposed to know. We was just supposed to get the boat part right.

"I tried to think of everything I knew about the boat part.

"I did know that *T-18,* which was assigned to Camp Hero on the South side of Long Island on the oceanfront west of Montauk Point was broke down and in the shipyard. I don't quite know why they called that 'Camp Hero.' As I understand this was where the 1898 vets were quarantined after they came back from Cuba, and more died wrapped up in a blanket with fever than ever was shot in Cuba. Even Teddy Roosevelt had to stay out there when he come back until he pulled some strings and got to go home down to Oyster Bay. Maybe that was the 'hero' part.

"I asked the station by radio if we were to proceed due south from our present position. The station acknowledged 'Roger.' Captain Al and I agreed our destination was now Montauk, a dozen miles further. The target boats could do about eleven knots, about half that with the tow, which was square so didn't exactly cut a fine line through the water. We went into Fort Pond Bay, which is where all the fishermen always went and is inboard from the point a few miles. Fort Pond Bay turned out to be wrong. We was supposed to go in to Star Island, which is in the old salt pond out near the end and which had apparently been dug out and made into a yacht harbor totally unbeknownst to me. We began to feel a little nervous.

"Eventually we picked up our target detail, itself as well as the target and the soldiers to heave on the hawser included a radio operator—for all the good he did. They also had an artillery officer who brought aboard a funny looking rack. It was like a rifle with a barrel and a stock to go against your shoulder, but there was a four-foot piece of wood with pegs in it that crossed the end of the barrel down where the sight would be.

"'What's that for?'" I asked. I thought it might be a cribbage board so we could kill a little time between tows.

"'It was,'" he informed me, "'the range finder.'"

"I begun to worry a bit about carting around a bunch of guys to get shot at from a place named Camp Hero."

· · ·

"We rounded Montauk Point, plowed into the open Atlantic out past Great Eastern Rock, which we left to starboard. Captain Al put her on the southwest course that the station ordered. About four miles out they had us pay out the hawser, and then the fun began. Camp Hero, like Fort Wright, had sixteen-inch guns.

"Now all this might have been all right, but *T-18*, the boat we were subbing for, customarily, as we later found out, towed with no less than twenty-two hundred feet of hawser. Our boat, *T-11*, only had eighteen hundred feet of hawser, all that was required in the Sound. No one that afternoon at Fort Hero ever seemed to be aware of this. Well, what's four hundred feet among friends? Especially as how they're only just learning.

"I don't think we actually got hit with any of that shrapnel, but it was falling into the water all around us. Al and I, we tried to stay on the far side of the cabin. I was steering, so I stayed steering. Just aft of the wheelhouse there was a good-sized smokestack back of me, with the muffler and all. I just kind of tucked down there. Al was tucked down, too. The soldiers were tucked down under the bulwark at the fantail, which was waist high. The artillery officer, he set his rack on that fantail rail and squinted along the barrel to the end, where he had the cribbage board with the pegs. He might as well have been playing cribbage because I don't think anything he was doing had a single thing to do with what was happening all around us. If it did, what he must have been trying to do was commit suicide. We only made one run, about an hour by the clock. It seemed a lot longer. I don't know if they were punishing us or what. Maybe they was looking for some more 'heroes.'

"Looking back on those days towing the target, you might wonder what the hell we thought we were doing out there getting shot at by our own men. I mean most of the 'Battle of the North Atlantic,' as people came to call it, was fought *under* the water, certainly all of it that was on this side of the ocean. It's a little hard to imagine exactly what the War Department had in mind would be the actual targets of these guns. It would seem it would have to be an invasion force. Since the Germans never even got so far as to invade Britain, it shows you how far ahead we were, or maybe we was still thinking of the Spanish fleet in 1898. In which case it would be how far behind we was. Maybe they were waiting for Captain Kidd to come by. Who the hell knows?"

. . .

"Anyway, for all that, I enjoyed target boat duty a great deal, but all good things seem to come to an end. I received a letter from President F.D.R. saying 'Greetings. We need you.' I had no idea for what, as that *greeting* business wasn't so famous then, and I sure didn't think *I* was all that important. By letter I was told to report to New Haven, Connecticut for screening on September 2, 1943. I was twenty-five. I managed to talk my way into the Navy by telling them about my boat experience. I was happy when the day ended. It was getting pretty chilly walking around naked all day in that building. Going from one doctor to another. In those days people you didn't know pretty much kept their clothes on. It was quite a sight.

"My enlistment papers told me to report to Newport, Rhode Island, on September 9, 1943, for boot training. I was assigned to Company 603 with a hundred and ten men and one instructor. Boot camp only lasted about three weeks. We were loaded aboard a train early in the morning, and off we headed for Camp Shelton, Little Creek, Virginia, which is in the same corner of the lower Chesapeake as Norfolk. The whole company was assigned to Camp Shelton, an armed guard school to train men to go aboard merchant ships to man the guns.

"There were only two armed guard schools in the States, Camp Shelton on the East Coast and one in San Diego. In those days submarines were slow under water and submerging was mainly a defensive tactic. Most submarine attacks then occurred on the surface, and the idea was that with a gun and a properly trained crew you might have a chance of slugging it out face to face. The men of Company 603 were assigned different positions on the base. I was sent to the laundry as instructor of what they called 'extractors.' I wasn't sure what that meant as it was a word I'd only heard in reference to awful things that happened to you in the dentist chair. *Hey, maybe I'll come out a dentist,* I thought. I'd heard about people being assigned strange things they never done, but who might come out later with training for life. Although to tell the truth, there wasn't that much emphasis on that sort of thing until after the war was over. The idea then was more just to come out of it alive. This 'extractor' business apparently had something to do with laundry.

"We trained men to operate the laundries aboard all types of Navy vessels. The laundry was not completed when we arrived so we were put to work pulling nails out of used lumber. 'Ah,' I think, 'this is the *extractor* part.' After a week of pulling nails we were told to put the lumber in piles and it was set afire. I don't recall what we had to do with the nails. There must have been a couple of tons of bent nails on the ground. Maybe the next crew was told to straighten them out. Some of them had come out pretty good and wouldn't need much more work on them. Maybe they went into scrap metal. In any case, we never was told and for one who had always worked in small crews on projects that required common sense, and where you pretty much always knew the beginning and ending of a job of work, the Navy was a new experience for me.

"The laundry finally opened. Never been in a *laundry* in my life. What we done was just wash our clothes like you'd wash the dishes in a small tub . . . a bar of yellow soap. Now they put me on a marking machine, marking the clothes. We were training the crews that would go to sea on the big ships, carriers and battleships. After a week I decided that fooling around all day with a lot of damp cloth and soap and steam was not for me. I put in for a transfer. I also asked for a five-day leave to go home to pick up my car, trailer, and wife. Lieutenant Hutchinson, my CO, said he would OK a seventy-two–hour pass. That was in the days before the interstates. I said, 'Fine. I can't make it in seventy-two hours, so I'll see you in five days and suffer the consequences.' He finally OK'd the five days. Things worked out fine. I got the trailer set up in the park outside Little Creek close to Camp Shelton.

"This was a good set-up. I was home every night, except when I had the duty, but even then a buddy, Frank Kladger, insisted he would stand my watches. He didn't have nowhere to go. This was good, too. I would invite Frank on weekends and holidays to have meals with us and go to movies, etc.

"My wife wanted to go to the dance hall. God, it was hot in there and they had these big electric fans that were all the rage. Big fans standing around the edge of the dance floor. My wife, she got some excited. I believe they called it a *fox trot*. Up goes your hand and down it goes, pumping water. I don't know why pumping water makes it a *fox trot*. Maybe that's when you see the fox: out in the back yard whiles you're pumping the water. Up and down. Up and down. Just as we goes by one of them fans she's in the up part. *Whack*. Jesus, she got mad at me. Blood all over the place, the walls, the band. She starts screaming. Thought I'd never hear the end of it, what with bandages and all. And what with the dress. I mean she didn't lose a finger or nothing. She didn't bleed to death. It sure gets some hot down there in Norfolk in them days so I suppose you need them fans.

"When I put in for a transfer I had no idea when or where I would wind up, and I didn't much care. It took about eleven months for my transfer to go through. In meantime it was pretty much hot, wet cloth and the steam and noise. It was too hot in that laundry. I was now in charge of the *extractors,* extracting the water from the clothes. Those extractors were pretty good size machines and Jesus: noisy. I don't know how, but they were screaming—big machines that took the water out of the clothes. We use dryers now, but with all that material, they used a kind of press to squeeze the water out.

"I couldn't get myself out of that laundry for the longest time. Here I got a master's license to run boats. It seemed more like I was in the war when I'd been a *civilian* out there towing targets and getting shot at. Our bunkhouse was part of the laundry, so we ate, slept, everything right there. That damp thing hanging in the air—as if Norfolk weren't damp and hot enough all by itself!

"I was never sure why they didn't put me on the boats right away. I wore glasses at the time. I guess they figured I'd be no good to stick my eyeball up into a binocular on one of them aircraft carriers. In the laundry, we were a bunch of what amounted to 4-Fs. I don't know why F.D.R., he took me off that target boat in familiar waters just so I could mark clothes in the Norfolk laundry and run my wife's hand through the dance hall fan."

. . .

And what was Captain Malloy, Sr., doing all this time on the home front? After his father's death Larry came across a letter the old man wrote to the bank that had owned the Harrison's Landing property in the depths of the war. The "1938 loss" refers to the Great Hurricane. Both Larry and I agreed you can hear the old man talking:

. . .

February 16, 1943

Mr L—:

I find that you are still sending me a bill for $20 which I have no intention of paying as my rent was paid up to date when I received orders to move. That I did just as soon as possible. I lived in that house between thirteen and fourteen years. During that time I never at any time called on [your bank] to do any repairs. All materials and labor was furnished at my expense. I consider that house was the most profitable to them they had up here.

Speaking about me owing you $20. I have a bill from 1930 on the little white house that [name of tenant] lived in for about $41 that I paid [recipient] for removing and replacing shingles around the chimney. After that time they changed the workes [sic] around but still I had to turn the water off and on when ever necessary as the plumbers they hired didn't know where the water was or the first thing about it.

You people worring [sic] about losing $20. What do you think about me losing $75,000 in 1938 and $6,000 in 1941?

I am writing you because I am unable to get into your offices. I either get there to [sic] late or too early.

Yours truly
Lawrence H. Malloy

"Much to my surprise I was eventually transferred to the Naval Air Station, Norfolk. The trailer park I was living in was halfway between Camp Shelton and Norfolk Air Station so the mileage didn't change. I didn't have to move.

"I was assigned to Assembly and Repair, put on a plane crew, doing minor engine repairs and all around maintenance of the shop. We worked mainly on PBMs and PBYs, that is: Patrol Bomber Martin and Patrol Bomber something else. These were seaplanes, meant to land only on the water. Some of them landed on the ground, but hey, that was a mistake.

"These planes had come to us right out of combat, mostly the English Channel. Given the year of the war, I'm not sure exactly what they was up to over there. But they had bullet holes all right. They weren't flying the big bomber runs over Germany. When you're in a war, you don't always know how everything else is fitting in. That was one of the big differences between being on the workboats. On workboats, I usually knew where we was going and why. Maybe it wasn't always a good idea considering what we was doing, but I understood that, too. Of course, part of it too was being young. When you're young you just look at the hand in front of your face.

"We were to put the planes back together, a complete overhaul. The plane crew's job was: repair the plane and fly it until it went through every phase of inspection. Only then could the plane be released for combat again. I don't even have any ideas how they got back overseas. I know they had a lot of British equipment on them. I know I got a set of English parallel rules and dividers that I used after the war navigating on the oysterboats. That is if you want to call oysterboats *navigating*.

"One day in the middle of summer we were doing a test flight. It was hot in those planes, so we'd run with the big cargo door open. I was sitting on a toolbox eating lunch. It was a chicken sandwich, if I remember. Since it was almost my *last lunch*, what it was sticks in my mind. We were in off the sea coming over the city of Norfolk, and it was very hot down there on the ground. I guess you get *pockets* in that kind of heat between the sea and the land. Next thing I knew I was just kind of floating out the cargo door, still chewing on my sandwich. Somebody reached out and grabbed me back in. It's a good thing those planes were so slow that you could step out a moment like that, and they'd still be there for you when you was ready to come back in. That way, I suppose they were a little like oysterboats when you fall overboard.

"I liked this job much better than the laundry business."

. . .

"When we returned from a test flight, as these were *sea* planes we would need the assistance of small *rearming* boats. They were called that because they were specially designed to take ammunition out to all sorts of other craft. These boats had a big pudding all around them because you don't want to go smashing into other hulls with a load of munitions. *Pudding*, that is, fenders. We used these boats to push the seaplanes and hold them in square to the ramp so that when the tow motors pulled them up the incline they were straight. *Tow motors* were real short tractors, mostly engine and a seat with a steering wheel and engine controls. We also had to hold the planes from squirming around in the water with the rearming boats while we put on the wheels.

"In those days the seaplanes didn't fly around with the wheels, and they didn't retract. You attached them each time just off the ramp so you could roll the plane up and take it wherever you wanted to on the base, the shop or a hanger or wherever. When you were ready to fly again, you rolled them to the ramp, down the ramp, and off a little bit into the water where the plane could float. Then you removed the wheels. There were three sets of double wheels, port, starboard, and one in the middle back by the tail. What you call now African Americans in black rubber suits would walk out up to their necks to set these wheels. I never could figure out why the men didn't float upside down. Maybe they had lead shoes; I don't know. The star-board wheel was my wheel, so we'd row out in the sharpie and climb up into the plane. Inside, you'd lean out the window and reach out and wiggle it up into the *well* where you'd secure it by a pin. There's a picture of me reaching out the window and grabbing the wheel in the *Norfolk Navy Yearbook*.

"So because of our working with the rearming boats and the seaplanes, I got to know where the boathouse was located on the base. I guess I talked to the right people, because in three days after I began my talking I was as-signed to the Boathouse, Operations Department.

"At last I had found the sort of work that I had been prepared to do!"

. . .

After half a century it was an obvious delight for Larry just to catalogue the boats from memory:

"Vessels at the Boathouse consisted of two Yard Salvage Derricks (YSD), *YSD 38* and *YSD 7*; two fifty-foot fireboats, six rearming boats; two sixty-three-foot Air Sea Rescue Boats (PT) with two 650 horsepower each Hall Scott gasoline engines. Since the most horsepower we'd ever had in a boat at home was forty this was quite a shock. Although the rumrunners out of Greenport had Hall Scotts of great power. These were the ones I used to hear come and go until dawn when I'd lie awake at night in the house on Stirling Basin."

When I queried L.H.M. on this over the phone, he began a rasping cough. "Wait a minute," he said, "till I get through dying."

"There was also one thirty-six-foot ASTR (Air Sea Rescue) with two 650 horsepower each Hall Scott designated 'First Rescue.' 'Second Rescue' was a forty-five-foot with two Hudson Invaders at 350 horsepower each gasoline engines which could make twenty-two knots. 'Third Rescue' was forty-five-foot bottom of the line. She wasn't much of a boat. She didn't even look like a boat. An awkward-looking thing.

"Boats at that time were built all over the place. Solomon Island up the Chesapeake Bay or wherever. If you were interested in that kind of thing you could tell where a boat was built just by looking at the workmanship. These weren't all government yards. They were just the regular yards that built the local workboats of their day. Back in those days, of course, you built anything just as quick as you could. Still, you could tell the differences, because some places just did it better even though they were in a hurry.

"There was also one forty-foot and one fifty-foot motor launch; two twenty-six personnel carriers, like speedboats, kind of fancy; they carried the pilots and people like that.

"The sharpie (rowboat) was important. In all these fancy motorboats, the most important craft sometimes was just a fourteen-foot, flat-bottomed sharpie that you rowed here and there short distances to connect jobs and fetch tools. Same thing in the oyster business back home. We always towed or carried a sharpie."

. . .

"One particular night I didn't have the duty. I was just driving with my wife along the shore road. You know, like it was an evening out with the wife— just relaxing, enjoying the view. Keeping away from the dance hall fans. We were going out to see the flowers, or something. We look out and see all the lights in the Bay. It looked real pretty. Like a carnival. Turned out it was the divers working. Hell, we didn't even know what we was watching. After a while, though, I began to get an uneasy feeling. I knew you didn't see a lot of lights like that out on the water. Not even in peacetime. Not unless there was something.

"November 1945. The *YSD #38*, what they call a Navy seaplane derrick, had sunk in a collision with a tanker in the Thimble Shoals Channel off Norfolk. They didn't get all of her up until February 25, 1946. The reason it was such a tragedy was that most of the men were in the shower getting ready to hit the beach. All thirteen men were lost. I'd been working on her, so knew most of the men that went down.

"We nearly had another disaster that I was a good deal closer to. The Boathouse received word that a seaplane base at Banana River, Florida, was sending a bunch of seaplanes to us to moor until a predicted hurricane had passed Florida. The planes had to be fuelled up, so we acquired a tanker motor launch of fifty feet from Naval Operations Base to do this job. The tank truck came to the Boathouse with a load of hundred-octane gasoline. After awhile one of the tank boat crew noticed the gauge on the tank. It was not registering, so he dropped a measuring stick in the tank. It was dry!

"So where had all that high-octane gas gone?

"They opened the forward compartment and saw everything floating around: life preservers, mattresses, and all sorts of equipment. Someone had put the fuel hose in the *vent* and not the fill pipe.

"Lieutenant Stafford told me to get aboard this tanker and run her out to a mooring in the bay, far away from shore. I told him I would get one of the rearming boats and *tow* the tanker to a mooring.

" He said why not just start the tanker up and run her out under her own power? After all, she was a diesel. I said: 'Yessir, but what *starts the diesel*?'

"The lieutenant looked at me a moment. I'd known him to be a good egg or I wouldn't have said what I said. If he weren't a good egg, I don't know what I'd a done. Probably just go and maybe blow'd up half the harbor. The problem was he'd been a diver and been down so long, so deep his eyeballs were screwed up. When he just looked at you like that, it was hard to tell just what he was thinking.

"Finally he said, 'Do it your way.'

"When he'd made arrangements for a tank truck to pump the fuel out of the tanker, and the fire department was in place, he had me tow the tanker with a rearming boat. That was one of the boats that had all that pudding around her so in case we bumped it would be, at least we hoped, *gentle*. I towed the tanker to the steel bulkhead as far away as we could get her from everything else. We tied her up with cable away from everything. The idea behind using cable was that if the tanker caught afire, they didn't want her to burn through her manila mooring lines and go visiting about the harbor. They did pump her out, but she was wood down in the cabin where they'd poured the high octane. The fuel soaks into the fibers, and you never really get it out. I'm not sure just what they did do with her, but I didn't see her around after that. And I didn't hear her blow up.

"Another dangerous thing on the rearming boats. When the seaplanes came taxiing in, we had to guide them to their assigned moorings. We had a great big sign we held up:

FOLLOW ME

"Now we could do twenty-two knots; the plane might come in doing a hundred. Even throttled back to a third of that, the plane doing a "Follow Me" could overtake you pretty quick.

"A lot of things would happen like that in the war. You'd be really involved in some little part of it that might even risk your life and then hey, that little part was gone. You was still alive and you just went on to something else.

"One of the side excursions we done was take a rearming boat out the back door of Norfolk down the Dismal Swamp Canal and out to Pongo Point Air Station near Elizabeth City, North Carolina. The Dismal Swamp was some kind of water like I never seen before, a regular jungle like you have in the Tarzan movies on Bank Street with George Sanford. But we didn't see no gorillas or Jane swinging out of the vines. Just mosquitoes, and we come back by truck.

"At the Boathouse we all lived together, so there wasn't much baloney. We could all sit down and talk together. There were quite a few watermen in our outfit that was from that area. Kindred spirits. At the Boathouse they was all pretty good boatmen. Couple of them run aground, but hey, that's how you learned where all the rocks are."

DECONSTRUCTING
WORLD WAR TWO

THE IMPACT OF the threat of the Spanish Fleet in 1898 seems largely forgotten a hundred years later, but the Malloys, while in the course of a salvaging job, made an interesting discovery that puts the system of coastal defenses protecting Long Island Sound into perspective. While the Spanish fleet was sunk off the southeast coast of Cuba in 1898, there had been several "sightings" of the modern armada from Nova Scotia to Florida. Coastal defenses dormant since the Civil War suddenly were the subject of much attention. Larry Malloy pronounces Fort Michie "Fort My-kee." It was named after Lieutenant Dennis M. Michie, who, according to Noank Captain Benjamin F. Rathbun's *Capsule Histories of Some Local Islands and Lighthouses in the Eastern Part of Long Island Sound,* had been killed in the charge on San Juan Hill on July 1, 1898. Michie had brought football to West Point, and the stadium is named after him. The fort was begun in April 1897 when some 250 men working for J. F. Hoffman & Company of Philadelphia spent two years transforming the seventeen acres of beaches, dunes, and scrubby upland into a seventeen-acre fort. In each subsequent war the fort was upgraded with more concrete, and eventually what Captain Rathbun describes as a "huge underground hanger" to house its mighty guns.

Captain Rathbun discovered that the biggest moment in the military history of Fort Michie was on June 11, 1941, when with its sixteen-inch 1920-era "disappearing" million-dollar naval cannon "it hurled a total of fourteen individual 2,100 lb. projectiles at a target nineteen miles distant. There were some references in the [New London] press about the noise, along with reports of one or two cracked windows in the Mystic area."

Prior to the government's military establishment, Gull Island was used as a vegetable garden for the keepers at the lighthouse on its tiny, barren easterly neighbor, Little Gull Island. There, Captain Rathbun tells us, Little Gull keeper Frederick Chase rowed over from his light station to maintain a garden of sixteen different kinds of vegetables and imported apple, pear, and cherry trees. He also had "a fenced-in pasture for his cows, oxen, pigs and geese as well as a barn to house them in winter." Captain Rathbun thinks that Keeper Chase also ran a small guest hotel on the side, all of which would have been condoned as legitimate means to augment the meager income of a nineteenth century lighthouse keeper. Before that, Captain Rathbun tells us, the chief fame of the island was that in 1637 Roger Williams suggested it might make a good place to imprison some troublesome Pequots he had rounded up.

Perhaps the most poignant story I ever heard illustrating the loneliness of the Gull Island community was something I ran across in the papers of the Waterford historian Robert Bachman years ago. It was an account of a Gull Island keeper who was instructing his son in the techniques of seal hunting. Having struck the seal with a harpoon, the mighty hunter fastened the slippery line around his waist, informing his son as he did so that this was the proper way to secure the catch. Unfortunately, the stunned seal came to and swam off, towing the father behind, leaving the boy to contemplate the vast waters of the tern and the gull and the wisdom of fathers.

. . .

"After the war, we wasn't done with the war, and that was a good thing. There was more money to be made from the war after it was over than when it was going on, and making money on a war when the war wasn't actually going on, hey, that was a whole lot easier on your way of life. At least so it seemed to me.

"Of course, I guess you'd say it wasn't just one war we was making money off of, but two or three. We had the scrap job out to Fort Michie on Great Gull Island, working for the Museum of Natural History, who wanted to make it out there in a way so that no birds would be nervous about coming and going. Coming and going and all those things birds do in *between* coming and going, although from what I see of birds out there that's mainly what they do: come 'n' go. . . . But I think that's not the part they was most interested in *studying*. What the Museum wanted was: *The In-Between Activities of Birds*.

"The reason I say that it was more than one war providing for us is after we get down to the ground level of junking I see on the sewer grates those numbers 1898. Well, I knew there wasn't nearly two thousand of them out there, so I thought it was maybe some sort of serial number. The government was great for that, putting serial numbers on everything and everybody. It finally occurred to me that number weren't no serial number. It was a date, 1898. I began to wonder what was so special about 1898, and when I was ashore one day a friend reminded me that 1898 was when we was fighting. But not the Germans or even the British. Damn, but it turned out to be the Spanish, although I don't think they ever did their part and show up. Leastways not in our area. More of that Camp Hero business. I think the Spanish preferred to concentrate on the Cuban situation. That was the war with Teddy Roosevelt running around in it and even my father had that story he told some people, but not me, about Teddy Roosevelt. From what I gather, Pappy's Teddy Roosevelt story seemed more to do with him and the president having a boxing match than anything to do with cannons, though.

"Fort Michie received its share of attention in World War One and Two, though to my knowledge it never did get the big guns they had across the Race at Fort Wright on Fishers Island. What they had on Fort Michie been chiefly anti-aircraft, which was why, I suppose, the Museum of Natural History figured that the birds might be nervous. The Museum had us take down everything that stuck up in the air at all, and like I said, we worked our way from up there as high as anything went on the island—all the way on down to the manhole covers.

"We were using Alice on this job. As far as junking goes, Alice, she was built down to Tottenville, New York, in 1910 as a bumboat. That is, she was built to go around New York harbor picking up old rope, paint, and bottles, and other junk from the ships out there. Always had a lot of business with bottles. Recycling wasn't just invented, you know. At least that's the story about our Alice as the bumboat. The Alice in Kochiss that's built in 1907 is already an oysterboat, hey, that's a different boat. We bought her in 1946 from an estate where she was pretty tired out on the beach in West Haven and took her to West Haven Shipyard where we done a lot of work on her.

"There were all kinds of valuable things on Fort Michie, some of them not so valuable one by one, but in a deckload, hey, they added up. This was true of doorknobs. Each door had two knobs on it, one for each side and there was usually two doors for each doorway, a regular door and a screen door. That made four knobs for every way of getting in and out of every building. Inside doors didn't need the screens, of course, but like any door worth its name, they all had two sides: two knobs. These knobs were all made in them days out of solid brass. Not like now when you're lucky to get a season from something that says, "brass" on it. We took a deck cargo of them brass doorknobs across the Sound, up the Thames to Harrison's Landing. Across the river, above the Sub Base up the Poquotonuck River there was a brass factory. There used to be a drawbridge over the Poquotonuck so the steamers could get up to the wharf at Happy Land, the big amusement park. The guy who ran that bridge lived near the park and you'd have to come ashore and go seek him out, but at least you could get up in there with a load. By the year we took the doorknobs up, however, all that was shut down: Happy Land, the drawbridge. So we had to ship the doorknobs by pickup truck. They knew what to do from there with door-knobs that nobody wanted to be doorknobs anymore. I suppose they made brass "plating" for all the new doorknobs people were going to be needing in the building boom after the war. But I can't really say that because we didn't hang around to see just what they did do with the doorknobs. We just hightailed it back to Gull Island for more junk. I do know, though, that when I was working for the New London Housing Authority later on some of those new doorknobs weren't half as good as they ones we lugged up the Poquotonuck to have them tossed in the pot.

"Of course everything we junked out from Fort Michie wasn't so handy as a doorknob, or even a handful of doorknobs. Because of the birds being nervous we had to get all the towers and tanks down and some of them structures was more than a handful. There were four big tanks. Thirty feet long each and eight feet in diameter, wrought iron, riveted. They were like submarines and damn near as big as submarines used to be and a good deal bigger than that Jap job they got up to the Sub Base. The soldiers used these tanks to hold the water for fire protection. The sanitary system flushed with sea water. Drinking water was in the tower. Of course the way we was tearing the place apart, there wasn't going to be anything *to* protect. As a matter of fact, one of the main ways we got the buildings down after we'd junked them out was to set them afire. You could do that in them days without some lawyer over in Connecticut calling you up on account of he's running for office on the southwest breeze.

"The fire tanks was inside a building on cast iron legs or chocks. We cut them loose, jacked 'em around out of the building and got the crane and cable on them. When they got going, I just let out the slack. Let 'em roll down to the boat. They got going a little faster than we liked to see big iron things rolling down on *Alice,* but thank God, they stopped before they sank us. We eased them into the water and got a hold of them with *Alice* and towed them back across the Sound one at a time to the Thames River. That was the nice thing about them old oysterboats. They got a big wheel [pro-peller] on them. They maybe was slow, but you put a big tow on them and they don't get much slower.

"When we towed those big tanks up into the Thames River, Whaling City Dock and Dredge latched onto them. They used them on what they called their 'steam barge.' This was a rig to hold the engine they made steam for their compressors with. There was a house up on it with boilers. It was a mighty rig and the tanks made pretty good pontoons. Everybody called it '*The Steamah.*'

"Stuff got passed around a lot in them days. That's how you ran a harbor. You didn't have words like 'recycle' and 'adaptive reuse.' Those were just things *you did*. You did whatever you could to keep everything and everybody working. Most of the stuff never got very far away, and even when it wouldn't float or roll or lift or whatever it was last doing, you shoved it in under you and improved your dock. The fuel tanks we got on the edge of the dock at the Landing come from Fort Michie. George Sanford helped with what went inside those. Let's leave that at that.

"We sold the cast iron tank legs to Calamari's down by the harbor in New London on Howard Street near Shaw's Cove. They was the main junker. Everything by the weight. We got paid by the Museum, but I can't remember any money we ever got from those tanks from Whaling City. Hey, I bet if you asked my brother Bill though, he'd know. The same can be said for some DC motors. Junking was tricky that way. You could work your butt off for weeks, and a lot of it was dangerous. I mean it ain't no good where it is, but that don't mean it wants to leave. You've got old stuff already half broken falling apart some more each time you handle it. You got to get under it at some point to handle it, and maybe it's still got a roll or a flop or a cave-in left in it just for you. And that's all sharp, heavy, dirty, rusty stuff.

"But how did the money go? Somebody would make a deal. Somebody would be there at some point with his hand out. Who did the work and who made the deal and who had the hand out, hey, they wasn't necessarily the same person. Seems so to me—come to think of it now, that it *never* was the same person got paid who actually done the work. You can probably guess who usually was what person, but hey, the jobs got done and here we all are.

"Bill and I lived out there for a year. Most of the time, just the two of us. The soldiers had lived in tents as well as barracks. We lived in the barracks. We'd come home on weekends in *Alice*. That is, if the weather permitted. Otherwise we just stayed out there and found something to tear down or at least bang on. Hey, I wasn't really that much of a bird watcher.

"In any case where I was living back at the Landing wasn't exactly a palace. What I done was tow that little trailer back from Norfolk. There was really no land to stick that trailer when we got home, so we made a berm out of oyster shells next to my parent's house. It was Pappy's pile from the war so it was a pile that had been washed out and picked over by the rain and the birds and rats so it didn't stink too much. And when we'd got it high enough and compacted enough and smoothed out along the top, we parked the trailer right up there on all them shells and by God, that's where we lived, the wife and me. It sure beat the trailer park in Norfolk and it was close to work."

NOTE

THE AMERICAN MUSEUM OF NATURAL HISTORY'S TERN PROJECT (p. 191) was begun in 1964. It was headed up in 1969 by the ornithologist Helen Hayes from the Linnaean Society, who was ferried to and from the mainland by Lawrence Malloy, Sr., on *Anne* until he retired and was replaced by Captain John Wadsworth and his various party boat named *Sunbeam*, which ran out of the Niantic River east of New London on the Connecticut side of Long Island Sound.

23

SHIPMATES

The many men who sailed with me

I could not name if heart were strong as brass

And tongue ten force, unflagging.

—Homer's *Iliad*, trans. N. P. Falorp

JOSH MOORE INTERESTED me, a faded name in a time book from 1932. Ezra Pound says somewhere in the *Cantos*, "and what fared they who sailed with Odysseus?" or something to that effect. We know exactly how fared Josh Moore for the week of May 4, 1932, but who was he ? Where did he come from? Where did he go after Mumford Cove?

"Josh Moore, he always got a full week. He lived next to us and did everything around the place: paint the house, paint the boat, shuck oysters—whatever needed to be done. You might say we imported him. He come with us from Greenport on the *Emma Frances*. With all his furniture: chairs and tables and a baby carriage. It was foggy. We was heading to go through the New York islands at Old Silas Rock. There's no buoys in there so that ain't the way most anybody goes but local workboats, and it's kind of taking a chance and we got off course. The tide was ebbing, running to the east'rd. I was up in the bow standing on the hunting cabin looking out. I knew we hadn't got anywhere near Old Silas yet, but I didn't want to miss it. That is, I didn't want to miss seeing it before we hit it. Kind of a squared-off boulder about the size of a refrigerator. Just big enough to stand on. You hear that people put people off on there as a joke, but that's not such a good idea because with the current in there sometimes it's hard to get back. I guess the glacier left it there because it's a little too big to have gotten there by itself. 'Old Silas' himself, I never knew him. Suddenly I see what looked like a haystack. It was The Ruins, one of the old forts. It was supposed to be way back there out on the spit at Gardiners Island. That's near three and a half nautical miles off we was. There was a breakwater in them days at The Ruins about even with the water. By the time I shouted out, we hit pretty good. The *Emma Frances,* she went right up on the sand and listed. Josh Moore's baby carriage nearly went overboard. We didn't have the brakes set, I guess. Or Josh didn't have them set. I'm not saying there was a baby in that carriage at that moment.

"There was only one way to get out, and that was the way we come in, over the breakwater, so I got back up on the hunting cabin in the bow where I'd fallen off of. From there I could see a little and found us some water. Fortunately by then we'd had that double planking job done on *Emma Frances* to stiffen her from being lengthened out all those times. If it weren't for those extra planks down below I know we would have had some breakwater sticking up in our bilge that night.

"We settled the Moores in the other half of our Harrison's Landing house, the one that had been once across the Thames River as a blacksmith shop at the Submarine Base.

"The old Submarine Base Blacksmith Shop was a two-family layout with the insides perfectly reversed, each side with its own fireplace. One day my little brother Bill, he was playing and he fell off the porch and landed on his back so he looked up and saw the smoke coming out of the roof. Josh Moore had been burning papers or something. Pappy and I had been coming home a long way the night before on the boat and so were still asleep. Bill woke us up, and Pappy grabbed the garden hose and went up on the roof, but nothing came out. The whole little village at Harrison's Landing was run off one well with a pump that pulled the water up to a tank for water pressure. The tank had a gauge so you could read it from outside. We'd come home from school and look up at that gauge. If it was low it was our job to start the pump up. The trouble was that tank was only the same height as the roof. The fire department finally came and wetted down all the parts of the house that *wasn't* burning and while that may be what you learn in fireman's school, Pappy, hey, it was his house, he snatched the hose from them, went back up on the roof and put out the fire right where it was actually burning. We had to move into the house that was next door, which was vacant at the time, and Josh Moore moved into our part of the house until we fixed his roof and the rest of the house that had been affected."

. . .

Apparently Josh Moore's carelessness with fire did not mar his relationship with his landlord and employer. He stayed on for several years in his previous capacity. A browse through the *Weekly Time Book* reveals that a "J.

Moore" made a trip in the early thirties all the way to Perth Amboy, New Jersey, in *Emma Frances*.

"That's a hundred miles just to Hell Gate," says Larry. "At maybe ten knots, that is, if you aren't banging into a westerly. Then you got to get through the City, or rather around it and up into these Jersey creeks. I bet they was bringing a load of coal back to the Potato House at Halyoake Farm. Which I know they done from time to time. Besides being in the coal business on that part of the island, Hallock had a lot of coal stoves, at least one in each greenhouse, to keep the young plants warm. Pappy seems to have taken just one man: Josh Moore. There wasn't much to do but just tie up the boat. The coaling, that was all automatic. When they brought the chute down all you had to do was have your mouth open to catch it.

"The point here is, if you look at the dates in the time book, you see it took them two weeks. I don't know why it took that long. You got to read between the lines. Seems so to me there was a hold-up at the coal dock. I don't see anything down for *repairs* to the boat, but you can bet they didn't just go dancing in Perth Amboy. I'm sure the old man had Josh Moore painting the boat, and as you know on a wooden vessel there's no end to that. Of course painting a white boat in a coaling port might have been a bit discouraging, but then you wasn't trying to come up with a *yacht* finish. Maybe the coal people made them wait; a fifty-ton coal order wasn't much for that place. Pappy received sixty-five dollars for the load. Now you figure beans and coffee for the crew and fuel and if you got a pencil with any kind of point on it, you see what that trip amounted to. But then this trip has to be understood in relation to the whole Potato House arrangement where there was a lot of *I do for you; you do for me* stuff.

"Eventually Josh Moore went back to Greenport because he'd gotten a good job working at the new Greenport sewage plant. That seemed a natural thing for an oysterman to do because it was all part of the same thing you were trying to do. The last time I saw Josh, Pappy and I was drudging at Pete's Neck by the Potato House. This was long after we had stopped docking at the Halyoake. In fact there already wasn't much of the old establishment left by then. They had been using that area as a dump for a long time and there was all kinds of things in there like ox carts and wheels and other things of no use to us, and there was Josh Moore. He drove by with his wife in a car. And we all waved. Hey, he had a better job."

· · ·

"There was the Chapmans. I think they was brothers. They never spoke to each other one word the whole day. I guess that was because they got all their speaking with each other out of the way before and after work. They lived together in a tiny house along the Thames riverbank. They didn't have radio or, of course, TV, and I don't think they read much. It was a house that they fished out from the river as it was going by. Not all at once, mind you. That wasn't the way a house would usually come to you. You had to *assemble* it. You know, a crate bottom here, a billboard there. Whatever would come to you, as it come to you, and you never knew exactly what it would be from day to day that would come to you. What the *order* was going to be. There was always the possibility something better might come by tomorrow for just what you was doing today. But hey, you couldn't count on that. Might be nothing for a long time, leastwise something you could use. At some point you'd have to say, 'This is it.' That made the over-all plan a little different than if you'd hired yourself an *architect*. That's how we got a lot of our stuff. You'll recall the telephone poles arriving at Harrison's Landing that way.

"In the thirties a lot of people lived that way along the river. There was a man named Blair up to Cow Point built small boats. His southeast wall was the railroad ballast that run along the river. There was a spring—not a bed-spring—water run out between the rocks and that's where he got his water. Anyway, the Chapman boys, they worked for Pappy pickin' up oysters. They lived in that little shack by the river and they never spoke to each other all day long on the boat. I don't really know that they said anything more at night."

. . .

The man who appears to have succeeded Josh Moore after the war was Walt. Without a pay book from that postwar era, Larry could not recall Walt's last name, and unlike Josh Moore, Walt was not a tenant of the Malloys. He did, however, live near the Malloys. "He was higher up out of the water than the Chapman brothers. He lived up the hill a ways from the Thames Shipyard, about halfway up toward Connecticut College. And had a regular house up in there. He'd come to work by walking down the bank path to the shore of the Vermont Central Line. That ran along the river. He'd just keep walking the rest of the way along the beach until he got to *Anne* at the dock. You'd look up, and he'd be there. I think, in fact, that's how he got hired, though maybe somebody said something out loud first."

The concept of Walt-as-Apparition rang a bell. "Is he the same Walt who was on *Anne* when I was aboard her thirty years ago with your dad? Quiet fellow, kept to himself on the boat. That is, wouldn't join us in the wheel-house when we were on the long runs between jobs. I think he had a pint, sat in the sun. Now was that the same Walt was with you a couple years back?"

"Yes. If I ask brother Frank I can find out what Walt's last name is."

In spite of not recalling Walt's last name, Larry remembered much about him. "He lived with his sister. Like a lot of the good workers he didn't have a lot of stitches in his pocket. One time when we was in the oyster shop I heard a big crash from the back room. Well, the back room was just that, if you know what I mean. Things happened in the *back* room that maybe didn't get to happen in the front room. Just after the crash, I hear a *crazy kind of laughter.* I rush in, and there is Pappy lying underneath a big rudder he had back there for repairs or something. Walt, well, he's just standing there laughing because Pappy couldn't get up. He couldn't get up because he's pinned under the rudder. All's Walt says finally is: 'It fell on him.'

"Well, I suppose it did.

"Walt had been in the Army—maybe that's how he got his head rattled. Forgot easy. He did more than just the boat work. He helped my mother plant the garden. What you'd call a 'handyman.' Paid by the day. All what they called 'days' were the same even though, of course, in that kind of work, they weren't. Days would be, in fact, very different. A *day* could be overnight on the boat to Greenport. A *day* might be six hours in the garden. It didn't matter, you got paid the same and you hoped it all worked out. Then there was rain. That could be a hard call. Walt often worked in the garden when it rained. After all, this wasn't painting. Long as it didn't rain too hard. Just what was *too hard* depended on a lot of things, maybe least of all the rain. If you worked by the week, it was twenty-four dollars a week, six days. There weren't contracts or anything. You work until you get sick of it and then you don't show up any more. And maybe nobody knows what happens next.

"Walt and Pappy they had an arrangement. Eventually Pappy put that roller on the hyster post, and that rig made it so, to tell the truth, he could handle *Anne* by himself. If Walt didn't show up by the time that Pappy was ready to set out, he'd just cast off the lines himself. The engine already been running, and he'd back her out of the slip, turn her around and head for the Grounds. If he see out of the corner of his eye that Walt was coming along the path, he'd always be sure to lean out the starboard side wheelhouse window and wave."

"And just keep steaming?"

"That's what I mean about rigging up with that vertical roller. You see the crew walking along the path after you set out, hey, you just keep steaming."

. . .

"There were other men, like Josh Moore with his late-life career at the Greenport Sewage Plant, went on to better things. One guy worked for us turned out to be Dave Burnett, who later started a landscape business that he sold for a lot of money. Then there was Johnny Bartlett, who turned out to be one of the big-time marine construction men in the area.

"Johnny Bartlett was not related to Bartlett Reef, least so far as I know. He come from downstate, Branford. When he was a kid he used to hang around the docks down there when we'd be working for Elijah S. Ball. You didn't have full tide at the docks there except over to the Yacht Club. We didn't go over to the Yacht Club. Even with flood tide at the docks you was susceptible to winds out of the west and southwest, so you moved out as soon as you was done loading or unloading.

"There was a lot of stakes out in the harbor then. That's how you moored in a lot of the harbors, including Noank over in the Mystic River. In Branford we had hickory trees which we kept putting in. You'd jet them with the washdown pump. Set the hose right alongside of the stake and blow your way down into the mud. Then you pull the hose out and leave the stake there. Mud comes in around the stake where the hose was, and that's as good as you need except in a hurricane, and in that case nothing much is going to work. When the stakes got a little rotten you just jet some more in. You never took the old ones out, so after a while you got a big bunch of them all leaning together toward the top, which made a better mooring as you had something from all directions like a buttress. Some people call that a dolphin, but a dolphin usually gets done all at once and looks a little neater. These things just kind of growed. You still see some parts of them along the edge of the channel down there."

I agreed. In the summer of the last year of the century Geoff and I had come into Branford Harbor on a towing job and there were all those spectral spiles along the right side of the channel. Most of the harbor had been gentrified with the latest marina-style appurtenances, but here was this ancient hickory grove, as if planted by Druids for sacrificial purposes.

"Anyway, Johnny Bartlett, he'd be there five in the morning before even we was up. Just wandering around the dock. And at first light he'd row out to us and climb aboard so's when we wake up, there he is sitting on the deck with his back against the wheelhouse. So you give him something to do and next thing you know, he's aboard as a deckhand."

· · ·

Larry recalled that the biggest crews were on the steamboats, with their need to make the relatively long runs from New Haven to Greenport. "This was strictly in winter. The oysters were less likely to freeze if covered. A crew of six, eight, ten with a cook, the whole show. The crew was mainly Polish. They can work!"

African Americans had arrived in Greenport to work on the menhaden boats before World War Two. Some sought employment in the oyster fleet, a common enough occupation for African Americans in the Chesapeake. Larry remembers two such men who had come to New London after the war when they were in the armed service. In this case he recalls only last names:

"Johnson and Scott, they was with me on *Anne* for quite a long time. Scott, he was a cook at the Sub Base. Johnson had been in the army. Got himself in trouble. At least twice his mother came up crying to get him out of jail. Had to have their pay every day and then the next day had to take time off to spend it. We had them forking and wheeling shells in the summer. Hot work. At one time we had as many as twenty men doing that work. We'd send Johnson and Scott down Main Street, New London, and they'd recruit. I don't know if they got kickbacks.

"Down at New Haven we made arrangements with the black owner of the bar just outside the gate at Mill River near the Chappell Street Bridge. He kept cash in the meat locker and arranged to cash the paychecks. 'If you have any trouble,' he'd say, 'just let me know and I'll take care of it.' He was the mayor of that part of town. I don't know if you'd exactly call that an *election*, but for sure he had the job. We'd arrange through him to provision the boat. Besides his wife, he didn't have any help at the bar. I guess he knew better.

"There was 'Wash' and 'Vet,' two 'colored men,' as they were called then from what *they* called 'Sheik-tick,' Virginia. I guess that's what some other people called Chincoteague. They took care of the engine, cooked, and loaded shells aboard. They worked on Monsell's schooner in Greenport. They also did a lot of steering.

"One day Pappy hitched a ride aboard Monsell's *Charles W. Lynn.* This is an eighty-four-foot vessel, some sixty tons gross, built at the turn of the last century as a schooner down to Patchogue, Long Island, near Blue Point. Johnny Monsell was running the boat. His brother Henry was skipper of Vanderbilt's *Rainbow.* And that's how we got that cleat on *Anne's* hyster post. Other Greenport sailors went into yachting. Anyway, Pappy and Johnny Monsell, they're going down just outside of Long Beach headed for Plum Gut. A routine run, like leaving your driveway to go to work. Pappy's up in the wheelhouse with Captain John when 'Wash' comes up and announces, 'Dinner's on the table.' Pappy and John, they go down below to the forecastle where there's a nice table. There's a hatch right over the table, and the sun is streaming in on the table. They assume 'Wash' is taking the wheel. Like I said: 'Wash' did do a lot of steering. And hey, it's a routine run just outside home port. They're eating when all of a sudden Pappy, he notices the sun's no longer on the table. Where it had been falling through the hatch on the salt and pepper. Johnny runs up the ladder and leaps over the shell pile and climbs up into the wheelhouse. The helm, it had somehow got out of the becket that 'Wash' had rigged it in when he went aft to oil the engine. I guess 'Wash' figured what with *two* captains aboard there was more than enough people around to steer the boat. Hey, there was only *one* guy to oil the engine."

. . .

The Malloys could never indulge in specialization, nor did they seem to care to. The pride was in doing whatever needed to be done. "There were people who never left the wheelhouse. Those people never worked with us. Those were the big companies where you could specialize in things like wheelhouse or engine room. We did everything; sometimes it seemed almost all at once."

Even the bookkeeper, Larry's mother, the former Henrietta Bennett, ran the garden and, of course, the house. In later years I often found Larry's sons Wayne or Larry, Jr., aboard *Anne*, heaving a line or helping out around the culling table. (There was a youngest son, Henry, who worked downriver in heavy equipment, and whom I never met.) They were both in their thirties when I first knew them and both always seemed cheerful, eager to please, and glad to be aboard. It was also clear, however, that their father had memories of their past performances that might have been, shall we say, a bit *shaky*.

Larry's sons' shipboard career was a history largely suppressed. Access to it never went on for more than a flash and was but a hard-eyed glance or the tone of a phrase. I got the impression from Larry that I was not to set too high a store on what I saw on that particular day when everyone was on company behavior. Yet every time I went out, even after I had become a familiar face, the young men's demeanor was exemplary. It was also clear to me that at least some of this skepticism about the younger generation had been inherited from Larry's father, who had been a good deal less tolerant. In those occasional glances I saw not only the father, but a shaft down into the bleak times that no amount of romantic sea haze could ever quite obliterate. To that past Larry maintained these stubborn, if uncomfortable, loyalties. On another level I just think that Larry didn't want me to be disappointed should something awkward occur. I came to wish that he didn't feel that way. His sons had a touchingly affectionate loyalty to *Anne*, beyond what merely dutiful offspring might feel about hanging out at the office with Dad. There was, sadly enough, something in Larry that seemed to prevent him from seeing this. Yet there was his lesson for all of us: if you were *really* going to do this boat life thing you'd better learn that if you didn't do it right, you die or go hungry.

. . .

As the Malloys became a rarer and rarer example of a workboat family, their uniqueness came to be noted by outsiders. Earl Gale came by the other day to sit under the maple tree at West Mystic Wooden Boat Company. He was just in time to contribute to a chapter about the Malloys' method of taking on their crews. I'd known Earl for years. He must have been one of the last people to *join the Navy to see the world* and after his retirement had merely kept on going. He'd just come in from Tonga, or rather an island off Tonga (actually it was an island off an island off Tonga), where he'd left his ketch. He was taking his Australian crew to the Smithsonian, which was, as he put it, "So far off Tonga we had to abandon the boat, at least temporarily."

Back in the 1970s Earl had been rounding out his education at a nearby university. While he was at it he continued his moseying about the waterfront, an activity that somehow turned up Captain Malloy, the elder. Through Earl one of his professors wangled an invitation to visit Harrison's Landing. They found the old man down at the oyster shack near *Anne,* much as I had done a decade earlier at Mort Wright's suggestion. Perhaps feeling a bit awed, the professor introduced himself as "Doctor So-and-So." The old man eyed him suspiciously. This was not the first professor in his life. As we have seen, all the professors so far had promised great scientific breakthroughs that would help the oyster industry. Not only had these breakthroughs not occurred, but the "doctors" had also quickly made it known that they'd pretty much gotten out of the old man what they needed and were moving on. This day aboard *Anne,* Captain Malloy, Sr., nevertheless offered Doctor So-and-So some of his old chestnuts: how he had seeded the oysters of Martha's Vineyard and many another remote cove at the behest of mysterious women; how *Anne* had come back for him when he'd fallen overboard, etc. The "doctor," of course, was enthralled and asked if maybe he might not come out and work as a deckhand for a few days. The professor, of course, had assumed that his toil would be unremunerated by the crusty captain. The old man nevertheless looked him up and down. "Listen, Sonny, there's hardly enough work in this boat for *me* to earn a living."

. . .

I checked out this bit of scholarship with Larry. He did recall his father's trip east to Martha's Vineyard in 1928 or 1929 during the time the family owned *Lieutenant.* But it was not *Lieutenant* that the Old Man initially took east, a trip he'd done as a favor to owners of a New London shipyard. And yes, Lawrence Malloy, Sr., had delivered a *yacht* to a woman on the Vineyard. Malloy, Sr., apparently was amenable to making this trip in someone else's boat only because *Lieutenant* was up on the ways of the shipyard. He was, however, very apprehensive that if he left his own boat during the work it would not get done right. The yard owners assured him they would see to everything. After all, by doing them the favor of the delivery, wasn't he, as they put it, *one of their own*? So Malloy, Sr., blithely steamed off on the Vineyard woman's yacht. When he got there she met him and inquired into his life enough to find out his chief line of work. Indeed she did request the oysters, which he eventually did indeed deliver in *Lieutenant*. In between, however, he had had to settle his yard bill for that vessel. Unfortunately, in his absence the yard had far exceeded his desires in attending to *Lieutenant*. They nevertheless presented him with a bill that more than covered their enthusiasm. "There was quite an argument," said Larry. "In fact Pappy punched out the yard owner."

I offered the opinion that "Pappy" sometimes had a hard negotiating style.

"You might say that," said Larry.

And what of the mysterious woman, now in possession of a deckload of oysters?

"I don't always know what Pappy done with women and oysters," said Larry, "and maybe that's just as well."

. . .

Through the years the name Tommy Watt had come up in Larry Malloy's yarns so many times and with such affection that when I had a chance to buy his old boat yard I jumped at the chance. It was all a bit more complicated than that, of course, but that is another story.

One day I was walking home from a regatta at the West Mystic Shipyard on Willow Point and strolled past the For Sale sign in front of a run-down, two-pier mudhole. The boat yard, such as it was, was tucked into an obscure corner of the Mystic River just below the railroad bridge. The place had often intrigued me as I had stood at the West Mystic post office and gazed eastward toward the river. It was especially charming in autumn when the rooftops of the three buildings then on the property peeked over the top of the golden phragmites in the late afternoon sun. When later I casually asked Larry Malloy about the yard, he said, "That was Tommy Watt's place."

There is a snapshot of Tommy Watt astride his bulldozer berming up land that now lies under our boathouse and that, thanks to him, now constitutes the highest spot on Willow Point. There is another shot of him looking rather sour and dour in a white shirt on the wall of our office. Above it is a photo of his dragger at the spindly pier out back. This vessel, according to Larry Malloy, was the *Lucky and Lady*. "Not *Lucky Lady*," Larry explained, "but Lucky *and* Lady. She was named for Tommy's two dogs. One was named Lucky—"

"And," I said, "the other was named—"

"You got it."

I gathered this was not the only joke that Captains Watt and Malloy had shared in their long life on the water together. The quintessential Watt portrait is the ragged snapshot of him in a floppy-brimmed fedora. He's standing well away from a chalky, nail-sick, hog-backed oysterboat. This is interesting enough in itself. A closer look, however, reveals something of the venue. It is a scene out of Shackleton's voyages. Slowly you realize that what he's standing on is a huge field of ice, and that vessel behind him beset in the rumpled whiteness is the sixty-year-old *Emma Frances*. "That was taken in Plum Gut," explains Larry Malloy.

"Plum Gut!"

"Plum Gut."

The tidal current goes through Plum Gut so fast ordinarily that it takes all you can muster from an old workboat engine to make it through against the flow. I've spent hours in there looking at the same rock, imagining myself ashore creeping on hands and knees at a faster rate than what my boat is making wide open and roaring. At such moments, the idea that ice could lock up the place is unimaginable. That this ice could be strong enough to support a man's weight, and furthermore, that he would actually climb over the rail, lower himself onto the frozen water, then walk that far away from the boat, sends a chill through me. (And who was taking the picture and where was he standing? This is no *National Geographic/Jacques Cousteau Special* with all its cinemagraphic *deus ex machinas* in place). I had heard of the Great Freeze of that year, a hundred-year phenomenon, but to think of someone, actually *see* a picture of someone standing out there in—*on*—Plum Gut gave me not only a new sense of that event, but an insight into the man in the picture.

"I wasn't on that trip," says Larry, who has the photograph. "Tommy was working for the old man and that's him in the wheelhouse of *Emma Frances*. Veronica, Tommy's wife, she not only played that old piano they had in the house at the boat yard, she was a telegraph operator in New London. That job come in handy when they was stuck out there in the Gut and running low on food, Tommy, he sent her a telegraph message. The tide shifted just enough and they could get ashore, but only at Plum Island. That was before the Animal Disease station out there and after Fort Terry, so there was only the lighthouse keeper. There wasn't a lot of extra food, so Tommy, he called his wife up. She was working at the telegraph office. Now you might think what could she do across all that water? What she did was she sent him back a recipe to use when you don't have much to cook. I don't know exactly what that was, but it seemed to work. Maybe it was dipstick rags and seagulls. Some kind of a trick that women have with food."

. . .

Like Larry Malloy, Thomas Watt was the complete waterman. He was what unliterary people used to call a "water rat." He was the last skipper of the Block Island Ferry when she still had a wooden superstructure. He had *Lucky and Lady*, with which he performed a variety of tasks. His daughter Jeannie showed me a newspaper clipping that gave him credit for saving some lives in Fishers Island Sound. It was he who got Larry Malloy into the target-towing business in World War Two. His daughter told me, "During the war sometimes he'd be out too late at sea, and they'd close the submarine nets. He'd have to lay outside them all night until they opened them in the morning. You know: all night on the wrong side of the net."

Tommy Watt wrote a letter of recommendation for Larry Malloy's 100-ton license:

The United States Coast Guard
West Mystic, Conn.
Marine Inspection
May 4, 1965

Officer in Charge

I have known Lawrence H. Malloy Jr. since 1920. He has worked under me as an A.B. and a Quartermaster on the following vessels *Block Island,* the *Pemaquid* and the *Yankee.*

I also certify that he has operated his own boat the *Alice* which is thirty gross ton since January 1959, up to and including this date of May 4, 1965 which is over five years continuous service. The boat *Alice* has been in the business of towing, oystering and freighting general cargo.

He has operated on the following waters; Block Island Sound, Long Island Sound, Peconic Bay, Gardiner's Bay, Westerly River [Pawcatuck River] Connecticut River, Thames River to Norwich, Hudson River, East River, and Providence River.

He has spent all his life on the water and is an outstanding boatman.

I highly recommend him for a motorboat license up to one hundred ton.

I am
Respectfully yours,
Captain Thomas E. Watt

"Of course," said Larry, "that's really only *two* vessels as the *Block Island* is the same vessel as *Yankee.* I suppose he could have put down 'the former *Block Island*' or parenthesis or something, but hey, you put stuff down like he done, the people in the office, they eat that stuff up. Hey, it's not like the *Yankee* didn't exist or I wasn't putting in the hours aboard of her at sea."

The Block Island ferry had originally been named after its port of destination but during Tommy Watt's captaincy was indeed renamed *Yankee*. Captain Joe Collins, like Tommy Watt, was pilot. Larry Malloy was quartermaster and Harvey Fuller was deckhand.

"One day Tommy gets this notice that we not only got to change the name of the boat on the stern and bow, which we had already done, but on all the life preservers, throw rings and the lifeboats. It's a good thing we didn't have towels and pillowcases. So he turns to me and says. 'Go do it.' Well, I was steering the boat, so I holler down from the wheelhouse to Harvey Fuller to do it. 'I don't know how to do names on boats,' he says. 'Well, you better learn,' I say. Next thing I knows he's got a job on shore and what he's doing is painting the names on half the boats all along the Mystic River, and we've got to get a new deckhand."

. . .

Harvey Fuller's boat name painting I recall. He was, without doubt, *the* man in the 1950s and 1960s to hire to lend significance to your vessel. This was not merely a matter of slapping on decalcomania or a quick stencil job. The idea was that you had a real artist, a man whose stuff hung in galleries, carrying out your semantic whimsy. Harvey Fuller also had a sideline with Pete's Fire House Tavern (now John's), a riverside establishment of great probity. Behind the bar were ceramic beer mugs, which for two bucks you could have decorated with your name and a sketch of your boat, if you had one, or your dog or whatever. Harvey Fuller also did the odd shore-side sign as long as there was some aquatic connection.

One day my father came back from his job at Mystic Marine Railway and reported that a new sign had appeared in the carpentry shop. The shop was built out over the water and thus had a kind of attractive nuisance dimension for local men of a loquacious nature. The next day I myself observed this sign, which was installed above the bandsaw. A number of men were standing about in mute bewilderment beneath the inscription, text by Ben Franklin, calligraphy by Harvey Fuller:

DO NOT BOTHER MEN

TIME IS MONEY

Harvey Fuller is a fascinating man in himself. Descendant of a Civil War general, nephew of Buckminster Fuller, Harvey went to the Art Students League in Manhattan in the thirties and developed a muscular, proletarian painting style. His oil of an accordion band playing in the Stonington Holy

Ghost Club is a classic of energy and joy. Other wonderful work by Fuller includes a dragger hauling nets off the southwest bluffs of Block Island, and a haunting view through the windshield of a 1930s car speeding through falling leaves at night on a high-crowned, black-topped, back-country road. Recently he has done a large-scale picture of Huck and Jim looking up from their raft just as a spark-spewing steamboat rounds the bend. He has also done a print showing several waterside vignettes from Kenneth Graham's *Wind in the Willows* that illustrate the Water Rat's famous dictum: "There is nothing, absolutely nothing, like messing about in boats."

The piano that Larry Malloy tells us Veronica Watt played was in the living room of the house (now our office) at the boat yard, and her husband's reed pump organ and Harvey Fuller's accordion complemented it. "We had some great sessions in this house," Larry told me one day, and pointed out exactly where the pump organ was and where "'Ron" had her piano. Bob Morse, the ship model builder, kept a wooden catboat at Tommy's in the fifties and remembers leaving the yard at sunset and hearing the reed organ floating through the sun-besotted phragmites. "And over all the croak and wail of Tommy's voice."

"What sort of songs did Tommy Watt sing?" I asked.

"You know that's a good question. Sometimes I thought they must be *religious*. Other times I was quite sure they were *not* religious. The thing was, in any case, it always seemed to be the same song."

. . .

When Larry Malloy was over in a New London nursing home recuperating from having a new knee, we got to talking. "Well, you know," I told him, "I had Harvey Fuller down to the yard one day last year and, while he did mention that he was happy to see the old place again, he got very nervous, kept looking over his shoulder. It was as if he were expecting something to happen."

"What was that thing Hitler said?"

I wondered to myself what Hitler had to do with any of this. "He said a lot of things, unfortunately."

"He said *where you have something, and I have something and we put it all in a great big pile together and now it belongs to both of us.*"

"Communism?" I said.

"That's it: Communism."

"Hitler was a fascist."

"Well, that's what Tommy Watt thought Harvey Fuller was: *Communist.* Harvey Fuller used to come down not just Saturday night, but several times a week to Tommy Watt's—when they had the piano and when they got the organ, too. But then they came apart because of what Tommy Watt thought."

I tried to explain that Harvey Fuller had been to the Art Students' League in New York in the 1930s, that his uncle Buckminster Fuller was one of the great social thinkers in the 1960s—that Harvey at one point was a painter in the proletarian tradition. "Harvey probably thought of Tommy and you as *proletarian*. Proletarian heroes. I've seen his paintings from that period."

"Well, that's the sort of talk made Tommy nervous."

"Did it make *you* nervous?" I asked.

"Seems so to me Harvey Fuller was more nervous about not having a license or something. A license to play music. You got to have a license for that?"

I tried to explain that in the 1940s and 1950s the Musicians Union under James C. Petrillo was very active.

"Maybe that was it," said Larry. "Anyway, after all that playing music, after all them trips on the *Yankee* and on the *Block Island* working together, Harvey and Tommy they split up over that sort of stuff. Is that what you call *politics*?"

. . .

Tommy Watt helped Larry build structures at Harrison's Landing and Larry helped him build what is now our carpentry shop.

"There was a load of green oak Tommy got a deal on. The shop's exactly that high because that's how long the planks was." In other words, not only were the rafters and beams oak, but the siding as well. (Now, to hang your hat on a nail you must drill.) "We didn't have any outer layer of siding, and we didn't have windows or portholes," says Larry, "but what with shrinkage you had enough slots to see through in case someone was coming." As for the contents, "Tommy, he was like me; he was a *junkie*. It wasn't too long before he'd filled that building so full of junk that he could hardly get into it."

In fact, the evening before Tommy died he had a great deal of difficulty getting at the welding oxygen to give himself a shot to get through the night. He had been heaving on a line with Frank and Larry Malloy, trying to get Frank's fishing boat off the mud bar just north of the slipway.

"He kept heaving and hollering all this '*with a heave and a ho*' stuff," says Larry. "Next thing I know he's sitting down on some blocking and breathing hard. I don't know whether that oxygen done him more harm than good. I mean that stuff's *oxygen*, but I don't think it's the right kind of oxygen, but it's what he had in that shed. Next day they come in the ambulance, and I see him in the hall on a stretcher at the hospital with them other sick people. It looked odd seeing him there like that after all the stuff we done together. Stuff that was, you know, a good deal harder than pulling brother Frank's boat off the mud. Suddenly he jumps up from the stretcher. 'Jesus Christ,' he says, 'I just shit my pants!' He's standing there with this look on his face with all those people around and then he falls over. Just like that. It's the end of Tommy Watt. We done a lot of jobs together here and there and in all kinds of weather, but standing there looking at him, hey, that was the hardest."

NOTE

MONSELL AND THE *RAINBOW* (p. 202): Larry Malloy dropped by a piece that illustrates the range of Greenport's boating families and how the oystering community of which the Malloys were a member was also the spawning grounds of the great J-boat crews, one member of which, Captain George Hiram Monsell, attained the highest acclaim of any American yachtsman. See appendix.

24

RACE ROCK AND G-2

In this pass you will go through the *Horse race*, where you have

a strong tide. The place breaks when there is any wind,

especially when it blows against the tide ... a stranger may be

afraid, the Race appearing like a reef ...

— *The American Coast Pilot,* 4th edition, 1804

The death of the *G-2* was an event packed with drama.

—Paul Tzimoulis, as told to Bob Cahill

AT THE HEAD of West Harbor on Fishers Island, up at the end of a series of turnings that would make a chambered nautilus proud, is a spot
known as Pirate's Cove. While the name may smack of a developer's brochure, it is here that the island's working boatmen—chiefly lobstermen
and building contractors—hide away their vessels from the transient
yachtsmen in the outer harbor and, more important, from hurricanes.
Plastered against the shore of the last bend is a rotting barge that seems to
have become part of the permanent shore structures. Grass and moss grow
up from its deck. Indeed, it is difficult to tell at what point the deck becomes the lawn that surrounds the building on the shore. The hull does not
rise on either wave or tide. You might not even realize that what you are
looking at was once an independently floating craft if it were not for the
two massive cleats that adorn the wooden bulkhead that defines the water's
mild edge. The sheer size of these pieces of iron bespeaks a magnitude of
operation far beyond any demands of this tranquil backwater. Yea, here is
the hardware to meet the surge of the open sea.

In an overly confident mood one day I challenged Larry Malloy. Had he anything at all to do with this particular, obscure, cast-off hunk of maritime culture?

"The lighter in Pirate's Cove?"

"Yes, all mossy and overgrown. Looks like it's been there forever."

"Actually only since 1954."

And we were off.

. . .

Perhaps this was Malloy's most spectacular improvisation. In the 1950s the Coast Guard contracted out the repair to the foundation of Race Rock Lighthouse. Begun in 1871, the light took another seven years to complete, under the most difficult circumstances. Race Rock was one of the engineering marvels of the golden age of engineering in the United States. The conditions are formidable. The 1777 chart warns in large italics that there is "*a great Ripple both Ebb & Flood.*" Subsequent charts label the area "the Horse Race" and indeed the almost continually breaking tops of the waves even in calm weather invoke ancient images of competitive equine agitation.

With four-knot currents running in the last hours of the ebb and open to long fetches from virtually all directions, the Rock itself, only three feet below water in one spot at low tide, presented the sort of challenge that only the greatest need would justify. Race Rock was at the eastern entrance to Long Island Sound and constituted the sort of menace that the great rock in the midst of Hell Gate presented at the western end. At first the idea was to solve the problem the way engineers had in Hell Gate: by dynamiting the rock. The 1869 underwater survey showed that the ledge was over 200 feet in diameter and of highly irregular depth. Various attempts to mark the hazard with mere spindles met with failure. The sea would simply overpower these pipe structures, which served (and continue to work) inside Fishers Island Sound. By the time the decision was finally made to build a major aid to navigation there, one large ship per year had been claimed for each of the preceding eight years.

Novelist-painter F. Hopkinson Smith (1838–1915) was named architect and drew up a kind of Rhineland fantasy. Smith, from Baltimore, was a writer of somewhat schmaltzy, pre-Faulknerian "southern" novels. He also did a book on Barnegat Bay. Mainly he seems to have been an architect and even an engineer. The great-grandson of a signer of the Declaration of Independence, Smith's most famous contribution had been the base of the colossal statue originally known as *Liberty Enlightening the World.*

The task there in New York Harbor was, of course, much simpler, as Smith was able to incorporate the existing foundation of Fort Wood on the dry land of Bedloe's Island in the protected bay. Among Smith's eventual achievements was the Block Island breakwater and the Staten Island sea wall. His other major aid to navigation was the plan for Mosquito Inlet Lighthouse at New Smyrna, Florida. Mosquito Inlet Light was completed during the building of Race Rock but cost seven lives, including the lighthouse engineer, Orville C. Babcock. Fortunately at Race Rock, Smith was able to bring Captain Thomas A. Scott as chief engineer on the project to subcontract the underwater portion of the job.

Scott came to New London from New York Harbor, at forty-one already a hero for his salvage work. He stayed on to run the premier maritime construction company in Eastern Long Island Sound until he died in 1907. Among his jobs were the waterfront facilities at all the island forts from Plum Island to Fishers Island, including Fort Michie. Scott had risen to fame when, as a deckhand on a New York Harbor ferry, he had literally thrown his body into the hole ripped by a passing vessel. From 1871 to 1878 Scott worked on Race Rock under as difficult conditions as had ever faced an American lighthouse engineer. It took him three years alone to get the foundation in. Here is Scott's account of constructing the foundation. His job was:

> To send divers down; chain and drag out from the center of the turtle's back [the rock itself] by means of heavy derricks all the rock that had been dumped in; to place these rocks thus rescued outside the circle of the proposed cone, piling them up as a breakwater, and after excavating down to the original sand of the bottom and uncovering the original Race Rock, to fill this water hole with concrete in the front of a great disc up to the level of low water, and upon this concrete disc to build the granite cone.

In 1897 architect Smith published a novel about the building of Race Rock Light, the climax of which was the setting of the keystone by his hero, whom he called Caleb West, Master Diver:

> Caleb thrust his hand into his haversack, grasped his long knife, slashed at the kelp of the rock-pile to see the bottom stones the clearer, and sent a quick signal of "All right—lower away!" through the life-line, to Lacey, who stood on the sloop's deck above him.
>
> Almost instantly a huge square green shadow edged with a brilliant, iridescent light sank down towards him, growing larger and larger in its descent. Caleb peered upward through his face-plate, followed the course of the stone and jerked a second signal to Lacey's wrist. This signal was repeated in words by Lacey to Captain Brandt, who held the throttle, and the shadowy stone was stopped within three feet of the gravel bottom. Here it swayed slowly, half turned and touched on the boulder.

Caleb watched the stone carefully until it was perfectly still, crept along, swimming with one hand, and measured carefully with his eye the distance between the boulder and the Ledge. Then he sent a quick signal of "Lower—all gone," up to Lacey's wrist. The great stone dropped a chain's link; slid halfway the boulder, scraping the kelp in its course; careened and hung over the gravel with one end tilted on a point of the rocky ledge. As it hung suspended, its lower end buried itself in the gravel near the boulder, while the upper lay aslant up the slope of the rock-covered ledge.

Caleb swims solicitously about the keystone for another two paragraphs, realizes that the stone is in a dangerous position, sends up for a crowbar, is visited by a blackfish, works the crowbar. Then:

the chain tightened; the bar, released from the strain, bounded from his hand; there was a headlong surge of the huge shadowy mass through the waving kelp, and the great block slipped into its place, stirring the bottom silt in a great cloud of waterdust.

The first stone of the system of enrockment had been bedded!

. . .

Noank Captain Ben Rathbun's 1999 account of the building of Race Rock Light sifts through Scott, Smith, the government reports, and contemporary accounts in the New London *Day:* Captain Rathbun not only researched the paperwork but has spent well over half a century making his living trolling the Race, with plenty of opportunity to weigh the practical aspects of the light's construction in its actual environment. He concludes that there were many false starts in the construction. The better part of one year had to be chalked up to experience:

Smith's original plans called for dumping overboard thousands of tons of random sized, irregular stone blocks that would then become a sort of foundation on which the concrete base of the lighthouse would be built . . . the concrete foundation was planned to be poured inside of a gigantic rectangular wooden caisson/form that would have been built in New London, towed to the site and then sunk over the top of the rubble base. . . . Smith's crew spent the better part of a year barging the stone out to the site and dumping it overboard before everyone concerned was forced to admit that the tactic was a dismal failure. Although the shallowest point was only three feet below the surface, it was almost a pinnacle and the steep-sloping sides of the rest of the outcropping allowed the strong current and pounding waves to force the rip-rap slowly downward and outward into the fifty-foot depths that surround the area on three sides. . . . Scott &

Company began the treacherous task of removing a greater portion of the rock they had just finished dumping overboard.

Starting literally at ground zero again, Scott built up the foundation to the point where they could begin the above-water work. Captain Rathbun continues:

This part of the job would seem to have been relatively easy after the undersea struggle to build the foundation but, starting as they were from the platform that was only 6 inches (1-foot?) above high water line, this too proved a difficult task until they got high enough to be out of reach of all but severe stormy weather. . . . Unfortunately, this work appears to have been started in the late fall [when] storm after storm [plagued] the workmen by washing away some of the construction shanties and emergency bunkhouses; sluicing the unhardened cement out of the joints between the stone blocks and toppling the wooden derricks; . . . [after] several of the winter gales the crew reported that they were in imminent danger of being swept out to sea and drowned.

. . .

Eighty years later, in 1954, the Coast Guard decided to do something about a crack that had developed in Smith and Scott's concrete. The flaw began in the platform and ran down like decay in a bad tooth to the root. Captain Rathbun tells us that Smith left the top nine and a half feet of the concrete "partly hollow to form an octagonal cistern with a capacity of 26,000 gallons of fresh water." He goes on to quote a newspaper account that said "if one removed the stone cover to the cistern during heavy weather, the noise of the waves transmitted up through the base, sounded like a freight train rushing through a tunnel at top speed." As one who has been aboard a similar off-shore light station during violent storms, I can attest to the overwhelming volume of sound such structures may transmit up through their roots.

The 1954 repair job was put out to civilian contract. Once again, as he had on Fort Michie, Larry Malloy found himself following in the legendary steps of Captain Thomas Scott. During the month of September, Larry and his crew, the former Branford stowaway Johnny Bartlett, lived aboard the boat. Every weekday Malloy drove Alice, the forty-year-old oyster-bumboat, to work from the staging area at the Coast Guard dock in Silver Eel Pond just around the corner to Race Rock a mile away to the west. They towed, pushed, and prodded the barge, or as Larry called it, "the lighter," now in Pirate's Cove. Because of the good weather, it was a pleasant commute.

Knowing the *Alice*'s layout below, I tried to understand a little more about the living arrangements he and Johnny had endured. Larry and I had spent a lot of time together in New England and tropic waters aboard the eighty-foot schooner *Sylvina W. Beal*. She was no "Love Boat," but an austere old girl built as a sardine carrier in 1911, modified slightly in 1983 for the passenger trade. Where there had been fish holds were now small cabins. Larry and I each had our own tiny space in which were jammed two bunks, a couple of clothes hooks, and a sink. There was a toilet around the corner. We met in common spaces such as the saloon up forward where there was a big table between benches and the galley with its stove and iceboxes. On deck was all kinds of space on either side of the booms. You could sit on one of three cabin tops. In port we often rigged a tarpaulin awning.

Alice, however, like many proper oysterboats I had seen, made *Beal* seem like a Love Boat. Typically the foredeck was occupied by machinery. There was almost no afterdeck. To go under cover you had the wheelhouse, with all its necessary gear for running the boat. It's true that running athwartships across the back of the wheelhouse there was typically a bench, which in theory might serve the skipper as a bunk. In practice, however, this "bunk" always seemed crammed with oil cans, tools, a portable stove, jackets, boots, and other items whose nomenclature has forever fled from me. If you stepped down from the wheelhouse and made your way aft outside on deck to the very stern, you could access the engine room through a small, shoulder-shredding aperture. Down there was just enough space for a small table between the companionway and the machinery. On either side there was one bunk under the side decks, a berth you have to kneel to get into—not the sort of place to while away the evening hours. You could not sit upright. You were either in the bunk, recumbent, or out of it, standing. Whenever I looked at one of those bunks I thought of Larry's story about how, when he was a kid and looked at his father's torn ear, he'd always thought, "It had been bit by a rat one night when he was laying down in one of them oysterboat bunks." (That the elder Malloy's ear had apparently been wounded in a South Street brawl at the turn of the century was cold comfort.) On the bulkhead of the engine room there might be, among the oil funnels and wrenches and spare gaskets and belts, a few cup hooks for a spatula or a bread knife and a few cups. The dipstick rag might serve as a pot holder. As for "facilities," there was the fantail.

"So, Larry," I said, apropos the Race Rock repair, "How did you get your dinners?"

"John Bartlett, he was cook. I think the Race Rock job is where he got a big boost up in how to handle the heavy marine construction which he went on to do."

"And you slept aboard *Alice* that whole month?"

"God damn it, Cap'n, you just don't get it. *We lived aboard of the boat.* That was our whole world. Hey, we had everything we needed—right there aboard. We had food. We had blankets."

"But at night?" I said. "I mean, where did you meet? In the engine room or the wheelhouse?"

"Actually it was usually the Pequot House," he said, referring to one of the two bars on Fishers Island.

"During the daylight we did whatever was needed. There was enough of that so that by dark, we wasn't bored doing nothing."

. . .

Once at Race Rock he would shift the lighter around in front of *Alice* and ease ahead, shoving the barge stern first up to the platform. Employing the same technique Smith described half a century earlier in *Caleb West, Master Diver,* Larry would then hold his vessel there—just so, adjusting helm and throttle to maintain the right pressure. Though they were lucky on the weather, even in the calmest of winds there was always a strong surge as the current swirled around the Rock. To hold the vessels kindly to the task they fashioned a great bridle from a pair of trailer truck tires. It was then they cabled one tire to each of those cleats now reposing in Pirate's Cove. They took another pair of cables and ran them from the tires to the lighthouse tower. The tires in between the cables acted like giant bungee cords, absorbing the shock of the sea. To hold the bow of the lighter, which was now turned away from the lighthouses, *Alice* would run out a pair of anchors to the north.

"The contractors working up on the platform threw bales of hay down the crack, you know, like farmers—bales of hay. Then they'd pour the concrete in on top. They used a tube to get it down below the sea, called a 'trummy' tube. Don't ask me to spell it. The idea was to keep the bubbles out. Then everything could set up."

For all its potential terror, Race Rock can be a glorious place, the very embodiment of the old Romantic sublime. The water boils around nearby Race Point, with its faded rose-brick fort, and in autumn the bluefish fleet is out under a cloud of gulls that makes you realize why the ancient Greeks thought that all significant knowledge came from the air. To the south is Gardiners Island. Behind it is Montauk and to the east is the open Atlantic, so that your eye is escorted out gently island by island to a soft infinity of ocean. And there was Larry Malloy with Johnny Bartlett, this man who as a boy had rowed out to the Branford stakes before first light and dozed aboard until dawn just for a chance to work. And there was the old bumboat now in slow-ahead on the swell of the Horse Race, tethered by trailer truck tires—yo-yoing between lighter and lighthouse, slow ahead on through the wheaty days of September, filling the hollow yelp of the sea in the great tower.

"Very pleasant out there, for a change," said Larry. "And to know that it could be pleasant and we could still make money. In fact, the more pleasant it was, the more we could get done. Ain't that the way it's supposed to be?"

They didn't always stay out at the lighthouse all day. Sometimes they did a lot of shuttling back and forth running errands for the project to some part of New London Harbor half a dozen miles distant. It was an hour's run unless they were towing the concrete lighter, when it could pretty much take half the day, depending upon the tide. Weekends they spent at home. It was one of the great times in his life.

. . .

Maybe the biggest operation Larry Malloy was involved in was the attempt to raise the 1910 submarine *G-2* from its berth in ninety feet of water in the Twotree Island Channel in 1954. Built in 1912 at the Lake Torpedo Company in Bridgeport, Connecticut, accidentally sunk in 1919 between the two world wars, and raised in 1954 after the second, the *G-2* would seem to embrace the entire history of what we would call the modern submarine. The whole salvage episode, however, reads like a parody of Edward Ellsberg's classic *On the Bottom*, a detailed account of the successful raising of another submarine of that era, the *S-51*, which had been sunk in a collision off Block Island.

To start with, unlike the open ocean off Block Island, Twotree Island Channel is an intimate back channel inside Bartlett Reef between New London Harbor and Niantic Bay. It is overlooked by the summer colony of Pleasure Beach, and in the period under consideration, the quarry at Millstone Point, now a nuclear power plant. Twotree Island itself is a thumbnail of glacial carelessness that at one point in some cartographer's career had accrued enough bird droppings to have provided the home for a couple of trees. I recall going past it during the period of Malloy's work and the island's boskage had been cut by 50 percent, which gave it the look of the archetypal islet upon which cartoon castaways exchange existential bon mots. Larry, however, says that there were no trees on the island since the 1938 Hurricane. When he was working the *G-2*, "On Twotree Island nothing but grass." Now it is just a handful of loosely associated rocks and cormorants. As a further point of parody, the voyages of *G-2*, according to Larry, were strictly experimental. Sometime between the two great wars, *G-2* was dedicated to serve as a guinea pig for the effect of depth charges. (There was no Niantic Bay Fisherman's Association to challenge this concussive endeavor.) The submarine was not flooded, but as typical in such experiments even years later, cranked down to the ninety-foot depth by winches on towboats. (It is interesting to note in the light of subsequent developments that on the most recent charts there is no ninety-foot depth in the Twotree Channel. The closest is eighty-four.)

One day, however, this 160-foot vessel that usually had to be forced by various windlasses and assays to the bottom for experimental purposes foundered all on her own. *Jane's Fighting Ships of World War I* shows the deck of the three-ship Simon Lake type G class as charmingly cluttered with hatches, cowl mouth vents, and other hostages to fortune. Over the more orthodox, solid conning tower is a flying bridge up on a half-dozen pipe stanchions complete with canvas spray cloths and a cambered canvas canopy and life ring that looks ideally suited to be a seaside beverage stand. Steve Finnegan, director of the Submarine Force Museum at the Groton Base, says, "It was so uncomfortable being below on those Lake class vessels that no one wanted to spend any time down there. The boats did most of their running on the surface anyway, so the men just kept evolving all these bizarre deck structures to make life up there more comfortable."

Larry Malloy remembers the story that the *G-2* crew was below at supper while anchored. "They had the aft hatch open. Apparently they didn't need to have shut it when they went below, but the wind can get nasty in Twotree Channel when the tide shifts. Those boats were built on purpose halfway in between sinking and floating anyway. The idea was not to have to work too hard to submerge. It only took a couple of seas slopping over. Later divers went inside of her and took out the bodies. The number three rings a bell. Why there weren't more, I don't know." (In what presumably is a study of a fully operational vessel, *Jane's* photo shows nine on deck and maybe five up in the snack stand.)

The hull remained in the Twotree Channel until after World War Two, when in 1954 a consortium of contractors including Larry Malloy was summoned to raise the vessel. "It was a period when everybody was hot to salvage stuff," said Larry. "You had what seemed to be great new technology from World War Two and you had no environmental regulations, no regulations about finding stuff that somebody thought out to be on a shelf in a museum. You just went at it with whatever surplus gear you had. No one really knew what the limits were. There used to be a guy followed us around hoping he could find out where we'd been salvaging that copper phone cable we had the contract for. It was a cable set in World War Two to connect gun emplacements on the [New York] islands. After the war, I guess they figured they either had better ways or didn't need no way at all. You never quite know with the government. Half the time they'll have you rip something out for one war and hurry up put it back for the next. Hey, it keeps you busy. For some reason this guy who was following us around thought we'd tell him where we left off so he could pick up the ends. Whenever we saw him steaming our way, we'd steam the other."

Steve Finnegan sent me the United Press account which in the February 8, 1957, *Hartford Courant* reported the *G-2* salvaging more soberly, if slightly inaccurately in regard to the arboreal name of the channel and depth of water:

> Another attempt will be made this spring to salvage the submarine *G-2* which lies in about 63 feet of water in Twin Tree Channel off Pleasure Beach.
>
> Several previous attempts to raise the vessel which sank July 30, 1919, have been unsuccessful.
>
> But William McGuire of the Wm. McGuire Co., a New York salvage firm, has no doubts about the task ahead.
>
> "We will do it," he said confidently.
>
> Some preliminary studies already have been made under the direction of Capt. Lawrence H. Malloy of Waterford, an oysterman who also does salvage work.

. . .

While "some preliminary studies" strikes him as a bit dry, Larry Malloy does remember McGuire. "On the *G-2* I was working for a fellow named William McGuire. Now he had one of these operations in Honduras. Surplus batteries, planes—you name it. I was going to work for him down there in Honduras, but he forgot the carfare. Anyway, on the *G-2* he was going to raise it up, get it ashore, clear her off, then put her on a flatbed railroad car and tow the thing around the country. In other words, make an exhibit of her, make an exhibition tour out of it. I suppose the fact that people died on it made it worth more.

"We were at it on and off for a couple of years. We had an eighty-foot scow we towed out with *Alice*. Once we found the submarine, we anchored the scow out over it. We got fastened to the wreck with wires hitched to four big hot water tanks for mooring buoys. In them days you didn't have all these nice rubber or plastic buoys. Sometimes, on smaller jobs, we used beer kegs. Of course, we took the beer out first so they would float.

"We were using a compressor on *Alice*. I still got that compressor in the cellar. Later we had to get a bigger one that we rented from Whaling City Dock and Dredge. The job was mainly weekends, as we was using hard hats off the navy salvage vessel *Sun Bird*. The hard hat divers, they found the hatch just after the conning tower rusted open. That must have been the one that killed her crew. They didn't find no hot dog stand thing like you got in the picture. That must have been something temporary just for summer cruising on the surface. Anyway [our] hard hats couldn't close the hatch.

"They brought the hatch up, and it was around here for a while until

McGuire, he took it away. Maybe somebody still has it. What we did to plug the hatch opening was get a truck tire and weld the rim. Seems like we was always using truck tires in them days: for bungee cords in the Race, fenders alongside the boats. Hey, for an all-around handy thing to have with you on a boat, seems you couldn't beat a truck tire. Beer kegs and truck tires, you could near run a salvage business with them. The hard hats set that tire down in the old hatch opening and pumped the tube back up so it filled the hole. We did get some good air into her then from the compressor up on *Alice,* but the pontoons we was using along each side to help raise her broke loose and left the submarine on the bottom.

"One day a hard hat diver named Jack Lehman was down on the wreck when something went wrong with his air supply. The sea was scuffing up a bit, and things started to come adrift. Jack Lehman, he knew he wasn't getting enough air, so he opened up a valve, but it was the CO_2 line and next thing we knew he was coming up to the surface. My Jesus Christ, but he was puffed up in his suit big as a dirigible. It's a wonder he didn't just shatter. When we got him out of the suit he was blue. He was OK, though. In fact, the next day he insisted he go right back down again. That's what those fellows have to do. Something about falling off a horse. And not only that, but last I knew he was still alive all these years later."

Here is the way diver Paul Tzimoulis described salvage action aboard *G-2* as filtered through reporter Bob Cahill's magazine prose:

> Exhaust bubbles flecked up through the salty mist. It was cold, and my eyes ached from peering into an endless stream of murky liquid. I could hear the mewing of Frank White's regulator as he gulped in deep breaths of metallic air. Although he swam close beside me, he was barely visible in the dimming depths. A fierce current pressed at our bodies, and caused our mouthpieces to flutter between our lips. We swam downward, deeper and deeper. Our destination was the green ooze that quivers on the floor of Long Island Sound off the coast of Connecticut. Somewhere in that ooze was one of America's oldest sunken submarines, the *G-2.*

. . .

The submarine itself, however, didn't make out as well. Eventually Bill McGuire figured he had already spent enough on the salvage and realized he'd never be able to break even on his proposed tour of the nation. He left the job and with him went Larry Malloy, who went back to his usual work with oysters and other acts of "junking."

"Next thing I know there's another contractor on the job and his idea is to blow the submarine up. Why they didn't just leave it there where it had been all them years I don't know. There's always the idea you got to do something to anything that gets into the sea. Get it back on land, even if all you're going to do is bury it all over again. I mean it wasn't like it was an environmental or a navigational hazard down there. The average depth in that channel is half what it is in that hole, even with the submarine in it. It probably made a good home for fish. As for environmental, I never heard that dynamite was all that healthy for the marine life. Anyway I was working in the river when I saw it come in on the barge like that—in pieces. My brother Frank, he remembers seeing her like that, too. I was going over after hours and see what they done to her up close. But you know, somehow I never did."

Photos provided by Steve Finnegan show the remains of *G-2*, complete with her number, lying in state upon the catafalque of the barge. The New London skyline is behind her. She looks like a combination of a locomotive boiler that has been in a train wreck and some kind of giant cephalopod that has suffered unspeakable writhings—a posture no doubt the result of the decades of torture suffered at the hands of her salvagers rather than any fatal impact with the Twotree Island Channel floor. In any case, she would seem better left, as diver Tzimoulis put it, "somewhere in that ooze."

"The scow we sold down to Dureay's lobsters at Fort Pond near Montauk," says Malloy. "As to the use of dynamite in the water, well, that wasn't a problem in the 1950s and it wasn't a problem even in the 1970s for Electric Boat. They used to set off dynamite right there in the Thames River. They called it 'shock testing.' They'd try out some sort of new part for a submarine, oh, most anything like, say, a reduction gear. They'd put it in a case and set it out in the river with dynamite on a line strung every twenty-five feet or so out from the case. They'd start setting off the charges at the outboard end of that line and work in to where something interesting happened. There was a man with a red flag on the boat to wave off passing boat traffic. That was the little towboat *Pilot*. Something interesting usually did happen: anywhere from a quarter ton to a half to some days a whole ton of striped bass would come to the surface belly up. Charlie Novelis, an old submariner, was the detonator expert. Me, I was the guy with the red flag."

NOTES

MOSQUITO INLET LIGHT DISASTER (p. 214): At 175 feet tall, "the tower was the second largest on the East Coast." The brick was shipped from Smith's home town, Baltimore. "Landing materials at the inlet was extremely dangerous, and during supervision of one of these landings, lighthouse engineer Orville C. Babcock drowned. The construction of Mosquito

Inlet Lighthouse took seven lives in all, casting a dark shadow over its otherwise jubilant lighting on November 1, 1887. *Guide to Florida Lighthouses* by Elinor De Wire, Pineapple Press, 1987, p. 28. It was from this sea mark that the fatal filibustering voyage so memorably rendered by Stephen Crane in "The Open Boat" took its departure a decade later.

JOHN BARTLETT, PAWCATUCK (p. 217): His obituary, from the October 10, 1999, *Mystic River Press*, follows:

John Clayton Bartlett, 60, of 15 Moss St., died Thursday, Oct. 21, at his home after a brief battle with cancer.

He was born August 17, 1939, in Haverhill, Mass., the son of Vernon Y. Bartlett of Pawcatuck and the late Ruth Clayton Bartlett.

Mr. Bartlett served in the Navy as a navigator aboard destroyers for more than five years. He then worked for various marine contractors before assuming operation of the Elliot & Watrous Co., of Mystic, in 1966, and later creating Bartlett Construction Co. He also assisted in shipbuilding and worked as a tugboat captain for Thames Shipyard in New London.

He was a charter member of the Ledyard Sportsman Club. He enjoyed the water throughout his life, working on oysterboats in Branford and New London as a teenager.

Here is John Bartlett, age twenty-five, writing a letter from his quarters on a storm-bound destroyer escort to his old mentor, a letter Larry Malloy was to keep in his oyster basket for thirty-seven years.

John C. Bartlett
U.S.S. *Hartley* DE. 1029
Fleet Post Office New York New York
Tuesday Feb. 4, 1963

Dear Lawrence,

How are you and how have you been? I have been meaning to drop you a line since last June but now I'm getting around to it. I guess you have figured out by now I'm in this outfit but if all goes well and they don't start any more war games I will get out in June 143 more days. I am counting them again for the third time. I am down in Jacksonville Fla. Right now we are waiting out a blow here and hope to leave for Newport as soon as it is over. I'm navigator on a small ship now and we don't stick our nose out in that rough water if we can help it. I plan on dropping down sometime soon on a weekend if I get a chance. So how have you been doing are you and Bill still in with the sandsucker or have you changed operations now? Last time I saw you he was over in Long Island with the dredge. Has Frank got use to those teeth yet he had just had them pulled last time I was up? How's Pappy and how did the [oyster] set come out last year? Have you got any more kids started last I knew you had more than I could count. I guess most of them are getting pretty big now I probably wouldn't recognize them all. I've been collecting a few charts of the sound home every now and then I bring some home. I been planning on bringing you down some when I get a chance. . . . Well I'm sure waiting for the day I get free of this outfit. I guess you remember when you was in and wanted to get out. Well, I guess there's not much more to say now. Say Hello to Helen & kids and everyone else around. Drop a line when you get a chance. I hope I see you soon.

Best of luck, John

SLIGHTLY INACCURATE SUBMARINE REPORTS (p. 221): There are a number of small discrepancies between the UP dispatch and either Malloy's account or information in *Jane's Fighting Ships*. The UP account does, however, agree with Malloy that the sinking was due to "carelessness."

25

WORKING ON OTHER PEOPLE'S BOATS

> How bitter it is I know
>
> to climb another man's stairs
>
> and eat another man's bread.
>
> —Dante, *Inferno*

BLOCK ISLAND HAS been one of the favorite escape places for people in southern New England and New York for well over a hundred years. My grandmother in her one-room schoolmarm days used to spend July and August overlooking the Atlantic on the veranda of the Spring House. As far as I can figure out, her time was taken up fending off a married bottle salesman and catching up on her reading. There was a pianoforte in the front parlor upon which she practiced her stirring renditions of such tunes as "Under the Double Eagle." Other visitors were not as sedate. Ferry boats ran from Providence, Newport (taken once by Ben Franklin), and Point Judith. The ferry from New London got most of the New York traffic. It was on this run that Larry Malloy went to work in 1947.

He began on the *Pemaquid*, a diesel-driven vessel with a steel hull that yet retained the old flavor in its wooden superstructure. His first job was deckhand, but he soon earned a battlefield promotion to quartermaster. In those days, as now, the New London run departed from downtown early in the morning, ran the seven miles east through Fishers Island Sound, out through Watch Hill Passage into Block Island Sound, and reached Payne's Dock in New Harbor in midmorning. It left the Island in midafternoon and was back in New London around suppertime. It carried cars and had a snack bar. On an average decent day the bluffs of Block Island are visible from Noank. In a bad easterly, the Island can seem as far off as Spain. Once inside the harbor your troubles were not necessarily over.

. . .

"We was coming in to Block Island, Payne's Dock—you know where they sold the salt-water taffy and the ridgepole is held either up or down by the seagulls; I could never figure out which. Cap'n Billy Evans was on the wheel. He was famous for towing targets off Norfolk in the steamer *Sprague Carol*, an old Block Island boat by now dying in Shaw's Cove, New London. Cap'n Billy Evans himself was getting on to be an elderly man, a bit frail and that was a great big steering wheel. Not much gearing going back to the rudder so you get the leverage from the wheel. You know—one of them steering wheels that look real good hanging up in the ceiling of a seafood restaurant as a chandelier. Except here's a man really trying to steer with it before it turned into a chandelier.

"My job was down on the foredeck. I was supposed to be getting a line around a spile at Payne's. I just done this and am taking up the slack, looking back up at the wheelhouse over my shoulder to get the signal from Cap'n Billy Evans as to when to take a hitch around the bitt. I see him for just a second, his little head in the window; the spokes are spinning and then he's gone! The *Block Island*, she's still in ahead, so I run along the deck and climb up into the wheelhouse and there's Cap'n Billy Evans on the deck of the wheelhouse. He's gotten himself thrown by the wheel!

"I grab a spoke and straighten everything up and then help Cap'n Billy Evans back to his feet.

"'That's good,' he says, 'From now on, I want you up here with me in the wheelhouse.'

"I done that from then on. They got somebody else to handle the lines. I left *Pemaquid* to work back on the *Block Island* because of a pay raise the *Pemaquid* wasn't willing to match, but Cap'n Evans wanted me to stay on. He even offered to pay the difference between *Block Island*'s offer and *Pemaquid* out of his own pocket. I thanked him, but didn't take him up on that.

"Sometimes they had the *Yankee* (former *Block Island*) working the Yale-Harvard Race, which was in June when the Block Island season hadn't really got underway. In 1948 I thought we was going to roll her over. All them passengers up on the top deck and when the rowboats go by, they all rush to one side. I was deckhand and thinking she'd topple a bit, but I wasn't all that worried. I figured the boat would just start spilling the spectators over a bit at a time until about half of them would be in the river. Then she'd come up again OK and be all right.

"Well, for some reason none of that happened, but something else did. Cap'n Jack Williams, one of those Vermont Central Railroad men, was the pilot. Tommy Watt, he was captain. We're coming through the Railroad Bridge with a lot of traffic roiling up the water all around. It was as bad as going through Plum Gut, wind against the tide. Right then we lose our steering. Harvey Fuller, later the famous artist, he's another deckhand. He and I break out the relieving tackle and the tiller, which was in a deck box, and we rigged up a block and fall with the relieving tackle to the tiller. That's why they call it 'relieving tackle' I guess, because it's supposed to re-lieve your mind. This gets us through the bridge opening and Cap'n Jack Williams wants to know if we can land these people somewhere along shore.

"'Land 'em where they'll know where they are,' I said. 'Land them where they think they was going to land anyway—at the City Pier.'

"'Ooh, that will be too hard,' he says. 'How am I gonna do that with the steering being done back down there on the fantail where nobody can see what they're doing?'

"I shout up that Tommy Watt can stand out on the wing of the bridge and so see both the helm and us. So OK, that's what we're gonna do. And, damn it, that's exactly what we was doing: Tommy Watt up on the wing looking down at where the boat's heading and then looking aft down at us signaling where to shift the tiller with the relieving tackle. And we're laying her right to the City Pier. Except Jack Williams, he didn't quite have confi-dence it was really working out all right. His mind, it wasn't *relieved*. He rings down the back-up bell. Now with all that pressure on the rudder going backwards the juryrigged tiller which is close down to the deck on the fantail—that tiller can sweep across your legs, cut your legs right off or put you in the river—with the boat backing over you. All's we can do is dance out of the way of the tiller—Harvey Fuller and me dancing at the Yale-Harvard.

"'Hey,' I shouts up to the bridge. 'Tell Jack to take it easy. He'll kill some-one here!'

"I look up to see if I can find Tommy Watt on the wing, but I don't see him! Without him we've lost our eyes!

"Somehow we gets her alongside the pier OK. It's one of those things that looking back you can't figure out just exactly how that part got done and you wouldn't believe it *did* get done except there you are: *done*.

"Tommy Watt, he finally comes back into view. He comes down off the bridge and he comes aft and he says, real confidential: 'You know Cap'n Jack, he called you every name in the book up there.'

"Now that really got me. So I walked up to the wheelhouse and told him we was just doing the best we could.

"He looks at me and he says, 'OK, you did a good job.'

"Just like that. Case closed."

. . .

"The thing was it took us a long time to figure out what had happened to the steering. And it kept on happening. We was running moonlit cruises up the Thames to Norwich. No place to lose your steering. And every time we'd go to turn back into City Pier, which was hard right rudder, she'd veer off and go to the left. One time we went all the way across the river over to the Pfizer Pier and laid a light pole down on the pier. Funny thing is we tended to lose the steering less when I was on the wheel. The only difference between me and the other fellows was *I'm a take-it-easy guy*.

"I can usually anticipate where she's gonna go and so I don't have to do a lot of hard spinning. Don't forget, I been steering these workboats since my Pappy put me up on that chopping block on *Anne*. *Yankee* had a new electric motor to help with the wheel. It wasn't like with Cap'n Billy Evans having to spin himself half to death on *Pemaquid*. *Yankee*, she had been steam, but when they switched her over to diesel they also added this new feature to do the work for you when you was rolling the wheel. We figured that this new electric must have been the problem, but we just couldn't find the exact problem *inside* of what was electric. One day we got the panel off and there, sure enough, was a little piece of welding rod that had gotten in there. You know how when you're welding and your rod gets down to a nub, you flip that useless nub overboard or some place. Well somebody welding sometime past done that *flicking,* only he didn't flick the nub far enough out of the way. If you rolled that wheel over real fast the magnetism got riled up and picked that flicked nub, that little piece of rod, sucked it right up off the bottom of the space back of the panel and flung it around so's it shorted out the steering and there you were—veering off God knows where!"

. . .

"From 1964 to 1973 I worked for Clarence Sharpe at Whaling City Dock and Dredge. The 'Whaling City,' of course, was actually New London, but Clarence Sharpe had his base on the Groton side of the Thames right there under the Gold Star Bridge. He had the biggest things going then in the private side of things as far as marine work went. He himself was a great big man who some people said looked a little like a whale himself. Funny thing is that Clarence Sharp was actually a *haberdasher* before he was an engineer. Leastwise that's what I think you call those people: *haberdashers*. We'd be up in that office where he had the spittoon. That was pretty famous, the spittoon. Clarence Sharpe chewed tobacco. In fact, to tell the truth, there was more than one spittoon. He had them here and there all over the office, though it was chiefly Clarence Sharpe himself that did all the chewing. We'd be looking at that spittoon and wondering about it, you know, things like *accuracy*. We was waiting for him to tell us where to go with the *Bateleur*. She was one of his tugboats, meant 'Happy Warrior' in some kind of language, ninety-eight feet long, four crew, built as a minesweeper in 1942 down to Solomon Island in the Chesapeake, I think. He'd throw a *cloth* around his shoulders, you know kind of wrap himself up in a bright cloth and say, '*There, you see, this is what I used to do.*'

"Well, Jesus, what would you say to that? What could you do? You'd have to just stand there and wait until he got done wrapping himself up and un-wrapping himself and got back to the subject of the tugboat *Bateleur*, 'The Happy Warrior,' ninety-eight-foot ex-minesweeper.

"He was a damn good engineer though. And he was always good to me. Even in winter when there wasn't always work he kept me on, if it was just to walk the dog. He had one of them little dogs. It was called *Jacques* to rhyme with shock. He carried that dog around with him everywhere, every place he went. It used to do his job right about anywhere, in the office. In other words, Jacques wasn't much more accurate than Clarence Sharpe with his spittoons. Wintertime when there wasn't much work on the water, Clarence Sharpe still kept us on the payroll. One of our winter jobs— Charlie Novelis, the dynamiter, and me, we used to take Jacques for his walk. We'd take turns, one with the pooper-scooper, the other with the dog. We'd walk out one way, and then come back switched over. When we doing the dynamiting, we never did that. It was always me with the red flag, Char-lie with the dynamite.

"In summer Clarence Sharpe, he had me running the 'See Submarines by Boat' tours. A pair of sixty-five-footers, *The Double D* and *The Sea Lion*, licensed for forty-eight passengers and two crew. What with that big flat truck wheel in the stern and the long open-well deck from the steering platform all the way forward, people figured they was surplus Navy liberty launches. Fact is, he actually had them built at Warren, Rhode Island, for just this purpose. We started out right there at Whaling City Dock and Dredge under the Gold Star Bridge and went north up the river to the United States Submarine Base. Then you turn around and come back down all the way to the Electric Boat Company. Everyone found this pretty exciting because it was the middle of the Cold War, and here was all our stuff all laid out. You could see folks looking around to see who might be a Russian, but hey, nobody in a big fur hat ever showed up.

"At first we had a spiel on the tape made by some radio announcer fellow. But damn, I had a hard time keeping up with the tape or maybe getting ahead of it. You know, a big vessel'd come by, and you'd have to quarter off on the wake so you wouldn't drown everybody that was there in that big open-well deck forward. Or you'd get in a head sea or maybe there was just too many other boats, and first thing you know the guy in the tape is talking about the submarines when you're going by the ferryboats. Besides I got tired of listening to the same thing every day, and some of what he was saying wasn't even true, not even if I had the goddamn boat in front of the right ship. So that's when I begun my career as an announcer myself. That way I could keep up with my boat and maybe even get some stories right about other people's vessels. I could also make a joke or two, which always helps. At least it helps me. Of course at Whaling City Dock and Dredge we done other things besides clean up dog turds and tell jokes. We dynamited fish, built docks, ripped up cables, tore apart lighthouses, and tugged submarines into dry dock. So I guess you could say it was the *full range of waterfront activities*.

"Then, of course, there was working for brother Bill down to Bridgeport Harbor all day and half the night on the mud-barge *Carnesee*. That was the worst job I ever had until I fell down the ladder on some grease going to fix something in the engine room and wrecked my knee. That was, you might say, the high point—hey, it got me off the job."

NOTE

BATELEUR AS "HAPPY WARRIOR" (p. 230): It is interesting to think how a man can be sustained day in and day out in his labors by a wrong definition, buoyed up by a poetry that is not only false, but as in this case, perhaps even less rich than that which was potentially there. "*Bateleur, n.* A common African eagle, *Terathopius, ecaudatu s.,* having a very short tail. F; mountebank, juggler" (*Random House Dictionary,* 2nd ed). "'*Le Bateleur,*' the conjuror, a reference to the Tarot card of that ilk" (Charles Nicholl, *Somebody Else: Arthur Rimbaud in Africa 1880–91*). Nicholl goes on to say how this idea of *le bateleur* as the conjurer in the tarot pack has sustained him on his travels in search of the nineteenth-century French author of "The Drunken Boat"—travels "to Charleville and Paris and Marcella, to Alexandria and Aden and Harar [Ethiopia]." One can only speculate, however, which is the stronger image, a gypsy card or a yard tug capable of moving otherwise hapless nuclear submarines about, any one of which could have commenced the destruction of the literal world.

As a minesweeper, *Bateleur*'s World War Two career had been no less precarious. After the war many were dispersed far and wide. According to Jane's *Fighting Ships of World War II,* some were scrapped or, like *Bateleur,* sold. Some were transferred to the Soviet navy, some to the Chinese navy. Only one, *Salute,* seems to have been lost in the war. Other names for World War Two minesweepers include: *Ardent, Competent, Heed, Motive, Token, Zeal, Threat, Symbol, Requisite, Disdain, Dour, Knave, Jubilant, Staunch, Strength, Reproof, Risk, Logic, Implicit, Bombard, Device, Scuffle, Gayety,* and *Hilarity,* names indeed to conjure with.

26

INVENTIONS AND OTHER GADGETS

Glory be to God for . . .

all trades, their gear and tackle and trim . . .

 —Gerard Manley Hopkins, "Pied Beauty"

But actual adaptation takes place on the local level, where particular individuals and groups come to terms with specific environments.

 —Lawrence J. Taylor, "Oystering on Long Island in

  Comparative Perspective," *Long Island Historical Journal*

I look at these pictures and see some particular piece of a rig and I say, "Now why do we have *that* ?" Then I think: sometimes it's just because we didn't have anything else.

 —Larry Malloy

IN NOANK EVERY Memorial Day there is what may well be the world's shortest parade. Among the virtues of a short parade is that it gathers people together who don't see each other that often and it doesn't exhaust them. It gives them enough time at the end in which to visit. Furthermore, you don't even need to see all of the parade. A lot of people bid it farewell when it crosses the railroad tracks and goes out to the cemetery and on down to the War Memorial out by Beebe Cove. Not only is that territory outside the village proper, but that is the region where the speeches tend to accumulate.

Fortunately there are a number of places to stop off in Noank after the parade, and even during the parade. There is the fire house where the star apparatus of the parade is stowed; the park, where the kids are whizzing about on their bikes in imitation of the apparatus, and Carson's front porch. Since 1914 Carson's has been known for its "Sundries, Newspapers, Candy and Ice Cold Ice." If there were no Norman Rockwell, Carson's would have called him into being. It was here I ran once again into Charlie Haines, or Doctor Charles Haines, as he is now known.

Charlie grew up down the street, but the last I had seen him was at the Royal Pink Princess or some such venue in Bermuda where we happened to be attending an international convention on wrecks. Charlie had begun museum work in Mystic at the Seaport Museum, gone on to the Buford, North Carolina, museum, and thence to the Philadelphia Maritime Museum. Somewhere in there he had earned a Ph.D. in history at the University of Delaware by writing a thesis on material culture, which explored the relationship between the use of wood and the changing roles in society of the workers who used this material.

Charlie knew Larry Malloy and had been keeping track of *Anne* in her days out on the Noank Grounds and more recently upriver in the West Mystic Shipyard where she was being rebuilt. I said that we had arrived at the point where Larry and I had been talking about inventions and how they came about in the oyster business. Over a couple of bottles of fruit juice Charlie jumped right into the discussion.

"In those days when there were hand skills involved, a man was defined not just in his job but in the community at large by his ability to practice these skills. Every one, male and female, young and old, knew who the stars were. These were the people you looked up to. These were the people you listened to at meetings whatever the agenda was. This was all fine until some technical device came along and replaced those human skills. Then that man, even if he had kept his job, even if he had maintained or improved his wage, he lost his prestige not only in the workplace, but after a while even in the community."

Charlie's insight hit home. Only a couple of weeks earlier Noank had celebrated the funeral of a wonderful old boat builder whose career had illustrated certain aspects of the thesis. In a tiny boat yard on the West Cove of Noank in the 1940s Bob Whittaker and Web Eldridge had built a handful of unpretentious down-home wooden fishing boats. Students of craftsmanship might call them "vernacular." By the end of the war few boats were being built anywhere and when they were constructed most were poured out of fiberglass. There followed a hiatus in wooden boat building lasting almost a full generation, before the advent of what is now known in retrospect as the Wooden Boat Revival. To make ends meet Bob Whittaker worked building submarines, where, according to some of the other villagers who toiled alongside him, he'd spend the day waiting for other union specialists to get out of the way so that he could squirt something in a hole: "It was a crying shame to see a man of his talent go that way." The other side of that sort of "employment," of course, was that there was now a good, steady wage with benefits. It turns out that this was the same dismal time on the water when Larry Malloy had worked "in housing" and later given his "See Submarines by Boat" tours.

"I got a lot from Lewis Mumford," said Charlie. "Mumford was one of the first to do the sort of analysis that showed the relationship between the way a person lived in a community and the way not only the tools, but the materials that the tools were designed to work functioned."

. . .

When Larry came by I asked him about innovations. Who made them? Under what circumstances? How did they spread ?

"Well, everybody tries to go modern, but that ain't always the best way. I already told you about the electric steering on the *Yankee*. OK, you go with electricity on a salt-water operation and you get what you ask for, but you take *hydraulics*. Suddenly everybody's got to have hydraulics. We had perfectly good wheel ropes, and hey, they was foolproof. So we put hydraulics on the steering on *Alice* and when something happened in the hose, Christ, where was it going on? It could be in the coupling or somewheres in the middle. In the meantime you are helpless. We'd gone modern and hid the hose and I had to knock a hole through the wheelhouse to find the damn thing. Then you got to replace the entire hose anyway. You also got to put the wheelhouse back together because you smashed it all apart to get at the damn hose. Before that, what with rope or chain, what you see is pretty much what you got and you can splice in a patch. You can fix it yourself, which is what you're always going to have to do out there anyway.

"As far as waterfront changes, hey, these days you go by some place you haven't been in two years, you're lost."

"But *fads* aside, we was always inventing something or other just to get done what we had to do with what we happened to have. It wasn't that we thought of it as *inventing* or nothing. It wasn't trying to be *creative* or *clever*. It was just *making do.* You didn't have a catalogue and a credit card. You had a piece of wood or iron and maybe some rope.

"As far as getting ideas from other people, well, sometimes we'd be in Co-ecles Harbor, say, and we'd see a guy come in with a different way of rigging a boom or something. We'd keep an eye on him and see if it was working out. If you'd see him again a little while later, and he was still doing it, then maybe you'd look a little harder. That's how the boom on *Anne* got re-rigged. Pretty soon, you'd see everybody doing it that way and you'd say, 'Hey, wasn't that always the way we did it?'

"That mast on *Alice,* by the way, that was nothing but the end of the Cup Defender *Rainbow*'s jib boom or something. Another item we got through the Monsells in Greenport."

· · ·

Sometimes change wasn't this seamless. There was, at least in the Malloy business, always the generational lag. The exchange between father and son was at all times a potential source of crisis, but when it came to innovation, the generational conflict usually was the determining factor.

"'If it works why change it?' says the old man. Well, you're forced to change. Wages . . . regulations. When you stop to think about it, the old man and I we never really did get along. I don't know if it was because I thought I knew everything. We had quite a go-round on the dock at Greenport. People came from all around to hear it.

"I already told you about the time my old man took me down to the Greenport Shipyard, picked me up and set me up on the scaffold so I could see. 'Don't fall in the hole,' he says. We were looking at *Anne.* There was a hole because they had her all opened up and were putting that tugboat or horseshoe stern in her. She'd had a square or *sloop stern* when she was built as a freighter, but *Anne,* she needed the structural strength of the tugboat stern—that kind of bracing—if she was going to do much towing. Now, I suppose you could call that 'innovation,' what Pappy was doing. To him making a fantail back there, a pretty shape—that was all just to make the stern stronger structurally so you could pull on it without having the back end of the boat fall apart on you. I don't know where he got that fantail idea, but you see a lot of the boats of that period got that done to them. 'Don't fall in the hole,' but my Jesus Christ, that must have been the last time we discussed anything halfway near an '*innovation.*'"

· · ·

To put this sort of family business hierarchy in perspective, I think of another local father-son fisherman combination of the same era. A man who was crewing on one of the other fish boats at the dock in New London in midcentury told me, "I see the son coming down the pier with his hand over his ear and blood coming out from between his fingers. Turned out his father and he had had an argument about if the wind was too strong that day to go out. The father thought the wind was just fine and to prove his point, he slashed his son's ear with a razor."

In *The Myth of the Machine* Lewis Mumford puts even more distance on the syndrome:

> Tradition was more precious than invention. To keep even the smallest gain was more important than to make new ones at the risk of forgetting or forfeiting the old. It was not nostalgia but the necessity for preserving the hard-won symbols of culture that made man treat the ancestral past as inviolable: at once too valuable and too valuable to be lightly altered. (p. 98)

. . .

Rebuilding would not in itself seem to be innovation, but it offers another look at the technology that preceded you. Museums are, of course, committed to restoration, not merely repair, but even they often debate the question of what they sometimes call *target date*. In other words, in the long life of this artifact what was the most characteristic moment, the instant when it was most what we have come to recognize it as? That there was (or in the display sense *is*) such a moment may well be the fatal assumption. After all, even in simpler days and before planned obsolescence the artifact was never designed to be a static response to its complex environment. The artifact was, after all, once a functioning device in a real, complex, and dynamic society. Catch it at any given time and it had been not only repaired but modified perhaps many times. And how many repairs modulated into modifications under the banner of "While we're at it, we might as well"? To what model number are we restoring? The schooner *Emma C. Berry* came back to Noank some hundred years after she'd been built in the village as a sloop. There was a great celebration at the shipyard aboard the schooner and then she traveled up the Mystic River to her "final resting place" at the Mystic Seaport Museum. There experts decided she should be "restored" to her original sloop rig. Down at Orion Ford's gas shack, Noank boat builder and master mariner Jack Wilbur argued with his characteristic sense of irony that this was patently nonsense.

"While it was true that *Emma C. Berry* had been launched as a sloop, this rig almost immediately had proved unwieldy, unsatisfactory. She was within her first years rerigged as a schooner, and it was as a *schooner* that she earned her living all those subsequent years. This was the very *living* that economically justified her maintenance and incidentally, it was this living that she earned under a *schooner* rig that preserved her long enough so that she was still around long enough to enable these 'experts' to be born, then educated and finally hired to make the decision they made."

Commercial mariners such as the Malloys are, of course, under no such archival obligations, but it is interesting to see in what way they do preserve the old ways, not out of nostalgia, but, as Captain Wilbur suggests, out of economic necessity. The case of *Anne*'s stern is a good example. When rebuilding her in 1999, Larry Malloy's successor, Thom Janke, who happened to have been a shipwright in the duPont Preservation Shipyard at Mystic Seaport, never even entertained the notion he might go back to her original 1884 "sloop" stern.

"It was more a question of how much we'd add to the freeboard of the 'new' fantail stern that Larry had seen his dad putting on in the 1920s," said Janke. "She had gotten so hogged that there was almost nothing above water back there. You'd step down from the wheelhouse feeling pretty good about things, but when you walked aft behind the engine house, it could be quite a shock when you came to the end of that house and found yourself only inches above the water. To put it another way, you know you're in trouble when you have to start putting bottom paint on your port of call. The word 'Anne' was still above water, but there was scum halfway up 'New London.'"

Thom and shipwright Walter Ansell added another foot of vertical staving above the old water line. "It's an old boat builder's adage," said Walter. *"If you can't lower the river, raise the boat."*

One day recently Larry was standing back of *Anne*'s stern when she was up on the poppets being worked on by Thom and Walter. "You don't know where to start so you flip a coin and start there. After a while, you say, 'Oh, shit! I shouldda started three feet more in.' Then you get so the problem is trying to figure out where to stop.

"We always made sure the deck was as tight as the bottom because lots of times we used the deck as the bottom, what with the load. By that I don't mean we was upside down. I just mean we was damn low in the water. In fact that got to be the thing. The lower you was in the water, the less of the boat you had showing, hey, the better you was doing. If you sunk the ship, you knew you musta done real well. We never did do quite that good."

. . .

I found a roll of film I'd taken in 1969 of a trip I'd taken on *Anne* with Larry's father, Walt, and Elmer Edwards of the Oyster Ground Committee. I showed Larry a picture of the galley, which shared the space with the engine room. He became a bit miffed, twisted the photo this way and that, even upside down, tromboning. "You sure you took this picture? You sure this was *Anne?*"

I attempted to assure him, fanning out several other snaps from the same shoot.

"That bulkhead, it looks too goddamn clean. Remember that big diesel's in there, too."

"Must be washed out by my flash."

"And that hand basin hanging on the bulkhead over by the foxtail—I don't remember we hung it there. There was a post—it's not in this view—ran down the middle of the cabin, had a nail on it. That's where we hung the hand basin so the water would drip down in the bilge."

"Well," I said, "these photos were taken at a time when you told me you were not on the boat. You were working for Whaling City Dock and Dredge."

"I guess so. And while I done that, *this must have been the time Pappy changed the way we hung up the hand basin.*"

"Hey, when the cat's away—"

. . .

We got to talking about wheelhouses. The wheelhouse, sometimes called the "pilothouse," is more than just the shelter for the helmsman. It is the very soul of the vessel. On oysterboats it is usually the grandiose structure that catches your eye and by which individual boats can be identified. By comparison, the other deckhouse, the protection over the engine, is merely a large, unornamented box tacked to the back of the wheelhouse, and apt to be barely visible above the bulwarks.

As on a tugboat, but not competing with a big funnel or stack, the oysterboat wheelhouse towers nobly from the deck just aft of amidships, culminating in a rounded front capped by a visor. On the top of the wheelhouse, set in their boards, are the required port and starboard running lights. Often it is just aft of the visor on each side that the name is displayed on a separate board. Within this formula there was a wide range of subtle variations. Larry Malloy noted, "There was all sorts of ideas about how deckhouses, wheelhouses, all that stuff should be designed. On *Commodore* the wheelhouse jutted way out over the foredeck. There was nothing under the floor but a couple of stanchions holding up the front end. You was standing pretty much on air, but for the floorboards. Running *Commodore* in winter you'd try to push as much of your load as possible up under the wheelhouse as insulation."

The present wheelhouse on *Anne,* for reasons discussed below, however, left something to be desired. Larry Malloy: "Now the windows in *Anne's* old pilothouse looked better, what with that overshot design, and they drained good, but occasionally they'd come down on you like a guillotine. That was on your fingers, not your head."

Thom Janke and Walter Ansel had set up new stanchions on *Anne's* deck. Stanchions have been around a long time. Captain Smith defines them in his 1627 *Sea Grammar,* and Richard Henry Dana takes a crack at them in his 1841 *Seaman's Friend* :

> upright pieces of timber, placed at intervals along the sides of the vessel, to support the bulwarks and rail, and reaching down to the bends, by the sides of the timbers to which they are bolted.

On an oysterboat there were traditionally spaces between the stanchions, cut-out slots in the bulwarks through which the oyster shells were shoveled, rather than lifted the extra couple of feet up over the bulwarks. On *Anne* the stanchions had formerly been the traditional wooden posts. It was because the rot that had infected the timbers below deck had begun in these structures that Thom had decided to make them out of stainless steel. Without the bulwarks yet being added to them, in the dim light of the boat shed the stanchions gleamed like dragon's teeth. Larry was standing next to me on the scaffold along the port side. I expected some comment from him as to the cost of these stainless steel extravagances, or perhaps something about the aesthetics, or trends in modern innovations, a robust satire on the younger generation. "Well," I said at last, "what do you think of those stanchions?"

"Hard on the shovel," he said.

It was a remark that only an old oysterman who'd worked the decks and not always hit the pass-through slot in the bulwarks could have made.

When Thom bought *Anne* from Larry, he had been slow at first to innovate. By the second year, however, he'd added an electric winch and a ventilator, and perhaps most alarming of all, a depth finder. It was only when I saw this strange blinking screen in the wheelhouse that I realized I had never seen one there before. "It's all well and good for Larry not to have a depth finder," said Thom. "Hell, he's got the whole chart of the bottom in his head."

This was true. I recalled being in the wheelhouse of *Anne* one day years before when we were going down the Thames River. We had just passed the United States Submarine Base to port and to starboard was the United States Coast Guard Academy waterfront. Ahead was the span of the Pequot Bridge.

"Here," said Larry, "take the helm. I have to go aft a minute."

I looked around for the channel markers. It was a wide part of the river. Nevertheless, we were probably a good fifty yards outside the channel. On the left bank above us was a huge housing project filled with the wives and children of naval personnel. It was here that today's nuclear technicians put their heads down at night. The aggregate knowledge of the most complex information on judging water depth that was on those pillows probably added up to more knowledge on this subject than in the previous history of man since Archimedes took his bath. I, however, had no certainty as to what was under our keel.

Fortunately it occurred to me then that *Anne* as an oysterboat had probably spent more of her life out of the channel than in it. I continued to steer for the same bridge abutment that had been dead ahead when I was given the helm. In a moment Larry was back. "I guess *Anne*'s spent more of her life out of the channel than in it," I said.

"That's right," he said. "She knows the river pretty good by now." Nevertheless he took the helm back.

"I'm glad you didn't fall off the stern," I said.

"I don't usually do that," he said.

. . .

Various nonmaritime contingencies cause modification. During a low point in *Anne*'s life a man got hold of her who was an admirer of the TV show *Love Boat*. To achieve what he thought was the same effect as he had seen on the tube, he got an old trailer and, having removed the derrick and culling table from *Anne,* placed the trailer lovingly upon the foredeck. The only problem, as the Innovator now saw it, was he could not quite see over the trailer from the wheelhouse. It was this wheelhouse that Larry Malloy had referred to in his discussion of overshot windows, and the one that had been in place when I'd first gone aboard her with Larry's father all those years before. Our innovator did not even have the sense, as had others in the area with similar gems on their hands, to turn the classic wheelhouse into a tomato stand or a summerhouse—or even a phone booth. He simply broke it up, overshot windows, staving, and all, and honored the Montville dump. In its place he stuck a bleak plywood enclosure of adequate height to permit him to peer over the beloved trailer. He even removed the old Roosevelt mahogany wheel with the locking pawl that had saved old man Malloy. In its place he put a gleaming chrome helm suitable for a plastic sailboat owned by an investments counselor.

. . .

Sometimes there is just no hope for the design that got handed to the Malloys in the middle of a job. Such was the case of the square-bow narrow skiff they had been using downstate in a dredging operation. The innovation, if you want to call it that, existed in the manipulation of the tool. Or, as Larry put it, "That barge come from Branford. The only way I could tow that sonofabitch here was all the way backwards."

Even in so apparently small a thing as packaging freight, innovation was necessary to adjust to the nuances of the season. As we have seen, in July potatoes were shipped from Halyoake Farm in barrels to protect the skins because bags would chafe off the outer layer. At other times they were freighted in burlap bags.

Sometimes the ability to innovate was a matter of life and death. In boot camp the Coast Guard lists "mattresses" as emergency caulking. While hearing things like this can be a charming moment in an otherwise grim period of one's life, I had never known anyone who'd actually employed this technique. "Oh, yes," said Larry. "Coming back around Point Judith one night the garboard come loose. You could tell by the way the helm staggered. I took a peek below. We shoved the mattress in. Hey, it wasn't like anybody was going to be sleeping much on it that night."

There were times, of course, when Larry's earlier maritime improvisations were not necessarily looked upon with favor. Jetting in spiles with the deck washdown pump instead of employing the cacophonous overhead hammer of other contractors was easier on the ears of waterfront residents but alarmed the DEP. Worse was the seemingly benign method of prop dredging, by which crucial quantities of harbor bottom might be quietly shuffled about to accommodate the draft of customers' boats. At a formative meeting of the Mystic River Watershed Association held at the Pequot Sepos Nature Center there was, as the minutes later read, "a wide spectrum of interests represented." Included were Captain Lawrence H. Malloy, Jr., and one Douglas Cunningham of the Connecticut Department of Environmental Protection. In my enthusiasm I introduced the two. There was an awkward pause. "We've met," said the DEP man.

"Yes," said Larry, "We've met. A little matter of dredging in West Cove, Noank."

"*Prop* dredging," said the DEP man.

"I've pretty much reformed," said Larry. "Or at least I should say: my customers have."

Then they both began to laugh and the DEP man slapped the old mariner on the shoulder.

NOTES

BOB WHITTAKER (p. 234): Unlike the typical craftsman in Charlie Haines's theory, however, Bob Whittaker had always maintained his prestige in the village. Fifty years later almost all of his boats were still around. One built in 1942, which I had bought for $3,500 in the early sixties and later sold for the same, was, some years later, advertised for ten times her 1960s market value. About the time Bob died, she had actually fetched $15,000. Only two years before, the Noank Historical Society had celebrated his accomplishments to a packed house. When he died there were as many people at his funeral as you'd get for a local banker and a good deal more than a recently arrived financial adviser from downstate might draw.

"SMALL-VESSEL DESIGN (p. 237) in the nineteenth century and earlier was a bit like folk music, similar yet different from town to town and from time to time." Jon Persson, "The Shadboat: The Past is Prologue," *The Ash Breeze*, Spring, 2000.

All photos from the collection of Lawrence H. Malloy, Jr. Line drawings by James Mitchell of Noank, salvaging photos by Captain Malloy.

Captain Lawrence H. Malloy, Jr.'s, license. The one the old man never bothered with.

Larry's younger brother Frank with his mother, father, and *Anne.*

Let's Go. A locally built oyster tonging scow is in foreground at Harrison's Landing, 1941. While Larry, Jr., oystered for Elijah Ball in *Anne* to the westward in the Sound, his father worked this sixty-five-foot boat in a variety of jobs, not including catching oysters. He did, however, use her for planting shell. The long boom is for the potato trade. When taking this vessel around Point Judith, Rhode Island, Malloy, Sr., went below to take a nap, leaned back against one of the hull's ribs, and broke it. Her flywheel was a foot wide and she turned only 150 r.p.m.

Sterling Basin, Greenport. *Anne* and *Emma Frances.* Both boats were lengthened to reduce draft. The Malloys lived directly behind Washington White's building. The house behind the automobiles was used to store liquor that had been run into Greenport in "go-thru" boats from Rum Row during Prohibition. It was in this berth that *Anne* rode out the infamous 1938 Hurricane.

Aftermath of the 1938
Hurricane at Harrison's
Landing. *Captain* (top) and
Emma Francis.

The demise of the *Captain* at Harrison's Landing, September 1938. Line drawing by James
Mitchell.

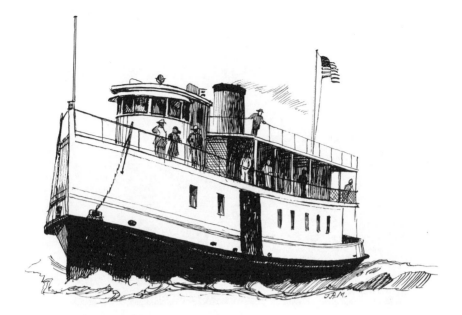

Block Island Ferry. Drawing by James Mitchell.

Home again. Discharged sailor Larry Malloy's car and trailer from Norfolk perched on a pile of Pappy's oyster shells at Harrison's Landing.

Anne in Three Mile Harbor, Long Island, sometime in the early 1940s, painted white and in her World War Two numbers. (As a documented vessel she did not in peacetime desecrate her topsides with numerals.)

Alice up in the ice, James Mitchell's re-creation of a Malloy photo taken in midcentury.

The conveyor on the pier to the right has loaded *Anne* with 750 bushels of oyster shells to go to Branford, Connecticut, for planting. 1951.

Anne still with her old wheelhouse in repose at Harrison's Landing. Vermont Central railroad line in background.

Dredging in Wickford Cove, Narragansett Bay, Rhode Island. The screw in front digs into the mud. The spoils are passed out the stern into the long pipe kept afloat by steel drums.

Alice and Anne on the ways at Thames Shipyard in New London, 1959. Although Alice was built as a motorized bumboat and Anne as a sailing freighter a third of a century apart, by now they look like sister ships.

Another moving performance for *Alice*. The bandstand was originally on Fishers Island, New York, and now adorns the village green at Mystic Seaport. "Captain's Row" in background.

Nearing Harrison's Landing at the end of an educational voyage aboard *Anne*. The old "professor" himself in the wheelhouse. The students are from Connecticut College just downriver from the derelict barges in the background. Schools now have their own state-of-the-art vessels, which are designed to simulate this sort of experience.

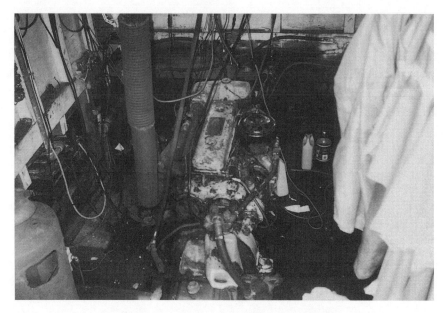

Anne's engine compartment. The foul weather gear is hung to the right in hopes that the heat from the engine will dry it before the wet from the clothes drowns out the engine.

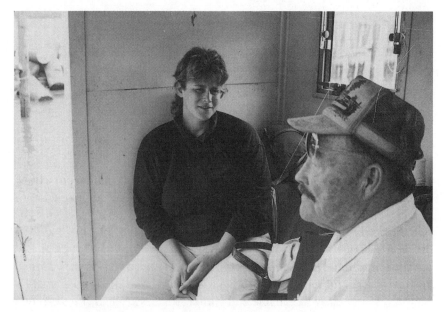

Larry Malloy and fan. Sina Wright of Noank sits on a pile of life preservers in *Anne*'s otherwise stark new wheelhouse.

Larry Malloy's son Larry, Jr., never afraid to get dirty in order to perform the task. July 14, 1989.

Imperturbable amid her handy work: Side-wheeler, steam spile driver *Walter Royal* at Hallock's dock, Orient Point, three-quarters of a century ago. Photo courtesy of Estelle Adams collection.

Part Three

SWALLOWING
THE ANCHOR

A seaman's ironic term signifying retirement ashore.

—*Falorp's Word Horde*

The fullest expression of husbandry is to be found in the care
of a ship.

—H. A. Callahan, *The Ship's Husband,* 1937

27

THE WORKBOATMAN IN WINTER

Our life is but the flight of the swallow as among the rafters of

the mead hall it passes in one window and out the other.

—The Venerable Bede, more or less

M OST OF THE time the monthly meetings of the Groton Shellfish Commission are attended only by the handful of commercial fishermen who, at least by Western Connecticut Standards, hold small lots. They sit just slightly apart, their caps low over their eyes, arms folded. Although he no longer owns any grounds, barring some sort of rasp or wheeze Larry Malloy will be there. He usually has a new cap, which he accounts for by claiming the privileges of a dark closet. Sometimes the lid of the cap gets very low and you wonder if he isn't in some sort of dark closet himself. This is a dangerous assumption.

Ten years ago he was more active and requested a plot in the Poquonnock for experimental purposes. One of the questions the experiment was to address was the range of surfaces that a Poquonnock oyster might be tempted to set upon. It was a problem that was part of a larger question his father had asked me thirty years before: "Why were Poquonnock River oysters stunted?" The set itself was wonderful. It was then that the famous scientist for the state was approached by Malloy senior and uttered in his German accent his maddening mantra: *"Hopping-stance."* Later, in the 1970s the Shellfish Commission had put out a couple dozen nylon bags full of scallop shells hung from the stringers on two deckless rafts. We followed the advice of Timmy Visel of the Marine Advisory Service at the University of Connecticut and caught the moment when the oysters released their spat. We had the bags in place in a fifteen-foot-deep section of the river up between the railroad bridge and the broken trolley bridge. One cold November day we loaded the bags on a barge, poked it through the broken trolley bridge, and moved downriver. We found a spot opposite the public beach where there was a gravel spit extending out into the river from the small state airport on the west bank. According to Visel, the set was thirty times greater than the Chesapeake when they were still bragging about their successes down there. In fact, so successful was the experiment that we got complaints from the bathers across the river. The manager of the airport on the west bank also began calling up to complain. He wanted us to control a situation that required him to order out the snow plow several times a week to clear the runways of the oyster shells dropped by the gulls. Sometimes, he noted, the blizzard of shells was daily. Nevertheless, in spite of the overall abundance, each individual oyster remained stunted. We were no closer to solving the problem than in the days of the elder Malloy.

Larry volunteered to get the answer, and the Commission granted him license to poke about on the east bank below the railroad bridge. It was there that I found him one day with his son, Larry, Jr. We now had three generations of Malloys seeking the solution to the mystery of the Poquonnock River stunted oyster. You could look at this as the carrying on of a fine old family tradition or as a maddening exercise in the futility of science.

One evening Larry brought to the meeting stones of various dimensions, shapes, and types, and other oyster shells that had attracted spat. Everyone at the table nodded wisely. Surely some policy decisions would arise from this research. But wait, said Larry, he had yet to display the winning substrate, the object that his research had shown to be, hands down, the unequivocal winner in attracting oyster spat. As the Commission sat up as high as their chairs permitted, from a brown paper bag Larry produced the dog collar, heavily encrusted. "I'm not sure what happened to the dog," he said. "But as you can see, the oysters are doing fine."

During the portion of the meeting when "comments from the Public" are encouraged, Larry will almost never say anything. As the meeting progresses he seems to be woolgathering. Sooner or later one of the Commissioners asks him a question. Sometimes it is to recover some ancient but suddenly relevant fact; sometimes it is to track the common sense of an idea. In either case, Larry is right there with a pithy contribution.

After an especially tedious run of speculation on the deleterious effects of occasional freshwater intrusions in the Poquonnock River, one of the Commissioners finally checked Larry as to the significance of the problem.

"Oysters are pretty smart," rasped Larry. "If something comes by they don't like, they just shut up."

One night an ominous, hulking stranger plopped himself down across the aisle from the usual shellfishermen. He was one of those physical specimens who, through a combination of skull size and shoulder slope, seem to have been cheated in the brain-to-brawn ratio. To enhance this effect, the man had trimmed his hair in the fashion favored by the barrel trundlers of Brueghel the Elder in those Flemish depictions of peasant life. During the first few items on the agenda (including "comments from the Public") the Brueghel man contented himself with wet-lipped warmups, mumbles, and heavy breathing. Suddenly he found his public voice.

Certainly one of the banes of serving on town boards and commissions is putting up with that citizen sharpshooter who, under the flag of public advocate of the oppressed taxpayer, will attend meeting after meeting, sniping and plinking away at an unholy mixture of good and bad points. This did not seem to be quite the Brueghelman's style. I can't remember even what the ostensible issue was upon which he sought to hang his cap. I do recall that none of us back of the table could figure out a way to help the man articulate whatever it was he was trying to say. Eventually we moved on. The next item he greeted with the same inchoate reception. I asked him if he could restate his complaint, if indeed that *was* his position: a complaint.

"*That's it!*"

The voice had not come from the Brueghelman. I looked over to the other side of the aisle. Larry Malloy was standing up, facing sideways, and jerking his thumb at the lout like a baseball umpire. "Come on. Out you go."

He motioned a few more times and advanced upon the hulk. No one moved.

We all sat transfixed as Larry grabbed the oaf by the ear and hoisted him out of his chair. Up the aisle they went—the hulk shambling ahead of his keeper, a man half his size, twice his age.

I followed them into the corridor. Larry continued to herd the man up the stairs. At the landing he shooed him out the door and down the steps. Outside he kept up the shooing—along the sidewalk under the trees and into the parking lot. There the big man fetched up against a car while Larry shook his finger in his face. Nowadays there is a security man on the door, but then there was only the janitor lurking somewhere deep in his lair of buffer and buckets. From the door I watched Larry and his charge. The hulk was standing immobile; Larry was winding down. Finally assured that the situation had deflated I went back inside. When I returned to the meeting there were a lot of open mouths, but no words were coming out. The rest of the meeting we kept a careful eye out the cellar windows, through which we could see two sets of knees standing about six feet apart. When the knees disappeared, I went upstairs again and saw Larry's car leaving the lot. After the meeting I called him from home. He was perfectly fine.

"Did you know that guy?" I said.

"Knew his father. Worked on the docks."

"I couldn't figure out what he wanted."

"He was misguided." There was a pause. "Then he got guided."

. . .

Larry brought lunch over today. Two Spamlike ham sandwiches on Wonder Bread and a tightly wound cinnamon roll, each individually wrapped in a plastic box sealed by one of those modern, bewildering lids. His beard had grown out. There were, however, scars up by his right temple from Dr. Wolf's skin spray, with which he's been treated for pre-melanoma.

"Well," I said, "at least the beard will defend that part of your face from the sun."

"It will also defend me from the razor," he said.

. . .

Defending oneself was certainly on his mind, as the following attests:

Larry came to visit me with a letter that had revoked his license, the one he'd earned that morning long ago in the New London post office when Mr. Brooks and Mr. Macdonald had grilled him. "It's not like I expect to be up there in the pilothouse of a commercial boat," he said. "It's just the idea of it. I had this since I was eighteen."

He had written out his defense on the yellow legal pad. The cancellation had been based on a high sugar level, but the basis of Larry's response was an emotional appeal centered on his long years of accident-free operation. It was a most poignant piece, but after a bit of poking at it here and there, I set it down. "You know," I said, "if I were back in the Coast Guard and I ever had a job involving licensing and this came across my desk—well, I might well want to buy you a drink or give you a lifetime achievement award. But I would not want to have it on my record that I had signed off on your renewal based on this. Let's take a different approach."

"My sugar varies from day to day," he said. "Especially when I'm off my feed."

"OK, get the hell back on your feed and when you think it's right, go back and get tested again."

He did all this and got a decent reading. We rewrote the letter, stripped of its emotional appeal, with just the medical facts. He was shortly reinstated.

"There," he said, laying the official Coast Guard acquiescence on the table. "You see, I ain't dead yet."

. . .

Once in the epistolary mood, Larry sat down at the kitchen table at the Landing and cranked out another one to the Coast Guard. For the past several months he had been lobstering on a friend's old cabin cruiser out of the lower Thames:

To Whom It May Concern
Oct. 17, 1994 Mon

Lawrence, B——, P——and S——left Crocker's Boat yard shortly after 10:00 A.M. to haul lobster pots. We pulled string of pots east of Pine Island and reset them.

We proceeded to area north of Vixen Ledge to haul second string of 9 pots. We were hearing a strange noise below deck in the stern, sort of a tapping sound. On arriving at this location, B—removed deck hatch and went below to listen for sound while I (Lawrence) shifted Starboard engine in and out of gear. B—thought that something was wrapped around Starboard shaft making the sound as the propeller shaft was turning. We had to postpone this operation because Coast Guard boat #41350 came up to us and requested to come aboard. Two male and one female Coast Guard personal jumped aboard. One man inspected boat equipment while the other man kept quite busy working some sort of new computer machine. The young lady present kept busy taking pictures of everything that moved also everything that didn't move. This boarding party's inspection results in another story. The C.G. Boat stood by off our stern while inspection took place. Inspection completed C.G. 41350 came along side to pick up three personal. Two Coast Guard personal stayed with the vessel during the operation. The first attempt to pick up the boarding party didn't work so they backed off and came in again. This time the personal succeeded in getting aboard their vessel and at the same time their vessel hit us a severe blow. I (Lawrence) heard the wood crack and managed to get their attention while they were backing away. They came back quickly looked at damage, handed B—a accident report form to fill out. Young lady took pictures of area of impact. This area being the Starboard quarter where the sheer strake and rub rail join the transom. Rub rail shows some damage protective metal oval on rub rail bent, screws bent and pulled out. Not sure what will be found on a more thorough inspection. The weather was very favorable this day for our operation. Wind was North app. 10 knots with a slight chop. A remark was made by C G. personal how nice the weather was, we all agreed. Also did not see anyone standing by with fender as they came along side.

Truly yours,
Lawrence H. Malloy Jr.

As one who had served part of my military obligation in the Coast Guard on just such forty-foot patrol boat inspections, I could only wince at Larry's devastating account. I pointed out that back in the early 1960s the Coast Guard had no money so we performed our boarding duty with only three "personal." "But I don't remember cracking anyone's transom," I told him. "Of course we had coxswains that grew up on boats on the Outer Banks. My job was the fender."

"Well nowadays you don't use anybody with any boathandling experience and you got to have one person on the camera and one on the computer, and I guess by then you ain't got any money left for the fender."

. . .

This entry maybe should come more under father-son relations or maybe even employee relations or even engines.

"I had a sixteen-foot power sharpie," he said one day. "I don't know if I ever told you about her. She had a one-cylinder make'n'break engine."

In thirty years he hadn't mentioned this boat, at least not as such, that is, as *his* boat. It might have been the vessel in such narratives as: "*Then we came alongside in the sharpie.*" Larry's personal sharpie apparently was his own foot outside the family circle. It represented independence and potential growth, to talk like a social psychologist. I am struck, however, with the autumnal nature of the sharpie story, especially the Sharpie & Dog story. Told to me the way he did, *when* he did, the story really was the kind of story an old man tells about his youth, the kind of yarn that maybe tells us more about the mood of his old age than the ostensible period under discussion. True, on the surface he seemed chiefly interested in the way the engine had worked half a century before. Indeed, the one-lunger make'n'break is an interesting development in engineering history. It is one of those moments when people looking back feel that this maybe was the last time when they could literally get their hands on the apparatus and bend it to their will, a moment enhanced perhaps by the fact that in that very instant, the machine could bite back. The stowaway Pomeranian is a rather strange breed for a workboat family in the 1930s. There is also a rather poignant note tucked in the middle of this reminiscence about yachting.

. . .

"The power sharpie was sixteen feet long, flat-bottomed, pointed at one end, and squared off at the stern, without much sheer. A flatiron. Unlike most sharpies of that size, however, it did not have an outboard, but an inboard, a real engine: a make'n'break, as was quite common in those days. Pappy towed it home from Greenport behind *Emma Frances*. That was around 1930, so I was what, about thirteen years old, and we were still well known in Greenport. Just before that I'd had a little sloop in mind, but that didn't work out. Boom and gaff rig. Eighteen foot. I thought it might be nice to just go sailing around like you see people do. Yachting! The power sharpie cost forty dollars and was never named. It was a numbered boat.

"To put one of those make'n'break in reverse you had to slow them down when they was in ahead. Then you'd flip the igniter from off the front of the engine and wait until the flywheel was slow enough to stop it with your hand so you could get her spinning the other way. Once the flywheel was spinning the other way, you'd drop the igniter back on and *put-put*—away you go in the opposite direction. Some boats with two cylinders, you'd just take the igniter off one cylinder when you was shifting. Some of the bigger boats had a string or a wire on the igniter so you could handle that part from above without necessarily standing on your neck. It took some thinking ahead. You always had the opportunity of not getting it right and cutting a swath up through the spiles and maybe lose your head or go overboard if you didn't duck.

"The sharpie was the only boat to survive the 1938 Hurricane. She didn't rate dock space, so she was out on the mooring. She did sink, that is most of her sunk, but she had a gas tank built in up in the bow, and I guess I didn't have enough money to keep her very full so there was plenty of room in there for air. You could just see her bow a foot, foot and a half sticking up above the water.

"So we just got her ashore and bailed her out. Because the engine was so simple there wasn't really anything to get ruined by a little dunking even in salt water.

"That was the boat I had the dog on. It was some kind of *Pomeranian* named Mike. I know a Pomeranian don't exactly sound like an oysterman's dog, but hey, he belonged to the neighbor. I'd come by on my bicycle and that goddamned dog would latch right onto my pants leg, and there I'm trying to keep from falling off the bike and he won't let go. Later the neighbors had to move, Navy people who were transferred, and they said, 'Why don't you take him? He seems to fancy you.' I told them I thought it was more my pants cuff he fancied. So then when he's my dog we get along fine, and he comes out with me on the sharpie, sits right up there in the bow. A good dog in the fog. He'd bark at rocks. You didn't need no compass or anything. He'd come out on the bigger boats, too, though he wasn't supposed to. He'd hide under a basket or a bag and not come out until we was below the railway bridge. That way he knew we wouldn't turn back. Come out wagging his tail. I guess you could say he was a stowaway. Even when he didn't come aboard and would wait at home, my mother could always tell when the boat, the *Emma Frances,* was coming home. He'd run down to the water and start to bark, and sure enough in ten to fifteen minutes the boat would appear. Must have heard us the other side of the bridge. Hey, that's a good ways. I guess a sound travels over water different, especially up or down a river, and of course, there wasn't all the noise of the trailer trucks and what not."

. . .

An oysterman friend was worried his product might suffer winter kill, so Larry discussed what actually happens to oysters in winter. "They can take a pretty good freeze. Them flats fall bare even at a normal low tide, never mind the moon and the wind. What happens is not the freeze, not if they can get down in the mud. What happened to us once was that the ice got them. Picked them up and carried them off. We lost 30,000 bushel of seed that way. Carried them right out to sea—or wherever the ice finally let 'em loose."

NOTES

NUMBERED BOAT (p. 263): The assumption here is interesting. "Named" boats, like *Anne, Alice, Emma Frances, Bateleur,* etc. are documented, which requires, by federal law, that they be named, and furthermore that that name be displayed on each side of the bow as well as the stern where the port of call must also be displayed. It is not that documented boats are not also numbered, but this number is hidden from sight below, much after the manner of an engine serial number on an automobile as opposed to the license plate posted out on the bumper. This maritime documentation number must be carved into the main beam, an interesting requirement when the fiberglass era arrived.

This quaint notion of identification and subsequent record-keeping by nouns rather than numbers has interesting implications in the personification of technology. As the Volstead Act created an inadvertent government subsidy to fishermen lucky enough to profit from smuggling, so the documentation regulation inadvertently kept alive the poetry inherent in the naming of ships. One can only imagine the bleakness of a history in which Drake's *Golden Hind,* a.k.a. *Pellican,* was, say, #3876; if Columbus sailed not the *Santa Maria,* but, say, the #2965; and that American democracy saw its first iteration in something called the "#29065 Pact." Try playing the same game with the #5732 sinking when it hit the iceberg; MacArthur signing the Japanese surrender on the deck of the #8754; Joshua Slocum sailing alone around the world in #6921; singing and swilling to that Great Lakes oarboat tearjerker "The Wreck of #35434." While there are certain legendary vessels who (that?) have come down to us by their numbers *PT-109,* being the most famous, these numbers seem to live on through the power of rhyme—an attribute not only totally accidental to the process of numbering, but usually thought to be antithetical to the quantification process that seeks to rinse away all emotional connection. (To be honest, I had to look up Edward Ellsberg's *S-51*, whose tragedy is examined in his great salvage book *On The Bottom*.) There is also the railroad song "Wreck of Ol' 99," and "Trouble in Mind" with "Gonna put my head on that lonesome railroad line / and let the 419 pacify my mind," in which the digit nine seems courted entirely on the basis of its chime.

DOG AND COLLAR SHOW (p. 258): According to Lorraine Chappell, this was the show Larry took on the road, or at least Hazelnut Hill Road.

THE MUSEUM OF WORKING
WATERCRAFT

OF ALL THE boats aboard which Larry Malloy had earned his living, *Alice* and *Anne* were the last to remain afloat. It was one of the ironies of maritime life that *Anne* should outlive her younger sister *Alice,* built a quarter century later. Twenty-five years is a long time in the life of any boat, especially one called upon to tow and lug. Because *Anne* and *Alice* had a similar look, even to the Pittsburgh Ivy Green housepaint job and seem often interchangeable in many of Malloy's stories, and because both vessels lived long lives, it is tempting to mix them up.

There is a picture on my desk of the two of them hauled one after the other on the marine railway at Noank Shipyard in the 1970s. The photograph makes a study of the nuances that separated their designs. *Anne* was built as a sloop to carry freight; *Alice,* the bumboat, was engine-powered from the start. However, the fact that one boat was constructed to be moved by sail and the other by engine did not make for the contrast that such differences in motive power would account for in the last half of the twentieth century. It wasn't until after World War Two that motor-driven vessels, especially workboats, outgrew their sailboat origins, particularly below the waterline. *Anne* was clearly built in an era that was solidly nineteenth century. *Alice* was built in 1910, the year that Virginia Woolf insisted was the date the modern era began. Ms. Woolf did not, of course, have in mind American workboats, but she was thinking of almost everything else—"the modern sensibility," as she called it.

The actual year a boat is built, however, does not necessarily convey the state of the art. Again, this is especially true of workboats, which until recently were the products of a more traditional culture than yachts. Yachts are more sensitive to societal fads and the need for competitive speed. *Anne* was, after all, a workboat built by the sort of all 'round handy man who farmed, fished, and did his own carpentry on what was then eastern Long Island only one generation after the Civil War. In strictly engineering terms then, the year 1883 should not in her case suggest such contemporary marvels as the Statue of Liberty, the Washington Monument, and the Brooklyn Bridge, but the sort of engineering that was going on back to the Civil War and before.

It is fitting, then, that it should be *Anne* who at this writing sits in view out off West Mystic Wooden Boat Company on her mooring. It is *Alice*, however, that is burned in my memory.

. . .

I had not seen *Alice* for some time. What with *Anne* around I had not even much thought of her until one spring we were down in Oyster Bay, Long Island. We had *Sylvina W. Beal* anchored off the Seawanhawka Yacht Club to be a background prop in Martin Scorsese's version of Edith Wharton's *Age of Innocence,* for a scene in the novel set in Newport. The set-up involved three days' shooting, hundreds of technicians, and a fleet of classic boats brought the hundred miles from Mystic. To mute the competition from the bright red mooring buoys, Scorsese had draped them all in burlap, giving the harbor the look of a Catholic Church in Lent. More impressive than his control of the yachting fleet was his takeover of the commercial fleet. He had somehow forbidden all harbor traffic during this period, which, at that time of year, was chiefly shellfishermen and eelers. Aboard the schooner, we were required to hide below so as not to upstage the actors on the yacht club veranda. (The entire background of classic boats ended up being dissolved to faint fuzz behind the heads of the actors having their tedious *tête à tête* on the yacht club veranda.) I took comfort in the fact that this was the port in which old man Malloy had encountered Teddy Roosevelt with the boxing gloves.

The next morning I woke up to a voice floating about somewhere nearby our stern. When I emerged on deck into the light dawn fog there was a large man hovering about in what seemed thin air. He struck me as more of a cinematic miracle than anything I'd yet seen from Scorsese. He was working a long pole, as if with luck it might somehow attach him to the earth, or in this case at least to the watery part. Dante must have had his medieval counterpart in mind when he wrote about Charon poling across the Styx. As I blinked over my coffee, this apparition hardened his edges into a clammer with a bull rake. The mist all across the harbor began to burn off, and there behind him some fifty yards was a small flotilla of ancient oysterboats, the very fleet that Scorsese had banished from the harbor. The boats all looked more or less like *Anne* and *Alice* except for the huge, grotesque hydraulic conveyor rigs that had seemingly pounced on their sterns like great reptiles slowly devouring the boat, wheelhouse and all. I recalled Sophocles had once described the sexual appetite as just such a beast clinging to one's back.

Mindful that the World Trade Towers were visible as you left the harbor, I was amazed at this flurry of shellfishing so close to the City. I knew that *Alice* had been sold down the Sound somewhere and wondered if indeed she might be laboring out there under the same disfigurement as one of those poor craft. I exchanged greetings with the nearby tonger. He said he was happy to be back at work, having been banned by the filming from the harbor for three days. I assured him I found the present spectacle of shell-fishing craft a good deal more interesting than the scene Mrs. Wharton had contrived. Was it possible, I inquired, that one of the boats I was looking at in the mist might not be my old friend *Alice*?

"That would have been *Alice* out there last week," he said. "But she was too rotten to take the new dredge rig. They got rid of her."

"Where did she go?"

"A couple of crazy old men from Connecticut come down here and took her back. If she didn't sink under them, she ought to be there by now."

. . .

"Yes, we nearly did sink," explained Larry. "There was the bilge pump. That's why she nearly sunk. It was a regular bilge pump, but I knew the whole way back she wasn't doing the job she was rated to, the job she was supposed to be doing. They claimed they had her all apart and back together again, and she was fine. Well, when we got home after we damn near sunk, I take that pump apart and I take apart the elbows as well. Them elbows was solid full of wood chips. You know old wooden boats gets that way. New ones too if you don't run the vacuum after the carpenters. On old boats, well, it's maybe not quite right to call them *chips* anymore. More like slivers of rot.

"We got her back because she was family—Hell, I don't know why we got her. We got her for a dollar.

"They ruined her with that goddamn *clam* dredge rig. Then they damn near burned her up with that stove they put in her. They wanted fifteen hundred dollars for that stove. I had a perfectly good way to do a stove at home. I didn't want a stove like that aboard of her. It's a wonder they didn't set her afire. They had lined the stovepipe with an *aluminum* sleeve. It was all scorched and melted in there. They must have had her stoked up pretty good. I got that pipe out in my yard. I don't know what good it's going to do me. At least it won't burn up no boats."

Next I knew of *Alice* she was working as a clammer on the State grounds off Sea Flower Reef in Fishers Island Sound outside New London Harbor for our friends Gilbert & Fellini's Briar Patch Shellfish Company of Stonington and Milford. While Larry and Frank Malloy continued to own her, she was skippered by a much younger man in the employ of Briar Patch.

"One day they decided to move her down to Milford," explained Larry, "and somebody picked a howling gale for that. Going out around Bartlett's Reef the west side of New London, well, you know you got to get pretty far out in the Sound to make that spindle and the current can rip pretty good there under the right conditions. *Alice,* she got the shit beat out of her, and they called the Coast Guard, and somehow she barely made it into Milford. I was in Georgia visiting my daughter Carol when I get this call informing me that my boat is hauled in Milford and too rotten to fix. I cut short my visit with my daughter and come all the way back up to Connecticut.

"I tell them: 'Looks to me like all you done is sprung the caulking between two planks on the port bow in under the roller post. Why don't you just through-bolt those planks, pull them back up and recaulk her?' They tell me there ain't nothing to caulk *to.* 'She's all rot,' they say. I say, 'Well, there's enough of her for what I just told you to do. Just go all the way through to the sealing on the inside.' Christ, the sealing on them boats ain't no interior decorating like you got on yachts these days. There's more to the sealing in a boat like *Alice* than you got in the outer hull of today's boats. So they do that, and sure enough there's enough bite and they pull them planks right back up so's when they caulk her she's just fine.

"By then that other younger skipper who punished her so going around Bartlett's, well, he's gone back to the hills. I guess he got a little punished by Bartlett's himself. Anyway, by now there's nobody to run her, so, hey, guess who's back at work running a boat at age seventy-three?

"The problem wasn't in running the boat. The problem was driving down to Milford every day in the car on I-95. We was working the State Grounds from off Milford to halfway to the New Haven breakwaters. The crew was both living in New London, and I'd pick them up on the way. She was moored in the Milford River, right opposite the State Shellfish Lab and, while that's an interesting place, it's a hell of a drive. I wasn't going to get up at five in the morning just to go *clamming.*

"Now, Pappy, for some reason, he never wanted anything to do with *clams.* It wasn't like we didn't run across them out on the oyster grounds. Like I told you, he'd say to people, 'Go out there and get all the clams you want. Just throw the oysters back.' Hell, I guess he figured anybody can raise a *clam.* Now if I was working the oyster beds and came across some clams I always kept them. Either brought them home for chowder or stopped on the way home and sold them. You know the odd bushel here and there at the back door. To me it was like what the draggermen call *shack money* when they used to sell the trash fish *by-catch* to the lobstermen for bait. Shack money was real good money because it was yours. It wasn't Pappy's, and I guess with some people, there wasn't none of it going to be any of the government's either."

At some point, evidently Larry got tired of the car ride part of the job and it was, as he said, "only clams."

. . .

The last time I saw *Alice* was only a few months later. I had not heard about what was happening to her from Larry himself. Word had leaked that his youngest brother Bill, the man with whom he had lived for a year while junking Fort Michie on Great Gull Island, had somehow gotten complete control of the Malloy waterfront at Harrison's Landing and was demanding that the oysterboats be destroyed.

It was not as if *Alice* had not been in trouble before at Harrison's Landing. There is a snapshot of her sunk at the dock in 1983. She is yet tied to the rotting wharf. You can just see her name above the water with her mast and upper part of her wheelhouse above water. I have heard variations on the cause of this, but am not sure I can untangle the story except to say that it was not the fault of anyone in Larry's generation. Something about the people on watch leaving for a saloon. . . . In any case, Larry and Frank were able to pump her out and restore her to another decade of active service.

Nor was it that Frank and Larry Malloy didn't try to dispose of *Alice* in as dignified a form as they could. They even drew up a good old-fashioned

BILL OF SALE

I, Lawrence H. Malloy Jr. of # 7 Harrison's Landing, Quaker Hill CT. 06375 and Frank H. Malloy of . . . each owning 50%, in consideration of the payment of one dollar ($1.00) and other good and valuable consideration, receipt of which is hereby acknowledged, do hereby sell, bargain, transfer, assign and convey to _____ of _____ the vessel "Alice," federal documentation number 207240, together with the equipment affixed to the vessel, now located at Harrison's Landing, New London, CT. 06320 covenants that we are the lawful owners of the Vessel, that she is free of mortgages, maritime liens and other encumbrances, that we have the right to sell the vessel and that we will defend that right.

Lawrence H. Malloy Jr. and Frank H. Malloy does not warrant the seaworthiness of the vessel or the condition of the Vessel's hull, machinery, equipment, engine, tanks or any other part of the vessel's suitability for any use or purpose, it being understood that the vessel is being sold and transferred in its current "As is, where is" condition without any express or implied warranty or representation whatsoever except as to ownership of the vessel by Lawrence H. Malloy Jr. (50% owner) and Frank H. Malloy (50% owner).

It was well after the demise of *Alice* that I discovered the reason behind the preparation of the Bill of Sale. The Brothers Malloy had been planning to turn their old bumboat over to a not-for-profit corporation that was, according to its prospectus, devoted to the preservation of the dying work craft of the region. The president of this corporation was one Manfred H. Rieder.

. . .

I'd first met "Rieder" when he was working in Westerly Rhode Island on the Pawcatuck River as the manager of a boat yard near where that stream flowed into Little Narragansett Bay. I was looking to acquire the pilothouse off an old lobster boat upriver named *Bobby D.* and was told that the man to see on this matter was downriver in another yard. I was wandering about in the downriver yard when a very well-organized man in his forties dressed in khakis came up to me and introduced himself as the yard manager. He had a neatly trimmed reddish beard and looked like D. H. Lawrence about the time when he had written that marvelous short novel *The Fox*.

The Fox was ostensibly about two women who lived together and had their relationship altered by their obsession with a fox that came prowling about their farm. One woman wanted to shoot him for his unrepentant depredations. The other woman wanted to feed him because she felt a deep blood-bond of sympathy for him despite his outlaw nature, or perhaps because of it, etc. Some of Lawrence's friends had said that *The Fox* was an allegory about two of his girlfriends and Lawrence himself, whose beard trim and mad, beady eyes made him look just like a fox. I did not explore this interpretation with Rieder, which in the long run may have been a mistake. Instead, we stuck to boats.

Because the *Bobby D.*, the boat whose wheelhouse I coveted, had once been a sailboat, we fell into a discussion about Friendship sloops versus Noank sloops and he at once proved his competence in this arcane field. From this discussion and other even more minute matters, it was clear to me he had worked in boat yards for dozens of years. Next I knew, he was selling foreign cars. He had one of those generalized Germanic accents that could slide off into whatever Teutonic tribe seemed most appropriate. Since he was dealing with my Fiat, he was that day Swiss. It was clear to me from our discussion that he had worked in automobile dealerships for dozens of years. We got into the nuances between the use of the hand throttle and the choke, neither of which, of course, had been seen on cars since my youth. This, however, was the extent of our nostalgia, for when I tried to reintroduce the subject of Friendship sloops he drew an absolute blank, and I had a moment when I actually thought that he was not the man with whom I had had that talk in the boat yard a few years before. When I returned a few weeks later to the dealership, the man called Rieder was no longer working there.

I next encountered Rieder's name on the framed restaurant review of a local seafood place I enjoyed. Looking at his by-line I thought I had learned at last that "Rieder" was not his first name, but his last, but I should add, as I subsequently learned, not his *last* last name. I was not exactly sure of the significance of "Manfred" in the Teutonic culture, but I had images of something out of Goethe, a kind of *Sturm und Drang* hero standing on a cliff, wind blowing the blond hair as great gulps of Atlantic ozone coursed through his body. Had I been a better Byronic scholar there would have been other warnings.

In any case, Manfred H. Rieder commenced the review by referring to "friends" who had put him onto this dining spot, which he somehow associated with a long-past rendezvous of "Tall Ships." The feeling was very much that of the laughing fellow rover, equally sturdy midst buntline and arpeggio. In the review of the food itself Manfred H. Rieder made finely nuanced distinctions between various scallop preparations. (I suspect in this case his former part of Switzerland was closer to the French border.) It was also clear that he had been writing restaurant reviews for years and that he was no doubt a graduate of a major European culinary institute. He also included several knowing remarks about the jazz band that played at the restaurant "at no extra charge" and described their style as "eclectic." In addition to the usually printed byline, the article was literally signed by *Manfred H. Rieder* in large script running diagonally up a good column inch of otherwise white space. It was clear that Manfred H. Rieder was not only an astute observer, but also someone who in himself deserved watching. It did not entirely surprise me then when Larry Malloy handed me Rieder's prospectus for the Museum of Working Watercraft.

I cannot say, however, that the discovery that the Brothers Malloy were about to sacrifice their *Alice* did not alarm me. It was not until much later that I realized that Larry Malloy had kept a whole file entitled "Manfred."

THE MUSEUM OF WORKING WATERCRAFT
A PROPOSAL

The following is a proposal for the creation of a museum of working watercraft. The term "working watercraft" is used to describe the focus of the exhibits and the vessels that will be featured. Working watercraft include all vessels formerly engaged in maritime commerce, fishing, transport of goods, passenger transport, towing, lightening and all activities having to do with maritime commerce. New England has a variety of museums such as the Mystic Seaport, Newprts [sic] Museum of Yachting, etc. but no museum thus far has given priority to the men and ships who were once the mainstay of commerce from Maine to New Jersey.

It is our goal to create such a museum and we have made great progress in beginning to collect vessels and memorabilia to get this venture under way as soon as possible. A list of ships already in our possession and a description of each is included on a separate page.

The proposal goes on to describe its desires. There will be dockage. "The water depth alongside cannot be less than eight feet." There will be "power requirements." Structures "will have to be able to house exhibits, work-shops and administrative offices as well as public restrooms." Parking for up to a hundred cars and highway access are addressed.

Exhibits

There will be two main areas of focus: Fishing and the history of New England commercial fishing and Coasting trade, exhibits exploring the tremendous history of coastwise commerce since colonial times. A large separate proposal and study is currently being prepared to outline the exhibits and general layout in detail. Since most of the preparation of this study is dependent on the site and location, it will be of little use at this stage of the planning.

The "funding" paragraph states that, while the organization will require "start-up funds," "we already have in excess of $500,000 of vessels ... that we would wish to accommodate." It goes on to use such phrases as "contin-ued growth," "our goal is to create an employment base and a tax base for the community," "good and paying neighbors," "Federal grants," and "our accounts."

A list of ships follows, some of which I knew, some not. The ones I know are described in a way that causes me to realize how poorly I have observed them. There is one with whom I was a next-door neighbor for six years. How could I have failed to realize that *Al-Mar*, my motorized neighbor at McGugan's Water Street Yard for a half dozen years, good old *Al-Mar* with all her plywood, was actually a "1908 dragger ... representing a traditional New England fishing vessel of the period"? I sift the pages anxiously, fear-ing that *Alice* will appear, but she does not. Yet.

"Other inventory" includes "more than 30 antique marine engines ... that range from 1890 to 1940. All engines are in working order." There is also "a small collection of nautical artifacts and exhibits ranging from compasses, sextants, blocks and rigging items to various small watercraft such as prams, yawlboats and fishing skiffs. More than 30 nautical paintings have been collected for future inclusion in the museum."

There are to be "other" attributes: "The Ship's Chandlery, a museum store selling maritime related gifts, collectibles, clothing, posters, memorabilia." There will be "The Ship's Galley, a snack bar or restaurant," a "Maritime Gallery . . . maritime art, books, charts and quality nautical antiques." And my favorite, "The Reading Room, a museum-run research library of nautical books, reference material, ship's logs, old charts, plans and other research-related items, available to nautical researchers, the press and educational institutions. (We already have more than 250 old charts and many other items for inclusion in this collection.)"

There are "Planned Museum Events" that include "music of the sea" performed "by New England musicians." Pulitzer nominee and Shelley Memorial award winner Leo Conellan, "an old friend," will read from his book *The Clear Blue Lobster Water Country.* Maritime art, lobsters, fishing meets, and, of course, an "in the water workboat show."

"Guest Exhibits?" Well, "We have spoken to the British Royal Maritime Trust and to the National Museum of Holland and have commitments for guest exhibits of considerable scope if we are able to accommodate them."

And don't forget the "Educational Programs," which would involve "interfacing" with the DEP, the Coast Guard, Woods Hole, and various civic and government groups. And a "maritime historical educational program which has to interface with local universities and other educational institutions."

"So," said Larry, "what do you think?"

"I don't know what to think," I said. "It sounds like what my son and I have been trying to do for ten years."

"Well, Frank and me, we already signed over *Alice* to him."

"I see." I proceeded to kick a few stones. "Well, I was moored next to *Al-Mar* for a half dozen years and I just never knew she was a 1908 sailboat. I guess it was all that plywood fooled me."

"People can do amazing things with plywood," said Larry. "Manfred's going to name the exhibit after Frank and me."

"Yes. Well, good luck with Manfred. He's a man of many talents. Good luck with Manfred and his Museum of Working Watercraft."

"Hey, it seemed a good thing at the time for the old girl and hey, we get a tax break."

A couple of days later he handed me a single sheet of typed paper. The signature at the bottom was nowhere near as bold as it had appeared under the restaurant/jazz review. It was also interesting to note that the Museum of Working Watercraft was vertically integrated in providing its own no-

tary public—a capability that was no doubt especially felicitous in the light
of future identity shifts.

Mssrs. Lawrence and Frank Malloy

Gentlemen

With this understanding, we the undersigned agree to take possession and
full responsibility of the oyster vessel ALICE with the understanding that
this vessel will be transferred into the trust of the Museum of Working Watercraft, currently organized in Bristol county, R.I. The Museum of Working Watercraft will give to you a statement of gift of $10,000 which can be
used on a one-time deductive basis or can be parceled-out to five consecutive years at your discretion. You will have to tell us how you wish the receipts to read.

I have further proposed to call the eventual exhibit the Lawrence and
Frank Malloy Oyster exhibit and your eventual guidance in setting up appropriate displays would be greatly appreciated.

Until such time as we can transfer our vessel to Bristol, we will dock
Alice at Lotteryville Marina on the lower Pawcatuck River in Westerly,
Rhode Island so that some of that work can begin immediately. Until such
time as you gentlemen will have received appropriate tax receipts and a letter from the directors of the museum, you may retain a $10,000 lien upon
the vessel which the undersigned hereby personally guarantee.

I hope this meets with your satisfaction!

Thank you very much

[signed]   [signed]
Manfred Rieder   Nancy Allen Rieder   May 4, 1993

MANFRED H. RIEDER
Notary Public
My Commission Expires March 31, 1994

. . .

My son Geoffrey said that when he was working on the schooner *Beal* out
on her mooring one day, *Alice* had come past with Larry Malloy and a
strange man in khaki in the wheelhouse. Larry had stepped out onto the
deck and shouted that this was Manfred, the man who was the president of
the Museum of Working Watercraft, and the man to whom he'd just signed
over the boat.

"I didn't quite know how I felt about that," said Geoffrey, "but I gave him
a wave and wished him well. I was working on my own transmission."

The next thing I heard about Rieder was a week later in the New London *Day*. I quote from Larry's file entitled simply "Manfred":

New London *Day,* May 18, 1993. A Groton man arrested last year for allegedly bilking four people out of $56,000 was charged last week with fourth-degree larceny, according to local police.

Manfred Kellersberg, 44, who had been using the name Manfred H. Rieder, but whose name has since been legally changed to Kellersberg, was arrested May 10 after he reneged on a deal with a Mystic business, according to Detective Peter Cleary of the Montville state police barracks.

Cleary said on Monday that Kellersberg, who was living on a boat docked at 293 Thames St. in Groton, was hired to build a wooden sign for the business for $750, but he cashed the check and never delivered the sign. Cleary would not identify the business.

Also arrested last week was Kellersberg's wife, Nancy Rieder. Ms. Rieder was charged by an inspector from the state Department of Motor Vehicles with 24 counts of issuing a bad check and larceny, Cleary said.

The charges involve the Motor Vehicle Extension Service—a business that Ms. Rieder and her husband operate on Thames Street. Cleary said the company, which is not affiliated with the state motor vehicle department, charges motorists a fee to bring cars to the motor vehicle office to be registered. [This service was lauded by the New London *Day* earlier as a breakthrough convenience concept demonstrating creativity.]

Last October, Kellersberg was charged with three counts of first degree larceny and insurance fraud by state police. At the time he was using the name Manfred H. Rieder, Cleary said.

Investigators said last fall that four customers gave him $56,000 in deposits for cars, but [he] never delivered the cars and failed to return the deposit money.

He had worked for numerous dealerships in the area. Police accused him of making deals on the side with clients, promising he could import cars for them.

WARRANT ISSUED FOR CAR SALESMAN

New London *Day,* June 12, 1993. A car salesman accused of bilking customers out of $56,000 in deposits was last seen at the Canadian border, heading north in his boat. ["His boat" was actually *Sunbeam III* on which Manfred had failed to complete payments to Willis Jones (no relation).]

Manfred Kellersberg, 45, who had been using the name Manfred H. Rieder, had just bought 500 gallons of fuel for his boat and paid for it with a bad check, according to a prosecutor in New London Superior Court.

Rieder was supposed to be in court Friday for a pretrial conference on his pending criminal charges. He was arrested last fall on several fraud charges and again last month for allegedly cashing a $700 check for a wooden sign he never built.

But the prosecutor said Rieder was seen Sunday traveling on his boat called the *Sunbeam,* the same vessel he had lived on when it was docked in the Thames River in Groton.

Rieder went through customs at a port in Canada near Maine, Assistant State's Attorney Kevin T. Kane said.

Kane said the courts sent Rieder a notice that he was supposed to be in court Friday.

Judge Joseph J. Purtill, smiling and patiently listening to Kane explain why Rieder wasn't there, said before ordering another arrest warrant for the man, "Think it might be futile to send another letter?"

Sunbeam III had been one of the gems of the local harbors. Built in 1939, before she came to southern New England she had served as a kind of floating missionary vessel to Maine lighthouses in the sixties. Her skipper's column in the then *Maine Coast Fisherman,* "God's Tugboat," was a regular feature, along with the innovative ideas of John Gardner that were laying the foundation of what would be called the Wooden Boat Revival. Replaced by a steel boat, she went, as Norwich *Bulletin* writer Tony Whyte put it, "through more hands than an old opera star." When *Sunbeam* came to live in the Mystic River her sturdy workboat lines were a daily joy to us between the bridges in downtown Mystic. Her owner at this time was an ex-Navy man named Kent who had retired from a TV and radio repair service to live on the boat with his wife. I happened to be rowing past the day Mr. Kent died below in his bunk. It was with considerable apprehension that I read of the vessel's abduction to foreign parts. Years later, after *Sunbeam*'s recovery, her then owner Willis Jones came to see me with the idea of chartering her out to the University of Connecticut at Avery Point for the dual purposes of science and keeping her afloat. Because of inspection and insurance issues we were not able to resolve anything as far as the boat's future was concerned, but he did tell me something of his bizarre chase into Canada to recover *Sunbeam* from a Nova Scotia fish dock. As he talked I could just imagine the Brothers Malloy involved in such an international tangle over *Alice,* a mind experiment that eased the pain somewhat of *Alice*'s actual ultimate fate.

NOTES

BETTER BYRONIC SCHOLARSHIP (p. 272): William Rose Benet's *The Reader's Encyclopedia* (2nd edition) informs us that Manfred was an 1817 "dramatic poem by Lord Byron. The hero, Count Manfred, sells himself to the prince of Darkness and lives wholly without human sympathies in splendid solitude among the Alps." My colleague Professor Margaret Breen, herself a child of the Alps, informs me that Byron clipped Manfred, concept and name, from Goethe, who called him on this, to which George Gordon, a.k.a. Lord Byron, shrugged something to the effect, "Oh, yes, well, you know I hadn't thought that."

BETTER MANFRED H. RIEDER SCHOLARSHIP (p. 272): Last night I went up to the restaurant reviewed by Manfred H. Rieder to see if the review was still there. The place was packed, as was the town, from the launching of the schooner *Amistad,* but I was able to press into the foyer where I had last seen the piece. It was no longer framed on the bulkhead wall, and I despaired of being able to confirm the scholarship. A pale, nursery-blue sky with scrap-paper seagulls occupied the space where once Manfred's review had blessed the premises. As the crowd pressed in, I was slammed up against the cashier's counter and all but had my nose shoved down onto the glass. There, lo and behold, reposed like John Hancock in the museum case, Manfred H. Rieder's signature! While not yet quite parchment quality, the newspaper clipping was yellowed and had a bit of the ear of the dog about its edges. But there it was in all its "eclectic" glory.

"Oh, that's been there a long time," said the hostess, whose husband was glowingly mentioned by the author and indeed was to be seen in the next room drinking with the jolly patrons, living evidence of Manfred H. Rieder's veracity. As I was solemnly trying to read the document, a surge of urchin, high on sugar and the back-seat squirminess of gridlocked tourist cars, attacked the decorative ship's wheel. It was tentatively affixed to the cashier's counter at my right elbow, and as the spokes flew just off my crazy bone, the father said, "Don't, Johnny. Can't you see the man's reading?"

Indeed.

29

ALICE R.I.P.

ONE DAY LARRY came into the boatyard with a spar lashed to the top of his car. It was, he said, the mast off *Alice*. We did not use the word *artifact*. We did not discuss Manfred's Museum of Working Watercraft.

Instead he muttered something about not wanting it to go to waste. It was eighteen feet long and six inches in diameter, "solid wood." On one end was what Larry called a *"with,"* that is, what the hardware catalogues call a *mast band,* a kind of galvanized collar, in this case with four strap eyes attached for rigging. At the other end a tenon had been chiseled out so that when the mast was stepped it would not squirm in its keel box. In its shaggy solidity the mast seemed the epitome of a traditional workboat mast. This, after all, was the mighty spar that had moved the Fishers Island bandstand to Mystic Seaport, participated in the rebuilding of Race Rock Light, the salvage attempt on the *G-2,* and numerous other deeds. We made modest plans for extending its meritorious service in using it at the West Mystic Wooden Boatyard as a stiff-leg derrick for stepping and pulling spars. It wasn't until a few years later Larry remarked that the mast had actually been the mere tip, "some kind of sail boom" for the Cup Defender *Rainbow,* part of the Monsell-Greenport connection (see Appendix).

"I just wanted to make sure this didn't go to the dump," he said. I could see he was not merely being wistful. He was miffed, but I couldn't get anything out of him beyond the fact that this particular part of *Alice* had been menaced. Granted, the mast of a vessel is a serious part of her, but some new steel version might at that very moment be adopted.

Eventually I found out that the younger brother had apparently issued an ultimatum. I was curious as to why I'd had to hear all this from other people. Larry usually called me once a week on one thing or another, but I'd had no word from him on anything for a month. He had not even attended the monthly Shellfish Commission Meeting in the basement of the Town Hall.

"It's time we went over and saw for ourselves," said Geoffrey.

I agreed.

. . .

What did we expect to do or even to observe?

In the pickup on the way over the Gold Star Bridge there was some talk about offering up our boatyard, although we did not really have the depth of water for *Alice*. There was talk of offering a mooring in our riparian rights area between the flats and the federal channel, a suggestion that was in fact eventually taken up with *Anne*'s new owner. In the event that all else failed, I was prepared to indulge a lust for her wheelhouse, for which I was, of course, prepared to pay. About this business of scavenging parts from these two great old ladies both my son and I felt much guilt. Hovering over us like the trailer trucks was the dreadful nimbus of the Museum of Working Watercraft. Geoffrey developed a mantra: *"I'd much rather keep both boats working."*

To which I, of course, uttered the required *amen*.

What gnawed at us was the way Larry had said nothing of this. It was not that he had never invited me into his privy council. Among the many matters we had consulted on was his last will and testament. In the case of the brother's ultimatum, I smelled some sort of recalcitrance on Larry's part, an attitude that demanded he be let alone to work out the solution. I was afraid I knew what this solution was and I deplored it. The whole thing reeked of the dying elephant seeking out the desolate shade. At best it seemed as if to drop in on the Landing at this moment would have the moral stickiness of an AA intervention.

It was not as if the younger brother could be painted with entirely dark colors. Having grown up in a family business, I was painfully aware of the sort of thing that might go on. Though Larry had often said that working for Bill on the mud barge *Carnesee* in Bridgeport Harbor had been the absolute low point of his life, Bill's projects were not always devoid of a certain charm. The *Carnesee* itself was a fascinating monster. She was not so much a ship as a piece of the industrial landscape unmoored. She was a great square gray box of a floating thing with a smaller box aloft as a wheelhouse. Looking up at *Carnesee*'s sides was like standing below the left field wall at Fenway Park, but it was not so pretty a moment.

She, or rather it, had been cobbled together out of two half vessels, one of which was a kind of heavy-duty pusher and the other the bow end of a modular barge system that allowed for as many as eight other "middle" sections to intervene. The sections were held together by pins you lined up on the bottom and hooks on the top that you drew together with come-alongs. Whaling City Dock & Dredge had bought a couple of sets of these components from a New York outfit that had employed them on the Hudson River and the Erie Canal. The steel ribs in the bow section were, unlike other vessels, laid horizontally rather than vertically, apparently, as Willie Malloy, Bill's son, and Larry agreed, to ease the pangs of the many benign collisions such pushing units would encounter in the locks.

It was, after all, Bill and his son who had moved the rebuilt Long Beach Point Light from the Greenport Shipyard the mile and a half out onto its old foundation, a spectacular and heartwarming sight. It was Bill in *Carnesee* challenging the famous Bascule drawbridge in downtown Mystic. Coming downtide with a bellyfull of ripe ooze, Bill informed the bridge tender that, regardless of the official schedule, he was about to pass through. Whether the bridge tender chose to open or not was entirely up to him. It would be a decision in any case that would have absolutely no effect on the outcome of his vessel's passage. Looking out of his operator's shack high above the traffic and seeing directly into *Carnesee*'s wheelhouse, the bridge tender, of course, saw the point. Ultimatums by the *Carnesee*, therefore, were not to be shrugged off.

As we turned right on Bella Vista I saw the boom of a big crane above Larry's roof. It looked as if it were set to pick the house up and do with it what it willed. At first I did not realize how far away it was—down the hill back of the house on a barge in the river. It was, in fact, set up on the *Carnesee*.

It took me a moment to find the two oysterboats. There were bushes between Larry's house and the waterfront. One had pretty white flowers, the sort of shrub you'd pose your girl in front of when you were both all dressed up going to the prom. The others were lurking spots for old driveshafts and propellers, somnolent chain, and the odd iron contraption that looked like it might be a bear trap, but was more likely a mooring puller. These were all valuable items, just the sort of thing you'd suddenly require in a pinch and not be able to find elsewhere, even with all the time in the world. The scrap metal value alone was worth considering, and Larry had recently complained that *"certain parties"* had been making depredations in these very bushes.

There was even what is called in the ads an "above-ground swimming pool," but even this suburban symbol could not change the character of the yard. Seen in that context it looked like an oil tank. Nevertheless, swimming pool it was. Larry and I had re-created our Caribbean experience one afternoon by creeping over the floppy lip and descending into its soupy waters during a light rain.

There was now a wheezing and clicking. Within stone-throwing distance a half dozen Vermont Central boxcars groaned by slow enough for a hobo to mount. But where were the oysterboats?

For a moment I thought we were too late. I knew that the Landing had a way of making vessels disappear. After all, buried to make the very dock-yard we were looking at were *Captain, Mary A. Brewer,* the barge *Useful,* and even Larry's first command, the venerable *Emma Frances,* a vessel that even thrice lengthening could not finally save from the axe. Once there had been at least a little identification: a bit of bulwarks here, a stanchion there, like the simple markers of a Flanders field. Now brother Bill's sheet piling at the edges had firmed up the backfill so smoothly that you might have been looking at a marina.

But then I saw them, two park-bench-green boats. They were in the usual slip. *Alice* was rafted outside *Anne. Alice* seemed much the larger, which was odd because, as you looked carefully, there was actually much less of her. How could this be?

The wheelhouse and all the deck gear were gone, but this made her float much higher than *Anne,* so that the bulwarks of *Alice* were a good three feet above that of her elder sister. In a moment I was to learn that all her below-decks gear had also been stripped: engine, tanks, hyster drums, bunks, and indeed most of the decking itself. Like a tubercular patient in the last operatic flush before succumbing, she looked marvelous. She was floating high, at last free of all earthly burdens—a pure and simple vessel.

Two old men were sheepishly sitting upon what of the deck remained aft.

"I've heard of you guys," I bellowed. "Down in Oyster Bay: *two crazy old men* on this very boat."

"Well, you're a little late," said Frank Malloy. "But come aboard anyway. Just don't kick the chain saw into the bilge."

The bilge looked a long way down, its weep holes yet trying to hold onto its secrets in the loud and deckless light.

There were other tools of a similar lack of subtlety: come-alongs, chain hoists, sledgehammers, crowbars, assorted minor pries. More disturbing, there lay an adze, that ancient nuancing tool of the one who builds, ren-dered here pathetic by its thuggish company. Larry Malloy sat among these instruments, his logo cap shockingly clean and rigged peak dead on. His feet dangled over the shattered edge of the deck and hung suspended over what had been the berthing quarters.

"Only the steering gear's left," chirped Frank. His cap sat upright as if it might just pop off, and the sunlight twinkled off his glasses. I was re-minded of a snapshot of him sitting on the break of the deck just under the wheelhouse of the *Virginia.* With characteristic precision Larry had la-beled it: *Gardiners Island August 3, 1940.* In the photo Frank's legs are dan-gling over the foredeck, which is stacked with cordwood. He is wearing a large straw hat, which he has pushed onto the back of his head, and he has a big grin. It is a portrait of a man quietly celebrating a day's work. "You can just see the steering quadrant back there," said the present Frank Malloy. He poked a pry bar in the relevant direction.

"But it won't be there for long," croaked Larry, breaking his silence. He patted the sledge on its head. "It won't be there for long." His jaw was set, and there was a wild gleam in his eyes that I wasn't sure I'd seen on him before. I had seen it in his old man's look when he'd get into his less attractive stories. It was the gleam of the South Street tough who pulled the beer wagon driver off his seat by the whip's live end and ended up punishing his attacker with the butt. It was the gleam of a man who you'd believe had his earlobe chewed off by a rat before he crushed it.

"That's right," said Frank. "You give the Malloy boys a job to do, and it gets done." He was almost as happy-go-lucky as he'd been in the 1940 photo.

"It's a good thing you came today," said Larry. "Because tomorrow night by this time, there won't be nothing left."

"I wish you'd let us know earlier," said Geoffrey. "When there was—"

"You mean there's not enough left?" said Larry. "You mean there's not enough of the *'old, rotten sled'* left?"

There was a kind of mitigating chuckle from Frank. "*'Old, rotten sled.'* That's what Bill called her."

"'Get rid of those *two* old rotten sleds.'"

I looked up at the *Carnesee*'s crane. It was over our heads like an industrial-strength Sword of Damocles. The height of the cab up there on a series of catwalks and ladders was enough to give you a nosebleed. It was as if a large section of the great shipyards downriver had steamed up into this humble nook of water and thrown everything else off scale. It was like when your brother comes into the sandbox with a big new toy he can actually sit on and that makes all your tinker toys, well, mere *toys*.

"You mean he's after *Anne*, too?"

"'Get rid of those *two* rotten sleds.'"

"He's not going to get *Anne*," said Frank. "Not if we have to take her out to sea and sink her."

I sputtered a bunch of our rehearsed schemes, fallback positions, and mitigations. Geoff contributed his mantra: "I'd rather see both boats saved."

"That's quite all right," said Larry when we were done. He levered himself up by means of the sledgehammer handle. "We got all the help we need right here." He patted the sledge head.

"Five loads to the dump already," grinned Frank.

"The wheelhouse?" said Geoff.

"First to go!"

"Now," said Larry, "I bet you thought we couldn't do that."

I looked down at the ground. We were enclosed, after all, in a dockyard made largely out of all those old oysterboats. Buried, they were still part of the structure: most of them in their day worked and lived on as much as *Alice*. I tried again to recall their names: *Captain, Emma Frances,* the barge *Useful* . . . and others I had forgotten, but neither of the Malloys had.

"I bet you thought we couldn't do that," Larry said again.

We agreed they could do it.

. . .

A decade after her menacing of *Alice,* the time at last came when *Carnesee* herself needed major repairs. The horizontal method of framing the bow proved difficult to duplicate because it required severe bending of the steel. While Larry was not the type to crow, this evidence of karma did not pass him unremarked. During his son's birthday party in 1999, Larry and his brother Frank sat under a comforting awning on the Harrison Landing porch and amid festive balloons and party food, gazed downriver, where over the great wall of the Thames Shipyard dry dock, the wheelhouse of the incarcerated *Carnesee* peeped. In Larry's lap was a folder of obits of colleagues and boats. Most of the people seemed to have made it at least into their eighties and the boats had all lasted at least half a century. There was a photo of the *Virginia* rebuilt by Long Islanders. "But she's gone now," sighed Larry, "sunk." There was also a big spread from the New Haven *Register* on *Carnesee* and her work in which Larry himself was mentioned as captain. She was touted as "probably the only self-loading, bottom dump, self-propelled dredge with crane in the United States."

"Well, self-propelled, yes," said Larry, "if you run up and down the ladder enough times between the engine room and the pilot house. Eventually I fell at the bottom of the ladder in the grease and self-propelled myself right out of that goddamn job. Nine hours dredging, two hours to the dumping ground, and three minutes to dump."

The article mentioned that while "a life at sea" might strike some as "romantic, all was not idyllic." No drinking of liquor, for instance, was allowed, and William Malloy even "frowned on the drinking of soda." I asked Larry about that. "I'm not sure dredging in Bridgeport Harbor qualifies as 'life at sea.' As for frowning on the soda, didn't you ever put something in the soda?" he said. "You see somebody with a can says 'Coca-Cola' all over it, don't mean that's the only thing in there."

There was a line in the newspaper story that said brother Frank "had chosen a career in painting" while Larry and brother Bill had "chosen a career in oystering."

"*Pappy* 'chose' my career," muttered Larry. "He said to me one day, 'You're *going oystering*' and that was that."

There was another yellowed article in which Malloy Sr. was interviewed on a number of subjects, one of which was the quaint topic of "pirates." Lawrence Malloy reported that in 1951 he had lost 5,000 bushels of oysters stolen from the grounds in Gardiners Bay. Surprised that I had never heard this story from Larry, especially when he was talking about poaching and Red Vernier, the quaint old oyster watcher with the duck gun and his gaff sloop, I read this excerpt out loud.

"That's right," said Larry.

"You lost all those oysters to someone who stole them from you?"

"That's right."

"Where was Red Vernier and his sailboat and his duck gun?"

"Red Vernier and his duck gun and his sailboat were long gone."

"And no one had replaced him?"

"We never planted another oyster in Gardiners Bay. We went out there and drudged around, and it wasn't long before we realized that there wasn't going to be anything. All the stuff we'd planted, everything we'd put down the year before had been stolen. It hadn't *died*. It had been *removed*. The funny thing was we went back home and next year got together a whole lot of seed and went right back to the grounds ready to plant it. Just as we were about to let it go, Pappy, he looked at me, and I looked at him. I don't know which of us said it: '*Why the hell are we planting here?*' That was it. We never worked those grounds again."

I stared at the yellowed paper a moment. Questions surged to mind. Had I missed all this in a mutter above the diesel that sunny afternoon back in July 1991 when we'd wallowed over those very grounds in *Anne*? How many other disasters had I missed between the grim grinding of gears and the chirping of colorful anecdotes?

Then there were the legal considerations. Hadn't there been an investigation? Was there any sense of who had done this? Where were the law enforcement officers? Who in that period had charge of the law enforcement? To take all those oysters. . . . This was no light-fingered filch of an instant, but an immense exercise in industriousness in itself, a task employing men and highly characteristic machinery—the work of how many days?

I had given up trying to find answers in the Malloy article itself, which had dribbled out into old-salty comforts. I had not yet abandoned searching the paper. There were ads for products no longer manufactured, news items about people long dead. I raised my eyes to the living around me. They were talking about potato salad and cake. *Comments* on potato salad and cake were being encouraged. *Decisions* had to be reached immediately in reference to potato salad and cake. Little side seminars on ice cream flavors and plastic forks sprang up. My questions about the past seemed trivial, if not unseemly. This was an old grievance worn too deep to ever surface. Or perhaps it had all worked out long ago in that exchange of glances between father and son when they'd agreed to give it up, a rare coming together of the two men, although only in the acceptance of defeat. In any case, there seemed to be no time or space to wedge in just why it was that a family business had virtually been wiped out by a crime. And what kind of a crime was this anyway? No one had broken into anyone's house or office. No one had been sapped or shot. Where were the masks and getaway cars? The witnesses? This was water and stuff under water. Your stuff's there and then it's not there. And isn't the water everyone's water, the sea?

Finally I found a moment in the festivities. "I mean, Larry, what did you *do* about it?

"We never worked those grounds again."

NOTE

WE DID NOT DISCUSS MANFRED (p. 279): One reason was that we did not know what had happened between Manfred's downfall and the present threat to *Alice*. We certainly did not want at that time to ask. A year or so later I asked Larry to fill in the gap.

"A friend spotted *Alice* moored down river below the bridges on the other side near the Hess Fuel Dock. He had just read that article in the paper about Manfred. Brother Frank and me, we got *Anne* and went down there and brought her home."

Later Larry said, "Brother Frank wanted to take her out to sea and burn her. I told him you can't do that no more."

IN THE TROPICS

Considering the lawlessness and loneliness of the spot, and the
sort of stories, at that day, associated with those seas . . .

—Herman Melville, *Benito Cereno*

THE TROPICS HAVE always presented a disturbing allure for New England mariners. World War Two was confusing in that a lot of men in our town actually got to go to these hot places. When they came back I heard the word *infested* applied to many of the locations formerly deemed paradisiacal. There was a brief flurry in our area of bars with tropic motifs, bare-breasted hula-hula girls swishing among the plaster pimples. During the winter of Larry's seventy-seventh year, my son and his crew sailed the schooner *Sylvina W. Beal* south for the season. Larry and I joined them on two separate occasions in Marigot Bay, St. Lucia, in the Windward Isles. "I know what you're after," said Larry's companion, Shirley.

We swam every day and there were often women, but the only one I saw without her top on was at a distance, backlit into near-obscurity by the light off the sea. When comparing notes later, Larry said to me, "Did you see that young man with the chest muscle problem?"

The schooner was moored, stern in, to a sandspit that divided the long, narrow bay on the leeward side of the high, round island. The land rose steeply on either side of the bay so that it had the dimensions of a shoebox open on the west end. The spit was about three-quarters of the way up inside the bay and ran about one-third of the way across from the east. On the spit were tall royal palms, and a local man named Mr. Lynch had been hired by the hotel to climb the trees with a cutlass to make sure that none of the coconuts fell the hundred feet or so upon the guests who occasionally reclined beneath the trees on lawn chairs.

History in the tropics can be as thin as the soil over the coral or volcanic rock. Indeed, who really wants more history than can fit on a placemat or back-bar mural? The story was this. At the time of the American Revolution, when the major conflict in the western Atlantic was actually between the British and the French over the Spice Islands, as the Caribbean was then known, Admiral Rodney had hidden his ships behind these tall palms or their ancestors and Admiral de Grasse had sailed past without knowing he was there. Clever Brits. Gullible Frogs.

More recently the Rex Harrison version of *Dr. Doolittle* had been shot there. The giant pink snail that figures so heavily in the plot had sailed out of the bay, but some of the prop façades were still part of the décor of the small hotel on our side of the harbor. They lent a whimsical air to the otherwise impassive jungle that rose, impenetrable, up the steep slope from the harbor. There were no automobiles on this side of the bay. There was a small, improvised pontoon ferry that ran from the spit to the other side of the bay, where there was another hotel and a store and where the taxis, called "transports," came down the steep hill from the international airport that was somewhere off on the far south side of the island.

The Windward Isles, unlike the low lands of the northern Caribbean, are chiefly volcanic. St. Lucia sports three beauts, two of them extinct cones called the Pitons, the likeness of which adorned the local beer label ("Pitons: The Power of Two"). The third was an active stink soup called Soufriere, which is French for steaming sulfur pot. In addition to these three there were many other eroded volcanic cones scattered about the place, and at night I'd sit up on deck fighting off the effects of Jamaican jerk sauce and listen to the dogs bark until the roosters woke up in the dark. I'd just read something about dinosaurs being nothing more than large chickens. Sitting there in a fever staring at those rumpled volcano parts right out of the scenic background in the Peabody dinosaur exhibit, I blinked an occasional tyrannosaurus out of the picture. Larry seemed to get by the heartburn problem, but he did mutter occasionally about his prostate. "Don't worry," I said. "Admiral Rodney had a bad prostate here, too."

The island's culture was an interesting mix of French, English, and what is euphemistically known as "local." The French and English had fought over the place numerous times. The title changed in double figures, not always the result of a local battle, sometimes merely the "player to be named later" in a struggle somewhere else. But local battles between the two European nations there had been, most famously between admirals Rodney and de Grasse. Rodney had been charged with watching de Grasse, who was over at the next island, Martinique. Rodney performed his duty a day's sail north from Marigot Bay, from a dead volcanic hump just off St. Lucia that is now called Pigeon Island, located at the entrance of what is now called Rodney Bay.

From time to time we made forays in the schooner down the St. Lucia coast from Marigot to Rodney Bay. When we were anchored in Rodney Bay, Larry and I rowed in to shore and climbed up the abrupt hump that was Pigeon Island. The place was so named from the use Rodney had made of those birds in his communications. At the top were cannons, and we marveled at the technology that could have hauled them up there. The side of the hill was steep rock veined with a bewildering network of two-foot-wide paths paved in clay, which even on dry days were slippery. Larry jumped right into the spirit of the place and tried to re-create the block-and-tackle system that would have got those cannons where they were.

"I don't see how Rodney did all this with a bad prostate," wheezed Larry. "Maybe they just used helicopters."

We could see across the straits to purple Martinique and imagine how Rodney could have maintained his watch. As it turned out, when De Grasse made his move north to what turned out to be the key development in the Revolution, the so-called Battle of Yorktown, Rodney was right on his heels. The struggle for the North American colonies, however, was only a sidebar to the major conflict over the Caribbean Spice Islands. At Cape Hatteras, George Brydges Rodney saw the opportunity to split off and go for England, ostensibly for prostate treatments at Bath. He also had some personal treasures that he might have thought to bank as well. In any case, he missed de Grasse's little blockade of Cornwallis off the tiny Chesapeake town of York. When he returned to the lower Caribbean he encountered de Grasse again, and with Samuel Hood defeated him in a good old-fashioned rousing sea battle off Dominica on April 12, 1781, and watched Hood taking the great gilded melon of a flagship, *Ville de Paris*. Rodney himself took de Grasse prisoner and maintained him in his grand cabin while he wrote smugly back to England that he had the French business in his pocket.

"In other words," said Larry, hand upon the parapet looking toward Martinique, "we are speaking English because of prostate trouble."

"You might say that. At least that's pretty much Barbara Tuchman's take in *The First Salute*."

"Who is this woman?"

I repeated her name.

"Well, do you think she'd be interested? I've got a touch of prostate problem right now myself."

"Only if, as a result, empires fall."

From the back of the parapet we looked down on the top of *Sylvina W. Beal*'s masts. On deck they were actually the size of telephone poles. From up on Rodney's perch they seemed like toothpicks.

"I wouldn't want to fall off here," said Larry. "Might get a schooner mast in my eye."

. . .

In March we celebrated Larry's seventy-seventh birthday back at Marigot Bay. Liz Prete, the cook, rode the "transport" torturous hours to the capital city, Castris, where there was a great market. There she bartered with her favorite women merchants, then lugged back special goodies. There were two other females in the crew, and "The Women of the *Beal*," as they called themselves, prevailed upon our hosts at the little restaurant to save the streamers and other baubles from one of their recent parties. With these they festooned the schooner's rigging. Nor was dressing ship the only decoration. "The Women of the *Beal*," also pulled from their seabags actual dresses and fluffed each other up, while "The Gentlemen of the *Beal*" made an effort to unsnarl their beards and find clean shirts. As the supper party wore on "The Women of the *Beal*" posed for pictures with the honored guest. "These will get me in trouble at home," said the man of the hour (and he was right).

. . .

A lot of stories got told under the tarp aboard the schooner down in the Windwards that probably wouldn't have got told back in New England. Some of these have been sprinkled through this book, but there was one that seemed destined for sharing far from home. Perhaps it was the stillness of the night, broken only by the cries of the locals communicating on either side of the harbor as the little pontoon ferry with the gingerbread canopy shuttled back and forth with its one running light, a flashlight that would have made a theater usher nervous.

It seems there was a period in Larry's career when no one thought anything of scuttling any old vessel that was yet able to float but promised no value to a scrapper ashore. Then there was a period when people still did this but worried about it. This was a story from the latter era.

Shaw's Cove in New London was the place where the city was first developed. Later nipped by the New York–Boston railroad line, the cove became a backwater where old ships came to die. The side of the cove up against the railroad tracks was like an elephant graveyard with the great old ladies of the passenger service wallowing out their last leakings. It was there the once-elegant *Sprague Carroll*, a Block Island boat run by the fabled Ray Abel, and others of her general size and type had expired. At some point, however, even the tiny Shaw Cove could no longer hold its dying, especially if the resident was a mere barge. Some local mariners were hired to dispose of just such a barge.

The idea was to smuggle this craft out of Shaw's Cove in such a way that there would be no record of its departing should it by some chance never reappear there or in any other port. To accomplish this, these mariners moved another comparable barge next to her, flooded the first barge and then shuffled the second barge over the top, having fastened them together with great cables. Then in broad daylight they simply hooked on a hawser and towed the barge(s) out of the cove.

The only problem was at the railroad bridge. This was a swing affair operated by a gentleman who found the demand on his time so minimal that it often seemed to make a good deal more sense for him to spend it elsewhere, preferably among cheerful companions on nearby Bank Street. This work ethic on the part of the bridge tender was not entirely unwelcome to our mariners. After all, there was no way they could really hide the cables strapping the two barges together if one cared to peer that way carefully and soberly. The mariners made sure they had their man off Bank Street at that delicately balanced point in his workday when he was still able to open the bridge yet not be excessively curious as to what passed through.

More to the point was the depth of the water at the bridge opening. As the bridge tender looked out the window he saw a strange thing. The barge being towed by the tug had suddenly stopped, even though the hawser was tight and the prop wash under the tug's counter was frothing manfully. This bewildered him, as he had seen, or thought he had seen, this barge pass easily in and out a number of times at what must have been various tides. But there it was, *stuck*. And there was his bridge, *open*.

Now if this were a mere backwater track, things might not have become so suddenly exciting. This, however, was the main line between New York and Boston, and if it weren't bad enough that trains ran from New York to Boston like that, they also ran from Boston to New York, which meant there were twice as many of them. Furthermore, while some of these trains stopped at New London and therefore slowed down passing Shaw's Cove, others were hellbent for Boston or New York and slow down they did not.

At the distance of Marigot Bay, it was not clear to me how the people of which Larry Malloy spoke ever extricated themselves from this problem. Such are the vagaries of classic storytelling beneath the lamp-lit tarp in the tropics, and, of course, because of the delicate nature of this tale of clumsiness, I have never again brought the matter up.

But extricate themselves they did, because we next see them towing the two barges out into Fishers Island Sound in what has become, in true sea story style, A GREAT STORM. The idea was to get out to the Race, where the water is a couple of hundred feet deep, and simply cut loose the bottom barge. The Race, however, as we have seen, can be a mean place without there even being a storm. By the time the merry little entourage had reached the outer fringes of the Thames Estuary the weather had, as the saying goes, deteriorated. Not only was the lower barge in danger of squirming down out of control and landing just anywhere at any angle, but there was the distinct possibility that it would take the floating barge with it. If that happened and the hawser could not be cut in time, the tug would for sure go too. Throwing theory to the all-too-literal wind, they decided to pick the nearest deep hole they could actually fetch and attempt to jettison the barge right there. (So many of Larry's stories seem to hinge on the depth of the water.)

There are not many deep holes inside Fishers Island Sound, but I'm not going to tell you which one they did find, lest, Gentle Reader, you go to that position with your fancy gear and in your literal-minded, litigious way attempt to prove our man either a liar or a criminal. But find a cozy hole they did and commenced cutting the cables.

Letting go a load like this is a bit like letting go of a tiger you have by the tail. You must sequence your activities crisply and be gone from the scene cleanly. The men working on each side of the top barge found it no longer to be their old stable friend of the Shaw's Cove backwater, but a slippery platform staggering and plunging. The precise moment when the cables had to be cut on each side could not be synchronized. One cable went before the other, and the top barge lurched—the full load borne on one side.

"Oh," said Larry, "and I forgot to tell you that by then it was dark and you couldn't see anything."

. . .

We were sitting around under the awning one evening in the dark listening to the locals shout at each other across the dark water. Next to us was the spindly landing of the ferry. The *Gingerbread Express* was a charming little craft in keeping with the cobbled-up World War Two culture of the Caribbean. It more or less floated on a couple of surplus pontoons over which a plywood platform supported a pair of benches that ran fore and aft. The chief character of the vessel was defined by the wooden canopy, whose valences had been cut into a Victorian gingerbread pattern. The engine was an outboard, the handle of which was lengthened into a long tiller by a windsurfer spar spliced on with baling wire. Our host told us he had originally had a quaint little yacht wheel arrangement for the helm. He'd set it up in the bow and run the cable system that connected the drum on the back of the helm to the tiller aft. Unfortunately this rig evidently proved too baroque for the young hot-rodders he employed to run the boat, energetic men who cranked the helm so dramatically they continually unpeeled the cable from the drum. Jolly as the little craft was by daylight, it was at best ill-lit after dark, and evoked a kind of Conradian menace as it sputtered across the narrow bay amid the rubbery volubility of the echoing local patois. Although the ferry was free and anyone could ride it as often as he or she liked, the chief local entertainment seemed to be to cross over and then volley interminable conversations with the people you had just left.

Their voices echoed in the steep-sided bay and we speculated on the content of their communication. Were these ominous messages? Or were they the trivialities of American teenagers using a telephone? Failing to get anywhere with that line of anthropology, I asked Larry about other vacations he might have had. What did a boatman do for a vacation?

. . .

"First of all, vacations weren't always around. Vacations when they did come around weren't always what you wanted. They was just days when you didn't have work. Or days when you did have work but couldn't get to it because of the weather. 'Down time,' they call it now. Mostly the weather, that's what planned your vacations for you. You didn't have *travel agents*. Not that *you* could plan it. You could have things set aside to do when the bad weather came. It wasn't money you saved for a rainy day; it was inside work. What you actually did was depending, of course, on where you were. Most of the time we was operating daytimes out from a base, Greenport or New London. That way you could get stuff done in the shop. But there were times when you were away and just had to make do. That coaling trip Pappy and Josh Moore took on *Emma Frances* to Perth Amboy in the thirties—I suppose some people might see that as a vacation: a little vacation to Perth Amboy, New Jersey. I don't think that's what you meant."

"It's interesting, but you're right. A coaling trip to Perth Amboy in the 1930s is not within the parameters of the vacation concept."

"Now I do remember a regular vacation once. That is, what shore people would call a vacation. I don't know about 'parameters.' Is that like 'perimeters'?"

"More expensive."

"I figured so."

"You were saying—"

"I was saying we took a vacation once. A real vacation. We took a trip on *Anne* with no other thing in mind than to just have this *vacation*. It was the middle of summer, which if you're not doing any shelling can be a slack time in the oyster season, and I guess we didn't have no other work, at least for that week. It was too early to run potatoes or maybe we wasn't running potatoes at all then. To tell the truth I don't know where Pappy even got the idea of a *vacation*. I don't think he grew up that way. Maybe he'd looked around at some of the yachts over at Shelter Island, and somebody explained it to him. Of course, even yachts to most of the people he knew were jobs, like Captain Monsell on the Cup Defender *Rainbow*. Maybe it was my mother's idea: a *vacation*. It's hard to imagine Pappy actually set aside that time if he did have any work.

"Not that we went all that far. We just went over into Gardiners Bay and anchored on the far side off Fort Tyler. That's the name of what's marked on the chart as "The Ruins." The spit connecting the fort to Gardiners Island was wider in those days. You could lay in there easy then because it was calmer. That was before the big blight in the thirties, and there was lots of eel grass to knock down the seas.

"In those days it wasn't what it became later: a bird sanctuary and bombing target. (I guess the birds got used to the hours.) Now it's not much more than a falling-down wall at the end of that long spit."

"Tombolo," I said.

"It tumbled down all right. I don't know what made it fall down and round off like that. Used to be all sharp angles. Was that the bomb range or the bird sanctuary done that? Them birds could do a job on you. Then there was cells inside and gates. I could never figure out why they had doors like you'd have in cells, you know, with bars. Looks so to me like it was a jail. Maybe it was to protect the ammunition, not to keep solders in."

"Captain Ben Rathbun has a story about that," I said, "how during the Portland gale of 1898, when they were building Fort Tyler against the Spanish, that a room just like that was where the workmen all huddled down against the storm. It was the only safe place. There was just one cot and the boss sat on that while all the other workmen stood around in thirteen inches of water."

"Well," said Larry, "even without knowing that story, just being in that room does make you feel funny, though. But the bombing tore it down. The bombing and the birds and the weather. That's what you call *time*, I guess.

"There was a pier off the north side of the Ruins, and we just tied up there, like I suppose you see people do these days at a marina. Not that we had power or fresh water or showers or a store or swimming pool or a restaurant or anything. Although the eel grass did make the Bay quieter then, we still didn't lay to the dock overnight, in case a breeze-o-wind come up out of the north. At night we'd go out around the Fort and anchor up in Cherry Harbor or run up north to Plum Island where there was a little harbor you could tie up at. Plum Island was a snug little place then and convenient because it was right in the middle of all the good fishing and being halfway across saved you a long running time out of Greenport for New London. Now, of course, that's all the Government Animal Disease Station there, and they'd either shoo you out or throw you in the cage with the sick giraffes and never let you out. And there's no good place now halfway between Greenport and New London. Of course boats are so much faster now, I guess you don't even think about halfway places.

"For some reason there wasn't anybody on Gardiners Island then. We just ran around all over the place whereever we wanted. There was deer and rabbits and turkeys and herons and hawks. And there weren't any ticks. There was just the Ruins and nobody else around. There were those rooms inside the fort like jail cells, but like I say, I think that was to keep people out of the ammunition. You read Captain Ben Rathbun's book you got all kinds of spooky stories about the place: *high tide and the storm raging and dark* and all that, but we didn't know any of them soldier stories like he tells in his book then. We just had to make up stuff. Captain Kidd, of course, he was famous for being out there back of Gardiners Island and maybe leaving some treasure behind, but that was all pretty sketchy to us. What you had as a boy running around out there wasn't so much names and dates, but just a kind of *feeling* that some things had happened that you wouldn't likely find at home. And maybe some of them things, they could start up happening again around the next rock.

"These days what we done you'd call it a *family outing*. We had my brothers, Frank and Bill, my mother and Pappy, and my sister Anna. There's no room below decks so we had a big canvas tarp that ran from the wheelhouse to the mast so you had the whole foredeck. Like we have down here in the tropics. Sometimes Pappy slept in the wheelhouse; it all depended on how hot it was. You could throw a mattress or some straw on the deck and get a night's sleep. As for mosquitoes, hey, you always got *them*, but you don't have so many out in the middle of the Bay like that. That's one reason you go out there: to get away from the bugs. We cooked our own food, went fishing, but not with a pole. You didn't have them fancy rods and reels then, even with the money. That started with the millionaires out to Montauk a decade or so later. We just used hand lines, tarred line you'd wrap up on a wooden hand frame like a kite string. If you was smart when the blues were running you'd find yourself an old glove for your right hand. I never caught a striper in my life. I know that sounds funny because every kid you meet nowadays has caught a striper. A whole bunch of stripers. Record-breaking *lunkers*. I don't think you can even call yourself a fisherman these days unless you caught at least *one*. I guess I didn't get to where they was. Ate a lot of *cunners* as big as blackfish. Nowadays you catch a cunner, you curse it and throw it back. When we used to lay in there at Plum Island, we'd catch cunners on purpose. You get a cunner eight to ten inches long you get pretty good eating. A bit boney, but, hey, you wasn't supposed to be gulping your food. There were no clams out around the Fort, but there was a good beach for swimming.

"Much later, after the war, we'd use *Anne* to watch the Yale-Harvard rowing races. I don't know if that counts as a *vacation*. Maybe that was only a *holiday*. Just chug out a bit from the Landing and set the dredge down.

With the dredge, you never had to anchor. There were plenty of fancy yachts all around, and they always had trouble in that silt bottom to get their anchors to hold. Any kind of a breeze—especially down under the bridge—and Christ, they'd be all over the place, blowing into each other. I don't suppose that made much of a holiday for them people, but we sure found it entertaining. Especially as we always kept upstream from them so we wouldn't have to keep fending off. Same thing with the fireworks down harbor when they started those city festivals. Except the yachts weren't quite so fancy any more. Expensive, yes, but not like the pretty ones you used to see at the Yale-Harvard in the old days. *Anne* was a steady platform, and if you got there earlier you could get a good seat for most anything that went on in the Thames River.

"Otherwise we had your holidays just like anybody else, in houses with whatever and whoever."

And then, maybe just to cool things off a bit in the heat of the tropical evening, he told me that story of the Christmas in 1941 just after war was declared—how, as he and his wife were setting out for home in a blizzard to Harrison's Landing from the little cottage at the Elijah Ball Oyster Company in Guilford, and his engine block had cracked.

. . .

All, however, was not idyllic in paradise. On an especially sultry evening in Marigot Bay, as was our custom after dark, we had created a little moat by easing ahead on our anchor, so that our stern was about a dozen feet off the wobbly pier next to the pier where the pontoon ferry landed. The moat was necessary because of some recent incidents.

Our host had had to fire one of the maids who worked in the bungalows after he had caught her thieving the fifth time. Her man, evidently counting on her income to augment his at-large status, had risen to the occasion by threatening to "lash" the wife of our host and "place her in *two* barrels." When Larry had heard this, frugal man that he was, he initially wondered at the need of the second container. "But I guess that's to get across the idea that when she's 'lashed' she'll be in more than one piece."

The second incident involved a sometime laborer called by his colleagues "Loco." He had been renting out the restaurant's beach chairs beneath the coconut trees as a kind of personal concession. When reprimanded for this by our host, Loco lured him in under a souvenir stand where locals sold "crafts" woven from fronds. There Loco reached up under the corrugated roof and produced a rusty cutlass with which he attempted to *lash*. When our host closed with him in under the cutlass Loco bit him in the nipple so hard as to nearly detach it. The most disturbing thing about this was that one of the more tranquil locals then joined in the fray, striking our host with a broken oar. Our host's wife noticed something going on and broke up the fray with a shot of illegal Mace, which she kept on her room key chain.

The constable in pith helmet and khakis came from the far shore on the *Gingerbread Express* and, brandishing his rattan swagger stick, marched Loco off to the jail. The constable then gave our host a ride to the hospital where he received a tetanus shot and had his nipple reattached. Loco was back on the beach loafing about his chair concession before our host returned from the hospital.

All this had taken place right within sight of where Larry and I were having our morning swim in the harbor. "Gee, I sure hate to miss a good fight like that," he said. Later we found out that three cutlass-wielding locals had jumped one of the visitors living in the bungalow inside his quarters.

The activity of the *Gingerbread Express* usually lasted until close to midnight, as the boat was the only way to get from the surrounding villages to the shore where the restaurant and a dozen associated hillside bungalows were. Through the evening, there was a kind of natural Curve of Obstreperousness which, if carried out, would lull you into complacency.

Down below it was too hot to shut the stateroom door all the way. To make sure that no one sneaked up on me in my bunk I had been in the habit of wedging a "pool shoe" under the partially opened door on my side. I was half-asleep when I awoke to a hullabaloo. Grabbing the cutlass from under my pillow, I removed the pool shoe and ventured into the passageway. Larry's door was still shut. It was with some apprehension that I climbed the ladder and stuck my head up out of the hatch. With my hands on the deck and my feet on the companionway ladder, I could just see over the after cabin top and under the awning overhead.

On the pier to which our stern line was attached, a crowd had gathered. In the dark it was difficult to count the number of people, but it seemed as if nearly the entire space on the pier was occupied.

Between the crowd and me was our own afterguard, consisting of maybe four. The awning partially blocked my view of the crowd. I could not see if any of our local friends were there. The afterguard bantered with what appeared to be a large woman who was frantically heaving and retrieving a round casting net into the narrow space between our boat and the shore. In my three weeks along the St. Lucia waterfront, I had not seen that type of fishing except in tourist brochures. Even there it was in sunlight on a shelving beach. Usually the night fishing at that Marigot Bay pier was conducted by an elderly local gentleman who, with a stick and bobber, kept to himself on a corner of the pier. Indeed, he was still there, conducting himself in the midst of all this din with his usual dignity. I had the feeling I had come in on the middle of an argument that had begun long before we had arrived on the island. It all might have been comic had not there not been those other incidents.

I had my sheathed cutlass flat on the deck beneath my chin. We had at times speculated on how we would deal with boarding and were armed with various utensils. In that discussion, however, the Captain advised Mace and told a story about watching an ancient local with almost no apparent muscle on his arm demonstrate how to cut open a coconut. "I had been beating the thing to a pulp with my cutlass. He severed it like a melon with one stroke that I never even saw fall."

I came up a step higher on the ladder and rested my elbows on the hatch runners. The awning was maybe three feet above my head. It gave me a false sense of security. Still no stirring from Larry below.

It was hard to know what the crowd behind the net-casting woman was prepared to do. Moreover, the ferry seemed to be bringing wave after wave of reinforcements and no one was making the return trip. No longer was it the beloved *Gingerbread Express,* but a sinister landing craft bristling with shock troops. As time wore on and my eyes became used to the darkness, many of the locals, so far as I could tell, seemed amused by the show. Others seemed downright bored. Was the principal actress in all this a leader of an insurrection or just a local crank, someone who could at best be guilty of attempting to politicize her nostalgia?

She was, in any case, making a big thing of having just come back home from spending a long time in Germany. Indeed, moping silently about behind her in the shadows was a thin blond man. Apparently in Germany she had learned of Yankee transgressions in Viet Nam. Now our schooner was taking over her childhood fishing spot. Our notion that we had been given permission was a phantasy. The man who had given this permission was a foreigner himself, a mere *renter.* Her net-casting style had less logic to it than her politics and contrasted comically with the serenity of the old bobber fisherman. He seemed totally oblivious to this bizarre dance, although, of course, all the ki-ying and splashing must have completely destroyed his own fishing.

I sensed someone behind me on the companionway. It was Larry. It was good to know he was there—a veteran of waterfront brawls. I recalled how he had handled the great lout at the Shellfish Commission Meeting. Old as Larry was, he would yet be a good man to have standing by you in the trenches. "Well," I said, unsheathing my cutlass and expecting a discussion of tactics, "what do you make of it?"

"I can't tell if she's trying to catch a fish," he said, "or just rinsing out a few things."

I waited a few beats in the companionway, then sheathed my cutlass. Twenty minutes later the net-caster had melted and with her departure the crowd had begun to ebb, ferry by ferry, until the *Gingerbread Express* shut down on the far shore in her night berth. Without the drone of her engine, all was quiet. The old man sat by his bobber in the darkness.

"Well, I guess that's what she was doing," said Larry, as he eased himself back down the hatch. "Rinsing out a few things."

. . .

Later we sailed down to St. Vincent, the next island south. Larry was at the helm for a long stretch across the channel between the two islands where the Atlantic rolls all the way in from Africa. We had the lee rail just awash and were going, as my father would say, *like a train of cars*. We passed all the modern ketches that had left the harbor before us. They were under reduced sail, their crews dressed as if they were off Gloucester, and their hulls were diving and plunging. We strolled about the deck and peeled fruit. Although Larry had spent 98 percent of his life steering powerboats, he had a good feel for the boat under sail. "What the hell, like I told you, we always had jibs. I also had a little sailing yacht before the war. An open-decked boat, you know. Nothing big. But a sailing yacht."

Toward the end of the light we came in under the lee of the volcano on St. Vincent. This great green hill had in 1902 blown the lake out of its top. Unlike Pelee on Martinique, which had killed so many in the same series of disturbances, it had not caused extensive human damage because there were fewer people living in its shadow. On the Atlantic side of the volcano, even as we passed, was the last settlement of the Caribs, the once warlike tribe that had subdued what seems to have been the indigenous population, the tragically peaceful Arawaks.

The locals who came to us in the pitch dark were not, presumably Caribs, or at least not purely so. They hung on our gunnels from the sanctity of their marvelous miniature Yankee whaling boats and offered to take our line ashore or sell us fish. We had caught a gorgeous miah-miah and showed them the tail, which impressed them. We told them to come back the next day and we would have something going on.

Because the shore falls so precipitously away from the shoulders of the volcanoes, one ends up tying the stern to something on land and anchoring in an average of 180 feet off the bow. Larry had spent most of his life in waters that only get to 80 feet and that in but a few holes. He stood on the bow and watched the chain run out endlessly into the darkening water. "You sure you got enough string on that anchor?" he asked.

We dispatched *Imp*, our own small boat, ashore with the stern line. I could see John Hope and Scotto, dancing about what looked like a giant pig on its back. When they returned to the schooner they informed us it was actually a great water tower that we later learned the locals had toppled as if it had been a statue of Lenin.

"Well," said the Captain, "let's hope they don't identify us with the water tower."

We kept a watch through the night to make sure no bright eyes and gleaming blades came over the rail.

. . .

The next morning the little boats were out in full force. About a dozen of the brightly painted double-ended pulling craft appeared off the beach, each rowed by a single bare-chested young man. We got a chance to examine the marvelous little whaling boats, most of which seemed about a dozen feet long. The oars looked even more homemade than the crafts themselves, and were thrust between thole pins that looked like the last teeth of an old, gummy man, an illusion perhaps encouraged by the usual choice of crimson for the gunnels. The concept of these boats had been based on the double-ended boats off Yankee whaling ships from the nineteenth century, and the local builders had merely reduced the dimensions of the hulls without changing the scantlings, so that they were planked out in wood massive enough for the original twenty-footers. Each was gaily painted with every excuse, every change in plank or rail, used to change a color.

Like their grim whaling counterparts, these gay boats, despite their size, were also vessels of commerce. If Stateside entrepreneurs speak of "positioning" themselves, these nimble craft justified their existence by putting their operators at the right place and time from which to exhibit their merchandise. Sometimes it was bananas (or more likely, given the export policies of their country, the *possibility* of bananas); fish; iguanas (live or dead); services as tour guides or line handlers or hull cleaners. Their North American urban counterparts are the much-maligned squeegee boys and hubcap traders.

"If you grew up down here," I asked Larry, "do you think this is what you would have done?"

"I don't see many *old* guys. Maybe they retire early in under them trees."

Like the rowing and sailing waterclerks of old in Northern harbors, the competition was keen, and speed getting out to the potential customer key. Since we had promised them some sort of activity the night before, the schooner captain decided to fulfill this declaration with what he called the "First Annual Cumberland Bay Rowing Race." Using the stern line as a literal starting line, we had everyone grab hold of the rope with one hand.

There was but a single buoy in the entire cove, apparently marking a fish pot, and it was about a half-mile away. That was to be the turning point.

The schooner captain and crew person Erin Haegan, Belle of the Lesser Antilles, stoked the Lyle gun. Larry prepared a solemn reading from his black-backed diary, which, while it looked like a pocket Bible, was actually a promotional gift from a marine construction company. Each day's entry had various bits of basic information and a short "inspirational" passage. Although I had stepped below and attempted to warm up by means of some lip-enhancing exercises on the mouthpiece of the ship's bugle, back on deck I played a faltering "Assembly Call," the fluffed notes returning to haunt me off the base of the volcano. Larry stood on the quarterdeck, his Hawaiian shirt covering his ample waist, his dark glasses and logo cap giving him the look of a Banana Republic dictator. All eyes were riveted on the black book, which he held at a solemn distance from the billow of his outrageous shirt as he intoned:

"As we go through the battle of life, let no man, desiring success, sound the faltering trumpet . . ."

There was a great cheer from the boat boys. It was a truly alarming response to something coming out of a little black book. I looked over at Larry. I could not see his eyes twinkle behind his dark glasses, but he raised his off hand in a quieting benediction, and I sounded a slightly less faltering trumpet on "Charge."

The Captain, having cleared the muzzle of the Lyle gun from admirers ("If you stay there, you will be *killed!*"), whacked the percussion cap with the carpenter's hammer.

Ka-boom!

The gun echoed off the volcano and no one moved. The entire fleet had dropped their oars and clapped hands over ears—all but the *Beal's* own entry, mate John Hope, in our relatively drab, flat-bottomed, flatiron skiff *Imp*. Because of this start, John Hope unfortunately led at the first turn. Scotto, however, had managed to borrow a local craft and was meanwhile upholding the integrity of the First Annual Cumberland Bay Rowing Race by flailing fatuously at the rear of the fleet. Still, those of us aboard the committee boat decided it would be politically wiser if neither of our entries actually *won* the contest. Not to worry, a brawny local lad eventually overtook John Hope.

First prize was a *Sylvina W. Beal* T-shirt, which the local lad immediately tried on and, finding it too small to encase his brawn, offered it up to Erin Haegan, Belle of the Lesser Antilles, who, having a sea bag full of them and no desire to become herself a trophy, modestly demurred. Second prize was a can of Budweiser and third prize was two cans.

"No, mon," said the third-place winner. "You got this prize bahk-waards. Should be *two* cahns second place; *one* cahn third."

"You haven't tasted Budweiser," said the Captain.

At the conclusion of the ceremonies I borrowed Larry's black book. "You made that quote up, didn't you, that bit about the *uncertain trumpet.*"

But he hadn't. There it was, by some obscure midcentury inspirational type who no doubt had uttered his advice with the full and certain knowledge it would not be employed literally.

. . .

At the next harbor on St. Vincent, with a name that sounded like a Bob and Ray character, Walli Balu Bay, we availed ourselves of the local services of two young brothers named Ron and Ronnie. They were near twins, to be distinguished by the number of front teeth. Ron and Ronnie did not have one of the local wooden craft, but something of which they were much more proud, an almost square fiberglass object, much patched, that looked as if it might have been happier as a sink liner. As for propulsion, they had what looked like a packing crate slat. They had worked out a division of labor: Ron paddled; Ronnie bailed. The patch was perfectly adjusted to admit just the right amount of water to balance the tasks.

The landing party was armed with two purposes: to go to the waterfall for a bath in fresh water and to find out more about a subject that had come to obsess the Schooner Captain: an iguana hunt.

Ron took us toward the waterfall up past the burning dump, up along the tumbling stream that the women had turned into a giant laundromat, using the bushes as dryers and the open air to exchange songs and gossip. In the deep hills the grotesque volcanic humps gave me no sense of scale. We were walking right into the Peabody dinosaur mural. An African cattle egret, its ancestors, as St. Lucian Derek Wolcott tells us, blown across the Atlantic on hurricane winds, flew just above us headed for the hills.

Hoping to pick up the local name, I asked Ron what he called the bird.

"That is a sea gull," he said. And then seeing I was struggling with this, added, "We call it a sea gull because that is where it comes from, the sea."

Descending the road from the waterfall ambled a thin old man with two thin old dogs out front. He carried a naked machete, here called a "cutlass," before him, his hands ceremoniously clasped just above the hilt as if he were carrying a candle in a cathedral. I had noticed this manner of transporting these potentially alarming tools on St. Lucia and assumed that a cutlass so borne was a cutlass come in peace. The old man identified himself as an iguana hunter and his hounds as central to this safari. I heard Larry mumbling something like, "I've got one of them at home." The Schooner Captain announced again that he was very much interested in the idea of an iguana hunt. Ron promised us that on our next visit he would organize such a thing. Larry repeated his phrase. I asked just where these exotic beasts would be found. Ron gestured to the grotesque hills up into which had flown the bird from the sea. We all stood there a moment enraptured by the thought of someday actually somehow going up into that remote country in quest of this creature.

"I've got one of those at home," said Larry again.

"What the hell are you talking about?" I said.

"An *iguana*. Isn't that what you call them?"

"They're talking about a strange lizardlike creature, a kind of miniature dinosaur thing," I explained. "Found in those remote hills." I pointed. "By the way, Ron," I said, "I can't get any sense of scale here. How far away are those hills?"

"Oh, that be very many, many miles," said Ron, "but I can someday take you there."

"Actually he lives in the attic," said Larry. "His name is Neil, and I didn't even know he was there until one night I hear this thump. I open the door at the bottom of the stairs and there he is. An *iguana*."

"An iguana is an exotic animal," explained the Schooner Captain.

"They live way high in the mountains," said Ron and raised his long finger unto the hills.

"Shirley's son had him up there in his room in the attic," said Larry, "for six months before I even knew it."

"At Harrison's Landing, on the Thames River, in Connecticut?"

"They said his name is 'Neil,' but I don't think *he* knows that." Larry looked at Ron. "Do iguanas know their own names?"

"In the high hills," said Ron. "I take you there some day."

. . .

When it was time to fly back to the States, we were in Elizabeth Harbor in Bequi in the Grenadines. To make our complicated travel arrangements work we had to get up when it was dark. I stooped under the tarp we had rigged topside and poured a bucket of warm harbor water over my naked body as Erin, Belle of the Lesser Antilles, sleepily gathered her mattress out of the way and eased past me. After breakfast the Schooner Captain rowed Larry and me across the harbor over to the St. Vincent ferry in the *Imp*. The ferry had a great list to starboard although there was no one yet aboard. Larry pointed out the tires on the side of the ship and, reminding me of his father's use of such devices, urged us to climb aboard in this fashion. Eventually a sleepy man collected our money and the vessel chugged away from the pier, still maintaining its alarming list to starboard. I thought of all those silly headlines through the years about Third World ferries. We plunged off into the open ocean, staggering and pitching. I found myself on the edge of seasickness for the first time in the Caribbean. Larry's eyes were glazed. We landed in Kingston, St. Vincent, in a jabber of port activity. The cab we somehow got our stuff into was, amazingly enough, also the one we got into, and the driver understood about airports. He even apologized for the chaos at the port. "It is Heroes Day," he said. "What we have instead of Columbus. Two Nobel Prize winners: the poet and the chemist." I assured him I had been reading Derek Wolcott if not the chemist. "This is a new thing," said the cabman, "*Heroes,* but it's hard on the transportation."

"Maybe you'll find some new heroes in the transportation," said Larry, clinging to the interior of the car.

· · ·

We took a puddle jumper, or rather a volcano jumper, across the old menace, over the St. Lucia Straits and into Huerinor, the international airport on St. Lucia. When we went through the examination, the official local girls began to laugh. Soon there were more local, official women coming out from back offices, all with their hands over their mouths in the vain attempt to suppress laughter.

"What is it?" said Larry.

"Excuse me," said one young woman. "But you are the 'Two Grumpy Old Men.'"

We had not yet seen the movie.

· · ·

Before midnight brother Frank met us up at the airport north of Hartford. It seemed brutally cold, and we wandered about in our thin, gaudy clothes for nearly an hour trying to find Frank's car in the vast, black lot.

"It ain't like a boat, you know," Frank kept saying.

Larry told a story about how he'd worked a dredge barge in a pond up near the airport. "We towed the barge up the Connecticut with *Alice,* then took it apart and transported it overland to the pond. It's around here somewhere."

"I tell you it ain't like a boat up here," Frank said again.

"It's a good thing it ain't a boat," said Larry. "If we'd been swimming around this long in this cold, we'd a been dead half an hour ago."

After awhile it got easy. Most of the other cars had left.

"Hey, you guys have been down there the better part of a month," said Frank. "Next time you've got to take me."

"I'll tell you one thing," said Larry, "we better not take Neil. They got a guy down there has a sharp knife and two dogs and all three of them look pretty hungry."

NOTES

FORT TYLER (p. 295): Captain Rathbun has an excellent account of the rise and fall of this bizarre boondoggle that was doomed by the sea. The Fort was named for John Tyler (1790–1862), tenth President of the United States, a man who, some half century before, had developed a grotesque connection with Gardiners Island. Tyler, the vice president of the campaign slogan "Tippecanoe and Tyler, too," is chiefly remembered as the first president to achieve that office by means of succeeding a president who has died in office.

NEIL, THE IGUANA (p. 303): When we got home from the Caribbean, Larry took me to a part of his house to which I'd never been—the upstairs. First he showed me the door at the bottom of the stairs against which Neil had so famously thumped his announcement of residence. At the top of the stairs was the room in which Neil moved (?) and had his being. He was in a large cage, head facing down river, a three-foot, inert, luminous green wrinkle. The conversation consisted largely of our pronouncing his name while he sipped our presence with what was apparently his only movable part, his long, quick tongue. Later that year he moved enough to fashion an escape. There were a few sightings on screen doors by startled citizens of Harrison's Landing before he vanished.

ERIN, BELLE OF THE (p. 303): Later Captain Erin Gabrielle Hagen, master of a commercial skipjack *Minnie V.* out of Baltimore. Also, among other billets, deckhand on Sea Education Association's blue water research schooner *Westward*, mate on schooner *Spirit of Massachusetts* during the Tall Ships Parade, and shipwright on the schooner *Amistad* project at Mystic Seaport.

31

ANNE REBORN

IN NORTHERN WATERS, there were other projects. Larry sailed with us on *Beal* to Newport to a rendezvous of the American Sail Training Association to be held at Fort Adams. He had the helm as we ran up before a pleasant summer sou'wester from Point Judith toward the yachting capital of North America. He had required no commands or corrections from the schooner's captain other than: "Take us to Newport." We were yet well off the Brenton Reef buoy near the Torpedo Range when he cried out, "What the hell is *that?*"

We all dropped what we were doing and searched near and far for something unusual. It was, after all, there in the Torpedo Range the crew had once sighted an enormous basking shark. There also might be retired Cup Defenders sporting about. We could see, however, nothing out of the ordinary. There to the left, spanning the West Passage, was the Jamestown Bridge. In the middle was the island with Beaver Tail Light and to the right the Newport Bridge spanning the East Passage.

"Right there," Larry said and pointed to the Newport Bridge. "How the hell long has *that* been there? "

"Since about the year I was born," said the Captain of the schooner.

Larry stared at the Newport Bridge. "I remember coming through the West Passage—running potatoes to Providence in the late 1930s. Not only wasn't there any Newport Bridge over the East Passage, they was only just building the Jamestown Bridge. They didn't have the central span done yet. I know that was before the '38 Hurricane because it was aboard the *Captain* and we lost her in the '38. They had it about half up when we went under it."

"You mean the *original* Jamestown Bridge," said the Captain.

"What have they done, gone and built *another* one?"

"Recently," the Captain assured him. "*Very* recently."

As part of the schooner's educational mission we took Girl Scouts out on the oyster ground and used Larry Malloy as an instructor. He gave us permission to attempt to pull up oysters under sail from his grounds at the mouth of the Mystic River off Noank. When I proudly showed him the gear I intended to employ he looked at it a moment. "You *do* realize that that is a *scallop* dredge?"

"Ah—"

"That's all right, I can modify it a bit if you give me a minute. We won't make any money this way, but at least we'll come up with something."

We did come up with things, dumping a gay assortment of wriggling benthic creatures onto the schooner's deck, some of which were actually Larry Malloy's oysters. Amid wriggling and squealing Girl Scouts, Larry opened a *Crassostrea virginica* with his oyster knife and offered it around to horrified faces. They would have been no more shocked if he'd opened up for their delectation the very palm of his own hand. To conclude the show, he slurped his prop and smacked his lips. Perhaps thinking she would be required to follow suit, one of the girls flipped the nearest oyster overboard. The Captain's youthful Labrador, Clyde, went immediately into action with a splash that threw water all the way back up on deck.

The oyster, of course, did not remain on the surface, and the dog kept circling where he'd last seen it. There was heavy traffic in the river mouth, and the Captain had to use all his tricks to back the schooner up to where his dog was frantically in aquatic orbit. Eventually the Captain got the boat alongside the dog. Four of us created a kind of impromptu set of dog davits and pulled the loose-skinned beast back aboard.

"That dog was even worse than the scallop rig," said Larry. "If we're going to be retrieving any more oysters, I can see I'm going to have to rig you folks a proper *oyster* dredge."

. . .

Larry served as emeritus operator of *Anne,* running the boat as new owner Thom Janke worked the dredge and the culling table. We made a movie for Public Access Television called: "*Anne:* Passing the Torch." On camera Larry quoted his father: " 'The only way you could ever know enough about an oyster was to be an oyster.' " Using a Radio Shack device, I dubbed in a whistling version of "There's a Hole in the Bottom of the Sea," which we were lucky enough to time to the somewhat shaky pavane of a horseshoe crab that had come up in the dredge for a cameo appearance. We ran the crab over the credits. The idea was that it was Larry whistling. At the premier he said, "I haven't been able to whistle like that in fifty years, so I'm glad you had the crab in there. People might believe he done it." Public Access played the film a couple of dozen times interspersed between interviews with a woman who had the inside track on dried flower arranging and a man in a Western string tie who had a toy bulldog on his desk, and like Huck Finn's father "went after the government." The film made Larry a local celebrity in the streets, or rather slightly above the street. "At least the highway bridge tender, he hollered down at me the other day when we was going through with *Anne*." The companion of Larry's son Wayne, however, had to hide the tape. "How many times can you see you guys on that old boat anyway?" she said. "And that stupid whistling crab!"

. . .

This was in the period when it seemed as if *Anne* could get by without a major rebuild. At that time she moored fore and aft just off the federal channel at Willow Point below the railroad bridge. Each Thursday Captain Thom would steam *Anne* downriver to the Noank grounds—those same beds where Larry's father had fallen overboard thirty years before. These were grounds that went back a hundred years, to when the 1892 *Atlantic Coast Pilot from Point Judith to New York* promises "A small Noank oyster steamer sometimes does towing." There, operating *Anne*'s ancient hysters from the wheelhouse, Larry would manipulate the dredge while Thom in his foul-weather bib overalls would manage the culling table. When they had twenty-three onion bags full of oysters, they would turn back upriver. Thom and his deckhands would load the bags from *Anne* down into a plywood Brockway skiff and bring them in over the flats to the floating pier at West Mystic Wooden Boat Company. The deckhands would then lug the onion bags up the gangway to Thom's pickup, which had a big fiberglass icebox on its bed like a St. Bernard kennel. It was then, while all this heavy lifting was being performed, Larry and I would sit in the shade on an old park bench with our backs to the bathhouse and he would annotate the proceedings.

At such moments, among our intellectual endeavors was the design of a running loop that would bring the fifty-pound bags up from the floats to Thom's truck. Our model was a ski tow with the onion bags of oysters simply replacing the ruddy-faced sports of the slopes.

"Not that I've ever gone skiing, mind you," said Larry.

Thoughts of cool mountainsides nevertheless eased the heat, and as for the guilt of watching others labor, there was always the notion that our invention would eventually lead to the ease of the young men's burdens—to say nothing of the possible alleviation of world hunger.

After a couple of years, however, it became clear to even the most *Anne*-besotted that she was in need of major work. The Schooner Captain offered his Bondo crew from the *Sylvina W. Beal,* but Thom rightly demurred and brought on Walter Ansel to head up a serious carpentry crew. Walter had the ideal talent and temperament to deal with the old girl. He was the son of Willet Ansel, author of *Rebuilding the Charles W. Morgan Whaleboats,* and the librarian and poet Hanneli Ansel. Walter's sister Talvi Ansel was winner of the Yale Younger Poets' award. His brother Peter, also a boat carpenter, worked on the *Anne* project. Besides building and repairing a variety of wooden craft, Walter had himself been a commercial fisherman in the Baltic as well as local waters.

The first year, Ansel kept *Anne* in the water at McGugan's new yard on Murphy Point across from Willow Point. By building a plastic shed over her, Ansel was able to get in a cozy winter replacing her deck. The next year, however, Thom faced the big decision and had *Anne* hauled at Willow Point's West Mystic Shipyard. This was a large yard next to us that had built iron gunboats for the Civil War, and at the turn of the century the five-masted schooner *Jenny Dubois.* Between the world wars the yard had manufactured a wild precursor to the Boston Whaler known as the Mystic Sea Sled. After World War Two the great Major William Smyth led the building, rebuilding, and maintenance of some of the finest yachts between Boston and New York, including duPont's powerful ocean ketch *Barlevento;* their *Maid of Honor,* the British admiral's barge from the Gibraltar fleet; the ocean-going yachts of Grosvenor Bell, chairman of *National Geographic* (formerly Blunt White's famous yawl *White Mist*); and an experimental sailboat for the Timkins of roller-bearing fame. Following the Major's retirement, a sequence of modern entrepreneurs took over the yard, marketing fiberglass sloops to the new clientele. Out of the sixty-some vessels that called the Mystic Shipyard home at the time of *Anne*'s coming ashore, perhaps only a half dozen were made of wood and none of these had remained workboats. The sight, then, of this venerable laborer of the waters, as day by day she was disrobed of her planking and even her horn timber, was an education to those who poked their head in her shed. People made pilgrimages to stand slack-jawed before her in the holy, diffuse light of the boat shed.

I must admit I was myself, even as a frequent traveler aboard her, shocked to see how much of a sled she was. There was almost nothing underneath her. It occurred to me that only her great breadth had kept her steady in a beam sea on a particular day off Bell Eight when we were coming back from Essex. Larry himself would drop by West Mystic Wooden Boat Company and occasionally we would stroll around the tree-shaded corner to visit *Anne.* He would fish through the trash barrels and almost always find some fragment of her he had once known whole. We were looking for locust trunnels, the "tree-nails" that had held her together far beyond the life of any metal fastening yet devised for boats. What we found were mainly iron bolts necked down by corrosion to mere wisps. Walter Ansel said he had indeed found some trunnels. "There were a few in the frames down under the engine."

"Locust?" I said, hoping to confirm the rest of the old legend.

Walter just smiled. "By the time we got them out all you could really say is that they had been trunnels. Whatever they had once been made of, they were now of some sort of wood-and-engine-oil composition."

One day as Larry and I stood there, I said, "I don't see how she ever could have been a sailboat, I mean one that would go to windward."

"You're forgetting she had a centerboard."

Of course. The aperture and trunk had long been replaced during the stretching exercise that had been performed on her to lighten her draft. But Larry remembered the old centerboard slot in the keel and the plug that had sealed that aperture. The term *sloop* in the nineteenth century almost automatically meant the sailing vessel was designed to deal with the problem of lateral resistance by means not of a keel but a centerboard. As the noted marine historian and architect Thomas C. Gillmer demonstrates in his monograph *Chesapeake Bay Sloops,* the rig was basically designed as a response to a nineteenth century need for a boat to haul a dredge over the shallow oyster ground. *Cutters* with keels did the yachting in deeper water. All the other business of racing and cruising for which sloops are now built came after.

As the relaunching of *Anne* grew nearer, excitement in the neighborhood mounted. People would drop by West Mystic Wooden Boat Company after having paid homage to *Anne* next door. The pilgrimage clearly was a venture to lift the heart. We were flanked by two neighbors, each yard with Virgin Marys in blue-tinted upright bathtubs. When Walter painted *Anne*'s new bottom a blue primer, the hue conspired to enhance *Anne*'s religious glow. In the dim cathedral of the boat shed, barn swallows tended their nests in the rafters.

. . .

Interesting as *Anne*'s reconstruction was, however, her being out of action for three years left Larry Malloy at loose ends. One afternoon he had me over to Harrison's Landing to meet an elder neighbor who had an old boat in his back yard. It was plywood, but had been built by the Franklin G. Post Company of Mystic in the 1940s and therefore had some integrity as a workboat. She also had an engine. She was, of course, a bit tired, as was her owner, and plywood when it is tired can be spooky in a way that traditional ship timber, no matter how rotten, never is. In any case, the owner dropped dead within a week, and the boat was taken away to the dump not long after. Larry continued to prowl the waterfront. One day he told me that he and his brother had a new boat.

"What's it called?" I said.

There was a pause as if he were thinking it up. Over the phone I heard the New York to Boston train run past in the distance and before the same train reached me out my window, he'd come up with it:

"*Dream.*"

. . .

In actuality *Dream* was, without doubt, the least interesting boat either Larry or Frank Malloy had ever been associated with in the some seventy years they have spent working on the water. (Make that a total of at least 140 years.)

To begin with, all those other boats, as we have seen, were made of wood. As such, each was unique, not only in its original form, but in the sags and sufferings in service and all those necessary probings, sisterings, scarfings, and reriggings that the Malloys performed to maintain that service.

Dream, on the other hand, was a twenty-eight-foot stock fiberglass affair, albeit originally designed after the wooden lobster boats of Maine. What made *Dream* worth the Malloys' attention was neither her design nor construction, nor even her little bit of history as a New London lobsterboat, but, as befits her name, her future.

The Malloys came across her in summer as they were poking about a boat yard next to the sewer plant a few miles downriver from Harrison's Landing. "She was one of three deadbeat boats about to be sawed up," said Larry. "Frank and me, we got the job of putting them out of their misery. Of the three, we figured maybe this one might be worth saving."

The Malloys themselves were flirting with the Great Chain Saw. Larry had just turned eighty and brother Frank wasn't far behind. Both had recently discovered the VA hospital and commenced to honor it with frequent visits.

Larry even took his brother Frank, who had been a POW of the Germans, fifty miles north to a Department of Veterans Affairs meeting and received this letter for his pains, addressed to one "Ernest Malley":

Dear Mr. Malley

It was a pleasure to have you attend the Former Prisoner of War Educational Symposium. . . . The number in attendance was very uplifting and exciting to see the interest expressed by this group of veterans. . . . I hope the information given by the panel members as well as the informational handouts proved to be beneficial to you.

There was an excellent exchange of ideas. As a means of further strengthening our relationship, we will be . . .

The two "Malley" brothers did not return to be further uplifted and excited, exchange ideas, or have their relationship strengthened, but they did go back for what they hoped might turn out to be straight medical work. So far, however, Larry reported, "They ain't found nuthin' I didn't know about before." Somewhat chagrined that they were not going to be invited to crawl into a federal bed just then, they had been left with only one alternative—to go back to sea.

"I got to watching reruns of this thing that's called 'Dallas,'" said Larry. "I never seen so many people with such trouble. But you know they also seem to have some fun, too. I realize this is a rerun, so I guess everybody else already knows all about it. I don't even know where I was when it come out. I musta been wasting my time on a boat somewheres."

Dream, a boat in any case, reposed about ten yards back of the TV set on the other side of the living room wall out in Larry's front lawn. He had recently added a picture window on the other side of the house. The view, which, of course, had always been out there, had now become more than spectacular. Why it had taken Larry so many years to admit this view into his house might tell us more than any other one thing about his life. For anyone involved in a low-tech maritime project such as the Malloys were, the looming examples of the Thames Shipyard, the United States Submarine Base, and Electric Boat Division of General Dynamics could not be dismissed as mere wallpaper, or as some decorators have come to call it: *the flavor of the sea.*

"I sit here at the kitchen table and I see the towboats taking those big lighters up to the Sub Base. Big lighters with big cranes on them. Something's going on up there. I used to swim across over there. And *back!* Downriver they're building those new high-speed ferries for export."

Even the side yard was bustling. Two hundred feet away in the final flatness of Harrison's Landing, just before the ground tilts sharply uphill, are the Vermont Central tracks. *The Montrealer,* the crack passenger train between New York and Canada, had been recently diverted from its old run to the west and came swishing and honking past Larry's house every night at eleven. For half a century these rails that once connected northern New England to New London harbor had seen nothing but the occasional sleepy freight. In fact, so relaxed was the operation that Larry picked up some loose rails and shipped them over to Willow Point for Tommy Watt's marine railway. We were looking at a photo of the old roundhouse down in East New London when he confessed. "That's where we got the rails that are now buried in the mud at your boatyard." He even had the name of the man who gave this permission and announced where he may yet be working. I put all this in because of my interest in maintaining fidelity to the Captain's narration. I'm not entirely convinced, however, that the man who gave the permission actually had the right to do so. In any case the statute of limitations has long run out.

To test Larry's narration after the winter storms and before the spring plankton bloom, I go out on the rope ferry that connects the floats on either side of the old railway slip. There in the lucent water is about a dozen feet of what might be one of the rails. I stop the rope ferry, fish down with the boat hook through the clear water and, yes, there is the metallic tap on the top of the rail. I reach in under the lip, being very careful not to flick the silt, and sure enough, I hook the flange. Sometimes, as I talk to Larry on the phone while I am looking out over the slipway, I can actually hear the old Vermont Central explode into life as *The Montrealer* roars on its way from New York to Canada.

But there in Larry's front yard sat the boat project. The front yard was about thirty feet deep, so the stern of *Dream* was right there in your face as you step off the front porch. Her bow overhung the gutter, that is, if there had been a gutter. Fortunately, Bella Vista Road, which ends a few feet from the Vermont Central Line, frayed out to an imprecise edge at the Malloy line so there was sufficient fiddle room around *Dream*'s bow.

As for the time dimension, immediate prospects for *Dream* were a bit indefinite as well. A photographer from the local paper came over one raw day and discovered the two old men, both fresh out of flu beds, just standing around. "We told her we could go down to the shipyard and borrow some wood shavings and scatter them about," said Larry, "you know, put a few in our hair. She didn't go for that. 'It can't be faked,' she said, and went off."

For one thing, there were holes in *Dream*'s bottom. Holes in a boat's bottom are, of course, always an embarrassment, especially up on land. "At least when they're down there in the water, you can stuff them with a mattress or something and you don't get no complaints from the neighbors, and after all, the boat ain't sunk. A good mattress and a good pump will see you through a lot of hole. But you can't get away with that up on land."

Holes in the bottom are particularly difficult in the case of a fiberglass hull. Such ruptures in the skein of modern technology are especially unsettling to men who are used to going with the flow of a material's innate tendencies.

"Now you take a plank of wood," said Larry. "Like on *Anne*. It's going to want to be where it's been, which is where it damn well ought to be. Especially after it's been there a while and got all its curves pretty much in mind. I mean, seeing how the plank's down in the water and it's wood, where's it going to want to go? Certainly not further down. Of course, you just got to be careful you don't get going so fast you run away out from the top of your bottom, that's all."

With *Dream* there was also the question of propulsion, a moot point as long as she remained in the cradle, but obviously something that was sooner or later going to have to be addressed if the project were to be taken seriously. People who know very little about boats as *hulls,* often have managed to accumulate an impressive amount of information about engines.

"Well, we have *two* engines," Frank reported. "And between them there should be enough to make one that will push her along pretty good."

And what was the specific mission that the two Malloy brothers had in mind for *Dream*?

"An oysterboat, of course," said Larry. "You hear about how this business is going to hell in so many ways. And from what I can see, looking back on what it was, it is. But it's also supposed to be coming back. And, seems so to me, that's true. All's we want is to be ready for the part that's coming back."

. . .

July 14, 1999. Today his sugar was 58, according to two of his machines, which also flash "err." "Which means, I guess," he says, "*Error.* I think I'm dead. In any case, I'm *fluctuated.* As for my blood, the red has gone out of it. It's kind of creamy."

In a property struggle with brother Bill, he considered hiring a surveyor who had recently become a shellfisherman. "I guess any shellfisherman who has another job should keep it."

I prod him again about innovations. "I keep thinking back and as I think about it all now, a lot of the things we didn't do was because it wasn't yet invented."

I'm confused when he talks about his brother bustling about the old Landing with the trucks of a group Larry calls "Connecticut Cotton." I have images of Mississippi levee scenes: sidewheeling steamers, African Americans, banjoes, the tunes of Jerome Kern. Turns out he means Connecticut *Carting.* I thought that in thirty years I had grown used to his accent.

. . .

July 15. Strolled over to Mystic Ship Yard to visit *Anne* with Earl Gale. Earl was fresh from some unpronounceable grunt of a Malaysian port, but nevertheless deemed *Anne*'s reconstruction a worthy addition to his world's tour of exotic vessels.

Guarding the door is the beagle Peanut who belongs to Shawn McGinnis, one of the carpenters. Religious light thin through high windows. Walter Ansel's crew going full tilt. Dramatic vapors wafting out of the steam box stuffed with burlap bags, heated by propane. The air is suffused with the pungent aroma of hot, wet, white oak and burlap. Walter and Rob Whalen, the caulker, armed with heavy gloves, grab the plank and run up the scaffold and vanish into the wispy clouds. The piece of oak is one big noodle. Shawn McGinnis and Peter Ansel slap it around *Anne*'s great fantail stern and start bolting it in. In a moment it is part of the boat, paralleling another similar piece below it. She is now, as Fitzgerald has Homer say, "oaken-waisted as Ares, god of war." I ask Walter what he calls this piece. "It's just the *guard*."

Of course. What else would it be, now that the magic of its affixing is gone? If *Anne* were an automobile this piece would be the rear bumper. Then Walter stepped back himself and saw this piece of work as if for the first time, the way it wrapped so beautifully around the vertical staving of the fantail stern. "I guess it *should* have a fancier name. How about the *After Guard*?"

Why not? Aren't there all those prints of the America's Cup racers over in the yard's Yachting Center, former site of Major Smyth's paint shop? But *After Guard* there, of course, applies to the brain trust, the captain, the sailing master, the navigator, the tactician.

Anne's owner, Thom Janke, is getting his hands very dirty and wet and hot. And while he had planned only to stay a minute, he is now part of the steaming gang. As the *Anne* project acquires more and more interest in town there is the question, whose boat is she? It's like the argument in Joyce Cary's *The Horse's Mouth*. Is it Sara Monday's portrait or is it Gulley Jimson's painting? Is she Thom's, the new owner whose money and vision and, on days like this, sweat, is invested? Is it Walter Ansel and his construction crew? Is it the longtime, legendary owner Lawrence H. Malloy, Jr.? Walter reports that Bill, the younger Malloy brother, was claiming her as *his* boat! This week, *Anne*, ex "old, rotten sled," is everybody's boat.

Then there are the kibitzers who find someone less knowledgeable to explain the whole affair to. Sometimes these experts du jour parade their wares to someone who actually knows more. The other day I saw a bearded man buttonhole Larry Malloy himself and explain to him all about Larry Malloy. The amazing thing is he knew that he was talking to Larry Malloy! We live in an information age.

· · ·

July 16. Run into Walter Ansel at the top end of the hedgey lane that runs between the deli and the Willow Point boat yards. He's buying grommet coffee for his *Anne* crew.

"So it's come to this?" I say.

"Hey, it's a week from today," he says. "Originally it was going to be Thursday, but Timmy Porter says he has a golf date then."

"Golf?! Golf and *Anne*?"

Timmy's a good fellow, brought up in an old Noank house I once lived in, but he has his weaknesses. Golf and *Anne* seem antithetical. We strain for a justification, and Larry says, "Well, brother Frank did work on a golf course that was where Connecticut College is now."

. . .

July 19. Everyone's telling Malloy stories now that the *Anne*'s relaunch is approaching.

The favorite seems to be about the time that old Captain Malloy fell overboard off *Anne* in February on the Noank grounds. The yarn now goes like this: The old guy climbed up out of the water by going hand over hand back up the oyster dredge rig! It takes Larry Malloy himself to straighten this out "The old man did *not* climb back aboard the oyster dredge rig. First of all, this would be well-nigh impossible. Exactly what part of the rig would he have? He'd have the cable swung out from a boom six feet higher than the water and stickin' out from the boat about that length. So you've got a seventy-year-old man been paddling about in that January water the length of time it took for the boat going less than 1, 000 r.p.m.s to get around. This man grabs the cable and shinnies straight up it fifteen feet to where it runs through the blocks to the boom. Then he reaches up and grabs the boom, which is about six inches around and goes hand over hand along the boom another fifteen feet. What Pappy really done was he climbed up on the tires he always had hanging over."

Larry's correction, however, only deflected the question as to *how many tires* were on *Anne* when the old man fell over. Here is a typical boatyard embellishment of the "corrected" story. "When the old gentleman fell over there was only one tire hanging off the boat, but when he got back home safely the first thing he did was put tires all along the side." This version, since it fits many people's idea of a colorful old salt story, delights the audience who nod and say, 'Ain't that the truth!' I repeated it to Larry Malloy who said, "No, we always had a lot of tires all along the rail. Why would we only have one? They was for fenders as well as to get back aboard. People who say we only had one tire out just don't understand what we was doing, how you have to go about doing it. That is if you're *really* going to do it."

. . .

July 20. Each day bringeth new FALSE HISTORIANS into the land. ONE MUST BE ARMED WITH THE TRUTH. I feel the need to grow my beard longer and carry a placard about the waterfront.

Anne facts gleaned from Larry yesterday (whose sugar is 120. Evidently his machine was off, thank God, although it scared us all to death yesterday.):

Malloys owned *Anne* starting in 1918 or 1919. Sold her to Washington White of Sterling Cove, Greenport, Long Island, in 1926 or '27. Bought her back from Robert Utz in 1940 or 41. (Contrary to false historians, who had her sunk under the highway bridge in New London, she did *not* sink in the 1938 hurricane, but stayed afloat in Sterling Basin. Says Larry: "When we went to buy her she was moored bow out to a pier just to the left of where you see her in that old photograph of Wash White's oyster house. Where the tennis court is now.")

Although strangers always pronounce her name "Ann," it's been Annie" since at least 1918, spelled *Anne*. And that's it. (Nearly lost a friend who is otherwise an expert on classic oyster boats over that one!) It is getting *dangerous* to know things about *Anne* that other waterfront experts do not know. I think of the blood nearly spilled a few years ago over *Hair-shoff* vs. *Her-a-soff*. This is much more intense because more local.

. . .

July 21. L. H. M. at Mystic Shipyard after looking at blue-bottomed *Anne* two days prior to launching: "I don't think these fellows today ever caught a load of oysters. I mean they got so much stuff on the decks these days there ain't no room for the oysters. I remember in 1951, you seen the picture, Johnny Bartlett and me we caught a load of oysters with *Anne*. That was on the Branford ground. We had a patch right in the middle of Elijah Ball's grounds. We had to quit when I couldn't get out of the wheelhouse to help Johnny with the dredge. We started that morning at seven o'clock and quit at noon. It took us five hours to get back up the Thames River. You can see Johnny in the picture lounging against the hyster post as if to say, '*See what we done.*'"

"Well, you had done it, hadn't you?"

"I suppose you could say that."

"Well, then what's wrong with saying it?"

"I dunno. Ain't it supposed to be: you don't go around saying it?"

"Then I'll say it. I'll say it just the way you just told it to me. *In one morning you and Johnny Bartlett caught so many oysters by noon that you couldn't get out of the wheelhouse and you had to steam home.*"

"Yes, we did. In 1951, Elijah Ball's grounds."

"In *Anne*."

"In *Anne*."

"This same *Anne*."

"Well, now you see, that's just it. The way he's got these bulwarks up so high now I don't see how he's going to swing the load over."

"Ah, so that's it."

"And how you going to back down to port with that scuttle hatch sticking up there so high? How tall a man you going to have going down below anyway? My father was six four and he didn't need a scuttle high as that."

"Perhaps there will be some modifications to the, ah, modifications."

"Perhaps the boat will be used differently."

"The main thing is that she's been saved."

"Yes," said Larry, "that *is* the main thing."

. . .

We were talking about the government. "It's getting so they tell you when to get up in the morning and when to go to bed," said Larry. Then he looked at the ground. "The scary thing about it, at my age I'm beginning to wonder if I don't need that advice."

. . .

There is the suddenly embarrassing problem of *Anne'* s engine. What with all the effort on the woodwork and the authentication of the design, the mundane matter of her propulsion has been neglected. During her convalescence she has not been exercised. The transmission has apparently seized. There has been much talk of lubricants, from the popular contemporary cure-all WD-40 through the panacea of midcentury youth, Marvel Mystery Oil, on out to potions and elixirs of the most exotic variety. "I've got an engine in my basement that will fit *Anne* just fine," says Larry Malloy. "When they run out of marvels and mysteries, they can come here and pay me for it. It's the old GM off *Alice.*"

Just how Larry Malloy came to have this particular engine in his cellar at the end of the millennium is a complex business of improvisation and horse trading that involves no less than four other different engines and, besides the late, great *Alice,* two other venerable vessels, and a farm on Long Island. The engines were an Atlas, a Kermeth, a Gardner, and a Caterpillar. The two other vessels were the forty-six-foot oysterboat *Sea Gull* built by H. C. Rowe of New Haven in 1905 and the Admiralty barge *Maid of Honor,* the elegant craft owned for a generation by the duPonts of Fishers Island. The Long Island farm (Halyoake) ended up using the Caterpillar to drive its irrigation pump.

Of these propulsion units, perhaps the most colorful had been the three-cylinder Atlas.

"Only thing against that engine was we had trouble getting it started. To get a lot of those old diesels going you'd use a blowtorch. Nowadays they got a variation on that built in they call a *glow plug.* Our *glow plug* was me holding a blowtorch on her to get the fuel loose. I was reaching across the batteries to get at the engine one day and then I set the torch down in such a way that it lit off the batteries, too. The explosion spat acid on my pants which for the remainder of the voyage commenced to shrink until when we come ashore I was near eligible for arrest. Up to that point I wasn't really worried. Hey, we was all among friends, and the main thing was that the engine had started. The fact that the batteries had blown up didn't matter at that point because once them engines got going, you could hardly kill them if you wanted to.

"For instance Pappy, Bill, and I was coming back from New Haven one day on *Alice* with the Atlas running on only two of its three cylinders. Each of the cylinders had a gadget that allowed you to meter the fuel going into it. We figured that this one cylinder wasn't quite getting the right supply, so Bill and me was *fine-tuning* it. Pappy's up in the wheelhouse steering for home. A little too much on the wrench and there's a whole lot of popping and snapping and crackling. 'Jesus Christ,' shouts Pappy from the wheelhouse, 'It's raining. The sun's out and it's raining!' What we done, I guess, was tighten up something too much, and she cracked the cylinder—sent all that water up in the air and down it come. We run her the rest of the way like that on two cylinders working, one just raining, the old man up in the wheelhouse hollerin' about the crazy weather. What the hell, that's all the cylinders was working anyway."

This narrative is a bit much for Thom Janke, who instead of buying into it opts for more Marvel Oil. His decision does not, however, affect *Anne*'s engine, which declines to spin.

. . .

In the midst of a heat wave and the biggest drought since meteorologists kept records of such things, the yard crew at West Mystic Shipyard under Timmy Porter's direction launched *Anne*. (The matter of the engine can be put off for the moment. It is inevitable, however, that sooner or later Thom will indeed purchase the old GM out of *Alice* and in so doing not only complete the resurrection of *Anne*, but like a surgeon performing a heart transplant, perpetuate a second life long thought lost.)

To fit in the travel lift slip, Walter Ansel had to leave her rub rails off. "She had guards on her sides when we brought her in last year, but they had been so worn down by, well, *guarding*, that she barely sneaked in. We knew, however, that she could not go back out if we put on proper guards, so we'll get them on next week. Of course that will mean she can never be hauled here again."

"Well, that's what them tires was for," Larry reminded him.

The launching was catered out of the back of a station wagon and included the sort of crustless sandwiches that encouraged wags to make yacht club jokes. A huge American flag was stretched across *Anne*'s wheelhouse and it covered from just under the windows down to the deck. The wooden boat community was well represented. I hadn't seen as many fine carpenters in one place since the funeral of the father of the boatbuilder Jeff Hall that spring.

Right next to where *Anne* lay was a huge plastic muscle boat, its hull decorated from stem to stern with the sort of gaudy iconography formerly reserved for motorcycle jackets. It was almost impossible to take a photo of the launching of the honored guest without including this object. During the middle of the ceremony a hundred-foot-plus modern ketch from Australia came up the river to dock at the Shipyard, but did not manage to upstage *Anne*'s moment.

Someone fired off a cannon and Peanut, the beagle, took off nor'noreast until it was gone.

"Damn," said Shawn McGinnis, "now it'll be after dark before he comes home."

Larry Malloy accepted congratulations from old friends and new acquaintances who were introduced to him as "*Anne*'s former captain." He deferred this homage by conducting an informal seminar, displaying on the hood of his Buick old snapshots of *Anne* in her former versions. He had also come up with a book, courtesy of brother Frank, that listed *Anne* in 1901 as "steam." This late-breaking bit of research caused many debates among the cognoscenti. Had *Anne* never been a sloop? Had she been converted from sloop to steam? Was this a likely transition, or would she have gone, as was previously held, from sloop to gasoline, thence to diesel, which was the more typical evolution of an oysterboat in the first part of the twentieth century? If she had never been a sloop, what about that centerboard plug Larry vowed he had seen?

From time to time we would turn away from Larry's display and stare at *Anne* herself, as if for an answer, but there she hung in the sling, her wheelhouse over the American flag, inscrutable as the Sphinx.

The sun hung low over the land, sending long shadows through the yard. The crustless sandwiches were all gone, and the caterer was closing up the back of her wagon. The beagle had not yet returned.

Somebody shrugged and said, "Well—"

"Wait a minute," said Larry, "there was something else I forgot."

All photos are from the collection of the author unless otherwise noted.

Larry Malloy at the helm of his *yot* heading back from the Poquetonnuck River. *Anne* is anchored by her dredge in the upper regions of the Thames just below Norwich, July 31, 1989. Larry had labeled this "outside Ledyard drawbridge," but alas, the drawbridge has not existed in decades and boats must slither under the railroad trestle.

Larry Malloy in his tropical shirt with the author and *Anne* at Harrison's Landing in the 1990s. The U.S. Navy Submarine base housing is on the far shore.

Sylvina W. Beal under way out of Block Island. Captain Malloy proved to be a good hand on the helm. Photo by J. J. Curran.

Anne rafted up with venerable wooden colleagues, 1911 sardine schooner *Sylvina W. Beal* and 1969 towboat *Lawrence,* in the Mystic River off Willow Point in the early 1990s.

In the slip at Harrison's Landing in the 1990s, Larry Malloy ready to come ashore. As his father did before him, he sports a clipboard to document matters pertaining to science and the government. The culling table is at left; the oyster baskets are by now wire. The "bridge tile" is on the deck and the new wheelhouse has replaced the old overshot version with the vertical staving. The plywood held by the stanchions on either side of the wheelhouse are to prevent crew from falling overboard upon stepping forth from the wheelhouse. The long-handled crab net is to retrieve smaller items that might have temporarily gotten away.

Larry Malloy atop Admiral Rodney's Pigeon Island lookout, Rodney Bay, St. Lucia. It was a long walk up from *Sylvina W. Beal* anchored below.

Steam box used to bend the oak guard.

Larry Malloy composing his memoirs under the elm tree at West Mystic Wooden Boat. Towboat *Lawrence* and Mystic River Railroad Bridge in background.

Anne today off West Mystic Wooden Boat. Thos. Janke's new Brockway-Persson skiff alongside. It was here that British Admiral Thos. Hardy's fire barges ran aground in 1812.

Stephen Jones and Captain Lawrence H. Malloy, Jr. Photo by Sina Wright.

APPENDIX

CHARLES MONSELL

I. Capt. Monsell Sails into Hall of Fame

Michael Gasparine, Suffolk *Times*, March 30, 1995

George Hiram Monsell, who died in 1951, [was inducted into the Suffolk County Sportsman's Hall of Fame.] Monsell [was] one of the most outstanding captains in the history of yacht racing. He gained fame by sailing *Enterprise,* the *Rainbow* and the *Ranger* to victory in international racing for the America's Cup, successfully defending the championship three consecutive times.

Monsell directed *Enterprise* to a 4–0 victory over *Shamrock V* of England in 1930, then captained *Rainbow* to a 4–2 victory over . . . *Endeavour* in 1934. *Endeavour* was considered the faster boat and won the first two races of the series, but Monsell and his crew rallied to win the next four . . . Monsell continued to frustrate the British in 1937, when he captained *Ranger* to a 4–0 victory over *Endeavour II*.

. . . At the age of 20 [Monsell] helped transport Teddy Roosevelt and his Rough Riders from Montauk to Cuba during the Spanish American War.

Monsell became the captain for Harold Vanderbilt's schooner *Vagrant,* and his association with Vanderbilt led to his selection as the America's Cup captain. In 1937, in the depth of the Depression, Vanderbilt financed the Cup defenses on his own and built *Ranger,* one of the fastest and most magnificent J-boats ever made . . . it was 90 feet on the waterline and nearly 140 feet long overall, with a 15-story mast and more than an acre of sail.

Monsell's nephew, Jim Monsell, said that one of the best things his uncle did was hire his crews from Greenport. "That was quite a thing," he said, adding that his uncle built one of the America's Cup pilot boats—*Bystander*—in Greenport, at the Greenport Basin and Construction Co.

"He was my mentor when I started sailing as a kid," said Bill Rich of Orient. "He taught me currents and racing tactics and all that, and did so much for Greenport by hiring the local guys and keeping the ships right. . . ."

II. The Monsell Collection: Bang the Drum Slowly

According to John Rousmaniere's *America's Cup Book*, the Starling Burgess-designed 127-foot *Rainbow* defeated Thomas Sopworth's *Endeavour* in 1934. "Aft, Vanderbilt assigned tasks to his four *amateur* [emphasis mine] assistants: he would steer at starts and upwind; somebody else would steer off the wind; one man— Sherman Hoyt, a wonderfully talented sailor—was in charge of sail trim. . . ." Hoyt also took over the helm in light airs when the Genoa job was set because he "had the best feel for the boat." Rousmaniere goes on to point out "there were three-man committees to decide on tactics, strategy and sail-selection. In short, her afterguard was a small model of the modern American corporation, and like the modern American corporation at its best, this company of mariners was successful."

This detailing of the "*amateur*" assignments would seem to preempt George Monsell's designation as "captain" of *Enterprise, Rainbow,* and *Ranger* as asserted in the March 30, 1995, Suffolk *Times* article. However, the discrepancy may be at least partially accounted for by a distinction between the racing afterguard and the crew that regularly maintained the boat. In a phone conversation John Rousmaniere addressed how he saw the distinction: "Mr. Monsell might best be thought of as a *foreman*. It was his job to recruit the bodies and train them. I believe he acted as paymaster. It's a bit of a stretch to call that job 'captain.' There is no question that the Harold Vanderbilt J-boats in the 1930s were *sailed,* that is conned, commanded during the Cup races by the afterguard of Harold Vanderbilt himself, Sherman Hoyt and the other amateurs. As for the crew Mr. Monsell managed to round up, I don't know where he got them all from. As for the Greenport workboat community, in the last Vanderbilt J-boat, *Ranger* in 1937, this professional crew was largely Norwegian. I don't think there was a word of English spoken."

The sepia photo that fills pages 82 and 83 of Rousmaniere's book shows a boom that is a deep, flat oval and in no way can be the future mast of the oysterboat *Alice* that is presently on the spar cart outside my window. However, lying along the leeward foredeck is a huge pole for what was then a new concept: the parachute spinnaker. It is an indication of just how large a J-boat was that but a third of its spinnaker pole could provide the entire mast for a forty-foot workboat. Actually, in examining Rousmaniere's photos of the three Vanderbilt-Monsell J-boats, I find the spar that looks most like what's outside my window is one of the two spinnaker poles on the deck of *Ranger* (p. 87), "the last of the J-boats." In his memoirs, *Rainbow* afterguard member Sherman Hoyt reveals how substantial was the boat's spinnaker pole. There were two halyards or lifts, and when one let go the results were as follows: "In this race we had several disastrous spinnaker mishaps. The first was when making a sharp luff across [British challenger] *Endeavour*'s stern, the inner spinnaker boom [pole] lift parted and the slide of the boom gooseneck, carrying away the stopper, let the inboard end of the boom plunge into the deck." In any case, Larry Malloy no doubt thought his mast was part of the *Rainbow*'s main boom because the only time he saw J-boats was when they had significance as salvage. Parachute spinnakers were not in his experience.

Another odd connection is that *Rainbow*'s designer, Starling Burgess, a gunner in the Spanish American War, later worked with Buckminster Fuller on what Rousmaniere calls "a three-wheeled automobile called the Dymaxion, which looked like an egg on wheels." Fuller was the uncle of Harvey Fuller, deckhand on the Block Island ferry when Larry Malloy was quartermaster, and chief accordion player in Captain Tommy Watt's West Mystic boatyard band.

One of the things that bothered me, however, was Rousmaniere's confident assertion that Vanderbilt's amateur afterguards were a "small model" for the best in modern corporations. This contrasted sharply with the paradigm of the Greenport workboat community, itself based more on the model of the extended family. A graduate of Union Theological Seminary, John, I thought, usually cast a wider social net and was certainly no apologist for the Robber Baron Society. It would, of course, be good, righteous proletarian fun to assert that the hardworking commercial watermen of Greenport were the true heroes of the America's Cup Defense at its most ostentatious. There may well have been a high percentage of Norwegians on *Ranger*'s 1937 crew, but Monsell's nephew's statement that his uncle "hired Greenport men" would seem at least applicable to the crews of *Enterprise* in 1930 and *Rainbow* in 1934. It is also true, as Rousmaniere implies, that much of the effort by the hired crew during the actual race consisted merely in applying various forms of closely directed mechanical advantage. There are, after all, those famous photos of long rows of men in what look like pajamas reposing somewhat uncomfortably on the windward rail as ballast, or even less at ease, upright pulling on lines (the application of the so-called 'Swedish [i.e., Norwegian] steam'). Nevertheless, as one who has tried to help keep an eighty-foot schooner afloat, I know that a wide range of crafts and skills is required to prepare and maintain such vessels in competitive condition. It was surely here that at least some of the men from the Greenport workboat community made, as Olin Stephens said, a contribution to the Vanderbilt "success" that was "active and necessary." If this classic relationship between grind and glory has been misunderstood, as either more or less than it was, the mistake is, alas, also a "small model" of something in the historical perception of corporate America.

. . .

On April 1, 2000, it so happened that the ninety-two-year-old Olin Stephens, America's premier yacht designer, was in town to sign his autobiography, *All This and Sailing, Too*. Here was the living source of much of what was in John Rousmaniere's book. Olin Stephens was the man who in 1937, at twenty-eight, had assisted the fifty-nine-year-old Starling Burgess in designing Mike Vanderbilt's J-boat *Ranger*. I left our little yard crew power washing an old Brockway oysterboat at West Mystic Wooden Boat Company, and drove up the mile or so to the Mystic Seaport Bookstore.

There indeed was Olin Stephens. At the top of the stairs above the bakery and gift shop he was sitting behind a stack of his autobiographies. My old friend bookstore manager Dedee Worth and her assistant Glenn Shea, the poet, were hovering about him evidently ready to stave off the overly enthusiastic. There was a small family group in line before me, and they were behaving with such frighteningly good manners that I thought Mr. Stephens must be made of porcelain.

When it was my turn I began by reminding him of our previous meeting and then asked him about the relationship between the Greenport workboat community and the Vanderbilt J-boats. He sat there a moment in his tweeds, and behind his spectacles his eyes twinkled. I had not seen him since the year before when John Rousmaniere and my friend and editor from the Norton days, Harvey Loomis, and I had had lunch at his table at the Seaport. I had no idea what would come out of him. A year at his age can make an amiable man difficult. But here after all was not only the the junior designer of *Ranger* but a man who had practiced with the crew all that summer of 1937 and *the* man who during the race against *Endeavour* had had the tactical calls. My question was phrased somewhat breathlessly under the pressure of my own rising obsession and the gathering crowd behind me. "What about Charles Monsell as captain?"

"Mike Vanderbilt [Commodore Harold's son] was very set on there not being a *captain.* He didn't want anybody to be called 'captain.' On *Ranger* in 1937, he himself was skipper and helmsman. There was an afterguard, which included my brother Rod, who handled sail changes and was a rover on deck and aloft; myself as relief helmsman and chairman of the tactical committee and Zenas Bliss who was the navigator."

"John mentioned a Willy Carson or some such."

"Willy Carstens." He spelled it. "As for direct communication with the crew, Willy Carstens was the mate over some twenty men."

"And George Monsell?"

"George Monsell was more of an administrator. He organized the crew, recruited them, and made sure they were housed, fed and paid."

"The Norwegians?" I asked. "The famous 'Swedish Steam?'"

"Yes, they were *winter* fishermen, fishermen who worked at that trade in the winter, and they came *through* Greenport and George Monsell. He was, of course, himself a boatman, but he did not have much to do with the sailing of the boat. Not to downplay what he did. He took a very active and necessary part in the operation."

"Ah." Somewhat emboldened, I asked, "Could a Vanderbilt J-boat spinnaker pole make a workboat mast?" To define "work," I added that the rig in question had moved the very bandstand outside the window of the building where we were and the pilot house off *Miranda,* which was at that moment being used as a phone booth. I pointed in that direction, but there were mainly people surging about buying images of whales and pirates and, from the dribbles of crumbs upon their faces and clothes, apparently the excellent, fresh cookies from the bakery below. I was aware of the line building behind me, polite readers waiting for their own scraps of wisdom from the great man.

"At forty feet those spinnaker poles were certainly tall enough," he said, "and they were big enough around to make a workboat mast even cut down. They were, however, I'm fairly certain *hollow*."

"I see, hollow." And hollow indeed I felt. There was no question that the spar on our cart that Larry brought in from *Alice* was solid as a telephone pole.

"Well," he apologized, "they had to be as light as possible."

"Yessir, thank you." I said. "Of course, *hollow*."

"A racing boat."

"*The* racing boat, sir."

"Well, there were others."

Others, yes. There was yet the cleat on *Anne*'s hyster post to hang my hat on.

On the way down the stairs, in classic *esprit d'escalier* fashion, I thought of some more questions. Driven by my obsession, I overcame my social reservations and returned. For the moment there was no one at his table. I apologized. I was trying to establish the provenance of at least the cleat on *Anne*'s hyster post.

"Where and when were the great J-boats of the thirties broken up?"

"During the war," he said. "In Bristol, at the Herreshoff factory, although *Ranger* had actually been built at the Bath Iron Works in Maine. You could see the transom of *Ranger* sticking out over the road there in Bristol that runs down by the harbor. It was very sad."

"So then a sympathetic man, a man with some *active and necessary* rights of sweat equity in the project might well come back to Greenport with a cleat or two under his jacket."

"I suppose so."

"And maybe a spinnaker pole on his pickup?"

"They were forty feet long, but I suppose they could have cut them down before they left Bristol."

"I certainly would have done so, sir."

"So would I."

· · ·

I went up the road a half-mile to the Pendleton Nursing Facility to visit Larry Malloy, who was making an amazing recovery after having been in something similar to hibernation for ninety days. He still could not talk, but he had corrected a mistaken date I'd given one of the nurses on the building of *Anne* by shaking his head and wiggling his fingers. "Eighteen eighty-four," I corrected myself and he nodded.

In came Willy Malloy, a lean man in his forties. He was Larry's brother Bill's son and was equipped with the long, lanky arms and hard eye of his grandfather. He proudly announced himself as a man with whom Larry had worked on many a waterfront project, including the infamous one in which they had rolled *Alice*'s rig down to the job and would have rolled her right on over if the rig had not broken.

"Yup, I done that," said Willy.

I told him Larry had informed me about that one, and Larry nodded.

"That was me, all right," said Willy. As if to back this up he pointed to a big bandage on his head that, while actually the product of a recent fall, seemed to provide documentation for the accident on *Alice* some thirty years before.

"What about that rig having come off the *Rainbow*?" I said.

"Sure," said Willy. "We had lots of that stuff."

Back at the boat yard, I was again trying to put all this together. There was what seemed to be the insurmountable problem of the solidity of the workboat's mast and the hollowness of the cup defenders' spinnaker poles.

Then, just as it was getting dark and I was staring out the window at the lights coming on across the river, something occurred to me.

· · ·

The "spar" that Larry Malloy had brought into the yard four or five years ago now was actually one of *two* spars, a mast and a boom used on the soon-to-be-broken-up *Alice*. And yes, while Larry had said "boom" he hadn't meant *Rainbow*'s; he'd meant *Alice*'s boom. *Alice*'s boom had "something to do with a jib or a big sail out front" of *Rainbow*. At the time I had been busy with something else, and Larry was rather vague about the whole business, mumbling and muttering, no doubt barely able to come to grips with the idea of cutting up *Alice,* not yet willing to admit that that was actually about to happen. Indeed, as recounted in the above chapter, he never said that he *was* cutting her up, not even when Geoff and I caught him sitting next to the chainsaw in the midst of his carnage. Meanwhile, both spars had lain on the cart among several other old spars for years awaiting suitable employment in some project not yet conceived. The closest they had come to finding a new use was a mile upriver to the Mystic Seaport in a kind of ephemeral shot at "immortality" as props in Spielberg's *Amistad*.

It was by now dark, but I ran downstairs and out into the dim yard. Why did I feel there was so much at stake?

I did feel that if I could establish that this was *Rainbow*'s spar, or that it was least from one of the J-boats, I would have demonstrated that some enormous coming together had happened—work and play, upper class and working class, the utilitarian and the poetic. The great synthesis seemed to hinge on the establishing of this single artifact. It was nuts, but it was Saturday night on the first of April in a New England boat yard, and the clocks were all springing ahead. The April 1 rolling over (or not!) of maritime insurance policies, environmental dredging permits, and boat registrations was all conspiring to make this night a veritable regulatory *Walpurgisnacht*. To top off the festival, I had spent the afternoon talking to

Olin Stephens and Larry Malloy, separated by less than a mile, two voices from the past amazingly somehow still with us. I had also met Larry's nephew, Willy, who immediately confessed that he had been aboard *Alice* working with his uncle Larry when they had so notoriously, but by now almost ceremoniously, bowed the rig to the work and sacrificially broken *Alice*'s mast.

The spar cart was beneath a big maple tree at the end of the gravel parking area. I stepped over the fist-sized links of an old mooring chain, around an L.S.T. anchor, and stumbled against the tongue of the spar cart. There were half a dozen spars lying on the cart like so many long logs. The weak light from the street picked up the last bit of flaking white paint from *Alice*'s mast. I rapped on it with my knuckles: *solid.* Next to it lay the slightly smaller spar that I recalled was indeed *Alice*'s boom. On each end were big pieces of hardware, one for the gooseneck to hold it to the mast, the other what Larry had called a "with," what the marine hardware catalogues call a "mast ring." This was a collar with four strap eyes, one every ninety degrees to hold halyard, two guy lines, and the load line. Clearly these were the sort of modifications one would make in converting a cup defender's spinnaker pole into a workboat boom. Because of these alterations I could not see down into either end of the boom. Under the circumstances, that left me with but two tests.

One assay was to lift the boom to see how it compared to its neighbor, the mast. First I tried the mast, holding it by the end with the notch for stepping cut in. With some effort, I got it to rise a foot or two off the cart. Next I grabbed the end of the boom by the gooseneck and the whole thing all but flew off the cart. Granted the boom was maybe three-quarters the diameter of the mast and maybe only three-quarters as long, and possibly made from lighter wood, but the discrepancy in weight clearly suggested that the boom was hollow. I then tried the second method available. I rapped my knuckles on the boom.

Boom indeed.

I advanced down its entire length tapping. If I had been an African with a couple of sticks I could have had a career. I went back to the mast and rapped it again.

Dud.

I went down each of the half-dozen spars on the cart, the solidity of which I previously knew—each tap was a clear confirmation of the knuckle method. It was like playing a huge, Mormon Tabernacle xylophone. The whole process was a strange kind of mixture of science and magic. In the dark, alone, I returned tentatively to the boom. Would it still resonate?

I rapped it again, the drum note coming back to me from various hulls and huts about the Yard.

A career?

I could have had a religion!

SELECTED BIBLIOGRAPHY, *with the Odd Annotation*

Bonner, William Hallam. *Pirate Laureate: The Life and Legends of Captain Kidd,* Rutgers University Press, 1947.

Bowditch, Nathaniel. *American Practical Navigator: An Epitome of Navigation and Nautical Astronomy.* Military Publishing, 1918.

Brooks, William K. Intro. by Kennedy T. Paynter, Jr. *The Oyster.* Johns Hopkins University Press, 1891. Paperback ed., 1996.

Bray, Maynard. *Mystic Museum Watercraft.* Mystic Seaport Museum, 1979. A rainy-day walk through a fine old boat yard without getting wet.

Bradley, Wendell P. *They Live by the Wind: The Lore and Romance of the Last Sailing Workboats.* Intro. by Howard L. Chapelle. Knopf, 1969. See "The Oystermen of Chesapeake Bay."

Carse, Robert. *Rum Row.* Rinehart, 1959.

Caulkins, F. M. M. *History of New London.* H. D. Utley, 1860.

Clark, Eleanor. *The Oysters of Locmariaquer.* Random House, 1959. Brilliantly written book about the culture of an oystering community in Brittany.

Decker, Robert Owen. *The Whaling City.* Pequot Press. Published for the New London Historical Society, 1976. A sequel to Caulkins's history of New London.

Fuller, Joseph J., Captain. *Master of Desolation: The Reminiscences of Capt. Joseph J. Fuller.* Edited with an introduction and notes by Briton Cooper Busch. Mystic Seaport Museum, 1980. A blue-water Yankee who sailed out of New London in the generation during which *Anne* was built.

Funnell, Bertha H. *Walt Whitman on Long Island.* Kennikat Press, 1971.

Gardiner, Sarah Diodati. *Early Memories of Gardiner's Island: The Isle of Wight of New York.* East Hampton *Star,* 1947.

Gribbins, Joseph. "For Decades Whaling Was King." New London *Day,* June 18, 2000.

Guthorn, Peter J. *United States Coastal Charts 1783–1861.* Schiffer, 1984.

Harwood, Michael. *The View from Great Gull.* Dutton, 1976. The account of the tern project with bits about Captain Lawrence Malloy, Sr.

Herreshoff, L. Francis. *An L. Francis Herreshoff Reader.* "Captain Charley Barr." International Marine, 1978.

Hohman, Elmo P. *Seamen Ashore: A Study of the United States Seaman's Service and of Merchant Seamen in Port.* See especially chap. 9, "The Human Equation: Seamen Ashore as Persons." Merchant Seamen Studies, Vol. 2, Yale University Press, 1952.

Jane's Fighting Ships of World War Two. Military Press, reprint of 1946–47 edition.

Karsnitz, Jim and Vivian. *Oyster Cans with Price Guide.* Schiffer, 1993. Not just a price list for flea market collectors, but history and excellent illustrations.

Kimball, Carol W. *The Poquonnock Bridge Story.* See chap. 8, "The River and the Sea." Groton Public Library, 1984.

Kochiss, John. *Oystering from New York to Boston.* American Maritime Library, Vol. 7. Published for Mystic Seaport, Inc., by, Wesleyan University Press, 1974. One of Captain Malloy's favorites, this book gives the technical side of all of the oystering activities and contains a glossary and helpful bibliography. The single best accompaniment to the present volume.

Lang, Varley. *Follow the Water.* Blair, 1961. Varieties of the waterman's life by a Chesapeake practitioner.

Lewis, Emanuel. *Seacoast Fortifications of the United States: An Introductory History.* Smithsonian, 1970.

Long Island Historical Society, Journal of. Fall, 1989.

Mitchell, Joseph. *The Bottom of the Harbor.* Reprinted as *Up in the Old Hotel.* Little, Brown, 1959. The classic book of waterfront reporting as literature. Contains a chapter on Staten Island oystermen and one on Captain Ellery Thompson.

Morton, J. E. *Molluscs: An Introduction to Their Form and Functions.* Harper & Brothers, 1958. Guts but not much glory.

Mumford, Lewis. *The Myth of the Machine: Technics and Human Development.* Harcourt, Brace and World, 1966. Charlie Haines's favorite.

Payne, Robert. *The Island.* Harcourt Brace, 1958. Gardiners Island history.

Peffer, Randall S. *Watermen.* Johns Hopkins University Press, 1979.

Persson, Jon. "The Shadboat *Brenda M:* The Past Is Prologue." *The Ash Breeze: Journal of the Traditional Small Craft Association,* Vol. 21, No. 3, Spring 2000. The journal is home to an ongoing discussion of key issues of traditional boat culture.

Rathbun, Benjamin F., Captain. *Capsule Histories of Some Local Islands and Lighthouses in the Eastern Part of Long Island Sound.* Published by the author, 1999.

Roberts, Mervin F. *The Tidemarsh Guide.* E. P. Dutton, 1979.

———. *Pearl Makers: The Tidemarsh Guide to Clams, Oysters, Mussels, and Scallops.* Saybrook Press, 1984. Roberts has served on his local shellfish commission for several decades and owns *Shellfish,* the retired State Shellfish Commission boat.

Smith, F. Hopkinson. *Caleb West: Master Diver.* Regent, 1897. Novelized version of the building of Race Rock Light by the architect.

Smith, John, Captain. Ed. Kermit Goell. *A Sea Grammar, with the plaine exposition of Smith's accidence for young sea-men, enlarged.* Originally published London, 1627. Demonstrates the ancient provenance of many sea terms.

Stephens, Olin J., II. *All This and Sailing, Too: An Autobiography.* See "Associations," "*Ranger,*" "War and Postwar." Mystic Seaport, 1999.

Suffolk County *Times.* Reports on Greenport, Gardiners Bay Area.

Thompson, Ellery. *Draggerman's Haul.* Viking Press, 1950. Yarns by a notoriously colorful painter-fisherman who worked much of the same water as the Malloys in the same era.

———. *Sea Sketches.* Stonington Publishing, 1958.

Tedione, David. Illustrated by Arf Ciccione. *The Complete Shellfisherman's Guide, Maine to Chesapeake Bay.* Peregrine Press, 1981.

Tuchman, Barbara. *The First Salute.* Macmillan, 1997. The effect on the outcome of the American Revolution of Admiral Rodney's prostate problems at St. Lucia.

United States Coast and Geodetic Survey. *United States Coast Pilot: Atlantic Coast, Part 4, From Point Judith to New York.* Second ed. 1892.

United States Government Printing Office. *United States Coast Pilot: 33, 40. Atlantic Coast, Section B, Cape Cod to Sandy Hook.* 1918.

Visel, Timothy Charles. "A Brief History of the Connecticut 'Natural Growth' Oyster Industry." University of Connecticut Sea Grant Fact Sheet, 1983.

———. "Life History of the American or Eastern Oyster *Crassostrea Virginica.*" *Aquaculture Center News.* Sound School Regional Vocational Aquaculture Center, New Haven, Conn., 1998.

Visel, Timothy C., Nancy E. Follini, Joseph J. Gilbert, and Lance L. Stewart. "Shellfish Bag Relaying Systems in Connecticut." University of Connecticut Sea Grant Fact Sheet, 1988.

Whitman, Walt. *Specimen Days.* New American Library, 1961.

Willoughby, Malcolm. *Rum War at Sea.* Treasury Department, U.S. Coast Guard, 1964. A good companion to Carse and Van De Water.

Van De Water, Frederic F. *The Real McCoy.* Doubleday Doran, 1931. As-told-to memoirs of the premier Rum Row schooner captain.

Volk, John H. "Connecticut Shellfish Program: Shellfish Sanitation Program." State of Connecticut Department of Agriculture, Bureau of Aquaculture and Laboratory, April 1998.

Wong, Edward F. M. "A Multiplier of Computing the Value of Shellfish." United States Department of the Interior Federal Water Pollution Control Administration New England Basins Office, Needham Heights, Mass., October 1969.